Challenging Behavior in Young Children

Understanding, Preventing, and Responding Effectively

THIRD EDITION

Barbara Kaiser

Judy Sklar Rasminsky

Foreword by Sue Bredekamp

PEARSON

Boston Columbus Indianapolis New York San Francisco Upper Saddle River
Amsterdam Cape Town Dubai London Madrid Milan Munich Paris Montreal Toronto
Delhi Mexico City São Paulo Sydney Hong Kong Seoul Singapore Taipei Tokyo

Vice President and Editor in Chief: *Jeffery W. Johnston*

Senior Acquisitions Editor: *Julie Peters*

Editorial Assistant: *Tiffany Bitzel*

Vice President, Director of Marketing: *Margaret Waples*

Marketing Manager: *Christopher Barry*

Senior Managing Editor: *Pamela D. Bennett*

Project Manager: *Linda Bayma*

Senior Operations Supervisor: *Central Publishing*

Operations Specialist: *Laura Messerly*

Senior Art Director: *Jayne Conte*

Cover Designer: *Bruce Kenselaar*

Photo Coordinator: *Lori Whitley*

Full-Service Project Management: *Saraswathi Muralidhar/PreMediaGlobal*

Composition: *PreMediaGlobal*

Printer/Binder: *Courier/Stoughton*

Cover Printer: *Courier/Stoughton*

Text Font: *10.5/12 Giovanni Book*

Credits and acknowledgments borrowed from other sources and reproduced, with permission, in this textbook appear on appropriate page within text.

Photo credits appear on page 329, which constitutes a continuation of this copyright page.

Every effort has been made to provide accurate and current Internet information in this book. However, the Internet and information posted on it are constantly changing, so it is inevitable that some of the Internet addresses listed in this textbook will change.

This book has been adapted from *Meeting the Challenge: Effective Strategies for Challenging Behaviors in Early Childhood Environments* by Barbara Kaiser and Judy Sklar Rasminsky. © 1999, Canadian Child Care Federation, 201-383 Parkdale Avenue, Ottawa, Ontario, Canada, K1Y 4T4. The authors wish to express their gratitude to the Canadian Child Care Federation for granting permission for its use.

The name WEVAS™ is a trademark of WEVAS Incorporated.

Tools of the Mind by Elena Bodrova and Deborah J. Leong. © 2007, Pearson.

Library of Congress Cataloging-in-Publication Data

Kaiser, Barbara

   Challenging behavior in young children: understanding, preventing, and responding effectively/ Barbara Kaiser, Judy Sklar Rasminsky.—3rd ed.

     p. cm.

   Includes bibliographical references and index.

   ISBN-13: 978-0-13-215912-8

   ISBN-10: 0-13-215912-0

   1. Behavior modification.   2. Early childhood education.   3. Classroom management.

I. Rasminsky, Judy Sklar   II. Title.

   LB1060.2.K35 2012

   371.39'3—dc22

2010048991

10 9 8 7 6 5 4 3 2 1

www.pearsonhighered.com

ISBN 10:   0-13-215912-0

ISBN 13: 978-0-13-215912-8

For Martin and Michael

About the Authors

Barbara Kaiser and Judy Sklar Rasminsky first teamed up two decades ago to write *The Daycare Handbook* (1991). Since then they've published a number of award-winning and bestselling books and booklets in the field of education, including *Meeting the Challenge* (named a Comprehensive Membership Benefit by the National Association for the Education of Young Children in 1999), *Challenging Behavior in Young Children* (winner of a Texty Award for textbook excellence in 2007), and *Challenging Behavior in Elementary and Middle School* (which won a Texty in 2009).

BARBARA KAISER has taught at Acadia University in Wolfville, Nova Scotia, and at Concordia University and College Marie-Victorin in Montreal, Canada. In addition to presenting workshops and keynote speeches on challenging behavior throughout the United States and Canada, Barbara has acted as a consultant for Mr. Rogers' Family Communications, Inc., and was the chief consultant for *Facing the Challenge*, an instructional DVD based on *Challenging Behavior in Young Children* produced by the Devereux Early Childhood Initiative in 2007. She holds a master's degree in educational administration from McGill University and founded and served as the director of two child care centers and an after-school program.

JUDY SKLAR RASMINSKY is a freelance writer specializing in education and health. Her work has appeared in numerous magazines, newspapers, and anthologies, and she has won awards from the National Association of Government Communicators, the International Association of Business Communicators, and the National Institutes of Health. For many years an editor at book publishers in New York and London, she has a B.A. from Stanford University and an M.A. from Columbia University.

Visit Kaiser and Rasminsky at www.challengingbehavior.com

Foreword

Even after decades in the profession, most teachers vividly remember their first year in the classroom. I certainly remember mine. In fact, my first *day* of teaching is imprinted on my brain. I can still recount in detail the many examples of children's challenging behaviors as well as my own inept and ineffective responses.

Desperate for answers, I enrolled in a course on guiding young children's behavior. I firmly believe that had I not taken that course when I did, I would have left the early childhood profession at the very outset of my career. I learned enough in that course and my subsequent studies to become a better teacher. However, teaching children with challenging behaviors continued to be a struggle for me throughout my years as a teacher. In looking back, I sincerely wish that I and my college instructors had had access to this outstanding book. Barbara Kaiser and Judy Sklar Rasminsky describe their book as a "survival manual." But I consider it an invaluable guidebook for teachers to make it possible for *all* children to thrive in early childhood programs.

In this third edition, Kaiser and Rasminsky fulfill the promise of the book's title by providing an eminently readable foundation for teachers to understand, prevent, and respond effectively to challenging behavior in young children. Readers will find no instant answers here, because there are none. Nevertheless, new and inexperienced teachers will be heartened to learn that there are research-based, effective strategies for working with and promoting the positive development of children with challenging behaviors.

The first four chapters clearly summarize the most current research about the causes of challenging behavior and the intricate relationship between risk and resilience. Chapter 4 presents highly compelling evidence about the brain and its implications for children's learning and development, particularly the effect of negative early experience on children's growing brains and its relationship with their later behaviors. All this research leads to essentially the same conclusion: Children's behavior is the result of a complex interaction between biology and environment. Interventions, such as prenatal care and social and mental health services, can and do effectively address biological risks but are usually beyond the purview of teachers. However, the environment—specifically, nurturing—is something that every teacher bears some responsibility for.

Understanding the roots of challenging behavior is an important first step that is too often overlooked in the middle of a specific situation with a difficult child. If they were completely honest, most teachers would admit that they just want the problem to go away or they dream of a quick fix so they can get on with doing their "real" job. But Kaiser and Rasminsky lay out specific steps that teachers can take to prevent or minimize challenging behaviors. This process begins with teachers' self-awareness because as they say, "Teaching isn't just what one does but who one is." When teachers are aware of their own temperament, values, and cultural perspectives, they can more successfully build a positive relationship with each child—the all-important foundation for preventing challenging behavior and promoting learning.

What I love about this book is that the authors do not just state the obvious—such as that relationships are important. Instead, they go deeper into how relationships are built and what they mean for children and adults as in: "Teacher relationships are made up of thousands of interactions every day" or "Start fresh every day. Whatever happened yesterday, let it go." Such guidance will help you be a better teacher for every child and is essential for children with challenging behaviors.

One of the many strengths of this book is how the role of culture and language in children's development and behavior is infused throughout. Culture is the framework for behavior that a group passes down from generation to generation. Therefore, it should not be surprising that expectations for appropriate behavior vary by cultural group, and yet ignorance persists. Understanding linguistic and cultural diversity is vital in America's schools where a large and persistent achievement gap exists for children of color and dual-language learners. These same children, particularly African American boys, are overidentified for special education and are more likely to be retained in grade or expelled from school. Given these disparities, it is essential that all teachers deepen their understanding of culture and gain cross-cultural competence—a goal that this book will help address.

Inclusion of children with disabilities and special needs is the law. Given that some children with disabling conditions or emotional disorders exhibit challenging behaviors, all teachers need to know the requirements of the law and be equipped with effective teaching strategies for children with special needs. This third edition includes a chapter on inclusion to help teachers understand the law and implement it successfully so that both children with disabilities and their typically developing peers benefit.

In addition to the knowledge that teachers need to understand and prevent challenging behavior, Kaiser and Rasminsky give teachers tools for dealing with challenging behavior in children that also apply broadly to *all* children. They stress teaching children emotional literacy and social skills, clarify the difference between guidance and punishment, and offer specific language and strategies for teachers to use. They never shy away from controversies such as time-out or reinforcement; teachers will find their honest discussion more helpful than the usual, simplistic proscriptions regarding these practices. Most helpfully, the authors provide detailed guidance for systematic, research-based approaches such as functional assessment and positive behavior support. The final chapter on bullying addresses an age-old problem about which we now have a large body of illuminating research to guide our practice. Bullies, victims, and bystanders (who are the same person at times) can wreak havoc in school and in the larger society. Teachers must be vigilant and create school communities that tackle this problem on multiple levels.

None of what Kaiser and Rasminsky advocate will be as successful without engaging families. When children exhibit challenging behaviors, building relationships with their families and communicating effectively can be particularly difficult. Again, the authors provide practical, useful recommendations for this essential aspect of early childhood education.

This book could not be more timely or more needed. The current economic crisis in our country has impacted children most severely with one in five now growing up in poverty. Given the multiple risk factors associated with poverty, the long-term consequences for children's behavior are highly predictable. Already the expulsion rate in preschool is three times higher than that in K–12 schools. Challenging behavior begins at a young age, and without early intervention, often grows worse over time. If every early childhood teacher were better able to understand, prevent, and respond effectively to challenging behavior, not only would we make a difference in the lives of children and families, but we would also make a major contribution to improving the outlook for our nation.

Sue Bredekamp, Ph.D.

Preface

Why a third edition? We continue to follow and share the latest about children with challenging behavior because children, families, and teachers are still struggling for answers. Why does this child behave this way? What can I do to change her behavior? Should she even be here? How do I teach the other children in my class? Every day, teachers are left feeling, "Nothing I do works."

The world around us is changing dramatically, and the stress affects children as much as adults. The ongoing economic crisis has cut budgets at schools and child care centers, inflating class size and endangering the quality of care. Inclusion is now a fact of life, but even with some special education training most teachers aren't yet prepared to work with children with disabilities. The number of children who speak languages other than English is also growing, baffling many teachers. State-based prekindergarten programs have expanded, bringing younger children into school, and No Child Left Behind testing continues to have pushdown effects. Children and teachers will face new challenges for years to come.

All of this is reflected in this third edition, which contains the following new material.

What's new in the third edition

- Throughout the book there is more about working with children in primary school—without losing focus on the preschool years.
- Chapter 9 features a new section on what makes a guidance strategy work, as well as descriptions of several additional guidance strategies, such as developmental discipline, teacher effectiveness training, and collaborative problem solving. There is also a section on what to do when a child loses control.
- Chapters 7, 8, and 10 seamlessly support the CSEFEL model and the TACSEI initiative.
- Chapter 6 has more material about the culture of school and child care, and there are new sections on dual-language learners and culturally responsive teaching.
- We've written new segments on autism and the IDEA requirements for assessment.
- We've greatly expanded Chapter 8, which deals with physical space, routines and transitions, procedures, and teaching strategies (including Tools of the Mind) appropriate for children 3 to 8 years old.

- New reflective checklists help students and teachers improve their practice.

- There are updates on brain research; temperament (which is increasingly recognized as crucial in challenging behavior); the role of peers in challenging behavior; and new approaches to enhancing resilience.

- A new *Instructor's Manual* is available for download to college instructors who register online at www.pearsonhighered.com, Educators. This manual includes interactive activities, discussion questions, learning outcomes, chapter summaries, and more to enrich a variety of college course formats—online, hybrid, and face-to-face.

Our mantra in this edition is *make the implicit explicit*. To behave appropriately, children must know your expectations. This is particularly important when it comes to culture, guidance, and preventing challenging behavior.

We can offer no magic fairy dust, no single theory or practice that will work for all teachers or all children. But we do offer you several effective, evidence-based strategies so that you can select those that suit who you are and what you believe in—as well as the child with challenging behavior in your own classroom. Every child has some kind of special need, especially children with challenging behavior. This book will help you to see each child as an individual, figure out where he's coming from, and build a meaningful relationship. In the end, that is what will help you the most.

Acknowledgments

This edition has required Judy's solitary sitting, Barbara's three decades of work in early care and education, and the help of a great many colleagues, friends, and family members.

Our heartfelt thanks go to Neil Butchard and Bob Spencler for their commitment to children and their willingness to share their wonderful WEVAS program; to Carol Patterson and Alida Jansen for passing along their vast experience and expertise in working with children and their families; to Carol Copple of the NAEYC and to Joan Duffell of the Committee for Children for believing in us from the beginning; and to Sue Bredekamp for making us feel as if our work was worth telling others about.

Barbara would like to thank all the participants and organizers of the workshops she's presented throughout North America over the past several years: You have taught us so much. Special thanks go to principal Marydine K. Emery and the staff at Donaldsonville Primary School in Ascension Parish, LA; Terry Caldwell and Jeannie Wilks, Le Blanc Special Services Center, Gonzales, LA; and Carolyn Knight, Washington Parish, LA, who opened their classroom doors, shared their experience and expertise, and made her feel part of a very caring community.

We very much appreciate the valuable feedback of our reviewers: Christine Hoffner Barthold, University of Delaware, Newark; Sharon M. Darling, Florida Atlantic University, Boca Raton; Francine Favretto, University of Maryland, College Park; Mary R. Gonzales, South Texas College, McAllen, and University of Texas-Pan American, Edinburg; and ReJean A. Schulte, Cuyahoga Community College, Emerita, Cleveland, OH.

For giving this book a special spirit, we owe thanks to our young artists, Joseph Belland; Suzanne Charbonneau; Vittoria Damiani; Samantha Handal; Emma

Harries; Toby Izenberg; Julia, Krissy, and Michael Keech; Alexandra Plaitis; Abigail Rasminsky; Emma Rubin; and Nathan Shepherd, as well as to their families.

We are very securely attached to our editor, Julie Peters, and the staff at Pearson—Tiffany Bitzel, Carol Sykes, Becky Savage, Linda Bayma, Laura Messerly, Saraswathi Muralidhar, et al.—who have all provided the sensitive, responsive care authors require.

It goes without saying that Barbara thanks her sister, Joan, who, in her mind, remains the best prekindergarten teacher on the planet, for her sense of humor and wonderful stories. Judy's brothers, Daniel and Zachary, sustained her throughout the writing process with their sage literary advice and unflagging support.

Barbara thanks her husband, Martin, for being there when she needed him and for cooking dinner every night. Judy thanks her husband, Michael, for making the brain chapter possible and for giving up many hours at the piano without complaint. She is also grateful to Abigail, Sonya, Oren, Toby, and Miri for putting up with their perpetually cranky and unavailable mother and grandmother. And Barbara would like to thank her children, Jessika and Maita, for reminding her of the importance of our work for all teachers and children.

Brief Contents

Contents

CHAPTER 3
_____

Protective Factors   43

CHAPTER 4
_____

Behavior and the Brain   53

CHAPTER 5

Relationship, Relationship, Relationship   65

Opening the Culture Door   90

CHAPTER 7

Preventing Challenging Behavior: The Social Context   119

CHAPTER 8

Preventing Challenging Behavior: Physical Space, Routines and Transitions, and Teaching Strategies   146

CHAPTER 9

Guidance   173

CHAPTER 10

Functional Assessment and Positive Behavior Support   197

CHAPTER 11

The Inclusive Classroom   217

CHAPTER 12

Working with Families and Other Experts 239

CHAPTER 13

Bullying 253

Reflective Checklists for Chapters 7 and 8   273

The Functional Assessment Observation Form   278

The Functional Assessment A-B-C Chart   282

Introduction

This book—and the 12 years we've spent finding ways to support children with challenging behavior—began 17 years ago with one child.

Barbara had been working in the field for 14 years when a 2½-year-old named Andrew turned her world upside down. The staff at the nonprofit community child care center she directed were all experienced and qualified early childhood teachers, but this child brought out every flaw in the program and taxed every skill they'd developed.

It was the first time the teachers lacked the ability to help a child regulate his own behavior. Because they couldn't keep Andrew from hurting them or his classmates, many of the children no longer felt safe, and several became anxious, copied his behavior, or were just too scared to do much of anything. These "borderline" children, as the staff called them, sometimes tried to provoke Andrew when things were calm. If they could get him to scream, hit, or throw things, they knew what to expect. When they were in need of attention themselves, they saw what worked for Andrew and followed his example. As a result, the group soon contained four or five children with challenging behavior.

The teachers spent their days putting out fires, consoling children, and saying no. They knew they weren't helping Andrew and, worse, they found themselves liking him and some of the other children less—a feeling that made them profoundly uncomfortable. As the year wore on, they began to feel resentful, burned out, inadequate, and full of self-doubt.

As Andrew got older, the problems got bigger. Because he had no diagnosed medical problem or medication, there were no treatment guidelines or extra money to help care for him. Large for his age, he had poor gross motor skills—and, aside from puzzles, he wasn't interested in fine motor activities either. Although he was extremely articulate, he had difficulty relating to other children, and the only way he could play or communicate was to kick, hit, or push. During transitions and free play, he worked the room, moving from one target to the next, pushing over block structures and grabbing toys. At snack and lunchtime, he selected a chair that was occupied and sat on the occupant. After a while, the children waited until Andrew was seated, then sat as far away as possible. If he got angry, he emptied the shelves onto the floor and flung chairs around the room. When the teachers tried to discipline him, he kicked and head-butted them.

Because Andrew's facial expressions and body language seldom reflected his feelings or intentions, his behavior seemed to come out of nowhere. One of his 4-year-old classmates said it best: "Andrew is like a volcano; he's calm on the outside and ready to explode on the inside."

The staff tried to encourage him when he was behaving appropriately, but positive reinforcement made Andrew nervous. If a teacher showed interest while he was concentrating on a puzzle, he shoved it to the ground or threw the pieces at her. Eventually, the teachers found themselves viewing his positive behavior as a chance to take a breath or be with the other children, who were receiving less and less care. The teachers were showing Andrew that the best way to get their attention was to behave inappropriately.

Some of the staff thought he shouldn't be there. They felt ill equipped and unwilling to have a child like Andrew in their group. Not only did he jeopardize the safety of the other children, but his presence compromised their ability to provide the program the children deserved. He consumed so much of their time and energy they had almost nothing left to give.

There were also some irate parents. Each day their children came home with stories about what Andrew had done, sometimes sporting bruises he had inflicted. The parents simply didn't understand why he was allowed to remain at the center. Barbara empathized with them, but she couldn't help wondering what would happen to Andrew if she asked him to leave. Would another center tolerate his behavior better? Or would he just bounce from center to center?

Barbara felt a sense of responsibility to Andrew, and she wasn't ready to give up. She brought in experts to advise them, but she had waited too long to ask for help, and the teachers were so stressed and defensive they couldn't hear the consultants' recommendations. They focused more on punishment than teaching, and they felt so overwhelmed they didn't recognize that any challenging behavior that persists over time is working for the child. When Andrew finally went to kindergarten, they felt they had failed.

Andrew's legacy

Barbara and the staff vowed they would never let this happen again. They attended workshops, read about challenging behavior, and devoted a portion of each staff meeting to discussing the research-based strategies they were learning about. It wasn't all smooth sailing. The nine teachers didn't always see things the same way. Some were eager to try everything. Others were still convinced that children with challenging behavior didn't belong in regular child care centers. Their emphatic responses reflected their diverse personalities, life experiences, cultures, philosophies, and attitudes toward children. Because teaching isn't simply what one does but also who one is, it was important to pay attention to what everyone felt, so they took it slowly and looked for solutions that felt comfortable to all of them.

Eventually the staff came to realize that Andrew hadn't actually been out to ruin everyone's day. His behavior had much more to do with the way he saw the world and the fact that he didn't know how to respond appropriately. More than anybody, he probably wished things had been different. Once the teachers recognized their job was to teach, not to police, they were on the right track.

The new approach

Three years later, $3^1/_2$-year-old Michael started at the center. During the brief orientation session for new children and their parents, he ran around screaming and grabbing toys from the other children. As soon as the children and parents left, Barbara and the staff held an emergency meeting. They talked about what Andrew had taught them and how they could help Michael develop social and emotional skills, impulse control, and self-esteem. Prevention was uppermost in their minds. To keep him from losing control, they decided he would become the partner of one of the teachers, they would place his cubby next to hers, they would give him focused and limited choices during free play, and they would assign everyone tasks at cleanup and seats at snack and lunchtime. Because they didn't yet know what would make Michael feel good about himself, they decided to reinforce his appropriate behavior by smiling, giving him thumbs up throughout the day, and letting him choose a song if he was doing well at circle time.

The teachers also talked about their feelings: their attitudes toward Michael's presence, his behavior, their different levels of tolerance, their verbal and nonverbal messages, and their confidence as individuals and members of a team. They knew it was important to be consistent, so they had to agree about which behaviors were acceptable and what they would do when Michael's behavior was unacceptable. As the meeting went on, it became clear that they all felt much more confident than they had with Andrew. They weren't helpless; they had strategies and plans.

It didn't take long for them to discover that Michael loved to have his back rubbed and that he grinned infectiously when they gave him a thumbs up. Within 6 weeks all the strategies they'd worked on were in place, they were feeling competent and comfortable about having him at the center, and he was able to play, share, and make friends. Instead of being anxious or frightened, the other children were learning to recognize Michael's strengths and weaknesses, and they enthusiastically encouraged his efforts to behave appropriately. Their support helped him enormously.

It wasn't all perfect. Any change in routine—for example, if his teacher was absent—derailed him. And no matter how much progress he made during the day, his challenging behavior reemerged when his mother arrived. You could feel her apprehension as she walked down the corridor. To help her see how well Michael was doing, the staff made a point of greeting her with a smile and telling her about something positive he'd done that day. As time passed, they encouraged her to spend a few minutes in the classroom before bundling him up for the trip home. Michael was delighted to have her sit beside him and meet his friends. He couldn't wait to tell her about the painting he'd made or the game he'd played in the gym. Eventually, even the hassles at the end of the day became easy routines.

After 2 years in the child care center, Michael went off to school. Although he's had some testy moments, he has made friends and is adjusting well.

Sharing the knowledge

Even before Michael came on the scene, we had decided to write a book together. The need for it was all too evident. Judy, a professional writer specializing in education and family issues, had been the first chair of the child care center's board of directors, and we had been coauthors for many years. She went along when the staff attended workshops on challenging behavior and read everything she could get her hands on, and we pushed each other to search out new ideas, constantly trying to understand more.

In 1999, the Canadian Child Care Federation in Ottawa published *Meeting the Challenge,* our 40-page booklet for frontline staff, which the National Association for the Education of Young Children in Washington, DC, distributed in the United States. But in 40 pages, we couldn't tell the whole story. Virtually every topic we covered demanded more explanation, and we believed it was vital to reach out to students, too.

Ongoing work by the Early Child Care Research Network of the National Institute of Child Health and Human Development (NICHD ECCRN) and others (Belsky et al., 2007; NICHD ECCRN, 2003, 2004) has shown that the time children spend in child care affects their behavior. And in 2005, a nationwide study of prekindergarten programs (Gilliam, 2005) found that 10.4 percent of teachers had expelled at least one child because of behavior problems during the school year, making it clear that many teachers are still not prepared to address children with challenging behavior. The first time a 4-year-old throws a four-letter word or a chair at them, they are stunned. Classrooms in today's child care centers and schools are filled with Andrews and Michaels. If we want them to succeed, we must make sure not only that children are ready for school, but also that schools are ready for children—all children.

Events at Columbine High School, September 11, 2001, and the economic downturn have changed our world forever. It has become increasingly apparent that teachers must have the knowledge, strategies, and skills required to help children with challenging behavior as early as possible. Although research shows that aggressive behavior in early childhood tends to persist throughout later childhood, adolescence, and even adulthood (Broidy et al., 2003; Côté, Vaillancourt, LeBlanc, Nagin, & Tremblay, 2006), it also shows that children with challenging behavior can learn appropriate ways to behave. Teachers who know what they're doing and why they're doing it can make an enormous difference in the lives of these children. As a teacher or future teacher, you have two choices. Either you can create an environment that welcomes them and *teaches* them how to become the best people they can be, or you can reinforce their growing suspicion that they have nothing to offer, will never belong, and cannot learn or cope with the demands of school.

Teaching today is highly demanding, and it may seem impossible to do all we advocate in this book. However, it is worth whatever time and effort it takes to build a relationship with every child, teach social and emotional skills, and develop a caring, inclusive classroom environment. In the long run dedicating a few minutes a day to preventing challenging behavior and creating opportunities for all children to succeed actually *saves* time and enables them to learn not only appropriate behavior but also the content of the curriculum.

By developing the ability to help children with challenging behavior, you are also helping the other children, who, in their presence are often frightened or excited and learn to become bystanders, accept the role of victim, or join in the aggressive behavior. When you are prepared, all the children will feel safe, and the difficult behavior will be less severe, less frequent, and less contagious. Then it becomes possible to make the commitment that everyone who works with children wants to be able to make: to welcome and help each child in your class. You, too, will benefit as you acquire competence and confidence, gain pride and satisfaction in your job, and feel more positive about the children you spend many hours with each day.

What is in this book?

This book is a kind of survival manual. Its aim is to provide the basic facts and skills you need to understand and prevent challenging behavior, address it effectively when it occurs, and teach appropriate alternatives. It brings together information and techniques drawn from neuroscience, psychology, psychiatry, special education, early care and education, child development, cross-cultural research, and proactive social and emotional skills programs. It doesn't provide recipes or formulas, because each child is unique and every situation requires a unique solution. And it certainly doesn't come with a money-back guarantee. But it does offer ideas and strategies proven to work time and again—and that *will* work if you give them a chance. Many weeks may elapse between the moment you first realize you need help with a child with challenging behavior and the day a consultation is finally arranged. These weeks are the time you are most liable to burn out—and the time the strategies here will be useful. But don't wait until then to try them.

We wrote this book for students and teachers who work with young children, but it can also be useful to administrators, who set the tone in schools and child care centers. Their backing for teachers as they deal with children with challenging behavior can make an important contribution to their success.

Nuts and bolts

This book falls into two parts. The first four chapters explain the background—some of the theory and research that underlie effective practice. They contain information about aggression, risk factors, protective factors, and the brain's role in challenging behavior. The nine remaining chapters are more practical. They describe strategies for preventing and managing challenging behavior. Each of these methods can be used alone, but they work extremely well together. The last chapter deals with a special variety of challenging behavior, bullying, and it comes at the end because it is a kind of summary: Addressing bullying effectively requires the use of virtually all of the techniques presented here.

Culture is a basic part of who children are, and we have tried very hard to make our book culturally sensitive. However, we are both European American, and in the end, we probably couldn't disguise that fact. It is important for you, as readers, to be aware of our bias.

Although challenging behavior is more prevalent among boys, it is increasingly common among girls. In recognition of this situation—and to avoid the awkwardness of "he or she"—we have called a child *he* in the odd-numbered chapters and *she* in the even-numbered chapters.

Many children inhabit these pages, but three are more prominent than the rest: Andrew, Michael, and Jazmine. Their stories illuminate the behavior and strategies that are at the heart of this book.

Hang in there

Here are a few hints to keep in mind as you read:

- Have confidence in your own abilities—you can handle this.
- View inappropriate behavior as an opportunity to teach. That will help with everything you do.
- Take it slowly, one behavior at a time, one child at a time. Build in success by setting realistic goals.
- At the end of the day, reflect on what went wrong and what went right. Make notes so you can figure out what to do next time.
- Train yourself to look for, measure, and record minute improvements—they are important signs of progress. Remember that you can't eliminate challenging behavior overnight.
- When you try a new approach, things may get worse before they get better. But if you don't see gains within a reasonable time, try another tack.
- If you work with other people, set common goals. Laugh together; support and compliment each other. If you work alone, seek out your peers. Everyone needs someone to talk to.
- Give yourself a reward, not a guilt trip. Eat that brownie or take that walk. Do whatever will keep you going.

CHAPTER 1

What Is Challenging Behavior?

Challenging behavior is any behavior that

- interferes with a child's cognitive, social, or emotional development
- is harmful to the child, other children, or adults
- puts a child at high risk for later social problems or school failure (Klass, Guskin, & Thomas, 1995; McCabe & Frede, 2007)

This book focuses on aggressive behaviors because they have such a vast and dramatic impact on the children who use them, their peers, and you, the teacher.

Aggressive behavior aims to harm or injure others (Parke & Slaby, 1983). It can be *physical* or *verbal*; it can be *direct* (hitting, pushing, pinching, biting, grabbing, spitting, hair-pulling, threatening, name-calling) or *indirect* (spreading rumors, excluding others, betraying a trust). Because indirect aggressive behavior endangers relationships, social status, or self-esteem, it is sometimes called *social* or *relational aggression* (Vaillancourt, 2005).

Aggressive behavior often overlaps with *antisocial* or *disruptive behavior*, which inflicts "physical or mental harm or property loss or damage on others" (Loeber, 1985, p. 6) and violates social norms and expectations (Walker, Ramsey, & Gresham, 2004). It includes defying rules, instructions, or authority; arguing, swearing, cheating, lying, stealing, bullying, or destroying objects; and acting in ways that are

War and Peace

Aggressive or antisocial behavior is not the same as conflict, which occurs when people have opposing goals or interests. Conflict can be resolved in many ways— by negotiating, taking turns, persuading, and so on—and learning to resolve conflict helps children to be assertive about their own needs, regulate their negative feelings, and understand others (Cords & Killen, 1998; Katz, Kramer, & Gottman, 1992). Aggressive behavior is just one tactic for dealing with conflict—in fact, some researchers consider it a mismanagement of conflict (Perry, Perry, & Kennedy, 1992; Shantz & Hartup, 1992). But most conflicts don't involve aggression.

abusive, coercive, or cruel. Many of the ideas and strategies in this book will also work with other types of challenging behavior—timid and withdrawn, for example.

We call these behaviors challenging because they are threatening, provocative, and stimulating, all at the same time. To begin with, they're challenging for the child. They put him in danger by preventing him from learning what he needs to know to get along with his peers and succeed in school. They're also challenging for him because he probably doesn't have much control over them. Even if he knows what to do instead—and chances are he doesn't—his ability to regulate his feelings and actions isn't yet up to the job. Improving matters will be an enormous challenge for him.

Challenging behavior is just as challenging for a child's family and teachers. In the face of this behavior, we often find ourselves at a loss. We can't figure out how to turn things around, make the situation tenable, or help him get back on track, behaving appropriately and feeling good about himself. But with the appropriate information and strategies, we can rise to this challenge and play a pivotal role in the development of a child with challenging behavior, helping him to avoid serious risk and blossom into the fully functioning person all children deserve to become.

Is challenging behavior ever appropriate?

Infants and toddlers begin to use aggressive, impulsive behavior in the first year of life as they become angry or frustrated and interested in controlling their own activities and possessions (Hay, 2005). For them, challenging behavior is developmentally appropriate. In one study, most mothers reported that their toddlers grabbed, pushed, bit, hit, attacked, bullied, or were "cruel" by the time they turned 2 years old. In an interview, Richard E. Tremblay of the University of Montreal put it this way: "The question . . . we've been trying to answer for the past 30 years is how do children learn to aggress. But this is the wrong question. The right question is how do they learn not to aggress" (Holden, 2000, p. 581).

With the aid of families and teachers, most children gradually stop using physical aggression after about 3 years of age—although as their language skills grow, they may turn to verbal aggression instead (Dodge, Coie, & Lynam, 2006). They learn to regulate their feelings, understand another person's point of view, and

A Rose by Any Other Name

Challenging is not the only label that adults have affixed to problem behaviors or the children who use them. Here are some others:

- High maintenance
- Antisocial
- High needs
- Bad
- Out of control
- Hard to manage

- Troublemaker
- Disruptive
- Aggressive
- Violent
- Impulsive
- Difficult

- Oppositional
- Noncompliant
- Mean
- A problem
- Attention seeking
- Willful

Labels are extremely powerful, which is why it's wiser not to use them—or if you do, to apply them to the behavior rather than the child. Employing language carefully makes a big difference in the way you see a child and think about what he can and cannot do. Negative labels can all too easily become self-fulfilling prophecies, preventing you from noticing the child's positive qualities and compelling you to lower your expectations of him. But when you can see a child in a positive light—as tenacious or persistent, rather than stubborn—he can see himself that way and act more positively, too.

utilize assertive and prosocial strategies to communicate their needs and achieve their goals. They are also increasingly able to delay gratification and decreasingly tolerant of other children's aggressive acts. By the time they enter kindergarten, most are relatively pacific and tend to remain so (Broidy et al., 2003).

All children continue to use challenging behavior once in a while when they're frustrated, angry, or having a bad day. Some even use it for an extended period when they're confronted with confusing and difficult events, such as a divorce, the arrival of a new sibling, a parent's illness or job loss, or a family move. But with extra support and understanding, they usually manage to cope.

What happens to children with more serious behavior problems?

There are some children, however, who have much more difficult and persistent problems, and they may come to rely on challenging behavior as the best way to respond to a situation. For this estimated 3 to 17 percent, aggressive and antisocial behavior continues (Broidy et al., 2003; Côté, Vaillancourt, LeBlanc, Nagin, & Tremblay, 2006); and some children start down a road that eventually puts them at very high risk for a delinquent adolescence and a criminal adulthood. Researchers call this type of aggressive behavior "early-onset" or "life-course persistent" (Broidy et al., 2003; Campbell, 2002; Moffitt & Caspi, 2001). The longer a child utilizes this behavior, the harder it is to change his direction and the more worrisome its fallout becomes.

Children with behavior problems often find themselves rejected by their peers—disliked, ridiculed, excluded from play in child care and school, and not invited to birthday parties or other children's homes. These experiences wound their self-esteem and self-confidence, leave them isolated and depressed, and deprive them of opportunities to develop and practice the social and emotional skills they desperately need. Instead they learn to expect rejection and may even discover that the best defense is a strong offense and strike out preemptively to protect themselves (Moffitt, 1997). Once rejected, a child will probably continue to be rejected and will have a hard time joining a new group (Campbell, 2002).

Behavior problems can lead to scholastic troubles, too. Because their social skills, emotional control, and language development are often below par, many children with challenging behavior aren't prepared for the most basic task of their early school years, learning to read (Coie, 1996). It doesn't help that their behavior may also be hyperactive, inattentive, and disruptive.

Teachers sometimes exacerbate the problem. They are more likely to punish children with challenging behavior and less likely to encourage them when they behave appropriately (Walker & Buckley, 1973); they call on them less frequently, ask them fewer questions, provide them with less information, and send them to the principal's office more often, causing them to miss many hours of class time (Shonkoff & Phillips, 2000). Not surprisingly, such children soon fall behind and are more likely to be suspended, expelled, held back, or tracked into special classes; they are also more likely to drop out (Kokko, Tremblay, Lacourse, Nagin, & Vitaro, 2006; National Institute of Child Health and Human Development Early Child Care Research Network, 2004).

Children who are rejected by their peers learn to expect rejection and may even discover that the best defense is a strong offense and strike out preemptively to protect themselves.

All of this primes children with challenging behavior to band together with their like-minded peers, raising their risk for delinquency, gang membership, substance abuse, and psychiatric illness. As adults, they find it harder to hold jobs or earn good wages, and they're more likely to commit violent crimes (Broidy et al., 2003; Côté, Vaillancourt, Barker, Nagin, & Tremblay, 2007). Their marriages are rockier, the boys may become batterers, and the girls, who are at high risk for early pregnancy and single parenthood, lack parenting skills and may be mothering the next generation of children with behavior problems (Odgers et al., 2008; Serbin et al., 1998).

What do the theorists say about aggressive and antisocial behavior?

The theory that dominates the study of aggression today is the theory we have just described: the theory of *early-onset, life-course persistent aggressive behavior* (Dodge et al., 2006). Emerging from the new field of developmental psychopathology, this theory holds that aggressive and antisocial behavior is the result of the ongoing interaction between a child's genes, experiences, and culture, starting from conception. We will examine all of these elements in more depth in Chapters 2–6.

This developmental theory also builds on earlier theories, such as the *frustration-aggression theory*, which maintains that when people are frustrated—when they can't reach their goals—they become angry and hostile and act aggressively (Dodge et al., 2006); and s*ocial learning theory* (Bandura, 1977), which is based on principles of conditioning and reinforcement and contends that people learn aggressive behavior from their environment. The father of social learning theory, psychologist Albert Bandura, argues that children observe and imitate the role models around them—family, teachers, peers, television. At the same time, they observe and experience the rewards, punishments, and emotional states associated with aggressive and antisocial behavior. When they see a behavior reinforced, they're likely to try it for themselves; and when they experience the reinforcement directly, they're likely to repeat it (Bandura, 1977). That is, when Zack hits Ben and gets the red fire engine, he will almost certainly try hitting the next time he wants something.

Social learning theory has spawned several sister theories that place more emphasis on cognition. According to the *cognitive script model*, advanced by L. Rowell Huesmann and Leonard D. Eron, children learn *scripts* or *schemas* for aggressive behavior—when to expect it, what to do, what it will feel like, what its results and consequences will be—and lay them down in their memory banks. The more they rehearse these scripts through observation, fantasy, and behavior, the more readily they spring to mind and govern behavior when the occasion arises (Dodge et al., 2006).

Psychologist Kenneth A. Dodge (2006) has proposed a *social information processing model* for aggressive and antisocial behavior. Every single social interaction provides a child with a mass of information to process and convert into a response. As each social cue comes in, he must encode it, interpret it, think of possible responses, evaluate them, and choose one to enact.

Most children learn at a young age that people usually have benign intentions and that situations rarely call for an aggressive response (Dodge, 2006). But children with very challenging behavior—perhaps because of their adverse life experiences— often lack the skills required to process incoming information properly, and they tend to see the world with a jaundiced eye (Dodge, 2006). When another child bumps into them in a situation most children regard as neutral, they think the other child did it on purpose—that is, they believe the child intended to hurt or be mean to them. Dodge calls this having a *hostile attributional bias*. Furthermore, they don't look for information that might help to solve a problem, and they have trouble thinking of alternative solutions. And because they don't anticipate what will happen if they respond aggressively, they often end up choosing passive or aggressive solutions that don't work (Dodge et al., 2006).

Seeing Straight
....

Researchers Kenneth Dodge, John E. Bates, and Gregory S. Pettit (1990) wanted to find out whether physical abuse affects the way a child processes social information. They showed roughly 300 5-year-olds a series of cartoon vignettes depicting unpleasant events—a child's blocks get knocked over, a child tries to enter a group and fails, and so on. In some of the stories, the event is an accident, in some it is intentional, and in still others it is hard to tell.

When asked about the vignettes, children who had been physically abused gave different answers from children who were unharmed. Those who had been maltreated paid less attention to social cues, more readily attributed hostile intent to someone in the stories, and thought up fewer competent solutions to the problems the stories posed. Their teachers also rated their behavior as more aggressive.

The researchers concluded that the experience of being physically abused leads children to see the world as a hostile place and impairs their ability to process social information accurately.

This pattern, which becomes stable in middle childhood (Dodge, 2003), grows out of their experience. Children who are harshly disciplined at home or rejected by their peers feel angry and alienated and learn to defend themselves by becoming extra vigilant and quickly resorting to force (Dodge, 2003). Children who respond with indirect aggression may also have hostile attributional biases (Crick, Grotpeter, & Bigbee, 2002).

Other researchers distinguish between two different kinds of aggression. Children use *proactive aggression* (also called *instrumental aggression*) to achieve a goal such as obtaining a desired object or intimidating a peer. Proactive aggression is more common among very young children because they don't yet have the words they need to ask for a toy or the teacher's attention. They aren't angry or emotional; they're just using the means available to get what they want. Proactive aggression is governed by reinforcement and thrives in an environment that fosters the use of aggression to reach goals. It often leads to later delinquency and violence (Hay, 2005; Vitaro & Brendgen, 2005).

Reactive aggression (also known as *hostile* or *affective aggression*) appears in the heat of the moment in reaction to some frustration, perceived threat, or provocation (Dodge, 2006; Vitaro, Barker, Boivin, Brendgen, & Tremblay, 2006). Angry, impulsive, and not at all controlled, it is often aimed at hurting someone. Children who are prone to reactive aggression may have an especially reactive temperament and live in a harsh environment (Vitaro & al., 2006). Because they also tend to make errors in social information processing, attributing hostile intentions to others in ambiguous or neutral situations, they are disliked by their peers (Vitaro & Brendgen, 2005).

Children who behave aggressively show some additional distinctive thought patterns. Aggression is perfectly acceptable in their minds. It doesn't hurt the guy on

Children with challenging behavior believe that aggression pays off, and in their experience it often does.

the receiving end, and it can enhance their reputation and make them feel good about themselves. Moreover, they believe that aggression pays off, and in their experience it often does (Vitaro & Brendgen, 2005).

Children who behave in an aggressive or antisocial manner may also lag behind in moral understanding. They can't see things from another person's perspective, insist on having their own way, blame others when things go wrong (Dodge et al., 2006), and continue to attack even when their target is clearly in pain (Perry et al., 1992). They may also inflate their self-esteem by overestimating their own popularity and social competence (Dodge et al., 2006).

Aggressive or antisocial behavior is more likely to occur if the environment considers it normal and acceptable and if it is part of a child's usual repertoire of responses (Brendgen, Vitaro, Boivin, Dionne, & Pérusse, 2006). When the environment devalues aggressive behavior and children have competent, effective, nonaggressive responses at their disposal, they have a far better chance of solving their problems amicably.

Does culture play a role in aggressive behavior?

Cultures vary in the way they view aggressive behavior, highlighting the importance of learning. When adults actively discourage aggressive behavior, the outcome is a peaceful society such as that of the Amish or the Zuni Indian (Delgado, 1979). When they encourage it, an aggressive society is the result. Anthropologist D. P. Fry (1988) studied two neighboring villages in Southern Mexico. In La Paz, the inhabitants

Roughing It

....

Teachers sometimes find it hard to distinguish between aggressive behavior and rough-and-tumble play, when children hit, chase, wrestle, and restrain one another for fun. Rough-and-tumble play is a normal activity, more common among boys, that once upon a time probably honed fighting skills and now helps children test themselves against others and learn to compromise, respect rules, and regulate aggression (Tremblay, Gervais, & Petitclerc, 2008). Rough-and-tumble play decreases with physical maturity. British expert Michael Boulton (1994) offers these tips on how to distinguish it from serious combat:

- *Facial and verbal expression.* In rough-and-tumble play children usually laugh and smile. When they fight for real, they frown, stare, grimace, cry, and get red in the face.
- *Outcome.* Children continue to play together after rough-and-tumble play, but after a real fight they separate.
- *Self-handicapping.* In a play fight, a stronger or older child may let his opponent pin or catch him. This doesn't happen in a serious fight.
- *Restraint.* In playful fighting, the contact between children is relatively gentle. When children are really fighting, they go all out.
- *Role reversals.* In rough-and-tumble play, children alternate roles—for example, they take turns chasing and being chased. This doesn't usually happen in a fight.
- *Number of partners.* Lots of children—10 or more—can participate in rough-and-tumble play. Usually just two fight when it's serious.
- *Onlookers.* Spectators aren't interested in play fighting, but a serious fight or bullying often draws a crowd.

frown on aggressive behavior, and there is very little of it. In nearby San Andres, the residents think aggressive behavior is normal, and when children throw rocks at each other, their parents don't intervene. The consequence is a homicide rate five times higher in San Andres than in La Paz.

A study of the behavior of children in six cultures—India, Okinawa, Kenya, Mexico, the Philippines, and the United States—found that, relatively speaking, American parents tolerate a fair amount of aggressive behavior among children (Segall, Dasen, Berry, & Poortinga, 1990). The United States is one of the most violent countries in the industrialized world (United Nations Office on Drugs and Crime, 2010). Just look at the homicide statistics: In 2008, the United States averaged 5.4 homicides per 100,000 inhabitants (U.S. Department of Justice, Federal Bureau of Investigation, 2009), compared with 1.8 for Canada (Statistics Canada, 2009). Homicide rates among American youth have been falling since the mid 1990s, but they are still alarmingly high (Centers for Disease Control and Prevention, 2009). In 2007, 6 percent of high school students brought a gun to school (Eaton et al., 2008).

Teacher's Choice

In *Preschool in Three Cultures,* Joseph Tobin, David Wu, and Dana Davidson (1989) vividly describe a Japanese 4-year-old who spends his preschool day fighting with the other children, ruining games, and loudly singing and joking. For the most part, his teacher ignores his behavior.

This is a deliberate choice. The Japanese teacher doesn't believe in confronting, censuring, excluding, or punishing. She believes children learn to control their behavior by interacting with their peers and that fighting among boys is inevitable, age-appropriate behavior that teaches children to deal with conflict and become more complete human beings.

The Chinese have a completely different perspective on aggressive behavior: They believe the teacher must intervene at once. "If you let a child behave that way in preschool," says one Chinese teacher, "he will think it is acceptable to be that way, and he will develop a bad character that may last his whole life." The responsibility for teaching appropriate behavior falls squarely on the teacher.

In the United States there is a third approach. Here, words solve the problem of aggressive behavior. Teacher and children talk about the rules and what each child wants, and little by little they negotiate a solution to their dilemma.

Although there are higher rates of violence among African Americans and Latino Americans than among European Americans (Kaufman, 2005), "ethnicity in and of itself should not be considered a causal or risk factor for violence," reports the American Psychological Association's Commission on Violence and Youth (Eron, Gentry, & Schlegel, 1994, p. 101). In these communities there is much more poverty, which is a significant risk factor for violence. When socioeconomic status is taken into account—along with community disorganization, joblessness, racism, and discrimination—the differences in violence rates are small.

There are no real differences in the rates of aggression between African American and European American elementary school children—or among young people ages 18 to 20 who are employed, married, or living with a partner (Dodge et al., 2006). This is an eloquent statement about intervention.

Regardless of their culture, race, or ethnicity, children need to feel safe, respected, and cared for to be able to learn. It's much more difficult to create the conditions that make learning possible when there's a child with challenging behavior in the classroom. The information in the following chapters will help you to understand challenging behavior as well as the children who use it. It will also enable you to develop the skills you need to prevent and manage challenging behavior effectively so that every child you teach can have the opportunity to learn and reach his potential.

W HAT DO YOU THINK?

1. In the text of this chapter, we say, "Negative labels can all too easily become self-fulfilling prophecies." Have you ever been labeled? How did the label affect your behavior and relationships? Can you think of situations when you have labeled someone else? Make a list of negative labels and find positive ways to say the same thing.

2. How can understanding the theories of aggressive and antisocial behavior help you to understand, prevent, and respond to a child's challenging behavior? Choose one of the theories described on pages 11–13 and explain how it would affect your response.

3. How are a child's life experiences related to the cognitive script and social information processing models of aggressive behavior?

4. "There are no real differences in the rates of aggression between African American and European American elementary school children—or among young people ages 18 to 20 who are employed, married, or living with a partner." Why do we say this is an eloquent statement about intervention?

5. Why do you think the United States is so much more violent than other industrialized countries?

S UGGESTED READING

Garbarino, J. (2000). *Lost boys: Why our sons turn violent and how we can save them.* Garden City, NY: Anchor.

Harris, J. R. (2009). *The nurture assumption: Why children turn out the way they do* (rev. ed.). New York: Simon & Schuster.

Kagan, J. (1971). *Understanding children: Behavior, motives, and thought.* New York: Harcourt Brace Jovanovich.

Newman, K. S. (2004). *Rampage: The social roots of school shootings.* New York: Basic Books.

CHAPTER 2

Risk Factors

Even if you're the most experienced and confident of teachers, you can find yourself filled with self-doubt when a child with challenging behaviors enters your classroom. As feelings of insecurity, inadequacy, and defensiveness come flooding in, your first instinct is often to blame someone—the child, the child's parents, yourself. When you feel this way, a wall goes up, and it's hard to ask for help and even harder to accept it. One way to break down that wall is to understand what's behind the challenging behavior.

Because challenging behavior allows children to meet very real needs, it usually serves them well. It will be easier for you to help a child meet those needs more appropriately—and address her behavior effectively—if you understand why she behaves as she does. When you can recognize that her actions stem not from a desire to ruin your day but from other factors in her life, you can then see her in a different light and figure out what she can do, what she can't do, and what she needs to learn in order to succeed.

What causes challenging behavior?

Challenging behavior is so complex that it isn't really possible to talk about its causes. Instead, researchers refer to "risk factors" that may predispose a child to act in an aggressive or antisocial way and "protective factors" that may enable her to avoid such behavior (Rutter, 2006a). Risk factors increase the risk of a particular outcome, but they don't determine it. Outcomes depend on a wide range of genetic and environmental influences (Rutter, 2006a).

Juggler

James Garbarino has been studying the impact of violence on children and youth for decades. In *Lost Boys* (1999), he emphasizes the danger of multiple risk factors:

> I look at it this way: Give me one tennis ball, and I can toss it up and down with ease. Give me two, and I can still manage easily. Add a third, and it takes special skill to juggle them. Make it four, and I will drop them all. So it is with threats to development. (pp. 75–76)

Similar risk factors can result in different outcomes; different risk factors can produce similar outcomes. And risk factors have a cumulative effect. A child who has one risk factor faces no more risk of developing challenging behavior than a child who has none. But a child who has two risk factors faces a risk *four times as great* (Rutter, 2000; Yoshikawa, 1994). Where risk factors are concerned, one plus one equals more than two.

Risk factors are often invisible, and families may not even know they're there. You can ask about them if it seems appropriate, but information will probably be hard to come by. At the same time, even though you're not a doctor or a psychologist trained to make diagnoses, you can learn a lot by observing a child and talking to her family. As you do, keep the risk factors in mind. You can rarely change them, but they will provide you with insight, empathy, and ideas about how to proceed.

People used to ask, "Which is more important, nature or nurture?" But experts now tell us that this debate has become "scientifically obsolete" (Shonkoff & Phillips, 2000, p.6). With the vast outpouring of research in neuroscience and child development in recent years, they have discovered that nature and nurture are inextricably entangled and work together in every aspect of human development. In this chapter, we will try to tease a few threads out of this intricately woven fabric so that we can examine them more closely, but we warn you that they won't come out neatly. Here we'll look at the threads that make up the risk factors for challenging behavior; in the next chapter we'll explore the factors that protect children against it.

We've arranged the risk factors for challenging behavior into two broad categories: biological and environmental. We've defined *biological* as anything that impinges on a child from conception to birth, beginning with genes. The *environmental* section starts with the family—a child's most intimate environment—and moves outward through Urie Bronfenbrenner's (1979) ecological circles of peer, school, neighborhood, and societal influences. Culture is such an important factor that we've given it a chapter all its own (Chapter 6).

Although we present these factors as if they were separate, this is an artificial construct. In fact, they are constantly overlapping and interacting. As we'll see in Chapter 4, each environmental influence has a biological counterpart, and everything comes together in the brain.

BIOLOGICAL RISK FACTORS

Genes

Scientists lean toward the view that a gene specifically "for" a disorder or condition such as antisocial behavior is very unlikely (Rutter, Moffitt, & Caspi, 2006). Rather, many genes—as well as many physiological, developmental, and environmental influences—are at work in almost all types of behavior (Rutter, 2006a).

Because there are so many elements interacting with one another in such complex ways, sorting out the influence of genes from the influence of the environment is extremely difficult. To unravel these different strands, behavioral geneticists use twin studies, comparing identical twins (who share all their genes) and fraternal twins (who share about half their genes). Researchers also study adopted children to see whether they are more like their biological parents (with whom they share genes) or their adoptive parents (with whom they share the environment).

These studies show that antisocial behavior is 40 to 50 percent heritable (Moffitt, 2005; Rhee & Waldman, 2002), leaving a considerable role for the environment (Dodge, Coie, & Lynam, 2006; Rutter, 2006a). However, when it comes to antisocial behavior that begins early in life, genes probably have a more powerful effect (Arseneault et al., 2003).

In addition, scientists have discovered that some genes interact with a particular environment to produce an effect such as aggressive behavior (Rutter et al., 2006); some genes are *expressed* or turned on (or not) because of physical, social, and cultural factors in the environment; and some genes—for example, those that influence difficult temperament, impulsivity, novelty seeking, and lack of empathy—may incline people to put themselves in risky situations. Genes even help to shape the environment. Genes influence how parents bring up their children, and genes affect the responses that children evoke from those around them—for example, a child who is irritable seems to make everyone else ill-humored, too; a child who hits and bites her brother almost automatically elicits harsh discipline from any adult in charge (Deater-Deckard & Cahill, 2006).

Nevertheless, heredity is not destiny. With the right environmental interventions at the right time, even a trait with a strong genetic foundation can be altered.

Double Dose

A study of children adopted in Iowa compared the biological children of parents who were diagnosed with personality disorder with the biological children of parents who did not have this problem. It turned out that the children who had both the problem genes and a problematic environment in their adopted home were much more prone to aggressive and antisocial behavior than the children who had only the problem genes or only the difficult environment. Their genes made them vulnerable to the environment or, to view it from another angle, their environment made them vulnerable to their genes (Cadoret, Yates, Troughton, Woodworth, & Stewart, 1995).

Gender

The experts agree: Boys are more physically aggressive than girls (Archer & Côté, 2005; Underwood, 2003). Boys seem more susceptible to many of the risk factors for aggressive behavior—difficult temperament, ADHD, and learning disabilities, for example (Campbell, 2006; Moffitt & Caspi, 2001; Rutter, Giller, & Hagell, 1998)—and by their first birthday, some boys have already started to use physical force strategically (Baillargeon et al., 2007).

This difference—the result, perhaps, of the male sex hormones bathing a boy's fetal brain—persists throughout childhood (Broidy et al., 2003). Boys hit, push, kick, bite, tease, and insult each other more, spend more time in rough-and-tumble play, and get expelled from prekindergarten 4.5 times as often as girls (Gilliam, 2005). Boys consider aggressive behavior more normal than girls do, and for first-grade boys aggression is positively related to peer acceptance (Dodge, Coie, Pettit, & Price, 1990). Physical aggression starts to taper off only as boys get older and develop more impulse control (Broidy et al., 2003; Maccoby, 2004).

Although girls usually begin to give up physical aggression at about 2 years, a surprising proportion attack their toddler and preschool classmates and use physical aggression well into adolescence (Archer & Côté, 2005). These girls face the prospect of school failure and rejection by their peers and are more likely to be depressed (Underwood, 2003). They often join groups of boys, fight with boys, and eventually date—and marry—boys who act aggressively.

Instead of using physical aggression, many girls turn to *indirect aggression* (also known as *relational* or *social aggression*) as early as age 3. Here the goal is to damage another's self-esteem, social status, or both (Underwood, 2003) with covert tactics such as exclusion, back-stabbing, gossiping, and belittling. Indirect aggression becomes more sophisticated and prevalent in middle childhood and is fairly widespread among girls during adolescence. But note—boys use it almost as often (Card, Stucky, Sawalani, & Little, 2008).

Temperament

In 1956, psychiatrists Alexander Thomas and Stella Chess (Thomas, Chess, & Birch, 1968) began a pioneering longitudinal study of temperament. By collecting data on a sample of 133 children from infancy through young adulthood, they discovered that each child is born with a distinct temperament—an observable, biologically based pattern of behavior and emotions, a characteristic way of experiencing and interacting with the world.

In the following years, other researchers confirmed and extended these findings, and we now know that temperamental traits are moderately heritable, emerge early, become relatively stable by about 3 years of age (Caspi, Roberts, & Shiner, 2005), and remain into adulthood, although by that time they may look entirely different, thanks to their experience in the environment (Caspi & Silva, 1995). This explains why a self-assured young woman who talks easily to strangers at a party may still regard herself as a shy person.

For Mary Rothbart, perhaps the most influential theorist in the field today, temperament is largely about emotion—about the inherent, very individual ways children react to their experiences (which she calls *emotional reactivity*), and the equally individual ways they manage these reactions (which she calls *self-regulation*) (Rothbart, 2004).

According to Rothbart (2004), each child has her own typical, involuntary responses to stimulation (for example, anger, sadness, fear, excitement) and her own typical, involuntary style of expressing herself (for example, persistently, intensely, slowly, impulsively) (Frick, 2004). Likewise, each child has her own distinctive manner of dealing with these responses and returning to equilibrium (by avoiding an event or paying attention to it, for instance). Development, attention, and motor activation all play major roles in this process (Putnam & Stifter, 2008).

Research has consistently found a robust association between temperament and challenging behavior (Frick & Morris, 2004; Rothbart & Bates, 2006). Rothbart describes three broad dimensions of temperament:

- *Negative emotionality.* Children with this temperament feel and express their negative emotions—sadness, anger, frustration, fear, discomfort—more readily. Often irritable, they are distressed by new people and situations and are difficult to soothe (Rothbart, Posner, & Kieras, 2006). Developmental psychologist Jerome Kagan (1998), who has studied this trait in hundreds of children, calls it *behavioral inhibition*; Thomas and Chess use the term *withdrawal* (Rothbart & Jones, 1998). Children with negative emotionality are at high risk of challenging behavior. Untamed, their negative reactions can make them defiant, bring on tantrums, lead to peer rejection, and—because they often feel threatened—impair the development of cognitive skills such as social information processing. In addition, a tendency toward anxiety and depression diminishes their chances of learning the social and emotional skills they need (Eisenberg et al., 2009; Martin & Fox, 2006).

- *Extraversion/surgency.* This dimension's qualities include positive affect and cheerfulness, curiosity and a desire to approach, a high activity level, impulsivity, a distinct lack of shyness, and a pursuit of high intensity pleasure, such as risk taking and novelty seeking (Rothbart, 2004). Children with this temperamental trait, who often display a hot temper, stubbornness, and aggression, are also at high risk for challenging behavior (Dodge et al., 2006; Eisenberg et al., 2009). Those who possess an extreme version—variously called *uninhibited* (Kagan, 1998), *daring* (Lahey & Waldman, 2003), and *callous-unemotional* (Frick & Morris, 2004)—aren't deterred by the threat of punishment or moved by others' distress; and they frequently seem unable to develop empathy, guilt, or a conscience (Frick & Morris, 2004). Their aggressive behavior is likely to be covert and instrumental.

- *Effortful control.* This dimension appears late in the first year of life and develops throughout early childhood as the brain's executive functions come online (Rothbart et al., 2006). It includes two key abilities: the ability to focus and shift attention voluntarily; and the ability to inhibit or activate behavior in order to adapt to a situation, especially when a child doesn't want to (Eisenberg, 2005). Effortful control grows in strength and influence as it interacts with the child's other temperament qualities and the people around her, enabling her to steadily improve her self-regulation. When effortful control is working well, a child can sit still despite distractions, face something she fears, and stop herself from hitting a boy who knocks over her puzzle (Eisenberg, 2005; Rothbart et al., 2006). Effortful control may come to the rescue of children at risk. A child blessed with strong effortful control can manage very powerful emotional and behavioral reactions, whereas a child who has little effortful control may struggle to regulate even relatively weak feelings and impulses throughout childhood (Eisenberg et al., 2004; Frick & Morris, 2004; Olson, Sameroff, Kerr, Lopez, & Wellman, 2005).

Fortunately, traits of temperament aren't written in stone. What matters most is how the environment—including teachers—responds to them. In their temperament study, Thomas and Chess (Thomas et al., 1968) evolved the concept of *goodness of fit*. Serious disturbances are more likely to arise, they found, when the temperament of the child and the expectations of the family or teacher are out of sync.

Teachers who are aware of their own temperament and go out of their way to understand and accommodate a child's temperamental qualities can gradually extend her capacity to cope—to regulate her emotions and behavior, maintain relationships, develop empathy and guilt, and follow societal norms (Frick & Morris, 2004). An fMRI study of Kagan's inhibited children showed that a particular area of their brain, the amygdala, reacted as strongly to novelty in early adulthood as it had when they were toddlers; but with the daily encouragement of their families and teachers, two-thirds of the young adults had succeeded in overcoming their fear and irritability (Schwartz, Wright, Shin, Kagan, & Rauch, 2003). Many uninhibited children had also learned to manage their disobedience, aggressive behavior, and impermeability to adult criticism. Children with more extreme temperamental traits find such learning more difficult, which makes it harder to teach and care for them. But researchers are finding new ways to bolster children's effortful control, which may make a difference in their behavior (Eisenberg et al., 2009). We'll tell you more in Chapters 3 and 8.

Survival of the Fittest

....

In 1974, medical student Marten deVries (1989) went to Kenya and Tanzania to collect information about the temperament of the children of the Masai, a tribe on the Serengeti Plain. Using temperament scales based on Thomas and Chess's criteria, he identified 10 infants with easy temperaments and 10 with difficult temperaments.

The area was in the midst of a severe drought, and when deVries returned 5 months later, most of the Masai's cattle and many of their people had died. Though deVries couldn't locate all of the babies, he found seven with easy temperaments, five of whom had died. On the other hand, all but one of six with difficult temperaments had survived.

What accounted for the survival of the children with difficult temperaments? DeVries credited several factors. First, the Masai admire their warriors and encourage aggressiveness in their children. Second, shared caregiving in the Masai's extended families makes it easier to deal with children with difficult behavior. Third, Masai mothers breast-feed on demand, and children who are fussy ask for—and receive—more nourishment. The qualities that European American middle-class families regard as difficult—loud and frequent crying, for instance—are an advantage in an environment of scarcity (Chess & Thomas, 1989; DeVries, 1989).

Although the environment has a sizeable influence on temperament, it is important to remember that biology comes first. Kagan and others (Kagan, Snidman, Kahn, & Towsley, 2007), who suspect that variations in neurochemical inheritance provide the basis for temperament traits, have found several physiological differences between inhibited and uninhibited children, including differences in heart rate and cortisol levels (Kagan et al., 2007; Schwartz et al., 2003).

Shaped by both biology and childrearing, temperament varies with culture and geography (Kagan & Snidman, 2004). Chinese and Japanese mothers spend a lot of time holding and gently soothing their babies, who tend to be calm and quiet. These practices reflect the high value their cultures place on early mastery of self-control (Ho, 1994). European American mothers use a more active, verbal parenting style because their culture values individuality, independence, and verbal facility. Interestingly, third-generation Japanese American infants are just as talkative and physically active as their European American peers (Ho, 1994). This demonstrates how temperament can change under the influence of changing cultural values.

Complications of pregnancy and birth

New longitudinal studies show that women who experience high stress during pregnancy are more likely to have pregnancy complications, early deliveries, and low-birthweight babies (Talge et al., 2007; Van den Bergh & Marcoen, 2004). Their children are prone to language and intellectual difficulties as toddlers (LaPlante et al., 2004); and later they may develop symptoms of ADHD, anxiety, aggression, and other behavioral and emotional problems (O'Connor, Heron, Golding, Beveridge, & Glover, 2002; Van den Bergh & Marcoen, 2004). Boys seem more vulnerable to these effects than girls (DiPietro, 2002).

Any child who is born prematurely or experiences delivery complications faces substantial risk (Bhutta, Cleves, Casey, Cradock, & Anand, 2002). Prematurity predisposes an infant to brain injury and deprives the developing brain of sustenance (Shonkoff & Phillips, 2000). Premature and low-birthweight babies are more likely to have low scores on cognitive tests and a higher risk for ADHD and aggressive behavior (Bhutta et al., 2002).

Early Birds

Like dinner guests who arrive early, premature babies and those with low birthweights can easily throw their unprepared parents for a loop.

When their babies have to stay in a hospital's neonatal intensive care unit, it's hard for parents to connect with them, and once they come home, they are more difficult to care for than full-term infants. Their cry is more disturbing and irritating, parents find them less satisfying to feed and hold, and parents' expectations of them are often unrealistic (Brady, Posner, Lang, & Rosati, 1994; Moffitt, 1997).

Improving prenatal care and promoting maternal health can reduce the risk of neuropsychological damage to the baby. In a study in upstate New York (Olds et al., 1998), nurses visited poor, young, or unmarried women at home at least once a month during their pregnancies. Fifteen years later, the children of these women had fewer arrests and ran away from home less often than the children of unvisited mothers. That is, the intervention lowered the risk for these children even though the nurses had never visited after they were born.

Substance abuse during pregnancy

Alcohol, tobacco, and drugs ingested during pregnancy can do considerable harm. How much harm depends on the fetus's stage of development, as well as how much, how long, and how often exposure takes place. The resilience of the fetus and the mother's health and prenatal care play a role (Shonkoff & Phillips, 2000), and so does the parents' behavior after the baby's birth. If they continue to abuse drugs or alcohol, their children may face the added danger of neglect, abuse, or chaotic, inconsistent, unresponsive caregiving (Bendersky, Bennett, & Lewis, 2006; Keller, Cummings, Davies, & Mitchell, 2008).

Alcohol

Alcohol is responsible for much more damage to unborn babies than any illegal drug. Drinking any amount at any time during pregnancy—especially heavy or binge drinking—causes lifelong damage to the developing brain (U.S. Department of Health and Human Services, Office of the Surgeon General, 2005).

The set of birth defects now known as *fetal alcohol spectrum disorder (FASD)* includes *fetal alcohol syndrome (FAS)*, which is characterized by facial defects, growth deficiency, brain abnormalities, and behavior problems, and *alcohol-related neurodevelopmental disorder* (*ARND*, also called *fetal alcohol effects*, or *FAE*), in which cognitive impairments just as serious lie hidden behind perfectly normal faces and bodies. FASD is the leading cause of mental retardation, and children with FASD have difficulties with learning, memory, attention, planning, problem solving, and motor skills (Mattson, Fryer, McGee, & Riley, 2008). Their self-control and executive functions may also be affected, and they have higher rates of ADHD. Easily overwhelmed by stimulation, children with FASD react impulsively, quickly become angry or frustrated, struggle with understanding and using language, and have trouble making friends (Harwood & Kleinfeld, 2002).

Tobacco and nicotine

The warnings on the cigarette packages are there for good reason: Smoking during pregnancy causes babies to be born prematurely and to have low birthweights and low IQs (Fergusson, 2002). Nicotine crosses the placenta and affects the developing nervous system, putting a child at risk for aggressive and disruptive behavior, attention difficulties, impulsivity, hyperactivity, and problems with language and emotional regulation (Cornelius & Day, 2009; Fried, 2002b; Huijbregts, Séguin, Zoccolillo, Boivin, & Tremblay, 2008; Olds, 1997). Once again, boys suffer from these effects more than girls (D'Onofrio et al., 2008).

WARNING
CIGARETTES HURT BABIES

Tobacco use during pregnancy reduces the growth of babies. These smaller babies may not catch up in growth after birth and the risks of infant illness, disability and death are increased.

Health Canada

All Canadian cigarette packages carry health alerts. This one warns of the dangers for the fetus of smoking during pregnancy. Large graphic warnings are required in countries all over the world, including the United States.

Health Canada, Tobacco Control Programme. This is a copy of an official work that is published by the Government of Canada and has not been produced in affiliation with, or with the endorsement of the Government of Canada. This use is licensed under Health Canada copyright.

Illicit drugs

Pregnant women who use drugs probably use more than one substance, raising the risks for their unborn child. Children who've been exposed to *marijuana* prenatally perform poorly on attention, memory, and verbal tests, and they are more likely to be impulsive and hyperactive (Fried, 2002a; Goldschmidt, Day, & Richardson, 2000). In addition, their executive functions may be impaired (Fried, 2002a).

The research on children exposed to *cocaine* or *crack* in the womb has yielded mixed results. Some investigators have seen no impairment (Chasnoff et al., 1998); others have found an association with aggressive behavior problems (Bada et al., 2007; Bendersky et al., 2006; Chasnoff et al., 1998; Shankaran et al., 2007), poorer executive functioning (Shankaran et al., 2007; Warner et al., 2006), and increased reactivity and decreased self-regulation, which lead to problems with attention and impulse control, especially in boys (Bendersky et al., 2006; Dennis, Bendersky, Ramsay, & Lewis, 2006).

Exposure to *methamphetamine* in utero—which is increasingly common—produces similar results (Smith et al., 2008). *Opiates* such as *heroin* cause prematurity and low birthweight and put babies at risk for attention and developmental problems.

Neurological problems

Children with challenging behavior often have difficulties with brain function. If the disability takes a recognizable form, the child may become eligible for special education services. But all too frequently, the problem remains undiagnosed or undiagnosable, and the teacher must find her own solutions. (For more about children with disabilities, see Chapter 11.)

Executive functions

Many children with challenging behavior have *executive functions* that don't work properly. This catchall phrase encompasses a series of interdependent skills that enable children to regulate their thoughts, actions, and emotions and perform any goal-directed activity, from taking a sip of juice without spilling it to entering a game of hospital in the dramatic play corner. The executive functions include

- planning and organizing behavior, including anticipating problems and figuring out strategies to cope with them
- sequencing behavior
- sustaining attention and concentration
- being flexible and able to shift from one mind-set to another
- inhibiting responses
- self-monitoring
- taking the perspective of others (Moffitt, 1997; Shonkoff & Phillips, 2000)

Executive functions emerge at the end of the first year of life as children start to inhibit certain responses. At about 2 years they can begin to use rules to guide their behavior, and from 3 to 5 years their ability to self-regulate gets better and better (Zelazo, 2005). These improvements coincide with growth in the brain's prefrontal cortex, where the executive functions reside (Anderson, 2002). When a child's executive functions are out of kilter, she can't control her behavior very well and is liable to act impulsively, without considering the impact on others (Moffitt, 1997). Many of the difficulties we describe next, which appear in order of prevalence, involve problems with executive function.

Attention deficit hyperactivity disorder

Challenging behavior very often arrives in the company of hyperactivity or inattention (Kutcher et al., 2004)—the hallmarks of attention deficit hyperactivity disorder (ADHD), sometimes called attention deficit disorder (ADD). A neurological disorder with a strong genetic base, ADHD has one additional core symptom—impulsivity—that combines with hyperactivity and inattention to create three different forms of the disorder (DuPaul & Stoner, 2003):

- *Predominantly inattentive type.* Children in this category have memory problems and difficulty focusing their attention. Because they can't block out unimportant stimuli, they see and hear things others don't, like the lawnmower on the next block.
- *Predominantly hyperactive-impulsive type.* Quick to anger when they're frustrated or reprimanded, children with this type of ADHD find it hard to sit still and wait their turn. They leap before they look, and although they often know what they should and shouldn't do, they just can't control themselves.
- *Combination type.* Children with the full-blown disorder exhibit all of its symptoms. Their behavior can be overactive, inattentive, impulsive, noncompliant, and aggressive.

These symptoms may appear early, but the diagnosis—which a doctor must make—may not be confirmed until a child reaches 5 or 6 years of age. More than twice as common in boys as in girls (Pastor & Reuben, 2008), ADHD affects 3 to 7 percent of school-age children (American Psychiatric Association, 2000) and is frequently accompanied by learning disabilities (Pastor & Reuben, 2008).

Children with ADHD often have trouble relating to their peers. They lose their tempers, argue, and fight; struggle to join groups and have conversations; and use aggression to deal with conflict. As a consequence, they may be rejected by their classmates and have no friends (DuPaul & Stoner, 2003).

Recent research has found that the brain's motor center matures more quickly in children with ADHD than it does in children who are developing typically, while the region of the brain that enables them to control their behavior—the prefrontal cortex, site of the executive functions—matures several years later (Shaw et al., 2007). Neuroimaging studies in children with ADHD show that this area is also less active during tasks that require cognitive control (Durston, 2008).

It is important to know that ADHD is sometimes mistakenly diagnosed when a child has experienced trauma and is actually suffering from posttraumatic stress disorder, which has similar symptoms (see page 38).

Learning disabilities

About 5 percent of school-age children have a learning disability, and another 4 percent deal with ADHD at the same time (Pastor & Reuben, 2008). The result of genetics and a neurobiological deficit, learning disabilities affect boys more than girls (American Academy of Pediatrics et al., 2009). The disabilities fall into two categories:

- *Verbal.* About 80 percent of children have the language-based disability known as *dyslexia* and have difficulty with reading and spelling.

- *Nonverbal.* Children in this group run into trouble with the complex conceptual skills involved in problem solving, understanding cause and effect, abstraction, and seeing the big picture (Vacca, 2001). In addition, problems with physical coordination and visual and spatial perception create difficulties with ordinary tasks such as drawing, cutting, and writing (Connell, 2003).

Children with both kinds of learning disabilities encounter frustration more often than most of us (Farmer, 2000), and their imperfect perception and inability to read social cues trip them up in social situations (American Academy of Pediatrics et al., 2009; Lagae, 2008). It is no wonder they tend to have low self-esteem, are often rejected by their classmates, and become verbally or physically aggressive (Haager & Klingner, 2005).

Although *sensory integration dysfunction* (also called *sensory processing disorder*) isn't formally designated as a learning disability, many children with learning disabilities (and those with autism) have trouble sorting out and integrating all the sensory information that comes their way (Kranowitz, 2006). Some hardly seem to notice sensory input; others overreact and develop strong preferences for such items as socks without seams that don't overwhelm their extra-sensitive systems (Greene, 2010). They are liable to be distractible and hyperactive (Ayres, 1979), and they often seem clumsy and uncoordinated, forever tripping and bumping their way through life.

Language and speech disorders

Studies report a 50 percent overlap between language delays and behavior problems (Campbell, 2002). Psychologists often discover unsuspected language disorders among the children referred to them with challenging behavior, and language specialists just as frequently encounter behavior problems among children with language delays (Coie & Dodge, 1998). According to psychologist Terrie E. Moffitt (1997), "The link between verbal impairment and antisocial outcomes is one of the largest and most robust effects in the study of antisocial behavior. The verbal deficits of antisocial children are pervasive, affecting their memory for verbal material and their ability to listen and read, to solve problems, and to speak and write" (p. 132).

Besides scholastic problems, children with language or speech impairments have social and self-esteem difficulties. Often teased or isolated, they find it hard to develop social skills and make friends. Because they may not understand the reassurances and instructions they get from adults, they can't convert them into tools for self-control, and they may try out many varieties of misbehavior instead. When using language is so difficult, problem behavior can be a much more effective way to get your point across.

Cognitive impairment

Cognitive impairment goes by many names, including *cognitive disabilities, developmental disabilities,* and *mental retardation.* It affects all cognitive functions, including thinking, learning, processing and using information, motor skills, complex reasoning,

Lost in Translation

It is easy to see how children without language and verbal skills might turn to challenging behavior. In *The Explosive Child* (1998), Ross W. Greene describes some of the barriers that such children encounter:

- *Understanding.* When a child doesn't understand the words of the people around her, she becomes confused and frustrated and finds it hard to respond appropriately.
- *Categorizing, labeling, and storing emotions and previous experiences in language.* If a child can't use language to classify and store her feelings and experience, she doesn't know how she feels or what she did the last time she felt this way.
- *Thinking things through in language.* When a child can't use words to think things through, she can't figure out what to do, even when she knows what she's feeling.
- *Expressing complicated feelings, thoughts, and ideas.* A child may have trouble going beyond simple language to articulate what's bothering her.

memory, and attention. Like children with ADHD, those with cognitive disabilities can't remember what needs to be done or how much time it takes to do it (Friend, 2005). They learn language more slowly, labor to grasp concepts, and fail to generalize what they've learned. They find schoolwork difficult, but they can learn more than people anticipate if they work harder and practice more than their peers (Friend, 2005).

Children with cognitive disabilities are also at risk for social problems. Because they are usually immature, often miss social cues, and easily misinterpret others' actions, their classmates tend to reject them and they feel lonely and isolated (Farmer, 2000; Leffert, Siperstein, & Millikan, 2000).

Autistic spectrum disorders

Autistic spectrum disorder (ASD), which affects nearly 1 in 100 children and four times as many boys as girls (Nicholas, Carpenter, King, Jenner, & Charles, 2009; Rice, 2009), is the name given to a group of neurodevelopmental disorders with the same tell-tale characteristics: problems with verbal and nonverbal communication, difficulty with social interaction, and repetitive behaviors or interests (National Institute of Neurological Disorders and Stroke, 2009).

Autism disorder, the most widespread, usually includes intellectual disability as well as moderately severe communication, social, and behavior problems. Children with *Asperger syndrome* develop reasonably normal language skills, but they don't know how to interact with others, despite their interest in doing so. Children with *pervasive developmental disorder not otherwise specified (PDD-NOS)* have trouble with social interactions and play and display repetitive behaviors.

Researchers are racing to track down the causes of ASD, which probably involves the entire brain, particularly the networks governing how brain cells grow and talk to each other (Munro, 2010; National Institute of Child Health and Human Development [NICHD], 2006a, 2006b). Both the environment and heredity play major roles, and siblings of children with the disorder are at high risk (NICHD, 2006c). A new study implicating more than 100 genes has found that each affected person has her own form of autism, genetically quite unique. The genetic variations can be inherited or arise spontaneously and often overlap with genes associated with intellectual disability. These findings should help lead to earlier diagnosis (Munro, 2010)—important because the sooner intervention begins, the more successful it's likely to be.

For children with ASD, communication is virtually always a problem, even if their language skills are relatively strong. They have trouble making their needs and desires known, as well as difficulty paying attention, taking turns, making believe, reading social cues, and understanding the feelings of others (Smith & Ellsworth, 2004). They may also have sensory issues, either under- or overreacting to sights, sounds, smells, pain, temperature, tastes, or touch; and they may learn in different ways—they are often strong visual learners but can't imitate what other people do (Smith & Ellsworth, 2004). Because children with ASD have a strong need for predictability, any change in routine may provoke tantrums, aggressive behavior, or self-injury (Thompson, 2007). For more information about autism see Chapter 11.

Emotional and behavior disorders

In 2005 about 20 percent of parents sought help for a son with an emotional or behavior difficulty, and another 16 percent wanted assistance for a daughter (Simpson, Cohen, Pastor, & Reuben, 2006). But not all of these children received treatment. It is difficult to distinguish appropriate short-term reactions to stress from a diagnosable disorder, which usually involves behavior that is frequent and intense, continues over many months, and impairs interaction and development (Campbell, 2006).

There are two broad classes of emotional and behavior disorders (called *emotional disturbance* by IDEA, the Individuals with Disabilities Education Improvement Act of 2004), some of which can be detected during the preschool years (National Scientific Council on the Developing Child, 2008):

- *Externalizing disorders,* in which the child acts out or directs her feelings outwards. This group includes *oppositional defiant disorder,* where children behave in negative, hostile ways, losing their temper, arguing, defying, refusing to comply, and deliberately annoying others; and *conduct disorder,* seen in older children who persistently break rules, bully others, and act aggressively (U.S. Department of Health and Human Services, 2003).

- *Internalizing disorders,* in which the child feels worry, anxiety, sadness, or fearfulness and withdraws or turns her feelings inward. Included here are *eating disorders; anxiety disorders* such as *separation anxiety, obsessive-compulsive disorder, posttraumatic stress disorder,* and *phobias;* and *mood disorders* such as *depression, bipolar illness,* and *schizophrenia* (U.S. Department of Health and Human Services, 2003).

Children with emotional and behavior disorders often have ADHD, a learning disability, or difficulty with language as well (Benner, Nelson, & Epstein, 2002; Handwerk & Marshall, 1998). As a result, they have great trouble in the academic realm (Sutherland, Wheby, & Gunter, 2000) and problems with social skills and friendships (Cullinan, Evans, Epstein, & Ryser, 2003).

ENVIRONMENTAL RISK FACTORS

According to the ecological systems theory of Urie Bronfenbrenner (1979), everything in a child's environment—her family, peers, child care center or school, neighborhood, poverty level, even her exposure to violence in the media and society at large—influences her development and can present potential risk factors for challenging behavior. In this section we've arranged these factors as if each could stand alone, starting with the closest to the child and moving to the most distant, but the truth is that all of these elements overlap and interact continually. Perhaps the best example of this phenomenon is poverty, which affects virtually all of the other risk factors, including those in the biological section.

Family factors and parenting style

Because families play so vital a role in their children's development, they are easy targets whenever challenging behavior appears on the scene. Raising a child is difficult and complicated work that requires a vast amount of time and energy—items in short supply in most families. It is important for teachers to understand the family's role in challenging behavior, but it is equally important not to blame them.

Any life circumstance that hinders a parent's well-being can put children at risk, including

- a young mother, especially one who had her first child in her teens (Gershoff, 2002; Tremblay et al., 2004)
- a mother with little education (Nagin & Tremblay, 2001)
- a mother who is depressed (Ashman, Dawson, & Panagiotides, 2008; Gershoff, 2002; National Institute of Child Health and Human Development Early Child Care Research Network [NICHD ECCRN], 2004)
- a mother with a history of conduct problems and aggressive, antisocial, or criminal behavior (Gershoff, 2002; Tremblay et al., 2004; Zoccolillo et al., 2005)
- marital conflict (NICHD ECCRN, 2004; Tremblay et al., 2004)
- financial hardship (NICHD ECCRN, 2004; Tremblay et al., 2004; Zoccolillo et al., 2005)
- single parent status (Gershoff, 2002; Joussemet et al., 2008; NICHD ECCRN, 2004)

Indirectly, all these factors influence the parent–child relationship, the first line of defense against aggressive behavior. According to *attachment theory*, first described by John Bowlby (1969/1982) and Mary Ainsworth (Ainsworth, Blehar, Waters, & Wall, 1978), a *secure attachment* to a sensitive and responsive primary caregiver provides the foundation for a child's emotional development, enabling her to learn to regulate and express her feelings, cope with stress, and see herself as an effective and loveable person. But when the primary caregiver is unavailable, unpredictable, insensitive, or rejecting, the child forms an *insecure* or *disorganized attachment*; and she doesn't trust adults to care for her or help her organize her world, has difficulty regulating her emotions, and feels ineffectual and unworthy of love. Because the parent–child relationship acts as a prototype for the child's future relationships (Bowlby, 1969/1982), children with an insecure or disorganized attachment have trouble getting along with their peers and teachers, and their behavior is often challenging and aggressive (Greenberg, Speltz, & DeKlyen, 1993; Zoccolillo et al., 2005). (For more about attachment, see Chapter 5.)

The more adversity the family is facing, the greater the chances a child will develop aggressive and antisocial behavior that begins at an early age and continues into adulthood (NICHD ECCRN, 2004; Zoccolillo et al., 2005). Parenting under highly stressful conditions—poverty, violence, depression, single parenthood—tends to become less warm and sensitive, undermining secure attachment. When parents are emotionally unavailable, they can't help their children learn social and emotional skills, regulate their feelings and behavior, or feel safe and supported (Ashman et al., 2008; NICHD ECCRN, 2004). Instead they may slip into childrearing methods that are harsh, hostile, punitive, and inconsistent, including physical discipline (Regalado, Sareen, Inkelas, Wissow, & Halfon, 2004), which is strongly associated with both direct and indirect aggressive behavior in children (Côté, Vaillancourt, Barker, Nagin, & Tremblay, 2007; Gershoff, 2002).

Gerald R. Patterson (1982, 1995) of the Oregon Social Learning Center has documented a cycle of interaction between parent and child that he calls "coercive." It can begin with a relatively trivial demand, such as a parent asking a child to do, or not do, something. The child ignores the request or refuses to comply. Then the parent responds more aggressively, scolding, nagging, or pleading; the child again refuses, whining or talking back. The exchanges escalate to yelling and threats, hitting and temper tantrums, until the parent finally gives up and gives in—or explodes into violence—and then the child stops, too.

When the parents give in, they are rewarding their child's negative behavior and increasing the chances she'll behave the same way again. Simultaneously, the child is reinforcing the parents by ceasing her own negative behavior (Coie & Dodge, 1998). When the parents explode, they are modeling the use of aggression as a way to solve problems. The child may do as they ask, but she is more likely to feel hostility toward them and to become aggressive with both parents and peers in the future, especially if they don't have a warm relationship (Coie & Dodge, 1998). Each time the parents use this tactic it will be less effective, and they will probably utilize greater force, which may eventually lead to abuse (Gershoff, 2002).

Whether they give in or resort to violence, the parents become demoralized. To avoid unpleasantness, they interact with their child less and less, missing opportunities to help her gain the emotional, social, and cognitive skills she needs to make friends and succeed at school. Children who live in families where this coercive cycle is the norm arrive in school with well-polished antisocial behavior. Because they challenge the teacher and don't follow instructions, it's difficult for them to establish good relationships and learn basic skills, such as reading (Biglan, Brennan, Foster, & Holder, 2004).

Biased social information processing also plays a role. When children are growing up with harsh, unpredictable discipline, they learn to tune into any indications of threat in their surroundings. Then they readily interpret others' actions as hostile, think of and use aggressive responses to deal with the situation, and regard their aggression as beneficial (Gershoff, 2002; Vitaro, Barker, Boivin, Brendgen, & Tremblay, 2006).

It is important to remember, however, that parent–child interaction is a two-way street. The child's temperament strongly influences the way the people in her life react to her, and each parent responds according to his or her own temperament. If the fit between them isn't a good one, poor parenting may be the result. A new study shows that children who are fussy at one year of age elicit both spanking and verbal punishment (Berlin et al., 2009).

Peers

As early as the preschool years, children have a powerful effect on one another. For their same-sex peers in particular, they act as important socializing agents (Fabes, Hanish, & Martin, 2003). Most children dislike playmates who act aggressively, especially if they lack verbal skills and have trouble controlling their impulses, attention, and behavior (Snyder, Prichard, Schrepferman, Patrick, & Stoolmiller, 2004). A child with challenging behavior often uses coercive tactics (e.g., teasing, name-calling, threats) as she tries to engage others and resolve conflicts, and her prosocial peers respond negatively in turn. It isn't long before the group rejects and excludes her (Snyder et al., 2008).

This process serves to escalate children's oppositional and aggressive tendencies (Dodge et al., 2003) and keep them from acquiring the social and emotional skills they need (Snyder et al., 2005). They may also become targets of harassment and victimization, raising their already high risk for aggressive and antisocial behavior, delinquency, and school dropout (Boivin, Vitaro, & Poulin, 2005).

Perhaps because they've been rejected, perhaps because they share an interest in rough play, or simply because children prefer to play with others like themselves, children with aggressive behavior tend to stick together (Estell, Cairns, Farmer, & Cairns, 2002; Snyder, Horsch, & Childs, 1997). As a result they spend more time in the company of others with aggressive and antisocial behavior, and a kind of contagion takes place: They expose one another to new antisocial ideas and experiences and adopt similar attitudes and behavior styles (Hanish, Martin, Fabes, Leonard, & Herzog, 2005). For example, in kindergarten they talk precociously about—and even role play—sex, drinking, smoking, stealing, cheating, swearing, and defying authority (Snyder et al., 2005). This provokes laughter, excitement, and approval, reinforcing the behavior and ensuring that it will continue and even increase (Snyder et al., 2008).

Not all children with aggressive behavior are rejected by their peers. Those who show little fear, use aggression proactively, aren't impulsive or disruptive, and have good verbal and social skills actually achieve high status and become the central players in a group (Snyder et al., 2008). Some of the most influential may rise to the

Under the Radar

At about 30 months, children begin to prefer playmates of the same sex (Fabes et al., 2003). Girls, who tend to play near adults, have numerous opportunities to practice self-regulation, follow adult rules, and gain adult approval (Fabes et al., 2003). But boys—whose activity is more rough, active, and physical—usually play in large groups away from adult supervision. Generating their own rules, they use aggression and power-assertive demands to establish a pecking order. This interesting, exciting play offers plenty of chances to lose control—and few to learn self-regulation (Fabes et al., 2003).

top of the social hierarchy by bullying, provoking fights, and defying the teacher—yet their peers consider them the coolest kids in the class (Estell et al., 2002).

Group norms that support aggressive and antisocial behavior—or fail to condemn it—foster this phenomenon (Boivin et al., 2005). A high level of aggression in a classroom breeds more aggression, especially in children who already have aggressive tendencies.

Child care and school

While children are attending child care, they have very little control over their own lives, and their individual needs often take a back seat to the needs of the group and the teachers (children may be required to nap so that teachers can have a lunch break, for example). Children who are inflexible or easily frustrated and children who are especially active or timid find this extremely hard, and it's harder when they spend the entire day there. Challenging behavior is their way of letting us know what they feel.

Research has shown that stimulating and emotionally supportive child care is associated with positive developmental outcomes for children. But in 2003, a longitudinal study of about 1,300 children by the National Institute of Child Health and Human Development (NICHD ECCRN) found a link between the number of hours that 4½-year-olds and kindergartners spend in child care and their social competence and problem behavior. As the children's time in child care increased, so did their problem behavior and aggression. A follow-up study (Belsky et al., 2007) showed that children who had experienced more hours in child care centers continued to display more noncompliant and aggressive behavior through grade 6. Both studies took into account quality of care, children's gender and temperament, mothers' education and sensitivity, and family income and ethnicity.

Because the effects detected by these studies are small and well within the normal range, it's tempting to dismiss them. But investigators have taken this research seriously, and they're digging deep to explain it, although their findings are often confusing. They have discovered that spending more time in child care creates "substantially greater behavioral problems" in children from low-risk, high-income White families (Loeb, Bridges, Bassok, Fuller, & Rumberger, 2007, p. 65); but it protects children growing up in high-risk, low-income, Latino, or African American families—provided the child care is of high quality (Côté et al., 2007; Loeb et al., 2007; Love et al., 2003; Votruba-Drzal, Coley, & Chase-Lansdale, 2004).

Other factors contribute to a rise in behavior problems, including low-quality care (Votruba-Drzal et al., 2004), changes in child care arrangements (Love et al., 2003), multiple child care arrangements (Morrissey, 2009), more time in the company of peers (see page 33) (Belsky et al., 2007; NICHD ECCRN, 2006), and primary school teachers who lack training and time to address behavior problems (Belsky et al., 2007).

Some investigators are wondering what will happen once a great many children who've attended child care reach school age. Will the small but widespread increase in problem behavior have cumulative effects? Will the school climate change? Will teachers have to spend more time on classroom management and less on instruction (Belsky, 2009)?

Research by Yale University researcher Walter S. Gilliam (2005) suggests they will. His study found that state-funded prekindergarten programs were expelling preschoolers "due to behavior concerns" at more than three times the rate that schools were ousting children in kindergarten through grade 12. Boys were thrown out more than four times as often as girls, and African American preschoolers were about twice as likely to be expelled as European American and Latino children. But, Gilliam discovered, the more access teachers had to the help of a mental health professional, the less likely they were to eject a child; and he recommended they receive enhanced support and better training in addressing problem behavior.

In the larger framework of a school, many more factors influence children's behavior. The wealthiest public schools spend at least 10 times as much as the poorest (Darling-Hammond, 2004), with the result that children in poor neighborhoods attend schools with larger class sizes and fewer books, computers, libraries, materials, extracurricular activities, counselors, and highly qualified teachers (Beam, 2004; Darling-Hammond, 2004). This shortfall affects students' behavior and their academic performance, which are often related (Gottfredson, n.d.).

The way a school is organized and run (including having clear behavioral expectations and rules that are consistently and fairly applied) also shapes school and classroom climate, hence children's behavior (Gottfredson et al., 2004). Corporal punishment is still allowed in 21 states, and in 2006–2007 more than 200,000 children were subjected to it (Human Rights Watch & American Civil Liberties Union, 2008). Emotional abuse—controlling students through fear and intimidation, bullying, sarcasm, ridicule, or humiliation—is equally harmful and has an impact on every child in the room (Hyman & Snook, 1999). Teaching quality, a subject we'll cover in Chapter 8, also influences behavior.

In addition, state and local policies and laws such as the federal No Child Left Behind Act of 2002 have a powerful effect. When the results of a test determine whether a child will move from one grade to the next or whether a school will be taken over by the state, the stakes are very high indeed. To raise their test scores, schools change their priorities, gearing their curricula to the exams instead of using developmentally appropriate content and practice. In the poorest schools in particular (Association for Supervision and Curriculum Development, 2004), teachers are spending more time on reading, writing, math, and science (the subjects tested under No Child Left Behind) and cutting back on subjects not tested—arts, gym, recess, and others (Mathews, 2005; Perkins-Gough, 2004; Tracey, 2005; Wallis, Thomas, Crittle, & Forster, 2003; Wood, 2004). Test preparation is replacing projects, themes, field trips, and hands-on, experiential learning—the ways that children learn best (Ganesh & Surbeck, 2005; Wood, 2004). One consequence of this narrow focus is enormous stress on everyone from the principal on down; another is an increase in behavior problems (Wallis et al., 2003).

Poverty and the conditions surrounding it

Because poverty affects families, peers, schools, and neighborhoods as well as individuals, it has an enormous effect on children's lives. Being poor creates a high level of family stress—nonstop anxiety about food, housing, jobs, medical care, child care, safety, and more. In high-poverty urban neighborhoods, people must deal with noise, overcrowding, substandard housing, air and water pollution, neighborhood and gang violence, homelessness, and illegal drugs; and they have little access to health and recreational services, mainstream role models and opportunities, and stimulating resources such as books, toys, and computers (Dearing, Berry, & Zaslow, 2006). They may also have little or no social support, formal or informal. It is hard to make and keep friends when you're living in a gigantic housing project, when people move all the time and you don't know your neighbors, when one person carries the full responsibility for the family, when people are afraid to go to church, the local store, even to school.

This "social disorganization" (Sampson, 1997), as the sociologists call it, is becoming more and more common in U.S. inner cities (Garbarino, 1999), and it carries with it an accumulation of risk factors for families and children. More than 35 percent of children who live in poor families have seven or more risk factors—versus 7 percent of those who live in wealthy families (Sameroff & Fiese, 2000). In these stressful circumstances, raising children is extremely arduous, and despite their best intentions, parents who suffer from anxiety, anger, or depression may parent in a way that's harsh, punitive, coercive, or withdrawn (Dearing et al., 2006). (See pages 31–32.)

A family belonging to a minority culture faces the additional stress of racial discrimination, which damages self-esteem and provokes feelings of rage and shame (Garbarino, 1999). In 2007, 34 percent of African American children and 29 percent of Latino children lived in poverty, compared with 10 percent of White European American children (Fass & Cauthen, 2008).

Families with young children are more likely to be poor (Dearing et al., 2006; Fass & Cauthen, 2008), and poverty has more drastic consequences for young children, both urban and rural, than it does for older ones (Duncan, Brooks-Gunn, Yeung, & Smith, 1998; Evans & English, 2002; Macmillan, McMorris, & Kruttschnitt, 2004). Because good prenatal care is often not available to low-income families, children are at risk even before they are born. Prematurity, low birthweight, and neurological damage—all players in challenging behavior—appear much more frequently in poor households (Dearing et al., 2006; Sampson, 1997).

Children living in poverty have a smaller chance of creating a secure attachment with their primary caregiver (Halle et al., 2009) and a greater chance of having emotional and behavioral problems, including tantrums, fighting, anxiety, sadness, noncompliance, impulsivity, and hypervigilance (Coles, 2008–2009; McLloyd, 1998; Xue, Leventhal, Brooks-Gunn, & Earls, 2005). They also struggle at school and are at high risk for grade retention and special education (Coles, 2008–2009; McLloyd, 1998).

Recent research attributes these difficulties to a surprisingly strong association between socioeconomic status (SES) and cognitive ability. Neuroscientists Daniel A. Hackman and Martha J. Farah (2009) put it simply: "SES influences brain function" (p. 68). In a series of studies, investigators have discovered that in comparison to children from middle-class homes, young children in low-income families do poorly on tests of language and cognition—especially of the executive functions that involve memory, working memory, planning, focus, and effortful control (Farah et al., 2006; Lengua, Honorado, & Bush, 2007; Li-Grining, 2007). In other words, through its effects on brain development, poverty can impair children's ability to regulate their own behavior. Fortunately, new interventions targeting these skills are showing remarkable success (see pages 51 and 163–166).

A natural experiment in North Carolina gave researchers a rare glimpse of the difference money can make (Costello, Compton, Keeler, & Angold, 2003). In the middle of the Great Smoky Mountains Study, an 8-year project involving 1,400 school-age children, a casino opened up on the Native American reservation where a quarter of the children in the study lived. Every 6 months the families on the reservation received a portion of the profits. Fourteen percent of them were able to climb out of poverty, and their children showed a remarkable 40 percent decrease in serious behavior problems—equal to the rate of children who'd never been poor. When the scientists tested factors that might account for this dramatic drop, they found just one: Parents who were no longer poor could provide better supervision for their children. Money gave them time, a scarce resource for people in poverty.

Hidden Threats

Because it is found in dust, lead-based paint, water pipes, and lead-based gasoline embedded in the soil, lead poses an especially potent threat to pregnant women and children living in old housing and poor inner-city neighborhoods (Jones et al., 2009). Through its link to hyperactivity, attention deficits, learning disabilities, lowered IQ, and problems with executive function, lead exposure puts children at high risk of aggressive, delinquent, and criminal behavior (Wright et al., 2008). In a recent study of young adults who'd been exposed to lead at an early age, an incredible 55 percent had been arrested at least once (Wright et al., 2008).

For many years a disproportionate number of African American and/or poor children have tested above the "acceptable" limit of 10 micrograms of lead per deciliter of blood set by the Centers for Disease Control and Prevention (Jones et al., 2009). And there is clear evidence that much lower amounts also inflict serious harm (Bellinger, 2008).

Malnutrition poses another serious danger for children in poverty. For optimal brain development, a child needs adequate nutrition both before birth and during the first 2 or 3 years of life, but some 17 percent of American children—and a much larger proportion of African American and Latino children—don't get enough to eat (Federal Interagency Forum on Child and Family Statistics, 2009). Malnutrition seems to hit hardest in the social and emotional realms (Shonkoff & Phillips, 2000). One study found that malnourished 3-year-olds are predisposed to neurocognitive deficits, which in turn make them prone to behavior problems throughout childhood and adolescence (Liu, Raine, Venables, & Mednick, 2004).

Exposure to violence

Violence is endemic in American life and culture. Children run into it in the news, in games and sports, in adult conversation, in Saturday morning cartoons, even in their own lives. A survey of children aged 2 to 17 found that 71 percent had seen or experienced violence (Finkelhor, Ormrod, Turner, & Hamby, 2005); and a study in a high-crime urban neighborhood revealed that 42 percent of preschoolers had witnessed at least one violent event. Over 20 percent had seen three or more (Linares et al., 2001).

A close encounter with violence makes a deep and powerful impression on children, even when they aren't its victims (Linares et al., 2001). It changes the way they view the world and "may change the value they place on life itself," according to Betsy Groves and Barry Zuckerman of the Boston Medical Center School of Medicine (1997, p. 183). Parents, who have the most power to help, may also feel traumatized and fail to recognize and respond to their children's distress (Linares et al., 2001). The younger children are, the more serious the effects, because exposure to violence can alter the developing brain (DeBellis, 2005).

Feeling stressed, unsafe, anxious, depressed, hostile, irritable, or threatened (Lynch, 2006), children exposed to violence find it hard to regulate their emotions and often behave aggressively—a response they've learned is an acceptable way to solve problems (Linares et al., 2001; Schwartz & Proctor, 2000). They struggle in their relationships with adults and peers and face a higher chance of abuse at home and rejection and bullying at school (Schwartz & Proctor, 2000). In addition, they may have trouble paying attention and remembering, which affects their ability to learn.

Some children exhibit symptoms of *posttraumatic stress disorder (PTSD)*. They may experience flashbacks where they replay the violent incident over and over in their minds; they may try to avoid thinking about it, experience emotional numbing, or become hyperalert to possible danger (Joshi, O'Donnell, Cullins, & Lewin, 2006). Rather than waiting around for something to happen, they may strike out first (Groves, 2002).

Even more toxic, violence that takes place within the child's family also evokes symptoms of PTSD and takes a toll on brain development (DeBellis, 2005; Groves, 2002). An estimated 15.5 million children—6 to 12 percent—witness intimate partner violence each year (Hamby, Finkelhor, Turner, & Ormrod, 2010; McDonald, Jouriles, Ramisetty-Mikler, Caetano, & Green, 2006). Even verbal conflict upsets them, and when it's combined with physical conflict it contributes to both emotional problems and aggressive, antisocial behavior (Maughan & Cicchetti, 2002). Children who live with family violence run a high risk of being abused—and of passing abuse along to the

Violence is endemic in American life and culture.

next generation (Kitzmann, Gaylord, Holt, & Kenny, 2003; Whitfield, Anda, Dube, & Felitti, 2003).

Child abuse and neglect are shockingly common—about 3.5 million cases were investigated in the United States in 2007 (U.S. Department of Health and Human Services, Administration on Children, Youth and Families, 2009). Younger children, African American, and Native American children are especially vulnerable. Because they live in a threatening, unpredictable environment, children who suffer abuse often form an insecure or disorganized attachment with their caregiver (Lyons-Ruth, 2003) and learn to react in a way that protects them at home but leads them into conflict with their peers and teachers (English et al., 2005; Maughan & Cicchetti, 2002; Schwartz & Proctor, 2000). In addition to being negative, angry, anxious, hypervigilant, or hyperactive, they may have difficulties with language, attention, memory, and abstract thinking (DeBellis, 2005).

Children who are abused have physical injuries as well. In infants, abuse accounts for most of the head injuries, which are particularly dangerous because they can result in behavior disorders, learning disabilities, and cognitive impairment (Christian, Block, & the Committee on Child Abuse and Neglect, 2009). Research connects them to violent and aggressive behavior later on: One study of 15 young murderers on death row found that all of them had had severe head injuries (Raine, 1993).

Many children are exposed to several types of violence. The type, the child's age, and the frequency, severity, and duration of the exposure all play a role in its impact (English et al., 2005).

Violent media

Many experts believe that when it comes to violence, the media exert as much influence as family and peers (Levin, 1998; Slaby, 1997). Eric Harris and Dylan Klebold provide vivid anecdotal evidence for this opinion: The teenagers who killed 13 students and teachers at Columbine High School in Littleton, Colorado, in 1999 played the video game "Doom" obsessively (Bai, 1999).

Children aged 6 months to 6 years log almost 2 hours a day watching television, videos, DVDs, and movies; using a computer; and playing video games; and about one third have a television set in their bedroom (Rideout & Hamel, 2006). African American children put in the most screen time, European Americans spend the least, and Hispanic Americans fall somewhere between.

In 1972, the Surgeon General's Scientific Advisory Committee on Television and Social Behavior concluded that there is a direct, causal link between seeing violence on television and aggressive behavior. In 2009, the American Academy of Pediatrics officially concurred, saying "the evidence is now clear and convincing: Media violence is one of the causal factors of real-life violence and aggression" (p. 1495). The association between media violence and aggressive behavior is nearly as strong as the association between smoking and lung cancer (Bushman & Anderson, 2001), and violence appears frequently in children's programs and video games (Wilson, 2008).

Researchers (Donnerstein, Slaby, & Eron, 1994; Slaby, 1997) have documented at least four effects:

- *Aggressor effect.* Children who watch violent media are more likely to engage in aggressive behavior, especially if they identify with aggressive characters or find the violence realistic and relevant to their own lives. Frequent viewing can shape and reinforce children's cognitive scripts about violence (Rutter et al., 1998). The more they watch, the more aggressive their behavior is likely to become and the more likely they are to think that aggression is an acceptable way to resolve conflict and achieve goals (Strasburger, Wilson, & Jordan, 2009).

- *Victim effect.* Watching television violence makes some children more fearful, anxious, and prone to nightmares. Most vulnerable are those who identify with the victim and perceive the violence as realistic. Heavy viewers of violence can acquire "mean-world syndrome," mistrusting people and seeing the world as more dangerous than it really is (Wilson, 2008).

- *Bystander effect.* Watching media violence desensitizes children and leads them to think that violence is normal, especially when programs present it as acceptable and without consequences. Instead of responding to real-life pain and suffering with sympathy, child viewers of violence remain indifferent.

- *Increased appetite effect.* When television violence is fun and exciting, children crave more of it. Children who behave aggressively watch more violent television in order to justify their behavior.

Recent evidence links early media viewing with bullying in school-age children (Zimmerman, Glew, Christakis, & Katon, 2005), with impulsive behavior and attentional and organizational problems at age 7 (Christakis, Zimmerman, DiGiuseppe, & McCarty, 2004), and with decreases in brain activity related to controlling impulsive behavior (Weber, Ritterfeld, & Mathiak, 2006).

Turbulent times

Violence in the lives of children takes on a new meaning during a crisis. On September 11, 2001, life in the United States changed forever. The extraordinary events of that day shattered everyone's sense of safety and security.

Human-made catastrophes (such as the September 11 terrorist attacks on New York and the Pentagon and the financial calamity of 2008) and natural disasters (such as Hurricane Katrina in 2005) create fear and helplessness, especially when they happen close to home. Because children depend on the adults around them to help them feel safe, their ability to recover is intimately connected to the ability of their families and teachers to comfort and reassure them.

Several factors influence a child's reaction to a disaster (Hagan and the Committee on Psychosocial Aspects of Child and Family Health, 2005): her age (both chronological and developmental), her temperament, her family's response to the event, the nature of the disaster itself (human-made disasters are psychologically more devastating), and how close she is to the disaster. Children who've lost family or friends or witnessed the event in person will be the hardest hit, but seeing

Soldier in the Family

About 800,000 preschoolers have felt the effects of war directly: One of their parents has been deployed to Iraq or Afghanistan (Chartrand, Frank, White, & Shope, 2008).

A recent study found that approximately 20 percent of these 3- to 5-year-olds showed how much they missed their parent with troubling emotional and behavioral signs, including hitting, biting, hyperactivity, anxiety, or sadness (Chartrand et al., 2008). Deployment in 2008 lasted for 12 to 15 months, a large portion of a young child's life.

it on television can also provoke a serious reaction. Boys take longer to recover and act more aggressively; girls express their feelings in words and ask more questions (Hagan et al., 2005).

Each child is different, but in general children respond to a disaster in distinct stages (Hagan et al., 2005). Immediately afterwards, they feel frightened and unsafe; a few weeks or months later, they may feel anxious, fearful, sad, apathetic, hostile, or aggressive. They may be cranky and easily upset, cling to their parents or teachers, and have little tolerance for frustration; and they may develop headaches, stomachaches, and difficulty sleeping. They're also liable to become hypervigilant, restless, and unable to concentrate. In addition, they may develop new fears—for example, children near the World Trade Center on September 11 became afraid of planes, of loud noises, or of being alone (Klein, DeVoe, Miranda-Julian, & Linas, 2009). To cope with these feelings, they may have a strong need to return to normal routines or recreate the disaster in their games and drawings.

Extremely sensitive children and those already burdened with stress will have a particularly hard time. Children who've experienced previous loss and trauma and children whose families are too upset to provide the reassurance and stability they need may be overwhelmed. Children whose behavior was already out of control may deteriorate further. In all of these cases, challenging behavior is often the result. If these reactions continue, children are at risk of posttraumatic stress disorder and later violent behavior (Hagan et al., 2005).

Understanding risk

This chapter presents a long list of risk factors, and after reading it you might feel that it's a miracle if any child manages to emerge from early childhood without challenging behavior. But remember that these risks have a cumulative effect. Each one you can counteract or help a child to avoid will make a substantial difference in her ability to cope. The simple fact that you understand more about who she is should increase your empathy and enhance the quality of your relationship—and the strength of your influence.

WHAT DO YOU THINK?

1. In this chapter we've separated biological and environmental risk factors, but in reality they are inextricably intertwined. Can you think of some examples of how they interact?

2. Temperamental traits are an important influence on the way people relate to one another. How would you describe your own emotional reactivity and your ability to control it? How do these traits affect your response to others' behavior in your own life? How do they affect your response to inappropriate behavior in your students?

3. Why do you think the NICHD Early Child Care Study indicated that the amount of time spent in child care is more important than the quality of child care when it comes to problem behavior? Why do you think spending more hours in child care has a greater negative impact on White middle-class children?

4. Some experts think the media play an extremely important role in increasing aggressive behavior. How have the news, films, and television programs you've seen shaped your attitudes toward other people and the world? How can you help children understand and deal with what they see in the media?

SUGGESTED READING

Flick, G. L. (2010). *Managing ADHD in the K–8 classroom: A teacher's guide.* Thousand Oaks, CA: Corwin.

Kleinfeld, J., & Wescott, S. (1993). *Fantastic Antone succeeds! Experiences in educating children with fetal alcohol syndrome.* Fairbanks: University of Alaska Press.

Kranowitz, C. S. (2006). *The out-of-sync child: Recognizing and coping with sensory integrative dysfunction* (Rev. ed.). New York: Perigee.

Kristal, J. (2005). *The temperament perspective: Working with children's behavioral styles.* Baltimore: Brookes.

Levin, D., & Carlsson-Paige, N. (2005). *The war play dilemma: What every parent and teacher need to know* (2nd ed.). New York: Teachers College Press.

McCord, J. (Ed.). (1997). *Violence and childhood in the inner city.* New York: Cambridge University Press.

CHAPTER 3

Protective Factors

After decades of trying to figure out why things go wrong, researchers came up with the idea of trying to figure out why things go *right,* even in adversity. Child development specialists, pediatricians, psychiatrists, psychologists, sociologists, and neuroscientists set to work studying children who were growing up in difficult circumstances—in war, in poverty, in families where there is violence or mental illness or divorce—to determine why some of them have the ability to cope successfully even when they encounter high hurdles.

The researchers named this ability *resilience* (Masten & Coatsworth, 1998; Rutter, 2000; Werner, 2000) and found that it is associated with a series of *protective* or *opportunity factors* that counter the impact of the risk factors in a child's life. In general, the more protective factors there are and the better they balance the risk factors, the more likely it is that a child will meet the challenges in his life and turn out to be a competent and caring individual (Werner, 2000).

Risk factors have a tendency to pile up, each one bringing others in its wake (Masten & Obradovic, 2006). A child who grows up in an unsafe neighborhood, for example, may overreact to his peers' behavior and pay little attention in school, which may lead to rejection, school failure, and low self-esteem—which in turn raise his risk for aggressive behavior, delinquency, and substance abuse. No teacher can change the fact that a family lives in poverty or a child's mother abused drugs when she was pregnant. But teachers can help the child (and maybe even his family) to deal with those risk factors more effectively. If we can bolster some of his protective factors early on, we may be able to minimize or even ward off some of the risks and divert him onto an entirely different developmental trajectory (Masten & Coatsworth, 1998; Rutter, 1987).

The further researchers delve into the subject of resilience, the more complex it reveals itself to be. Resilience is not a static state; it is a dynamic, developmental process that takes place over time and depends heavily on context (Luthar, Cicchetti, & Becker, 2000). Protective factors may protect a child in some domains but not others (Luthar et al., 2000), at some times but not others (Rutter, 2006b), at some levels of risk but not others (Masten & Obradovic, 2006), for some outcomes but not others (Rutter, 2006b), in some cultural groups but not others (Cauce, Stewart, Rodriguez, Cochran, & Ginzler, 2003; Richards et al., 2004). Factors that protect children in one context may actually render them more vulnerable in others (Luthar, 1999). And paradoxically, adversity that isn't overwhelming can protect a child from stress later on (Rutter, 2006b).

No child is truly invulnerable (Masten & Obradovic, 2006), but each is an active agent in his own development, and resilience involves constant interaction between him and his environment (Masten, 2004). All of this makes it hard to generalize and impossible to say, "This factor is universal and works for everyone" (Fergus & Zimmerman, 2005). On the other hand, it has become easier to say that there are many pathways to resilience (Luthar & Zelazo, 2003). Any outcome almost certainly involves multiple risk and protective factors.

In this chapter we describe four distinct waves of resilience research. In the first, investigators identified individual, family, and community factors that protect children from risk. In the second wave, researchers emphasized process, trying to figure out how these factors work. In the third wave, prevention and intervention entered the picture. In the fourth, which is ongoing, biology has come to the fore, as researchers attempt to knit the many strands of resilience together.

The first wave: Which qualities help a child bounce back?

Initially, resilience researchers focused on identifying people with natural resilience and created a striking portrait of a child who seemed to emerge unscathed from beneath a stack of risk factors as tall as he was. His family and teachers described him as "very active, affectionate, cuddly, good-natured, and easy to deal with" (Werner, 2000, p. 120). He was extremely responsive to everyone and everything around him and had a wonderful ability to seek out and relate to other people (Osofsky & Thompson, 2000). As developmental psychologists Emmy E. Werner and Ruth S. Smith put it in *Vulnerable but Invincible* (1982), their pioneering study of resilience, "To the extent that children [are] able to elicit predominantly positive responses from their environment, they [are] found to be stress-resistant or 'resilient,' even when growing up in chronic poverty or in a family with a psychotic parent" (p. 158). Because almost anyone who meets such children will happily bend over backwards to help them, they probably have little need for challenging behavior.

But what about the children who elicit negative responses from their environment? They are especially vulnerable, and their behavior is far more likely to challenge us. The question is How can teachers accept the vulnerable children for who they are and help them to become more resilient? What secrets of success do the children with natural resilience hold, and how can we bottle them for everyone's use? The first wave of resilience researchers identified three sets of protective factors: some in the child, some in the family, and some in the community (Masten, 2004).

Individual factors

Children differ enormously in how they respond to adversity, with genetics, physiology, and temperament all making a contribution (Ellis, 2009; Rutter, 2006b). As we've seen, children who exhibit resilience often have an outgoing temperament and the ability to engage the people around them in a positive way. They communicate easily with others, have a good sense of humor (Rutter, 1987), and tend to be flexible and empathetic. Their above-average intelligence enables them to do well at school (Masten & Coatsworth, 1998)—and indicates that their executive functions are in good working order. Their ability to pay attention, plan, think critically and creatively, and evaluate the consequences of their behavior makes them capable problem solvers (Curtis & Cicchetti, 2003; Rutter, 1987). In addition, they are able to regulate their emotions and behavior effectively and recover quickly from negative events and feelings (Curtis & Cicchetti, 2003). They have good control over their impulses and can do what needs to be done, even in difficult surroundings.

Children with resilience seem to have a strong sense of *self-efficacy* (they believe in their own worth and abilities) and possess what psychologists term an *internal locus of control* (they ascribe their success to their own efforts and abilities, not sheer luck) (Brooks, 1994; Luthar, 1999).

With varied talents, interests, activities, and coping strategies, they choose and build environments that reinforce their competencies, feel motivated to persevere and succeed (Masten, 2001), and have an optimistic outlook for the future (Wyman, 2003). They may also have a spiritual side that adds meaning to their lives (Masten, 2004). A recent study showed that inner-city youth who practice their religion privately—by praying, reading religious literature, watching or listening to religious television or radio programs— have a lower rate of problem behavior (Pearce, Jones, Schwab-Stone, & Ruchkin, 2003).

Even a child with challenging behavior is likely to possess some of these attributes and skills in an embryonic or unconventional form, although it may take extra thought and insight on our part to dig them out. One key to enhancing

Children with resilience seem to have a strong sense of self-efficacy (they believe in their own worth and abilities) and possess an internal locus of control (they ascribe their success to their own efforts and abilities, not sheer luck).

Photograph by Rachel at Rachel B. Photo Studio, LLC.

Pride and Prejudice

Experiences of discrimination and structural racism pose serious risks to the health and development of African American youth (Spencer, Fegley, & Harpalani, 2003).

In a longitudinal study of almost 600 African American adolescents, researchers (Spencer et al., 2003) found that Black pride helped boys to cope successfully. Those who believed in the importance of African American history and culture had significantly higher scores on emotional well-being, felt more valued by others, had more positive feelings about the future, and perceived themselves as more popular with their peers than boys who weren't interested in Black pride.

There are some indications that ethnic pride may protect children in other cultural groups as well (Szalacha et al., 2003). It's important to remember that children begin to construct their racial and ethnic identity during their preschool years (Derman-Sparks & Ramsey, 2006).

resilience is to search for these strengths—what psychologist Robert B. Brooks (1994) calls "islands of competence" (p. 549)—and use them to build new skills and self-esteem. Instead of noticing what a child does wrong, stop and think about his strengths and likeable qualities, what he's good at, what positive contributions he can make, and how you can create opportunities for him to realize whatever he has to offer.

At the same time, be careful not to blame a child who seems short on these attributes. Even the characteristics we usually consider inherent—intelligence and temperament, for example—are subject to the influence of the environment (Luthar, 2006).

Family factors

Again and again, research confirms that high-quality parenting offers the best protection to children in hazardous situations (Luthar, 2006). A loving relationship with one consistently supportive and responsive person who provides warmth, structure, high expectations, and age-appropriate limit-setting and monitoring (Masten et al., 1999) protects children at various stages of development and with many kinds of risks (Luthar & Zelazo, 2003). This relationship lays the groundwork for a wide range of skills, including well-regulated emotions, a sense of self-efficacy (Yates, Egeland, & Sroufe, 2003), academic achievement, mastery motivation (Luthar, 2006), and sociability with peers (Masten et al., 1999).

If the parents can't provide this crucial bond, someone else can. What matters is that at least one caring person—a grandparent, an older sibling, a cousin—accepts and supports the child (Rutter, 1987; Werner, 2000).

Unlike children at low risk, African American children in the inner city benefit from strict parenting (Cauce et al., 2003). When families spend more time with their children, chaperone them closely, and limit the places they go and the time they spend with antisocial peers, children perform better at school and witness less violence, decreasing their risk for emotional and behavioral problems (Cauce et al., 2003;

Poster Child

We know her as a successful talk show host, actor, and magazine publisher, but Oprah Winfrey is also a model of resilience. She overcame great adversity to become who she is today.

Her parents separated soon after her birth, leaving Oprah in the care of her grandmother on a Mississippi farm ("Oprah Winfrey," n.d.). At the age of 6 she moved to Milwaukee to join her mother. Their stormy relationship—and the sexual abuse she suffered at the hands of male relatives and friends—led her to run away when she was 13.

Oprah ended up in Nashville with her father, and this was perhaps the turning point of her life. A strict disciplinarian, her father had high expectations. Each week she had to read and write about a book; each day she had to learn five vocabulary words or go without dinner ("Oprah Winfrey," n.d.). Although her father's parenting techniques may seem extreme to some, in fact this structure and close supervision acted as a protective factor for Oprah. She joined her school's drama club, won a college scholarship, and at age 19—while still a sophomore at Tennessee State University—became the co-anchor of Nashville's evening news program. The rest is history.

Richards et al., 2004). In dangerous neighborhoods, this strong control is an expression of concern as well as an adaptive strategy that brings order, predictability, and safety to children's daily lives (Luthar, 1999).

Community factors

The community can also play a powerful part in fostering resilience (Werner & Johnson, 1999). When children receive support in such places as churches, community centers, and boys' and girls' clubs, they feel connected to other people and the core values of the community.

Community backing usually comes to the child in the form of relationships. Like parents, caring and competent teachers, neighbors, coaches, or friends can act as positive role models, make a child feel loved and valued, and even help compensate for a difficult family situation (Luthar & Zelazo, 2003). By believing in the child, expecting a lot of him, and supporting him as he extends his reach, a caring adult can help him to believe in himself, develop competence and confidence, and expand his ability to cope with stress. For young children at risk, having a supportive relationship with a teacher is significantly related to competent and appropriate behavior with peers (Howes & Ritchie, 1999). Support from teachers is especially effective for African American children (Meehan, Hughes, & Cavell, 2003), children in poverty (Luthar et al., 2000), and children with learning disabilities (Margalit, 2003).

High-quality child care and a strong bond to school—the only safe haven in the lives of some children—can also protect them against a wide range of risks, including aggressive behavior and academic failure (Hawkins, Smith, Hill, Kosterman, & Catalano, 2007). Researchers have identified several factors that increase school

Teachers, coaches, or friends can act as positive role models and make a child feel loved and valued.

bonding—proactively teaching expectations, routines, and procedures, interactive teaching, reinforcement of positive social behavior, teaching social and problem-solving skills, and giving students lots of opportunities to participate actively through cooperative learning groups.

Overcoming the Odds

In 1955, Emmy E. Werner and Ruth S. Smith (1982) began a landmark longitudinal study of 698 newborns on the island of Kauai in Hawaii. The fathers of the children were mostly semiskilled or unskilled laborers, many of their mothers didn't graduate from high school, and about half of the families lived in chronic poverty.

Among them were 72 children who faced enormous obstacles—four or more risk factors before the age of 2—who nonetheless turned into "competent, confident, and caring adults" (Werner, 2000, p. 119). "When asked who helped them succeed against the odds, the resilient children, youth, and adults in the study . . . overwhelmingly and exclusively gave credit to members of their extended family (grandparents, siblings, aunts, or uncles), to neighbors and teachers who were confidantes and role models, and to mentors in voluntary associations, such as 4H, the YMCA or YWCA, and church groups" (Werner & Johnson, 1999, p. 263).

Peers can furnish protection, too. With a friend, a child can experience intimacy, trust, and support; and being an accepted member of a group diminishes the risk of aggressive behavior posed by poverty, marital conflict in the home, and harsh discipline (Criss, Pettit, Bates, Dodge, & Lapp, 2002). Peers can also meet a child's need for connectedness and teach social skills (Criss et al., 2002). Friendship is especially helpful for children who've been maltreated (Bolger & Patterson, 2003) and children with learning disabilities (Miller, 2002).

The second wave: How do protective factors work?

In the second wave of research, investigators began the difficult task of uncovering the processes and mechanisms behind resilience (Luthar et al., 2000). The child's own history and genetic endowment both play major roles, and during periods of rapid change—for example, when children enter school—new strengths and vulnerabilities appear (Luthar et al., 2000), offering opportunities to redirect the course of development (Masten, 2004).

British child psychiatrist and resilience expert Michael Rutter (2006b; Rutter et al., 1998) has proposed eight possible ways that protective factors may contribute to positive outcomes. They could

- *reduce sensitivity to risk* (e.g., coping successfully with previous adversity helps a child meet new challenges)
- *dilute the impact of risk* (e.g., parental supervision can prevent children from spending time with antisocial peers)
- *reduce the negative chain reactions that follow exposure to risk and perpetuate its effects* (e.g., support from adults can enable children to deal successfully with the results of early stress)
- *increase positive chain reactions* (e.g., positive relationships with adults encourage children to explore, which in turn allows them to increase their competence)
- *promote self-esteem, self-efficacy, and problem-solving skills* (e.g., succeeding in an important task builds self-confidence)
- *neutralize or counter the risk directly with compensatory positive experiences* (e.g., a warm relationship with a friend's parents can buffer the effects of marital strife in a child's own home)
- *open up opportunities* (e.g., trying a new activity gives a child a chance to learn new skills)
- *support positive thinking about negative experiences* (e.g., focusing on the positive aspects of a difficult situation makes adjustment easier)

Context and culture both make important contributions to process. When basic human adaptational systems function normally, children can usually find the resources they need to cope, even in adversity (Masten, 2001). But children whose environment doesn't contain the appropriate resources may have to pay a price to achieve some measure of well-being. For example, for most children, emotional responsiveness and close relationships build positive adaptation. But children exposed to maltreatment or a mother's depression at home seem to fare better when they develop a more restrictive style of emotional self-regulation—when they're less open, less empathetic, less responsive, less connected. Distancing themselves emotionally from their parents enables them to handle their distress (Cicchetti & Rogosch, 1997; Wyman, 2003).

Logically extending the notion that children achieve resilience differently in different contexts, some researchers are coming to believe that resilience itself can have different—and sometimes startling—faces (Kaplan, 1999; Wyman, 2003). Psychologist Arnold Sameroff (2005) writes, "It must be noted that resilience is not the same as positive behavior. In stressful circumstances with limited resources, one individual's gain must be at the expense of someone else's loss, a zero-sum game. In such situations, resilience may take the form of antisocial behavior, such as resources gained by criminality in inner-city environments" (p. 4).

It's important for a child to have a range of strategies at his disposal (Rutter, 2006c). By recognizing and supporting the strengths a child employs to survive his everyday life, teachers can aid him in identifying areas of competence, control, and power that he can build on. For example, helping others is a talent that enables children to nurture their self-image. And having choices and a say about their own world allows them to feel valued for who they are (Ungar, 2004).

The third wave: Integrating prevention and intervention

Third-wave investigators started using prevention and intervention to shore up resilience—and test hypotheses about it at the same time (Masten, 2007). Effective programs focus not only on the child but also on the child's environment. The Seattle Social Development Project, a universal intervention designed to work with teachers, children, and parents in high-crime neighborhoods, reduced aggressive behavior and boosted commitment to school, academic performance, and family management skills (Hawkins et al., 2007). Targeting children at risk for conduct disorder, the Fast Track Project provided interventions on several fronts as well. Evaluations show improvements in children's social, emotional, and academic skills (Conduct Problems Prevention Research Group, 2004).

The Devereux Early Childhood Assessment (LeBuffe & Naglieri, 1999), known as the DECA, utilizes a different approach. Teachers and parents assess behavioral concerns and three key resilience factors: attachment, self-control, and initiative. Then teachers implement a strength-based intervention linked to the assessment results. A pilot study showed a significant rise in protective factors and a significant decline in behavior issues (Lamb-Parker, LeBuffe, Powell, & Halpern, 2008).

The fourth wave: How does everything fit together?

With new technologies at their disposal, many fourth-wave researchers are beginning to investigate the role of biology in resilience. In addition, they are striving to integrate work from the three previous waves, looking at how neuroscience, genetics, development, and experience interact to produce adaptation (Masten, 2007).

Some investigators are concentrating on emotional regulation and problem-solving skills that involve the executive functions and the prefrontal cortex of the brain and provide crucial brakes for aggressive and impulsive behavior. The prevention curriculum called PATHS (Promoting Alternative Thinking Strategies), which bolsters social and emotional competence, is based on neuroscientific principles. In a recent study (Greenberg, 2006), second and third graders learned self-control strategies, and their teachers learned to help them use the strategies whenever conflict arose at school. A year later, follow-up tests showed that the children's executive functions—particularly inhibitory control and verbal fluency—had improved significantly, along with their behavior (Greenberg, 2006). The *Tools of the Mind* curriculum, developed by Elena Bodrova and Deborah J. Leong (2007), also enhances self-regulation and behavior, largely by focusing on play (Barnett et al., 2008; Diamond, Barnett, Thomas, & Munro, 2007). (See pages 163–166.)

Other researchers are attempting to sharpen executive attention directly. After 5 days of training, 4- and 6-year-olds performed significantly better than children who didn't receive the training on tests of attention and intelligence (Holmeboe & Johnson, 2005; Rueda, Rothbart, McCandliss, Saccomanno, & Posner, 2005), indicating that it's possible to train executive functions. This study also looked at a gene involved in executive attention, one of many for the neurotransmitter dopamine. Children who carry a long form of the DAT1 gene seemed to have better effortful control than children with the short form (Rueda et al., 2005).

In the meantime, researchers observing mothers and babies (Bakermans-Kranenburg & van IJzendoorn, 2006) were examining another dopamine gene, DRD4, to connect resilience, biology, and the environment. These scientists made an astonishing discovery: Sensitive parenting seemed irrelevant for infants with the gene's short form. They were what the Swedes call "dandelion children," who do reasonably well in any environment. No matter how their mothers treated them, they had the same moderate level of aggressive behavior. However, for babies with the long form of the gene, sensitive mothering meant everything. With proper care, these "orchid children" became blooms of unusual beauty (Ellis, 2009)—when their mothers responded appropriately to their signals, they had little problem behavior. But under unfavorable conditions they wilted, reacting to insensitive mothering with the most difficult behavior in the study (Bakermans-Kranenburg & van IJzendoorn, 2006).

Similarly, other researchers found, children with low emotional reactivity—dandelion kids—flourished whether or not they received high-quality child care. But orchid children with high emotional reactivity were deeply affected, both negatively and positively, by the quality of care. Low-quality care produced challenging behavior, whereas high-quality care engendered strong social competence (Pluess & Belsky, 2009).

As ever, resilience is complex. As Bruce Ellis (2009) of the University of Arizona points out, it depends on who is being cared for, and one size does not fit all.

The results of these ambitious multidisciplinary efforts are just beginning to emerge. While we wait, we can incorporate what we already know about resilience into the classroom by creating strong relationships with children, enhancing their strengths and potential resources, promoting competence and emotional regulation, and paying close attention both to context and to what children tell and show us. Remember, the environment plays a powerful role in fostering a young child's resilience, and you are a large part of the environment.

Shifting the Balance

E mmy E. Werner (1984) makes these suggestions for teachers and others who spend time with children:

- Accept children's temperamental idiosyncrasies and allow them experiences that challenge, but do not overwhelm, their coping abilities.
- Convey to children a sense of responsibility and caring, and in turn reward them for helpfulness and cooperation.
- Encourage a child to develop a special interest, hobby, or activity that can serve as a source of gratification and self-esteem.
- Model, by example, a conviction that life makes sense despite the inevitable adversities . . . each of us encounters.
- Encourage children to reach out beyond their nuclear family to a beloved relative or friend. (p. 71)

W HAT DO YOU THINK?

1. Have you or has anyone else in your family ever had to deal with adversity? Think about your own risk and protective factors. Is there an activity or a person in your life who made a difference—a parent, a friend's parent, a teacher, or a neighbor who helped you to recover from a trauma or sustained you through a stressful period? How?

2. There are advantages and disadvantages to knowing about a child's risk and protective factors. How could this knowledge change your attitude and your behavior toward a child or his family?

S UGGESTED READING AND RESOURCES

Braschi, G. (Producer), & Benigni, R. (Writer/Director). (1998). *Life Is Beautiful* [Motion picture]. Italy: Miramax Films.

Devereux Early Childhood Assessment Program, LeBuffe, P. A., Naglieri, J. A., & Koralek, D. G. (1999). *Enhancing social and emotional development.* Lewisville, NC: Kaplan Press.

Masten, A. S. (2001). Ordinary magic: Resilience processes in development. *American Psychologist, 56,* 227–234.

Werner, E. E., & Smith, R. (1992). *Overcoming the odds: High risk children from birth to adulthood.* Ithaca, NY: Cornell University Press.

Werner, E. E. (1984). Resilient children. *Young Children, 40,* 68–72.

Chapter 4

Behavior and the Brain

Ultimately all behavior is a result of brain activity, so it is only natural to wonder about the brain's role in challenging behavior.

Every risk and protective factor in a child's life, before and after birth, can have an impact on the brain, although we often don't know why or how. The development of the brain is perhaps the most complex phenomenon in all of biology (Nelson & Bloom, 1997), and despite the astonishing progress of the last 20 years, work that uses the techniques of neuroanatomy, molecular biology, molecular genetics, neurochemistry, neurophysiology, brain imaging, and the like does not easily translate into statements about complex human behavior such as aggression (Kandel, Jessell, & Sanes, 2000; Shonkoff & Phillips, 2000).

By observing children carefully, researchers have amassed a great deal of valuable information about behavior and the brain (DiPietro, 2000; Nelson & Bloom, 1997), but much of what we know about the brain's wiring and development comes from studies of animals. Although those findings can provide extraordinary insights, we must use caution when we apply them to human beings.

These days neuroscience is bringing some wonderful new tools to the quest to link behavior and the brain, including *magnetic resonance imaging (MRI)*, which provides exquisitely detailed three-dimensional pictures of brain structure; *functional MRI (fMRI)*, which can show the brain at work on specific tasks by tracking metabolic activity in a particular region; *positron emission tomography (PET)*, where radioactively labeled compounds can illuminate specific areas of brain activity or pinpoint the whereabouts of a particular neurotransmitter; and digitalized *electroencephalography (EEG)* and *magnetoencephalogy (MEG)*, which record electrical and magnetic activity from the scalp.

The techniques that don't require radiation can be adapted for research with children, and National Institute of Mental Health scientists are currently compiling an atlas of normal human brain development by using MRI to look at the brains of more than 500 children ages 3 to 18. Using new leads from the map of the human genome, researchers are also investigating neurodevelopmental disorders such as ADHD, autism, schizophrenia, and bipolar disease, as well as the effects on the brain of child maltreatment, prenatal alcohol exposure, maternal depression, prematurity, and even video gaming.

This chapter will look at some of the connections between behavior and the brain. We begin with early experience and the brain and conclude with a tour of the parts of the brain involved in aggressive behavior.

EARLY EXPERIENCE AND THE BRAIN

How does the brain develop?

Not long ago, people believed that genes completely controlled brain development (Shonkoff & Phillips, 2000). Now it's clear that the environment plays an equally enormous role and is even involved in turning on genes that may otherwise remain inactive. The brain is the manifestation of gene–environment interactions. Brain alterations influence how a child interacts with the environment, and those interactions lead to more brain alterations (Monk, 2008). This is where biology and environment, nature and nurture, merge. Genes may provide the grand plan, but experience organizes and structures the brain's circuitry (Nelson & Bloom, 1997).

The infant brain arrives in the world equipped with 100 billion brain cells, or *neurons*, but relatively few of them are connected. As babies interact with their environment, their brain cells send and receive signals, making 1,000 trillion connections, or *synapses*, by the time they turn 3 years old. These connections wire the brain

All Roads Lead to Rome

....

How can we link behavior with brain processes? One example of convergence comes from psychiatry. Researchers have demonstrated that two different treatments for obsessive-compulsive disorder—one that used behavior therapy and another that used drug therapy—had identical outcomes. The patients' behavior changed in the same way with both treatments.

The patients' PET scans showed that their brains had also changed in the same way, allowing researchers to see how the brain and behavior relate to one another. What's happening on the outside mirrors what's happening on the inside (Schwartz, Stoessel, Baxter, Martin, & Phelps, 1996).

for present and future feelings, thoughts, and actions. As neuroscientist Joseph LeDoux (2002) puts it, "You are your synapses" (p. ix).

During childhood and adolescence, the brain undergoes a second major round of growth, when the neurons sprout countless new branches and connections (Giedd, 2004). In preadolescence, the synapses begin to thin out, the result, scientists hypothesize, of genetics and the "use-it-or-lose-it" principle. The frequently used connections survive, and those with little or no traffic gradually wither away (Shonkoff & Phillips, 2000).

At the same time, a fatty white substance called *myelin*, which begins to coat and insulate nerve fibers even before birth (Lenroot & Giedd, 2006), accelerates its work in order to create a streamlined system where information travels quickly and efficiently throughout the brain. The brain achieves an adult number of connections and finishes its reorganization only in our 20s (De Bellis, Keshavan et al., 1999).

How does experience affect brain development?

From the very beginning, an individual's experience has a major impact on how her brain develops and who she becomes. In fact, development depends on the environment (Goleman, 2006a).

William Greenough and his colleagues have identified two ways that nerve cells use experience to make connections and forge nerve pathways (Greenough, Black, & Wallace, 1987). They call the first *experience-expectant*. Some experiences—such as hearing speech and seeing light and patterns—are readily available in the environment; and as the brain develops, it "expects" to use them to form the connections it needs (Nelson & Bloom, 1997). When experiences occur as expected, brain cells connect and systems organize themselves normally; if the experiences don't occur as expected, neural organization is abnormal.

Nobel Prize winners David Hubel and Torsten Wiesel provided the classical evidence for this pattern in the 1960s. They were intrigued by the observation that children whose cataracts weren't treated promptly remained blind in the obstructed eye even after their cataracts were removed. To explore this phenomenon, Hubel and Wiesel performed experiments where they closed one eyelid of newborn kittens. When they reopened it three months later, the kitten could not see with that eye because its nerve cells hadn't made the proper connections in the brain, despite the fact that the eye itself functioned normally (Bruer, 1999; Shatz, 1992). The brain needed the normal experience of exposure to light and patterns in order to connect with the eye and interpret the information coming from it.

Hubel and Wiesel had discovered a *critical* or *sensitive period* for the visual system— a limited time when experience has a particularly powerful effect in shaping brain circuits (Knudsen, 2004). If the nerve cells in the kitten's eye failed to make the appropriate connections in the brain during that sensitive time, the kitten lost sight permanently in that eye (Kandel et al., 2000). There is also a sensitive period for vision in humans, as well as a sensitive period for sound (Kuhl, Williams, Lacerda, & Stevens, 1992), motor (Bruer & Greenough, 2001), and language sensory systems (Knudsen, 2004). This is why it's essential to detect and treat all vision and hearing problems early.

Sensitive periods for development are rarely brief or clearly defined, and they vary from one brain system to another (Bruer, 2001). They seem to be important only for systems that develop in the same way for all members of a species (Bruer, 1999; Nelson, 2000). For example, all human beings have a visual system, so there is a sensitive period for vision. But not everyone reads, so there is no sensitive period for reading; one can learn at any age (Bortfeld & Whitehurst, 2001).

Greenough and his colleagues (1987) noticed that experience guides brain development in a second way, which they call *experience-dependent*. Humans need to acquire a great deal of information that is unique to their own environment—how to relate to the individuals around them and navigate in their physical surroundings, for example. Again, experience triggers nerve cells to make connections, but this process isn't subject to sensitive periods. The brain is constantly restructuring and refining itself to reflect its new experience. In this way, a child actually participates in the development of her own brain (Gopnik, Meltzoff, & Kuhl, 2001). Experience-dependent learning goes on throughout life. Because the brain is so plastic—malleable—human beings are incredibly adaptable and attuned to their environment.

The brain is constantly restructuring and refining itself to reflect its new experience. In this way, a child actually participates in the development of her own brain.

How does early stress influence the brain?

We can get some idea of how experience affects brain development by looking at the *stress system*, which roars into action when we are threatened or frightened, getting us ready to freeze, fight, or flee. As the steroid hormone *cortisol* floods the brain, a whole cascade of changes takes place to prepare body and brain for the immediate threat and simultaneously shuts down activities that in ordinary times ensure long-term survival (Gunnar & Cheatham, 2003). When the threat recedes, cortisol levels and other activities return to normal.

But if a threatening situation lasts too long or reappears too often, the stress system gets reset. The result is an extra vigilant animal or human who is quick to experience fear and anxiety and has a hard time turning those feelings off (Gunnar, 2000). A brain in this state is vulnerable to the toxic effects of cortisol itself, which in large amounts may destroy neurons in brain regions concerned with memory, emotional regulation, and successful adaptation to stress (Gunnar, 1998; McEwen, 2005).

Scientists have found that caregiving has a remarkable effect on the stress system: It actually programs its development and lays the foundation for emotional regulation (Gunnar, 2006). For example, rat mothers maintain the correct level of the rat equivalent of cortisol in their pups by licking and grooming them and nursing in an arched-back position. Michael Meaney and his colleagues at McGill University (Meaney, 2001) have discovered that when mother and pups experience short daily separations in the first weeks of life—as long as they'd be apart in the wild—the mother's behavior becomes more organized, and she licks, grooms, and nurses more effectively. In turn, her pups develop more cortisol receptors in their brains and have more control over cortisol production. They are less fearful and anxious and less easily unnerved by threat, and their stress systems turn on and off quickly. But if mother and pups are apart for too long, the mother becomes disturbed and disorganized, and the pups become hypersensitive to stress. This early experience influences how the animal will react to stressful stimuli for the rest of its life (Liu et al., 1997).

In children, the connections between caregiving and the development of the stress system are just as powerful (Gunnar, 1998; Gunnar & Cheatham, 2003). During early development, stress regulation is "embedded in caregiver–infant interactions," says Megan R. Gunnar, a leading stress researcher (2006, p. 106). In fact, one of the most important responsibilities of a primary caregiver is to help a child cope with stress successfully so that she can learn to do this for herself. The caregiver acts as an extension of the child's own regulatory system, and each time she enables the child to return to a contented state, information about managing this crucial transition is reinforced and stored in the child's neural networks (Cozolino, 2006).

Normally, cortisol follows a regular daily rhythm. It begins to rise as soon as a child wakes in the morning, reaches its peak in 20 to 30 minutes, and gradually falls over the course of the day (Gunnar & Cheatham, 2003). When children experience high-quality caregiving and are securely attached to their primary caregiver, they have normal cortisol levels even if they're distressed, whereas children who are insecurely attached maintain high levels (Gunnar & Cheatham, 2003). Babies under the care of a strange but sensitive and friendly babysitter don't show a rise in cortisol, but babies left with a cold and distant sitter do.

Typically developing children find child care—being without their primary caregiver and learning to get along with their peers—a stressful experience. Younger children and those with less supportive teachers show larger rises in cortisol over the day than children who receive individualized, responsive care (Gunnar & Donzella, 2002). Temperament also plays a role. Children with less *effortful control* (the ability to suppress a response that they're ready to perform) have higher cortisol over the day (Dettling, Gunnar, & Donzella, 1999), and preschoolers who have the most trouble with emotional and behavioral control and are rejected by their peers have the highest cortisol levels in their class (Gunnar, 2006). They tend to need—and benefit more from—sensitive, responsive care (Gunnar & Cheatham, 2003).

What happens when caregiving fails?

But for children who lack a responsive, supportive caregiver or live in a threatening caregiving environment, there is no buffer for the developing stress system. When they are subjected to abuse, neglect, violence, trauma, or parental depression, the stress system is at the mercy of the environment—and the brain becomes susceptible to a whole host of serious problems: emotional and behavior problems (including aggression, anger, tantrums, and posttraumatic stress disorder); difficulties with self-regulation, arousal, attention, and hyperactivity; cognitive, memory, and learning problems; flawed decision making; trouble with relationships; and a sense of self as helpless, ineffective, and unlovable (Cook, Blaustein, Spinazzola, & van der Kolk, 2003; Shackman, Wismer-Fries, & Pollak, 2008).

Children who have a disorganized/disoriented attachment relationship with their caregiver—which is typical when a child has been abused or neglected or the parent is depressed—have elevated cortisol levels (Loman et al., 2009); and even years later, children suffering from posttraumatic stress disorder after experiencing abuse still have high cortisol levels that correlate with the duration of the abuse (De Bellis, Baum et al., 1999). Growing up with a depressed mother also raises a child's risk for high cortisol (Ashman, Dawson, Panagiotides, Yamada, & Wilkinson, 2002). Without a mother who interacts with her in a sensitive, positive way, she will have difficulty learning to regulate her emotions and is more likely to develop challenging behavior (Dawson et al., 2003).

Children in Romanian orphanages in the 1970s and 1980s faced severe deprivation from infancy, and many who were adopted after the age of 6 months had very high basal cortisol levels many years later, indicating a real confusion of the stress system (Gunnar, 2006). The longer they'd lived in an orphanage, the more serious their behavior problems (Maclean, 2003). Even 8 years after their adoption, they had trouble paying attention; and in a study of Canadian adoptees, 29 percent were diagnosed with ADHD, versus none of the children in a comparison group (Maclean, 2003). The Romanian adoptees also found it hard to get along with other children, and a substantial minority hadn't formed an attachment with their caregivers—instead they were overly friendly and all too ready to walk off with a stranger (Rutter, O'Connor, & the English and Romanian Adoptees Study Team, 2004). At age 11, they had more marked emotional difficulties (Colvert et al., 2008).

Researchers speculate that the adoptees' problems stem from the conditions in the orphanage, where stimulation and interactions with peers and adults were few and far between (Maclean, 2003). In particular, not having one consistent person to care for them at this early stage put their social development at risk (Rutter et al., 2004). The implication is that at least one close relationship with a caregiver in the first few years is vital for normal brain development.

What role do genes play?

At least 60 percent of our genes are expressed in the brain, and their impact, direct and indirect, extends far and wide, touching even our attitudes and social behavior (Rutter, 2006a). Because we each carry a unique mix of gene variants, we all respond and adapt to our environment in different ways (Moffitt, Caspi, & Rutter, 2006). In fact, genes code not for behavior itself but for proteins whose interactions eventually give rise to behavior (Lenroot & Giedd, 2006).

As we have seen, genes and experience are intertwined in such a complex manner that it's hard to know where one leaves off and the other begins. The gene

Turning the Tide

When children are placed in foster care, it's usually a sign that caregiving has fallen short. Frequently neglected at home, these children face the prospect of multiple brief placements with nonresponsive foster parents. Their predicament takes a toll: Children in foster care tend to have atypical cortisol levels, a consequence of chronic stress (Fisher, Gunnar, Dozier, Bruce, & Pears, 2006).

When foster parents were trained to respond consistently and sensitively to their behavior, toddlers and preschoolers experienced better attachment security, fewer placement failures, and fewer behavior problems. In addition, their cortisol patterns became more normal (Fisher et al., 2006). Foster care interventions like this provide hopeful evidence that responsive caregiving can reverse some of the effects of early adversity.

for the enzyme monoamine oxidase A, better known as MAOA, is a good example. MAOA is responsible for breaking down some of the *neurotransmitters* in the brain, a process that's essential for the normal use and recycling of these chemicals, which carry messages between nerve cells. When the gene for MAOA is defective, it doesn't produce normal enzyme, and the result is often disturbed neurotransmission, disrupted development, and aggressive behavior that lasts a lifetime.

Researchers noticed that children who suffer from abuse at an early age sometimes develop the same symptoms, including aggressive behavior that persists into adulthood (Caspi et al., 2002). But maltreatment doesn't always have this effect. The scientists wanted to know why. The answer lay in the faulty MAOA gene. Maltreatment almost seemed to activate it. Boys who carried the defective gene and had been abused as children were at extraordinarily high risk: 85 percent developed some form of antisocial behavior, and a disproportionately large number were convicted of violent offenses. On the other hand, boys with the flawed gene who'd escaped maltreatment did not behave aggressively; and boys who'd been abused but lacked the defective gene ran only a slightly higher risk of behaving aggressively (Caspi et al., 2002). Either their environment or their genetics protected them.

WHICH PARTS OF THE BRAIN ARE INVOLVED IN AGGRESSIVE BEHAVIOR?

Children who have trouble managing their emotions run a high risk of developing behavior problems (Eisenberg et al., 2001; Eisenberg et al., 2005). Where in the brain does the capacity for self-control—and the risk of aggressive behavior—reside? Several anatomical regions and neurochemical systems play crucial roles.

The amygdala

The *amygdala*, an almond-shaped structure deep within the temporal lobe of the brain, acts as an early warning device alerting us to danger (Goleman, 2006a). Its job, which it performs at top speed, automatically, and without our awareness, is to scan all the information our sensory systems relay from the outside world and, at any sign of a threat, to trigger our freeze-fight-flight reaction. In effect, it can hijack the brain and get us to act before we have a chance to think about whether we're doing the right thing (Goleman, 1997). The amygdala responds zealously to fear and other negative emotions in faces and voices and ultimately gets cortisol flowing (Cozolino, 2006).

Amygdala impairment interferes with this vital ability to recognize and judge emotion, particularly fear (LeDoux, 2002). Perceiving another's distress usually inhibits aggressive behavior (Decety, Michalsky, Akitsuki, & Lahey, 2008), but it doesn't seem to have that effect on antisocial adult criminals, children with disruptive behavior disorders, or children with callous-unemotional traits (who show no guilt or empathy [Frick et al., 2003]), all of whom display reduced activity in the amygdala (Cozolino, 2006; Decety et al., 2008). Inappropriate social behavior and communication difficulties also accompany amygdala damage (Cozolino, 2006).

The frontal lobe

Under normal circumstances, the *frontal lobe*—the part of the brain that makes us human (Giedd, 2004) and one of the newest from the point of view of evolution (see Figure 4.1)—rides herd on the amygdala. But this large region, which allows us to think about what to do instead of acting impulsively, automatically, or aggressively, is a late bloomer. Although it starts to mature in infancy, enabling young children to begin regulating their emotions and following rules, it isn't yet very efficient and must work hard to inhibit inappropriate behavior. It continues to mature throughout childhood and adolescence and doesn't finish developing until well into the 20s—which is why rental car companies refuse to rent cars to people under the age of 25!

Three frontal lobe areas work together to control the amygdala: the *prefrontal cortex (PFC)*, the *orbitofrontal cortex (OFC)*, and the *anterior cingulate cortex (ACC)*.

• The *prefrontal cortex*, a small area just behind the forehead, acts as the brain's executive or CEO. It controls the brain's most advanced functions—including its executive functions—organizing and coordinating highly processed information from all over the brain in order to plan, reason, and regulate affect and attention (Cozolino, 2006). The PFC can make use of several different neural circuits to manage the amygdala's impulses, allowing us to respond flexibly and appropriately to a situation, even when we're upset (Goleman, 2006a). The PFC also takes charge of *effortful control* and *delaying gratification*, a capacity that increases dramatically between the ages of 3 and 4 years (Zelazo, Carlson, & Kesck, 2008).

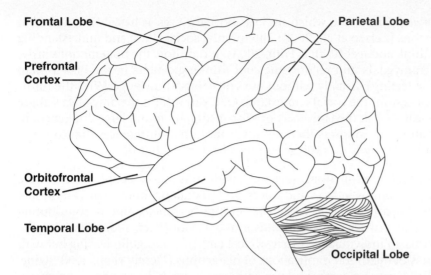

Frontal Lobe

Parietal Lobe

Prefrontal Cortex

Orbitofrontal Cortex

Temporal Lobe

Occipital Lobe

FIGURE 4.1 This view of the brain from the side shows the frontal lobe, which is important in the control of social behavior. It includes the prefrontal cortex (PFC), the orbitofrontal cortex (OFC), and the anterior cingulate cortex (ACC), but the ACC can't be seen here because it's on the interior surface of the frontal lobe. The amygdala isn't pictured because it is deep within the temporal lobe.

Damage to the prefrontal cortex interferes with decision making and leads to a breakdown in the use of emotional information to guide thoughts and actions (LeDoux, 2002). Because the PFC has a high density of serotonin receptors, some scientists suspect that malfunction in this area might alter serotonin metabolism and make aggressive behavior more likely (Davidson, Putnam, & Larson, 2000). One PET study of murderers who acted impulsively (as opposed to those who planned their crimes) found that impulsive murderers had less activity in the PFC (Davidson et al., 2000).

Inhibition Disbarred

The case of Phineas Gage was one of the first to link antisocial behavior with the frontal lobe of the brain. Gage worked as a dynamiter for the Rutland and Burlington Railroad in Vermont. Considered an efficient, reliable, and capable man, he was the foreman of a construction gang and had no history of violent or antisocial behavior.

In 1848, an explosion rammed an iron rod through Gage's head, damaging his left frontal lobe. He survived, but he became an entirely different person—impulsive, irreverent, profane, obstinate, and antisocial (Raine, 1993; Phineas Gage's Story, 2006).

• The *orbitofrontal cortex*, which sits just above the eyes, is heavily implicated in making decisions (Zelazo et al., 2008), interpreting social clues, and understanding what others think and feel (Frith & Frith, 2003). It monitors the hot emotions arriving from the amygdala and recruits the cool thinking centers in the PFC to help evaluate these feelings, usually without our conscious knowledge. With the information it gleans from the social context, the OFC can inhibit the amygdala's angry impulses. Researchers at the University of Wisconsin have found large differences in individuals' ability to suppress their negative emotions—differences that coincide with orbitofrontal activity on fMRI scans (Davidson et al., 2000).

When the OFC malfunctions, social behavior runs amok. People have trouble identifying the emotions in faces and voices; and risk taking, impulsivity, emotional outbursts, and impaired interpersonal relationships become common, contributing to the development of aggressive and antisocial behavior (Beer, 2007). Harming the OFC also harms an individual's capacity to feel empathy and guilt, leaving her with little awareness of the moral implications of her actions (Decety et al., 2008; Raine, 1993). Studies have shown that adults with aggressive behavior have deficits in activating both the OFC and the ACC and that children with serious externalizing behavior lack frontal activity in their brains when they're asked to inhibit a response (Lewis, Granic, & Lamm, 2006).

• The *anterior cingulate cortex* lies on the interior surface of the brain where the two hemispheres touch one another. Concerned with regulating both cognitive and emotional processes, the ACC controls and adjusts behavior in difficult situations (Tarullo, Obradovic, & Gunnar, 2009; Zelazo et al., 2008) and is a key player in self-monitoring, noting errors, and making complex judgments (Lewis et al., 2006). When we're in danger of being rejected, it registers in the ACC—in the same area as physical pain (Lieberman & Eisenberger, 2006). EEG studies show that self-control tasks turn on the ACC, which becomes more active between the ages of 3 and 6 years as children get better at resisting impulses and waiting for rewards (Posner & Rothbart, 2000).

Damaging the ACC leads to inappropriate social behavior, higher stress responses, impulsiveness, and decreased empathy (Cozolino, 2006). A baby's cry usually lights up her mother's ACC, but a defective ACC will stay dark (Goleman, 2006a).

Neurotransmitters

Neurotransmitters—the biochemicals that transmit information from one brain cell to another—also provide powerful links between emotional regulation and aggressive behavior (Viding, Williamson, Forbes, & Harir, 2008) and profoundly influence the creation of neural networks early in life (Cozolino, 2006).

• The *dopamine* system, which is integral to the development and functioning of the PFC, enhances working memory (Pihl & Benkelfat, 2005) and participates in both cognitive and behavioral inhibition, especially when rewards are involved (Viding et al., 2008). Adverse early caregiving disturbs development of the dopamine system, and scientists believe that abnormalities in it contribute to ADHD, drug addiction, and schizophrenia (Stanwood & Levitt, 2008), as well as early-onset antisocial behavior in children with ADHD (Caspi et al., 2008).

• *Serotonin* is equally essential in inhibiting aggression and regulating mood and emotion (Viding et al., 2008). It is perhaps most famous for its association with the antidepressant drugs known as SSRIs—selective serotonin reuptake inhibitors—which make more serotonin available for the brain to use. Glitches in serotonin transmission can trigger impulsivity and aggressive behavior (Pihl & Benkelfat, 2005) and even affect the structure and wiring of the ACC (Viding et al., 2008). Chronically high cortisol levels influence serotonin regulation, putting children who've suffered maltreatment at high risk for behavior problems (Tarullo, Quevedo, & Gunnar, 2008).

What does all this mean?

At about age 2, most children begin to practice calming the amygdala, reinforcing and strengthening these important neural circuits (Goleman, 2006a). But for children who've been abused or neglected or who've lived in other extremely difficult circumstances, "normal" circuits may develop differently. To remain safe, they may require an amygdala and a stress system set on high (or low). Because they haven't had the opportunity to learn to read others' emotions or to regulate their own, they haven't acquired these skills or shaped these circuits in the brain (Shackman et al., 2008). Instead, they've learned to pay more attention to anger, react to it fiercely, and even see it when it isn't there (Pollak & Tolley-Schell, 2003). They feel overwhelmed and unable to redirect their negative feelings or hold back their impulses. All of this makes it hard for them to focus on school-like tasks (Ayoub & Fischer, 2006).

Damage to the brain areas involved in self-regulation can occur through genetic susceptibility, injury, trauma, caregiving failures (such as abuse and neglect), environmental dangers (such as poverty), or any combination of these factors. No matter how it happens, this damage changes the way the brain works. Aggressive or antisocial behavior is often the result.

Although people and their brains continue to develop throughout their lives, when it comes to social and emotional development, early experience is crucial in shaping the brain's circuitry (Davidson et al., 2000). Research on both the brain and behavior shows that nurturing and stable relationships with adults are essential for young children. This means that teachers may have an unparalleled opportunity to make a difference in children's lives. It may not be too farfetched to say that consistently offering high-quality care may help to change children's brains and make children more resilient. How we respond to youngsters with challenging behavior and difficult temperaments, who need extra help in learning skills to regulate and cope with their feelings, is especially critical.

W HAT DO YOU THINK?

1. What is a sensitive period?
2. Can you think of some examples of learning that are experience-expectant? Can you think of some examples of learning that are experience-dependent? For example, what about learning a language, learning to swim, or learning to ride a bike?
3. What role does caregiving play in managing stress? Why is it important for teachers to understand the impact of stress on children's brain development?
4. How will learning about the parts of the brain involved in aggressive behavior help you to support children with challenging behavior?

S UGGESTED READING

Goleman, D. (2006). *Social intelligence: The new science of human relationships*. New York: Bantam.

Gunnar, M. R., & Quevedo, K. (2007). The neurobiology of stress and development. *Annual Review of Psychology, 58*, 145–173.

Rutter, M. (2006). *Genes and behavior: Nature–nurture interplay explained*. Malden, MA: Blackwell.

Tarullo, A. R., Obradovic, J., & Gunnar, M. R. (2009). Self-control and the developing brain. *Zero to Three, 29*, 31–37.

CHAPTER 5

Relationship, Relationship, Relationship

Research into the brain and resiliency reveals that consistent, nurturing relationships are a child's best protection against risk—including the risk of challenging behavior. Families have first crack at creating such relationships, but they don't have exclusive rights. Because teachers spend so much time with a child, they, too, have a natural opportunity to forge a strong, positive relationship—and thereby boost resilience. This role is particularly important when family relationships are wobbly. As Carollee Howes and Sharon Ritchie put it in *A Matter of Trust* (2002), "The quality of children's early relationships with their teachers [is] . . . an important predictor of these children's future social relations with peers, their behavior problems, and school satisfaction and achievement" (p. 6).

Part of this chapter has been adapted from *Partners in Quality, vol. 2/Relationships* © CCCF 1999, written by Barbara Kaiser and Judy Sklar Rasminsky based on the research papers of the Partners in Quality Project. With permission from Canadian Child Care Federation, 201–383 Parkdale Avenue, Ottawa, ON, K1Y 4R4.

The caring connection

Your connection with a child is the most powerful tool you have as a teacher. In a safe, caring relationship with an adult, a child finds a secure base for exploring the world. He learns to value himself and believe in his own personal power. He discovers that he can influence the people around him and that they will help him fulfill his needs. With a sensitive, responsive adult as a guide and model, he can learn to understand and regulate his own feelings and behavior, and he can learn to care about other people, see things from their perspective, and understand their feelings, too (Shonkoff & Phillips, 2000).

When problem behavior enters the picture, this crucial relationship may falter. The behavior gets in the way, blocking your view of the child and making it a challenge to like him and establish a connection with him (Birch & Ladd, 1998). Yet it remains essential to create that bond—because the relationship is the key to success. When you and a child care about each other, he has a desire to learn and a model to emulate, and you have more understanding, patience, and persistence. All of this enormously augments your ability to help him learn to behave appropriately.

This chapter describes four facets of creating a relationship: understanding yourself, understanding the child, establishing a relationship with the child, and establishing a relationship with the child's family.

UNDERSTANDING YOURSELF

"Who are you?" said the caterpillar

So how do you forge a relationship with a child with challenging behavior? How can you come to accept him for who he is and care about him no matter how he behaves?

It takes two to have a relationship, and as an adult, you have the responsibility for creating and maintaining that caring connection. You are the mature member of this duo, the one with the ability to size up the situation and adjust your teaching style to enable all the children in the classroom to function and feel comfortable.

Knowing the child well will certainly help, but to begin with, you have to understand where you are coming from yourself. The reason for this is simple: How you relate to the child depends on what you see when you look at him—and what you see depends on who you are. Whether you're aware of it or not, everything about your teaching—how you approach and respond to the children, set up your room, choose and present activities, even your knowledge of child development and theory—filters through the prism of your own emotions, family background, education, temperament, beliefs, values, and culture (Bowman, 1989). That is why it's important for you to discover who you are, to know what matters to you, to understand your reasons for doing this work, to figure out your philosophy of child care and education, to know what kind of people you want the children in your care to become. Knowing about yourself allows you to see the child much more accurately.

Your connection with a child is the most powerful tool you have as a teacher.

There are other reasons to look inward. When you're with a child with challenging behavior, it's critical to stay cool and collected. If you become defensive and stressed and allow him to push your buttons (or hijack your amygdala), you can't think clearly and act rationally. It's also vital to show the child that it's possible to accept, control, and express strong and negative feelings in direct and nonaggressive ways. He needs to see that you aren't afraid of his intense emotions and won't punish, threaten, or withdraw from him (Furman, 1986).

Knowing yourself won't give you magic powers, but it can bring you more control, and it will allow you to accept and talk about your feelings, to be honest with yourself and the children, to see the child and the environment more clearly, and to empathize and respond more fully and appropriately.

What influences the way you relate to a child with challenging behavior?

Without question, negative feelings produce the highest barrier between you and a child with challenging behavior. He evokes plenty of them—fear that someone will get hurt, frustration that you can't do the activity you'd planned, anxiety that you won't be able to manage his behavior, anger, guilt, resentment, inadequacy, and blame. He may remind you of qualities you don't particularly admire in yourself, such as a tendency to act without thinking, or he may bring back unwelcome memories, such as the terror you felt in the presence of that boy who bullied you in the second grade.

Seeing Is Believing?

In "Seeing the Child, Knowing the Person," Nancy Balaban (1995) gives this striking example of how feelings can distort a teacher's view of a child's capabilities:

> A teacher of seven-year-olds disliked the way Tim followed her and whined "teacher, teacher" many times during the day. The teacher was particularly repelled when Tim picked his nose and rolled the mucus into balls.
>
> One day the teacher brought in some sand and . . . screens for the children to explore. She recorded the activities of a small group, including Tim, as an exercise for a course she was taking. The record contained Tim's words: "Hey, the sand comes out faster when the holes are larger!" Reading the record aloud . . . the teacher disregarded this statement until several members of the course called her attention to Tim's discovery. The teacher's prior judgment about Tim had prevented her from seeing the child's achievement. (p. 50)

Source: Nancy Balaban, Infant and Parent Development and Early Intervention program, Bank Street Graduate School of Education. Reprinted by permission.

In addition to influencing your attention, memory, thinking, problem solving, and motivation (Sutton & Wheatley, 2003), negative emotions are contagious (Goleman, 2006a). When you don't like a child, he knows it, and he probably doesn't like you much either. The result can be a coercive cycle that escalates the negative feelings on both sides (Hamre & Pianta, 2005). Although feelings usually intensify reactions, they can also be strong enough to render you numb, unable to respond at all. If you aren't tuned in to these feelings, it's hard to control or change them, and they can easily distort your perceptions of a child's behavior and capabilities.

Your early relationship and past experiences with your own family make a substantial contribution to the way you respond to a child (Pianta, 1999). His behavior may open old wounds and reactivate feelings you had with a parent or sibling, making it difficult for you to respond in a rational way.

Those long years in school also have a profound influence on how you view children's behavior (Bowman, Donovan, & Burns, 2001). If you were a model student, you may have a hard time conjuring up patience and empathy for a child who misbehaves—you'll remember all too well how frustrated you felt when your classmates acted up ("Oh, no, not again!"). Or you may be following the example of the teacher who sent you out of the room at least once a week. As Carl Rogers and Jerome Freiberg say in *Freedom to Learn* (1994), "We tend to teach the way we've been taught [and] discipline the way we've been disciplined" (p. 241).

Your temperament gets into the act, too. If you like to slow things down to ensure that every child has an opportunity to talk, children who need more activity may respond by creating extra stimulation for themselves. If you're a person with intense moods and reactions, some children may be frightened and act unpredictably; or if

Barriers, Obstacles, and Filters

A child with challenging behavior evokes all kinds of feelings, attitudes, and assumptions. Here are some common reactions:

- He shouldn't be in this classroom.
- I'm not trained to work with children like this.
- I can't keep the other children safe.
- The other children aren't getting what they deserve.
- That child is out to get me.
- I can't help him—look at his parents.
- Children have no respect any more.

These feelings provide you with a learning opportunity—they allow you to become aware of what pushes your buttons and do something about it.

you have an aloof style, you may find that children who need a lot of emotional contact are always in your face (Pianta, 1999).

Your values and beliefs also have a powerful effect (Vartuli, 2005), but because they're usually part and parcel of your culture and upbringing, you may not even be aware of them. When a child won't look you in the eye, it's easy to label him as rude if you don't realize that in his culture eye contact with an adult can be a sign of disrespect, contempt, or aggression. Or if you've been raised to believe that children should do what adults say, you may be offended by a child who is always asking why he needs to sit on his bum during story time.

Left to their own devices, these barriers work full time, influencing the way you see the children, skewing your expectations of them, affecting the way they see themselves—and the way they behave. Fortunately, such obstacles aren't necessarily permanent. When you take the time to think about who you are and what you believe, it becomes possible to alter or remove them.

What is self-reflection?

In the past few years, you have probably done a lot of thinking about what's important to you. You've faced the gigantic question of choosing the work you want to do, which meant figuring out what and where you'd study as well. To make those decisions, you had to scrutinize your interests and talents and weigh them alongside family and financial considerations. As Rogers and Freiberg (1994) say, "We are [all] engaged in a struggle to discover our identity, the person we are and choose to be. This is a very pervasive search; it involves our clothes, our hair, our appearance. At a more significant level it involves our choice of values, our stance in relation to parents and others, the relationship we choose to have to society, our whole philosophy of life" (p. 52).

The Inside View

"Greatness in teaching . . . requires a serious encounter with autobiography: Who are you? How did you come to take on your views and outlooks? What forces helped to shape you? What have you made of yourself? Where are you heading? . . . . Of all the knowledge teachers need to draw on, self-knowledge is the most important (and least attended to)," William Ayers writes in *To Teach: The Journey of a Teacher* (2001, p. 124).

Source: To Teach: The Journey of a Teacher by William Ayers. Copyright 2001 by Teachers College Press. Reproduced with the permission of Teachers College Press via Copyright Clearance Center.

This thinking is called *self-reflection.* It is both an attitude and a method—a strategy for increasing your skill and a willingness to dig deep into yourself and your work and to act on what you find. *Why* is at the heart of the matter: Why am I doing what I'm doing the way that I'm doing it?

When you think about your feelings, values, and beliefs and how they affect your behavior, each interaction with a child becomes more meaningful. You have more self-respect because your actions are more intentional, and you have more control and ownership of them. You are working from a position of strength inside yourself.

How do you reflect?

The process of reflection is a messy mixture of the rational and the intuitive, of melding knowledge of yourself with knowledge from your training and experience and information gleaned from families, colleagues, and written sources.

In *How We Think* (1933), the philosopher and educator John Dewey, the father of reflective thinking, recommends cultivating three attitudes:

- *Open-mindedness,* which is the "active desire to hear more than one side; to give heed to facts from whatever source they come; to give full attention to alternative possibilities; to recognize the possibility of error even in the beliefs that are dearest to us" (pp. 30–32)
- *Whole-heartedness,* which is a willingness to throw yourself totally into the endeavor
- *Responsibility,* which is a form of integrity; a willingness to consider the consequences of possible changes and go forward if they're consistent with your beliefs

It is easier to reflect on what's going on between you and the children if you dedicate some time to becoming aware of your own personal history and culture. Think of yourself as an anthropologist setting out to explore that most fascinating person of all: yourself.

Think about your own childhood. What was your family's childrearing philosophy? Who took care of you, and how did those caregivers respond when you needed help or comfort? What role did your extended family play? How were you disciplined? Did your parents encourage you and make you feel special, or did you promise yourself that you'd never use their methods with your own child? If there are things about your early life that you don't remember or understand, talk to your parents, siblings, grandparents, aunts, uncles, or cousins.

Take a look at your education, too. Which teachers did you like, and which couldn't you stand? Why? What did they say and do, and how did they make you feel?

Can you see the child you used to be in the person you are today? It's likely that he or she is nearby when you are interacting with the children in your classroom, affecting your perceptions, interpretations, and behavior.

When do you reflect?

Ideally, a teacher should always be thinking about what she's doing, why she's doing it, and what she feels. Robert Tremmel (1993) likens the process of listening to your feelings to the practice of Zen Buddhism—paying attention to the here and now and investing the present moment with your full awareness and concentration. Janet Gonzalez-Mena (2008) advises: "Tune in on what is bothering you instead of just ignoring it and hoping it will go away. Work to identify what specific behaviors of others make you uncomfortable. Try to discover exactly what in yourself creates this discomfort" (p. 60).

Any time a disturbing incident occurs—whether it is major or minor—some reflection is in order. Before you forget what happened, sit down and focus on the event, recollecting what took place, what you felt, and how you reacted. If you can figure out what triggered your emotions and where they came from within you, you can see how they affected your work and how you can begin to improve things. Even if you don't know exactly what caused those feelings, you will have more control over them if you're aware they exist—and perhaps next time you'll notice them early enough to reframe them. At the same time, devote some thought to the values, goals, and teaching tools you might have invoked in this situation (Curtis, 2009).

It takes practice to do this well, but it is definitely possible. Whether or not you've located the source of your unease, you can use a behavior therapy technique to stop yourself from wallowing in destructive thoughts, put some mental distance between yourself and the situation, and refocus your attention where it belongs. When you find yourself thinking, "There he goes again; now I'll never finish this lesson," take a deep breath and shout inside your head: "Stop. These thoughts aren't helping me." (Alternately, you can concentrate on the soles of your feet, imagine yourself on a beach in Hawaii, or visualize the trigger thoughts floating away from you—anything that quiets the storm within.) Then replace your negative thoughts with a positive coping one: "He's testing my limits. I know what to do. I'm going to stay calm." Once you get past your own knee-jerk reaction, you're ready to take the next step and consider the child's needs: "He must have had a rough morning at home. I'll go sit beside him and see if I can help."

Once in a while, you and a child have a particularly hard time getting along together. You expect him to be nothing but trouble, and he obliges. You feel frustrated and out

Who's Got the Button?

Ms. Williams had been teaching for years, and she felt confident working with children with difficult behaviors: With her sense of humor and knowledge of kids, she always managed to help them realize they had skills and something special to contribute.

But Ms. Williams was at her wit's end when Joseph entered her class. No matter what she did, his response was always "%#@% off !!!!" or "%#@% you!" Although she tried to control herself, whenever Joseph shouted those words she lost her temper. She knew he had found a button to push, a vulnerable spot that grew out of her upbringing, but she didn't know what to do about it.

One day a friend suggested she shout the words at herself in a mirror until they lost their meaning. Since nothing else seemed to work, she decided to try. That evening she went into the bathroom, closed the door, and began shouting at herself in the mirror, "%#@% off, %#@% you!" A few minutes later her husband knocked frantically on the door, asking "Are you all right?" She realized she felt better and began to laugh. When she returned to the classroom, she found that she could respond calmly and appropriately to Joseph's outbursts and focus on his feelings instead of her own.

of control, and it becomes increasingly difficult for either of you to have a positive thought about the other. In fact, when you're in a relationship like this, you probably won't even notice the child's positive behavior.

These feelings—which show in your body language and tone of voice despite your efforts to conceal them—warn you that something is desperately wrong between you and the child. In the words of psychologist Robert C. Pianta (1999), your relationship is "stuck" or "locked up," and it's likely to prevent you from teaching effectively.

This situation offers an opportunity for you to take a hard look at yourself and try a fresh approach. The idea, says Pianta (1999), is to identify what you're feeling and understand how it's connected to what you do (for example, it's difficult to respond positively if you take things personally and think the child is out to get you). What's most important is to shake up your fixed ideas and open yourself to new feelings, perceptions, and interactions. Talking with colleagues can aid in this process; so can observing what's going on in the classroom, looking expressly for positive behaviors. The technique called banking time, which is described on pages 82–83, can also alter your point of view.

Are there any techniques to help you reflect?

Several tools can assist you in the process of reflection. One traditional way is to keep a journal. It is both a record and "an instrument for thinking about teaching and children in a critical, sustained way" (Ayers, 2001, p. 38). It allows you to return to a situation, to construct a whole out of many bits, and to increase your self-awareness by forcing you to put your thoughts in writing. When you write for yourself, without worrying about what others will say, feelings and ideas have a way of spilling out unbidden, bringing insights in their wake.

You can concentrate on daily events, difficult or memorable incidents, one child or several, one topic or many. If you're using a notebook, try dedicating one side of the page to record keeping and the other to reflection. Carry it with you or keep it in a handy spot in the classroom. If you set aside a regular time each day to write in it, you're more likely to be faithful to the task. When you have a child with challenging behavior in your class, writing in a journal can help you to identify what's working, what isn't, and why.

Though some people consider reflection a personal matter, others like to have a sounding board. When you're reflecting, questions inevitably arise, and it's useful to have a safe, supportive environment for sharing your doubts, feelings, and experiences. One way to arrange this is to fix a regular time to get together—in person, on the phone, via email—with friend or colleague. Staff meetings, case consultation, feedback from supervisors, and occasional talks with the school counselor also provoke useful reflection. Formal meetings where you have the freedom to explore your feelings about the children and your own style and needs are especially useful, because they give reflection and relationships the priority and status they deserve (Pianta, 1999).

We tend to pay attention to problems, but remember to give equal time to your successes. Positive reinforcement works just as well for teachers as for children, and your triumphs can tell you as much about your practice as any difficulty.

Be patient with yourself. As you become comfortable with the process, you can expand into more sensitive and difficult areas. The goal is to turn reflection into a reflex, an instinct that sits quietly at the back of your mind weighing pros and cons and whispering, "Why should I do that?" Eventually this effort will enhance your competence, confidence, and ability to work effectively with children with challenging behavior (Vartuli, 2005).

UNDERSTANDING THE CHILD

You are one partner in the relationship equation; the child is the other. And just as you bring your entire history into the classroom with you, so does he. The history of a child with challenging behavior is shorter than yours, which means that it's less entrenched and may be more amenable to change, but the baggage he's carting is still very weighty and no doubt includes some of the risk and protective factors we've already mentioned. As you start to build a relationship, you may want to see what those suitcases contain.

What is the role of attachment?

One of the most important items that any child carries with him is his relationship with his primary caregiver. This person is usually his mother but may also be his father, grandmother, or someone else entirely. This very first relationship is the basis for his relationship with you.

What we know about early relationships began with John Bowlby, whose ideas are so much a part of our thinking today that it's hard to imagine how revolutionary they seemed just 50 years ago. Infants are emotional beings who naturally form strong bonds with their caregivers, Bowlby recognized, and the way those special adults interact with their baby wields a powerful influence on how he turns out (Ainsworth, Blehar, Waters, & Wall, 1978; Bowlby, 1969/1982).

Bowlby (Ainsworth et al., 1978; Bowlby, 1969/1982) realized that human infants, like other animal species, are born with instinctive behaviors that help them to survive. Acts such as crying, smiling, vocalizing, grasping, and clinging keep babies close to their primary caregivers, who respond to their gurgles and wails, feed and soothe them, shelter them from danger, and teach them about their environment. These behaviors help to create *attachment*—children's vital emotional tie to their primary caregiver or *attachment figure* who provides them with protection and emotional support (Ainsworth et al., 1978; Bowlby, 1969/1982). In pioneering studies in the 1950s and 1960s, American psychologist Mary Ainsworth (Ainsworth et al., 1978) confirmed Bowlby's theory by documenting for the first time the emotional impact of parents' everyday behavior on their children. In Uganda and the United States, Ainsworth meticulously observed mothers and babies at home, watching the process of attachment unfold over the first year of life as the babies came to recognize, prefer, seek out, and become attached to their primary caregiver.

These observations enabled Ainsworth to make a critical discovery: A baby's sense of security depends on how his attachment figure cares for him. During the first year of life an infant evolves an *attachment strategy*—a way to organize feelings and behavior—that is tailor-made for his own unique caregiving situation, a strategy that will enable him to cope best with his particular circumstances and bring him the most security and comfort (van IJzendoorn, Schuengel, & Bakermans-Kranenburg, 1999; Weinfeld, Sroufe, Egeland, & Carlson, 1999). All attachment strategies are normal, adaptive, and functional; the trouble is that what works best within the child's family may not work outside it (Greenberg, DeKlyen, Speltz, & Endriga, 1997).

How does attachment affect behavior?

According to Bowlby (1969/1982), infants construct *internal working models* of how relationships work based on their experience with their own attachment figure. Although these models aren't conscious, they prepare the foundation for social and emotional development; guide how children see themselves, other people, and the world; and serve as templates for future relationships, including their relationships with teachers and peers.

Children who are *securely attached* (Weinfeld et al., 1999) receive consistently warm, sensitive, and responsive care from a primary caregiver who enjoys their company. From this experience, they develop internal working models of other people who are there for them, and they see themselves as capable of eliciting whatever they need from their environment. They tend to have a positive view of life, know

Infants construct internal working models of how relationships work based on their experience with their own attachment figure.

Photo by Abigail Rasminsky

how to manage and express their feelings (Honig, 2002; Karen, 1998), and possess good social skills, many friends, and high self-esteem. Because they are also good problem solvers who can ask for help when they need it, they do well in school (Howes & Ritchie, 2002). About 55 percent of children are securely attached (van IJzendoorn, 1995).

Children who are *insecurely attached* experience two different kinds of care: *resistant/ambivalent* or *avoidant*. The primary caregiver of a child who has a *resistant attachment* responds to his signals unpredictably (Ainsworth et al., 1978). Because he can't rely on her to provide comfort and security, he develops internal working models in which he can't get what he needs by himself and can't trust others to help him. It is no wonder that children who are resistantly attached become clingy, dependent, and demanding (Weinfeld et al., 1999). In longitudinal studies, L. Alan Sroufe (1983; Weinfeld et al., 1999) found they were angry, anxious, impulsive, and easily frustrated; and their low self-esteem made them easy targets for bullying. They often focus on the teacher, creating conflict in order to keep her attention (Howes & Ritchie, 2002; Karen, 1998). About 8 percent of children have the resistant/ambivalent attachment pattern (van IJzendoorn, 1995).

The early experience of a child who is *avoidantly attached* creates yet another set of internal working models. His primary caregiver is rejecting, angry, irritable, and hostile (Weinfeld et al., 1999). Children growing up under these conditions consider themselves unworthy of love and don't believe other people will be available to them (Karen, 1998; Renken, Egeland, Marvinney, Mangelsdorf, & Sroufe, 1989). To protect themselves from rejection, they turn off their feelings and act as if they don't care, but beneath their tough facade they are hurt, sad, and angry—likely to act aggressively and strike out preemptively (Kobak, 1999). Approximately 23 percent of children are categorized as avoidant (van IJzendoorn, 1995).

The primary caregiver of a child with *disorganized/disoriented attachment* usually has serious problems of her own—she may be mentally ill, severely depressed, addicted to drugs or alcohol (Lyons-Ruth & Jacobvitz, 1999). Sometimes she is frightened, unable to manage her life; and sometimes she is frightening—angry, hostile, distant. Very often she abuses her child—48 percent of children who have been maltreated have a disorganized attachment pattern (van IJzendoorn et al., 1999). At one and the same time she is the source of danger and safety, alarm and comfort (Lyons-Ruth & Jacobvitz, 1999). From this confusing experience, children derive internal working models of people who can't be trusted to care for them or organize their world (Lyons-Ruth, 1996). They are sad and anxious, with poor social skills, self-control, and frustration tolerance. Because they haven't developed an organized strategy for handling stress or strong emotion, they often have serious behavior problems, acting unpredictably and aggressively with their teachers and peers (Lyons-Ruth, 1996; van IJzendoorn et al., 1999).

Although children living with the most difficult conditions—trauma or severe conflict, for example—tend to remain disorganized (Moss, St-Laurent, Dubois-Comtois, & Cyr, 2005), most children with disorganized attachments evolve a new strategy by their early school years. To make their relationship with their mother more predictable and less frightening, their behavior becomes *controlling* (Humber & Moss, 2005; Moss et al., 2005), creating problems with peers and teachers, who find them bossy and inflexible (Greenberg, 1999).

Avoidant and disorganized behavior often appear together, and both are associated with peer rejection and poor emotional and school adjustment (Granot & Mayseless, 2001). But it is the children with disorganized attachment (especially those with the controlling variety) who are most likely to behave aggressively (Lyons-Ruth & Jacobvitz, 1999; Moss et al., 2005; van IJzendoorn et al., 1999). About 15 percent of children in middle-class families display disorganized attachment, but in families where there is poverty, maltreatment, or substance abuse the percentage can be two to three times as high (van IJzendoorn et al., 1999).

Attachment strategies are not immutable—they can change along with life circumstances (Weinfeld et al., 1999). When a child's environment remains stable, attachment and working models probably remain stable, too (Hamilton, 2000; Moss et al., 2005; Waters, Merrick, Treboux, Crowell, & Albersheim, 2000). But high-risk conditions and difficult experiences can have a powerful impact on parents' ability to parent, and attachment may change as a result (Waters, Weinfeld, & Hamilton, 2000; Weinfeld, Sroufe, & Egeland, 2000). Perhaps more importantly, children can form new relationships with teachers and other adults that modify their view of themselves and the world. It is also useful to bear in mind that attachment is only one factor among many that influences a child's outcome—in itself it is neither necessary nor sufficient to cause later behavior problems (Greenberg et al., 1997).

Is attachment culture bound?

Although most research on attachment has taken place in the European American culture, Bowlby conceived of it as universal, the outcome of an evolutionary process that ensures the survival of the human species (van IJzendoorn & Sagi, 1999). Ainsworth studied mothers and babies in two cultures, Ugandan and North American; and cross-cultural researchers have provided support for Bowlby's ideas by finding the three basic attachment patterns in Israel, Japan, Africa, China, and Colombia. The majority of children are securely attached, even in Israel's kibbutzim, where children live collectively. It seems likely that attachment occurs everywhere, regardless of race, gender, or social class (Posada et al., 1995; van IJzendoorn & Sagi, 1999).

Of course, when children go to child care or school, their attachment status doesn't appear in their file—an expert has to assess it and there is little reason to collect this information, apart from research. But whenever a child with challenging behavior appears in your classroom, it is a good idea to remember that attachment issues may be lurking underneath, particularly in children at high risk (Howes & Ritchie, 1999).

The Chicken or the Egg

Some researchers believe it is temperament, not attachment, that accounts for the different attachment classifications—that children with secure attachments are actually children with easy temperaments and children with insecure attachments are in fact children with difficult temperaments (see Karen, 1998).

Dymphna van den Boom of the University of Leiden in Holland (1994, 1995) shed light on this controversy with her research on irritable babies—babies who smile less, fuss more, and get less fun out of interacting with their mothers. In a few hours of individualized instruction, she taught the mothers of one randomly selected group of fussy babies to respond sensitively to their infant's signals. In follow-up studies, these babies were more sociable and better able to soothe themselves than the babies whose mothers had not been trained. More than 60 percent became securely attached, as opposed to 28 percent of the untrained group. At age 3, this gap remained (van den Boom, 1995), indicating that attachment and temperament are not identical and sensitive caregiving can override temperament.

Temperament certainly influences what a baby requires and how a caregiver responds. But several studies have found that babies with a difficult temperament are more likely to become securely attached when their mother has solid social support (Crockenberg, 1981; Jacobson & Frye, 1991). In the end, it seems clear that both temperament and attachment play important roles in challenging behavior.

ESTABLISHING A RELATIONSHIP
WITH THE CHILD

How does a secure attachment to a teacher protect a child?

A relationship with a supportive adult can play a key role in building children's resilience (Werner, 2000). This special person can provide a child with all that a secure attachment entails: the chance to learn that other people can be trusted, to regard himself as a valuable human being worthy of love and respect, and to adjust his internal working models to embrace this new, more positive view of the world (Howes & Ritchie, 1999).

Most children become attached to more than one person (Ainsworth et al., 1978; Bowlby, 1969/1982), and because each attachment relationship is unique and depends on the way the adult responds to the child (van IJzendoorn & DeWolff, 1997), a relationship with you can become an important opportunity, providing a secure base for exploration, a safe haven when a child is upset, threatened, or afraid, and interactions that help him regulate his emotions (Pianta, 1999).

A close relationship with a teacher brings children other "strong and persistent" benefits (Hamre & Pianta, 2001). They like school more, participate more actively in the classroom, and perform better academically (Birch & Ladd, 1998; Hamre & Pianta, 2001; Ladd & Burgess, 2001; Pianta & Stuhlman, 2004). They get along well with their classmates, engage in more complex play, have better social skills, and exert more control over their emotions (Howes & Ritchie, 2002; Peisner-Feinberg et al., 2001). Above all, their behavior is less challenging and aggressive (Howes, Matheson, & Hamilton, 1994; Peisner-Feinberg et al., 2001). All of this protects them from risk (Pianta, 1999).

On the other hand, a combative relationship with a teacher increases a child's risks. It makes school an unpleasant place (Birch & Ladd, 1998), and he is more likely to have attention and learning problems (Ladd & Burgess, 2001), low frustration tolerance, and faulty work habits, which, for boys in particular, adds up to a poor academic performance through grade 8 (Hamre & Pianta, 2001). Children who have a rocky relationship with their kindergarten teacher have behavior problems for years to come (Pianta & Stuhlman, 2004; Hamre & Pianta, 2001; Silver, Measelle, Armstrong, & Essex, 2005); and they act more aggressively with their peers, who often reject or victimize them (Howes & Hamilton, 1993; Ladd & Burgess, 1999).

Teacher Template

When children develop a secure attachment to the very first teacher or child care provider in their lives, other secure attachments are likely to follow. In one longitudinal study, children's relationships with their first teacher predicted how they would get along with their teacher when they were 9 years old (Howes, Hamilton, & Phillipsen, 1998). Perhaps children develop internal working models of teachers, too.

When conflict with their teachers is chronic, their misconduct increases (Hamre, Pianta, Downer, & Mashburn, 2008), and they may have disturbed thinking and lack social information processing skills (Ladd & Burgess, 2001). Even children who aren't at risk may develop behavior problems when they have a conflictual relationship with a teacher (Ladd & Burgess, 2001; Pianta, Steinberg, & Rollins, 1995).

For children with challenging behavior, discord with a teacher is especially common and influential (Silver et al., 2005). Teachers react to them with anger, criticism, and punishment (Coie & Koeppl, 1990), and their teaching becomes colder, less responsive, and less encouraging (Fry, 1983; Sroufe, 1983). The other children take their cue from the teacher and also turn against the child with challenging behavior (Hughes, Cavell, & Willson, 2001; White & Kistner, 1992). Feeling dislike and hostility all around him, he is likely to respond with more misbehavior and noncompliance.

But a supportive teacher can change all of this. A study of temperamentally bold, uninhibited children—who often lack impulse control and self-regulation skills and may act aggressively in social situations—found that having a sensitive teacher reduced their negative and off-task behaviors, in marked contrast to their bold peers in a classroom with a less sensitive teacher (Rimm-Kaufman et al., 2002). When teacher and child build a close relationship, a teacher can interrupt a coercive interaction cycle with a child (Hamre & Pianta, 2005), help a child with a disorganized attachment to be accepted by his peers (Zionts, 2005), and lower the likelihood a child will be retained or referred to special education (Pianta et al., 1995). For children at high risk, a close relationship diminishes aggressive behavior and boosts academic achievement (Hamre & Pianta, 2005; Silver et al., 2005).

A close relationship with a teacher brings children other "strong and persistent" benefits. They get along well with their classmates, engage in more complex play, have better social skills, and exert more control over their emotions.

How can you develop a positive relationship with a child with challenging behavior?

Relationships are actually made up of thousands of interactions (Pianta, 1999). If the teacher responds sensitively, promptly, and consistently, over time these interactions add up to a secure attachment—an emotional investment, a positive and supportive relationship, and an organized way for teacher and child to relate to one another (Howes, 1999). All the while, these interactions are building brain circuits vital to self-regulation—circuits that are reinforced each time a teacher helps a child return to a regulated state (Cozolino, 2006).

But constructing such a relationship with children with challenging behavior is not an easy matter. Their internal working models of adult–child relationships (which remain unknown to us) accompany them to child care or school, where the strategies that protect them from rejection or haphazard caregiving at home may provoke exactly the behavior they are supposed to ward off, alienating them from their teachers and classmates (Fearon, Bakermans-Kranenburg, van IJzendoorn, Lapsley, & Roisman, 2010; Howes & Ritchie, 2002). As psychologist Robert Karen (1998) writes, "The behavior of the insecurely attached child—whether aggressive or cloying—often tries the patience of peers and adults alike. It elicits reactions that repeatedly reconfirm the child's distorted view of the world" (p. 228).

But, Karen (1998) concludes, "If adults are sensitive to the anxious child's concerns, they can break through" (p. 228). Howes and Ritchie (2002) call this process "disconfirming" what the child has learned from previous experience. It depends, they say, on "careful observation and listening to children and on a teacher's reflecting on her or his own practice, examining missteps, and trying again. . . . In order to disconfirm maladaptive interactions, teachers must be able to think about why the patterns of behavior are occurring and consciously work to change them" (pp. 73, 75).

Sensitive, responsive care

Where a child with challenging behavior is concerned, we tend to keep our distance, limiting ourselves to the necessary, saying no, or feeling annoyed. But if we're going to help him learn to act appropriately, we have to put our interactions to work for us.

The research literature, starting with Bowlby and Ainsworth, returns again and again to two critical features of interactions: *sensitivity* and *responsiveness*. As Ainsworth (Ainsworth et al., 1978) saw it, this involves

- being aware of the child's signals
- interpreting them accurately
- responding to them promptly and appropriately

Building a secure relationship with a child who has an insecure or disorganized attachment is a long and arduous process requiring many doses of sensitive, responsive care (Howes, 1999). If a child doesn't trust adults to come through for him, the teacher must be, as Sroufe (1983) puts it, "patiently, inevitably, constantly" available (p. 77). If the child expects to be rejected and the teacher excludes him by putting him in time-out or sending him out of the class, then his expectations are confirmed (Karen, 1998). In contrast, if a teacher reacts empathically, it becomes possible for the child to believe that people actually do respond to his needs (Weinfeld et al., 1999).

Remaining physically nearby and emotionally accessible enables the teacher to act as an organizer for a child's classroom experience (Howes & Ritchie, 2002). By consistently acknowledging his efforts and responding positively to his questions, comments, and problems, she is helping him learn to regulate his own emotions and organize his own behavior.

Ainsworth also noted that sensitive, responsive caregiving is warm, tender, affectionate, and cooperative—caregivers don't interrupt the child's ongoing activity but guide without controlling or coercing; and they modify and space their interactions to synchronize with the child's cues. Others have found that children are securely attached to teachers who rate high on responsiveness and involvement—teachers who hold and hug children to comfort them, play with them, talk with them for long periods, ask open-ended questions, listen reflectively, and teach in teachable moments. On the other hand, children are insecurely attached to teachers rated as detached, intrusive, harsh, critical, punitive, or threatening (Howes & Hamilton, 2002).

Instead of waiting for an obvious signal like an explosion, sensitive and responsive teachers keep an eye out for subtle signs that appear in a child's body language or tone of voice as well as his words—stiff shoulders, gritted teeth, tooth-grinding at nap, lashing out at peers (Honig, 2002). These signs indicate that instead of feeling competent and confident, he's feeling anxious and uneasy, and it's time to show him you care.

Tell-Tale Signs

We can prevent challenging behavior by catching it in its earliest phase, anxiety. The signs vary with the child. You can't know for sure what a child is thinking or feeling, but you can make a good guess by knowing him well and watching him closely (Butchard & Spencler, 2000).

- *Physiology.* Tears, frequent urination, clenched teeth, blushing, pallor, rigidity, rapid breathing, sweating, fidgeting, vomiting, squeaky voice.
- *Behavior.* Downcast eyes, withdrawing, twirling hair, sucking thumb, fingers, hair, or clothes, hoarding, clinging, biting fingernails, whining, being noisy or quiet, screaming, masturbating, smirking, giggling, crying.
- *Thoughts.* No one loves me; no one wants me; I'm no good; I don't like it here; I don't have any friends; no one will come to get me; I can't do it; I'm bad; I want my mommy.
- *Feelings.* Concerned, distressed, troubled, afraid, nervous, excited, expectant, sad, irritable, grouchy, insecure, frustrated, worried, confused, panicky.

Teacher talk

In their observations of children with difficult life circumstances, Howes and Ritchie (2002) identified another effective technique for helping children trust the teacher and believe they're worthy of affection: *teacher talk.* Teachers used certain phrases over and over to support the child and explain what they were doing. A teacher would say, "I'm going to help you," "I'm going to stop you," or "I'm going to say no" to remind a child to try to control his own behavior and tell him that she's available to help him help himself and keep him safe during a difficult time: "I'm going to help you because it's time to put the blocks away." As children gained problem-solving skills and needed less direction, teachers began to *ask* if they wanted help: "Do you want me to help you, or do you want to do it yourself?" (Howes & Ritchie, 2002).

Talk openly about feelings

Open communication about feelings is also crucial to building a relationship. Children who've had difficult relationships and children from violent neighborhoods or abusive or stressed families often find it dangerous to show or express negative feelings, and as a result they shut down their anger, anxiety, sadness, frustration, and fear. But the feelings do not go away and may surge out unexpectedly in stressful situations. When teachers accept and validate these emotions and give the child language to label and talk about his feelings ("I know that makes you mad," "That must be scary"), they tell him they're listening, help him to cope in the classroom, and shore up the teacher–child relationship (Pianta, 1999). With the teacher acting as an emotional coach and modeling self-control, children can develop the ability to soothe themselves and to regulate and express their emotions in appropriate ways (Howes & Ritchie, 2002; Pianta, 1999).

Positive outlook

Being positive is another way to improve your relationship with a child with challenging behavior. This may not be easy if your joint history leads you both to expect discord at every turn, but it's important to give the relationship priority. If you notice his positive feelings and behaviors and respond positively to his requests, it becomes easier for him to behave positively, too (Elicker & Fortner-Wood, 1995).

Perhaps the best way to interact positively with a child is simply to spend time with him one on one. When you keep an eye out for moments to connect, they seem to appear miraculously in the daily routine, whether he's helping you with snack, pounding the play dough, or putting on his boots for outdoor play (Elicker & Fortner-Wood, 1995). (For more ideas, see "Savings Account" on page 83.)

If the vibes between you and the child always feel negative despite your best efforts, experts recommend a special kind of interaction, called *banking time* (Pianta, 1999) or *floor time* (Greenspan, 1996). A technique that introduces new interactions, perceptions, and feelings into a relationship, it is based on the notion that positive experiences with a child protect the relationship against conflict and tension, in the same way that money in the bank provides a buffer against extra expenses. Psychologist Robert C. Pianta describes its basic rules (Driscoll & Pianta, 2010; Pianta, 1999):

- At least once a week, the teacher sets aside 5 to 15 minutes to spend with the child one on one. She should arrange the time regularly and in advance, not use it to reinforce or punish behavior. It's a good idea to recruit a second adult to assist with the other children.

Savings Account

Good teaching practices, such as remembering to smile, starting every day with a clean slate, and listening carefully whenever children try to communicate, provide the basis for positive interactions. Researchers and teachers on the front lines offer these additional tips:

- As each child arrives in the morning, greet him by name and let him know you're pleased to see him: "Hi, Michael, I'm so glad you're here today."
- Learn about the child's family—who lives with him, the names and ages of siblings and pets—so that you can begin to enter his world: "What did you and Francesca do this weekend?" (For more about families, see the next section and Chapters 6 and 12.)
- Try to discover what the child likes, what's important to him, and what makes him feel good about himself. Create opportunities for him to share his memories, experiences, and feelings, and respond as if his words are vitally important. Keep track of these contacts so that you'll know which children you're missing or avoiding and can fill in the gaps.
- To show your respect, use his name often.
- Join the child's play, following his lead.
- Tell the child you care about him and think about him when he's not there. Call his home if he misses a few days of school, send him a letter if you're away, bring things into the classroom that you know will interest him ("I found a book you're going to like").
- Share your own interests, experiences, and feelings. This lets him know the relationship is reciprocal and you are a person as well as his teacher.
- Catch him being good. When he's behaving appropriately, give him extra time and attention.
- Perform kind and helpful acts for him, and assign him reasonable responsibilities of his own. Children feel important when they can help.
- Use gentle and affectionate touch—pats, hugs, high fives—to convey warmth and reassurance. But be sure he's comfortable with these gestures.
- Make comments that give the child the message you see and hear him ("You're wearing your favorite baseball cap today, Aidan!").
- Create a special signal, exclusive to you and the child. A secret sign, handshake, or password makes it fun to communicate.

- The child decides what the teacher and child will do together, choosing from a wide range of materials selected by the teacher. The child leads and directs the play.

- The teacher doesn't teach, direct, reinforce, or focus on the child's performance, but remains neutral and objective. In an interested tone of voice, she becomes a kind of sportscaster, describing what the child is doing and labeling his feelings.

- The teacher conveys no more than three simple messages (such as "You are important," "I will try to be consistent and available," or "I am a helper when you need or ask me") chosen to disconfirm the child's negative beliefs and expectations about adults and help him to use the teacher as a resource and a source of safety and comfort. The teacher reinforces these messages by communicating them in ordinary situations throughout the day ("I'm happy to help you. Teachers are helpers").

- When the session is over, the teacher records what happened and her feelings about it so that she can reflect on it.

Putting the child in charge allows him to behave in new ways and show you different competencies. He can become more interested in you, care more about having your attention and approval, and begin to believe that an adult can be available, responsive, and accepting. You, in turn, may well find him more agreeable, interesting, competent, and amenable to guidance.

When you know a child well, you are on firmer ground. You know how to make your interactions more sensitive and responsive, how to incorporate his interests into your activities, how to build on his strengths and teach him the skills he needs. If you pay close attention, you'll know that when Will is sitting alone, looking at the floor, tugging at his hair, something is wrong. If you put a hand on his shoulder or smile at him and he sits up straight and begins to do his work or talk to his neighbor, you can see that your intervention, subtle as it was, did the trick.

Keep in mind that you are a giant player in this game, the adult who has the responsibility and the one who's most capable of reflection and change. Whenever you examine your own feelings and actions and think about how they're affecting your relationship, the child benefits and your own practice becomes more rewarding.

ESTABLISHING A RELATIONSHIP WITH THE FAMILY

Remember those suitcases the child with challenging behavior lugged into your classroom earlier in this chapter? Well, his family probably occupies most of them—a fact that makes building a relationship with the family essential to building a relationship with the child.

Thanks to the ecological theory of Urie Bronfenbrenner (1979) (which urges us to look at the child in the context of family, community, and society) and family systems theory (which reminds us that family members are all connected to one another), we now know that child and family are one big package, an integral whole. By supporting families, teachers are supporting children's well-being and development.

Here are some of the basic ideas behind this family-centered approach (Chud & Fahlman, 1995; Gonzalez-Mena, 2010; Keyser, 2006):

- Families are central to children's lives—their first and main teachers and the experts on their own child.

- Families have their own strengths, competencies, resources, ways of coping, and goals for their children.

- Every family must be respected and accepted on its own terms, without judgments or preconceptions.

- Each family's values, beliefs, race, culture, ethnicity, religion, language, and socioeconomic status must be acknowledged and respected.

- Services and programs are effective to the degree that they support the family in meeting the needs it has identified itself.

In its new position statement on developmentally appropriate practice, the National Association for the Education of Young Children (2009) stresses the importance of shared decision making and responding to family choices without abdicating responsibility to support the child's development and learning.

Three decades of research confirm that when families are engaged in their children's education, children of all ages do better both academically and socially, no matter what the family's income or background (Hoover-Dempsey et al., 2005; Weiss, Kreider, Lopez, & Chatman, 2005). In fact, No Child Left Behind, the NAEYC, Head Start, and other groups consider family involvement a priority. The more teachers and families communicate, the more support and sensitivity the teacher displays with the child (Owen, Ware, & Barfoot, 2002), and the safer the child feels (Gonzalez-Mena, 2010; Keyser, 2006). Families learn about child development and their child's program and feel more supported and comfortable with their child's care and education (Gonzalez-Mena, 2010; Keyser, 2006). Teachers understand children and families better, improve their practice, and acquire more confidence, respect, and job satisfaction (Keyser, 2006).

What keeps teachers and families apart?

Many obstacles stand in the way of productive collaboration, especially for low-income families and families of different cultures (Trumbull, Rothstein-Fisch, Greenfield, & Quiroz, 2001):

- Time, a precious commodity for all families, is an enormous barrier. Most parents must work, and some may hold down two jobs and work odd or irregular shifts to keep afloat.

- Families may feel uncomfortable or intimidated, perhaps because they grew up outside of the United States and don't speak English well, perhaps because they had little education themselves (Trumbull et al., 2001), perhaps because they carry painful memories of their own school days.

- School and child care policies, programs, and ways of communicating, however well intentioned, may put families off. All too often educators are unaware that their efforts to involve families grow out of cultural values and knowledge families may not share—and may find puzzling, alien, even inappropriate (Trumbull et al., 2001). (See Chapter 6.)

- Many working-class and low-income families, as well as families with different cultural backgrounds, believe that school and family lie in separate realms. They view teachers as professionals with specialized knowledge who are responsible for education (Lareau, 2000); whereas their own role is to send their children to school on time and teach them to behave properly and be good people (Trumbull et al., 2001). Because they don't usually socialize with the parents of their children's classmates, they have little of the inside information that middle-class families easily accumulate and utilize in their dealings with the center or school (Lareau, 2000).

It's important to remember that even when families don't participate in traditional ways, they make a vital contribution. By stressing the importance of education, asking about their child's day, and providing high expectations, pride, understanding, and enthusiasm for their child's school experiences, they enhance attention, persistence, and motivation and decrease problem behavior (Fantuzzo, McWayne, Perry, & Childs, 2004; Ferguson, 2008).

Getting to know you

The families who are hardest to connect with may very well be the ones you most need to get to know—those whose children will benefit the most from a close relationship with you. When you know where the child is coming from, you'll understand him better, have more empathy for him, and make a stronger connection. If you can establish some trust with the family, you will have a much better chance of helping one another—and the child—when there's a problem.

How can you establish a positive relationship with families? Research provides some clues. A school-based study shows that parents become more involved in a child's education if they believe they can help him to succeed. Serious and sincere invitations from teacher and child are also "key motivators" (Hoover-Dempsey et al., 2005, p. 110). Such invitations are especially influential when parents doubt they'll be helpful or believe it's not their role to be involved.

These findings emphasize the importance of the teacher. Some parents will be involved no matter what you do; some have neither the time nor the inclination and will never be involved. But some may respond if you approach them the right way. What's required is a strong, clear message that their involvement can really help their child and that you truly value and respect their views.

Getting to know families takes time, so start as soon as possible. One way to begin is to develop your own welcome letter and enrollment form. Address the form to the "adults responsible for the child" and provide spaces for several names and signatures (Keyser, 2006). Ask where the family comes from, what languages they speak, and some specific questions about their culture, routines, discipline, and childrearing practices as well as their child's temperament and preferences. Be sure to ask whether there's anything else they want you to know about their child.

In your letter, tell the family something about yourself: your cultural background, your language proficiency, whether you're married and have children—whatever you'd like to share. Describing who you are will enable them to see you as a person as well as a teacher. Tell them, too, what the children in your class will be learning this year, and let them know they can call you whenever they have questions, concerns, or suggestions. If you're comfortable with the idea, give them your home phone number, or tell them how they can reach you at school. Diane W. Kyle and her colleagues (2002) recommend another strategy: Take a walk in the neighborhood where the children live. Watch a basketball game; go into the church; buy something at the drug store; have a snack at a local eatery; talk to people about the community. Try to spend some time there each week, check out street fairs, celebrations, and other activities that families enjoy, and draw a map showing the resources that you and the children can utilize.

Every contact with family members helps to build trust, so talk with them as often as you can. Because polite greetings and conversation are absolutely essential to communication, make a point of smiling and speaking to each adult at arrival and pick-up time and treating each of them as a distinct person in her or his own right, not just as Jackson's mother or Ava's father. Families often want to keep their private lives private (Powell, 1989), but, paradoxically, they may also want teachers to be interested in them as people (Powell, 1998). Like their children, they have their own temperaments, needs, and preferences. It's hard to converse when everyone arrives at once or you're comforting an unhappy child, so record your daily interactions. If you haven't managed to connect with a family all week, plan to phone or chat with them early the following week.

In a school setting, you may not meet until parent–teacher night. To make families feel at home on that occasion, set aside time for some informal talk, perhaps around coffee and cookies. In the meantime, keep in touch by sending home notes and information about what you're doing in class. You can even create a website to communicate with them.

Going home

Try to arrange to visit the family in their home before school starts or early in the year. A home visit is definitely worth the effort. You'll get to know the family members a little, obtain valuable insights into their childrearing practices and the child's development, and send the message that you value the family and their culture (Keyser, 2006). The child will feel proud to have you in his home, and the family will feel honored to have you as a guest.

With a colleague, prepare for the visit by discussing questions you might ask and doing some role plays to practice, ward off anxiety, and discover possible pitfalls. Make your arrangements in advance—write or call to let the family know why you're coming and tell them that a short visit is a regular part of the program, offered to everyone. Agree on a date and time and say you'd like to meet the whole family and you're open to anything they want to show you or talk about. By paying attention to the family's cues and your own comfort level when you're in their home, you can choose the right moment to leave. Visits can be as short as 15 minutes and as long as an hour.

Families who've had negative encounters with social services, immigration, or other authorities may feel uneasy with any kind of visit, and some families may not want you to come to their home. Offer to get together somewhere else—at a local coffee shop, park, library, community center, McDonald's. If they don't respond to your initial invitation, follow up with a phone call; but if the meeting doesn't come off, be careful not to blame the family or hold it against the child. Wait a while, then ask again.

As Kyle and her colleagues (2002) put it, the object of a visit is "to learn how I can help your child more" (p. 62), so it presents an opportunity to learn about the family's strengths, knowledge, talents, and resources, as well as their hopes and dreams for themselves and their child. Begin with polite small talk, say how pleased you are to have their child in your class, and thank them for welcoming you into their home by presenting a small gift of fruit or cookies (Ginsberg, 2007). Let them know up front what you'll be asking, and be sure they understand that they don't have to answer if they don't want to. You might ask about how the child spent the summer, what his talents, interests, and favorite activities are, how he helps out at home, and who his friends are, both in and out of school. Ask about what upsets him and how they help him to deal with it; and ask about the skills they'd like him to develop this year (Kyle et al., 2002). You can also ask about what they feel comfortable doing to help their child learn. Although direct questions are considered

Diplomacy at Home

In *Bridging Cultures between Home and School*, Elise Trumbull, Carrie Rothstein-Fisch, Patricia M. Greenfield, and Blanca Quiroz (2001) describe culturally diplomatic ways to communicate with parents.

> Diplomatic questions do not appear invasive, because they are based on background knowledge rather than ignorance; the teacher can use this knowledge to make her information-seeking more indirect. . . .
>
> For example, if a teacher wants to ask an immigrant mother how far she went in school, she can first ask two nonthreatening questions: "Where are you from?" and "How old were you when you came to the United States?" As an example, the mother may answer that she is from rural Mexico and that she was educated there. The teacher can now use her knowledge of Mexican schooling to transform what could be a threatening probe into a welcoming one: "I know that some places in Mexico do not have schools available, or they exist only up to sixth grade. It must have been difficult for you to get an education in Mexico." It is important to notice that this probe is *not* in the form of a question. The statement shows relevant background knowledge, rather than ignorance, making it a socially competent conversational move, not an intrusive probe. (pp. 108–109)

Source: Bridging Cultures between Home and School: A Guide for Teachers by Elise Trumbull, Carrie Rothstein-Fisch, Patricia M. Greenfield, and Blanca Quiroz. Copyright 2001 by Taylor & Francis Group LLC—Books. Reproduced with permission of Taylor & Francis Group LLC—Books via Copyright Clearance Center.

rude in some cultures, you might ask an immigrant family indirectly about their home country and how they like living in the United States.

As you chat, look around and ask about what you see—pets, photos, artwork, books, musical instruments. They will elicit stories and give you clues about the history and interests of the family members and the child himself. Answer any questions they may have, and plan to spend some time with the child. With permission, you might take a photo of the family in a location of their choice to document the visit and display in your classroom (Keyser, 2006).

"Without a doubt," Kyle and her colleagues (2002) conclude, "we all agree that visiting the family . . . is by far the most valuable experience we have had in teaching. Nothing comes close to doing what visits can do" (p. 75).

W HAT DO YOU THINK?

1. On page 68, Nancy Balaban provides a dramatic example of how feelings can distort perceptions. Have you ever noticed how your own feelings alter what you see or how you act? Can you give one or two examples? Were you able to correct or clarify the situation later?

2. Have you ever kept a diary or journal? How did it help you to see the things around you differently? Try keeping a journal of your experience in this class. How does it influence what you perceive and learn?

3. Why is it so important to develop a relationship with every child (and especially a child with challenging behavior)?

4. Even if you don't know a child's attachment status, why is it important to know about attachment and the way it affects children's behavior with their peers, teachers, and others? What do you think your own attachment status might be? Do you think it has changed over the years?

5. Visit a classroom and watch how the teacher creates relationships with individual children. Has she taken advantage of the opportunities she's had? What did she do well? What could she have done better?

6. When you're doing home visits, you may encounter families who feel you're judging them, and the visit may not go as well as you hope. With other students, role play a home visit to work out an appropriate approach.

S UGGESTED READING

Ayers, W. (2001). *To teach: The journey of a teacher.* New York: Teachers College Press.

Gonzalez-Mena, J. (2010). *50 strategies for communicating and working with diverse families* (2nd ed.). Upper Saddle River, NJ: Pearson.

Honig, A. S. (2002). *Secure relationships: Nurturing infant/toddler attachment in early care settings.* Washington, DC: National Association for the Education of Young Children.

Howes, C., & Ritchie, S. (2002). *A matter of trust: Connecting teachers and learners in the early childhood classroom.* New York: Teachers College Press.

Karen, R. (1998). *Becoming attached: First relationships and how they shape our capacity to love.* New York: Oxford University Press.

Pianta, R. C. (1999). *Enhancing relationships between children and teachers.* Washington, DC: American Psychological Association.

Weigand, R. F. (2007). Reflective supervision in child care: The discoveries of an accidental tourist. *Zero to Three, 28,* 17–22.

CHAPTER 6

Opening the Culture Door

More than 40 percent of children in preschools and public schools come from a diverse culture or speak a different language (Livingston, 2006; U.S. Census Bureau, 2010). Yet the vast majority of teachers are unilingual White European American women (Ray, Bowman, & Robbins, 2006; Strizek, Pittsonberger, Riordan, Lyter, & Orlofsky, 2006). Even teachers with a different cultural origin usually become acculturated to mainstream ways of thinking during their education and training (Trumbull, Rothstein-Fisch, Greenfield, & Quiroz, 2001). This culture difference affects our expectations of children and our relationships with them, influences their self-esteem and behavior, and cuts us off from their families, a vital resource when challenging behavior appears.

This chapter has been adapted from *Partners in Quality, vol. 2/Relationships* © CCCF 1999, written by Barbara Kaiser and Judy Sklar Rasminsky based on the research papers of the Partners in Quality Project. With permission from Canadian Child Care Federation, 201–383 Parkdale Avenue, Ottawa, ON, K1Y 4R4.

In *Culturally Responsive Teaching* (2000), Geneva Gay points out that students of color, especially those who are poor and live in urban areas,

- get less instructional attention
- are called on less frequently
- are encouraged to develop intellectual thinking less often
- are criticized more and praised less
- receive fewer direct responses to their questions and comments
- are reprimanded more often and disciplined more severely (p. 63)

We can take a giant step toward bridging this culture gap by getting to know more about our students' culture and our own. This chapter will help you to do that by describing what culture is; what happens when home and school meet; the connection between culture and language; and finally, some characteristics of specific cultural groups.

WHAT IS CULTURE?

Everyone has a culture, but most of the time we can't see it. As Eleanor Lynch points out in *Developing Cross-Cultural Competence* (2004a), culture is like a "second skin" (p. 20), and it becomes visible only when we brush up against one that's different.

"There is not one aspect of human life that is not touched and altered by culture," says anthropologist Edward T. Hall (1977), one of the foremost authorities on culture. "This means personality, how people express themselves (including shows of emotion), the way they think, how they move, how problems are solved, how their cities are planned and laid out, how transportation systems function and are organized, as well as how economic and government systems are put together and function" (pp. 16–17). Our culture is the framework for our lives.

It's important to remember that there are many variations within each culture. Educational level, socioeconomic status, occupation, temperament, and personal experience all influence our values and beliefs. So do race, language, ethnicity, religion, gender, family, workplace, age, sexual orientation, lifestyle, political orientation, and immigration history (Lynch, 2004a).

What does culture have to do with identity?

Our culture is an integral part of our identity, whether we know it or not. We learn it from our families (who learned it from their families) effortlessly and unconsciously, and it is reasonably well established by the time we turn 5 years old (Lynch, 2004a). "There is nothing in a young child's day that comes separate from the cultural context," point out Janet Gonzalez-Mena and Judith Bernhard (1998), experts in multicultural child care. "Culture is not directly taught but grows out of the interaction between caregiver and children" (p. 15).

There are no "best" childrearing methods, no universal norms, or expectations (Chud & Fahlman, 1985). Parents naturally pass along the ways of doing things that people in their own culture need to survive and succeed (Lubeck, 1994; New, 1994). Emotional display and affect, moral development, gender roles, even cognitive abilities depend on what competencies the culture requires of its citizens (New, 1994). Each child brings her own set of culturally based skills and values with her into the classroom.

Teachers have long understood the importance of developing a positive self-concept. We believe that children have the need and the right to feel good about themselves. But we have only recently begun to realize how essential a child's culture is to her self-concept—to recognize that children also have the need and the right to be proud of their cultural heritage and the language, abilities, values, attitudes, behaviors, history, and "ways of doing" that are inseparable from it (Barrera & Corso, 2003; Howes, 2010).

Children begin to construct their identity—to understand who they are—from understanding their place in their own family and culture and by responding to how others relate to them. To form a positive self-concept, children must honor and respect their own family and culture and have others honor and respect them, too. This is a vital human need. When we don't recognize a child's identity, we can actually harm her by putting her self-concept at risk. If her surroundings don't reflect and validate her family, her culture, and herself, she feels invisible, unimportant—and ashamed of who she is (Barrera & Corso, 2003; Derman-Sparks & Edwards, 2010).

To form a positive self-concept, children must honor and respect their own family and culture and have others honor and respect them, too. This is a vital human need.

Are cultures really so different?

In a word, yes. Mainstream American culture—that is, White European American, middle-class culture, which is based on Western European culture—is different from most other cultures in the world. To start with, it is *individualistic*. It values the individual over the group and considers the individual's independence the greatest possible virtue. It sees each person as a unique and separate being who is born with needs, rights, and an identity all his or her own, and it teaches its citizens to assert themselves, take the initiative, make their own choices, explore, compete, and achieve.

Children in individualistic cultures begin to practice independence when they're very small. Their parents put them to sleep alone in cribs in their own rooms; supply them with objects so they can amuse and comfort themselves; transport them in their own strollers and car seats; deposit them on the floor to play alone; give them finger foods and cups so that they can feed themselves; and leave them with babysitters when they go out because they, too, are individuals with separate lives. When children go to child care and school, parents and teachers encourage them to become independent, critical thinkers (Rothstein-Fisch & Trumbull, 2008).

But in about 70 percent of the world's cultures, this notion of the separate, individual self is "a rather peculiar idea," writes anthropologist Clifford Geertz

Breaking the Code

Each culture has its own communication style. Perhaps you've encountered some of these varieties:

- In face-to-face conversation, the European American culture expects eye contact, which conveys honesty, attention, and trustworthiness. But African American, Asian Pacific, Latino, and American Indian cultures consider direct eye contact aggressive, disrespectful, or impolite.

- Some cultures, such as the Mediterranean, display emotion openly and spontaneously; others, such as Chinese and Japanese, consider emotional restraint polite.

- European Americans laugh or smile when they're happy or amused. But in many Asian cultures, people smile when they're embarrassed, confused, or even sad.

- In Latino, Middle Eastern, and African American cultures, people stand close together to converse; European Americans like to stay an arm's length away. Asian Pacific Islanders also prefer more space.

- Whereas frequent touching is an important part of communication in Mediterranean cultures, the Japanese, Chinese, and Korean cultures avoid physical contact (Chud & Fahlman, 1985; Lynch, 2004b).

(as cited in Kağıtçıbaşı, 1996, p. 53). Outside of the European American culture, people value *interdependence*—being closely connected—and they are first and foremost members of a group. In these *collectivist* cultures, children learn that they are part of an extended family and a community and that they are responsible for looking after one another. They value harmony and cooperation and base their self-esteem on their contributions to the good of the whole, not on their individual achievement—which collectivist cultures view as selfish and as a rejection of the family (Lynch, 2004b).

As Lynch (2004b) puts it, "The majority of people throughout the world have nurtured children for centuries by having them sleep in the parents' bed; following them around in order to feed them; keeping them in close physical proximity through holding, touching, and carrying long after they can walk alone; or taking them wherever the adults go" (p. 52). Parents know their children will eventually grow up to become self-sufficient, so while their children are young, their idea is to forge a bond so strong it will never break (Gonzalez-Mena & Bernhard, 1998). When children go to school, their families want them to help one another, learn from one another, and cooperate with one another, because cognitive development is inextricably tied to being a good person (Rothstein-Fisch & Trumbull, 2008).

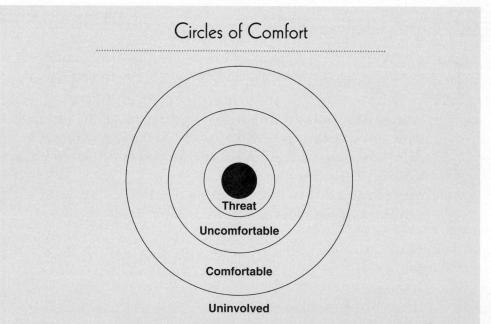

Circles of Comfort

Threat

Uncomfortable

Comfortable

Uninvolved

FIGURE 6.1 A comfortable distance between two people is a cultural matter, especially when a child is angry and out of control. If you're standing too close, or if you're trying to make eye contact, the child may feel threatened and her behavior may escalate. When you shout at her from a distance, she may feel you don't really care. Children and adults listen and communicate at their best when you find their comfort zone.

Source: © 2000, WEVAS, Inc. Reproduced with the written permission of WEVAS, Inc.

Of course, in the end, every culture needs both group and individual loyalties. The question is, Which takes priority (Gonzalez-Mena, 2008)?

Communication is another area where there are important cultural differences. Hall (1977) distinguishes between what he calls *low-context cultures* (such as Western European and North American) and *high-context cultures* (such as Asian, South Asian, Southern European, Latino, African American, and American Indian). In low-context cultures, words are primary, and communication is direct, precise, and linear. Speakers focus on the content and include relevant background information—that is, all the context necessary to ensure that their listeners understand them (Delpit, 2006). In low-context cultures, babies quickly learn to attract attention by crying or babbling, and their parents usually answer them by speaking (Gonzalez-Mena, 2008).

But in high-context cultures, words do not stand alone. Nonverbal cues (such as facial expression, gestures, and movement), contextual cues (such as shared experience, history, tradition, social status, and the relationship of the parties), and indirect ways of communicating (such as pauses, silences, empathy, storytelling, analogies, or talking around a subject) play a far greater role in communication (Gonzalez-Mena, 2008). Meaning is mostly implicit, and it's considered unnecessary, even insulting, to say what everyone already knows (Delpit, 2006). Always ensconced on a lap or in someone's arms, babies in high-context cultures learn to communicate with their bodies. Their tensed muscles or a change in position sends a clear message to their caregivers, who quickly calm them, feed them, put them on the toilet (Gonzalez-Mena, 2008).

People in high-context cultures don't focus on objects or information as things in themselves—rather they derive meaning from the relationships and emotions surrounding them. To a Latina child, for example, an egg isn't a collection of attributes (a shell, a white, a yolk); its meaning is embedded in its history and associations, such as her relationship with her grandmother, who taught her to cook eggs (Rothstein-Fisch & Trumbull, 2008).

The melting pot and the salad bowl

The United States has always considered itself a *melting pot*, a place where people from all over the world have gathered to become one nation, under God, indivisible. In the past when newcomers settled into the new land, they gradually assimilated, taking on the characteristics of the dominant, mainstream, White middle-class European American culture and giving up their own. But as the world grows smaller and the United States becomes more multicultural, our goals are changing. Members of many cultures are seeking ways to succeed while maintaining their cultural identity, and we are increasingly recognizing the rich contributions this diversity brings to our lives. Recently, some people have begun to rethink the metaphor of the melting pot. They would prefer to liken the United States to a *salad bowl*, or a mosaic, where the separate pieces mix but retain their own identity. Perhaps we'll see that vision realized sometime in the future, but until then, the dominant culture—what scholar and educator Lisa Delpit (2006) calls the "culture of power"—will define our thinking and pervade our institutions.

Anthropologist John U. Ogbu (1994) has developed an influential theory about why different cultural groups have different attitudes about assimilating into the dominant culture. Some are what he calls *voluntary* or *immigrant minorities*, who move to the United States by choice. They believe they will have more freedom, more opportunity, and a better standard of living in this country. Although they would like to preserve their own culture, they realize they will have to learn some aspects of the European American culture in order to succeed in it, and they don't feel their cultural identity will be threatened if they do. Their children usually do well in school.

Other cultural groups are *involuntary minorities*, Ogbu (1994) says—"those groups (and their descendants) who were initially incorporated into U.S. society against their will by Euro-Americans through slavery, conquest, or colonization. Thereafter, these minorities were relegated to menial positions and denied true assimilation into the mainstream U.S. society" (p. 373). American Indians, African Americans, and Mexican Americans (because the United States conquered and annexed their territory) make up this group.

Because the United States tried to wipe out the cultures of the involuntary minorities and because they are aware of the racism in American society, members of the involuntary minorities have defined themselves in opposition to the attitudes, beliefs, and preferences of the dominant culture. As a result, they feel they cannot adopt the dominant culture's ways without losing their own culture. Students with these beliefs and attitudes may not wish to succeed in European American schools. Those who do may be accused of "acting white" and face repudiation from their peers (Ogbu, 1994; Tatum, 1997).

This theory has prompted considerable discussion. Some scholars see the cultivation of a distinct racial or ethnic identity not as a rejection of the dominant culture's standards of achievement but as a source of strength, creating a sense of belonging, connection, and solidarity, as well as providing mechanisms for critiquing and coping with inequality (Carter, 2005).

WHEN HOME AND SCHOOL MEET

To teach any child—and a child with challenging behavior in particular—you have to understand where she is coming from. That means you have to understand her culture. But just as your feelings and beliefs create barriers, so does your own culture. Paradoxically, the first step in understanding someone else's culture is to become aware of your own. Then you can see how it influences your interactions with others—and that it isn't the only valid way to do things.

How can you see your culture?

People who belong to the European American culture often have the mistaken idea that they don't have a culture. That's because their way of thinking shapes our society and they're surrounded by people who think the way they do. For the same reason, they know less about other people's cultures. But people who belong to a less powerful culture have to learn more about the dominant culture—it's a matter of survival for them (Tatum, 1997).

Becoming aware of your culture requires careful observation and reflection. To start with, try to be mindful whenever you come into contact with a different way of approaching the world—that is, whenever you talk with people of a different gender, race, ethnic group, religion, nationality, age, or even family. Don't expect them to think, feel, or act like you, but listen closely to what they have to say and try putting yourself in their shoes (Eggers-Pieróla, 2005). If you raise your antennae in these encounters, you can begin to get a glimpse of your own assumptions.

Here are some questions to help you think about your own cultural beliefs and experiences (Chud & Fahlman, 1985; Derman-Sparks & Edwards, 2010):

- Do you remember the first time you met someone from another culture or ethnic group? How did you feel?
- Do you remember how you first learned about your own ethnic identity?
- What is important to you about this aspect of yourself? What makes you proud and what gives you pain?
- Have you ever experienced prejudice or discrimination for any reason? How did it make you feel? What did you do? Thinking about it now, would you change your response?
- Can you think of a time when you experienced privilege because of your color, class, or ethnicity? Were you aware of it at the time? How did you feel, then and now?
- Do you and your parents agree about ethnic, cultural, and religious issues? If your beliefs are different, how did they evolve? What did you learn in school? What will you teach your children?
- If you've traveled to another country—or even to a different area—how did you feel in those unfamiliar surroundings?

Now You See It, Now You Don't

About being a member of the dominant White culture, Janet Gonzalez-Mena writes (2003):

I am white and I see the world from a white perspective. I always thought that I was colorless, normal, regular. I didn't think of myself as having a color, a race, a culture. I understand now that view of myself relates to my having unearned power and privilege. Doors open for me that don't open for people of color. If I go register for a motel room and they tell me there is no vacancy, I don't have to wonder if they are lying. If I'm treated poorly in a restaurant, I put it to rudeness not racism. If my kids come to school tired, dirty, or in worn out clothes, someone may think I'm a neglectful parent, but no one will condemn my whole race. My view is the dominant view and is reinforced on all sides. My culture is the dominant culture and therefore invisible to me.

Source: "Discovering My Whiteness" by Janet Gonzalez-Mena, 2003. Used with permission of the author.

The culture of child care and school

"Education is as much about being inculcated with the ways of the 'culture of power' as it is about learning to read, count, and think critically," says sociologist Prudence L. Carter (2005, p. 47). Our schools and child care centers naturally teach the European American values of individualism and independence, self-direction, initiative, and competitiveness (among others), using European American methods of communication and learning.

But as we have seen, these values and methods are not universal, neither right nor wrong. Other cultures in the world—including several with deep roots in the United States—bring up their children according to different beliefs and values. And when the children of these cultures enter European American child care and school, we all face new challenges. Here are some examples:

- *Being an individual.* European American schools expect students to work independently, stay in their own seats, respect each person's private property, and compete for rewards (Rothstein-Fisch & Trumbull, 2008). Even in child care, children put on their own coats, eat their own lunches, and nap on their own cots. Individual children receive positive reinforcement for individual achievements ("I like the way Isabel is sitting with her legs crossed and looking at me"). Each child has numerous chances to make choices of her own—of a book, a learning center, a behavior—including the choice to be alone in a private space. And the first theme of the year is often "All about Me," which is intended to boost self-esteem (Rothstein-Fisch, Trumbull, & Garcia, 2009). Collectivist cultures, on the other hand, don't single anyone out but bring up their children to "fit in, not stand out" (Trumbull et al., 2001, p. 5), work together, help one another, and contribute to the well-being of the group. Children feel uncomfortable alone and prefer to stay close together (Howes, 2010). As for choice, collectivist cultures emphasize adapting to what is available in the environment (Gonzalez-Mena, 2008).

- *Passive-receptive posture and interaction.* In the mainstream classroom, the teacher talks and children respond when they're called on. To show they're listening, they sit still and maintain eye contact (Gay, 2000; Kochman, 1985). Circle and story time in child care centers require the same behavior. But in many interdependent cultures, direct eye contact is considered rude, and children may be reluctant to speak in public—instead, they are expected to watch and listen, because adults are regarded as the source of knowledge (Trumbull et al., 2001). These mainstream expectations create a different problem for African American children, who learn primarily through intense social interaction. In their culture, a speaker is a performer who's making a statement, and her listeners join in with gestures, movement, and words. No one needs permission to enter the conversation, and the discourse is fluid, creative, and emotional (Gay, 2000; Kochman, 1985).

- *Dispassionate approach and deductive style of inquiry.* In the European American culture, teachers and students strive to be rational and objective. They believe that emotion interferes with open-minded inquiry and accuracy and communicates a dangerous loss of control. They take a deductive approach to problem solving, emphasizing detail, moving from the specific to the general, and building a whole from the sum of its parts. Collectivist cultures solve problems in a different way: They use inductive means, focusing first on the big picture and moving from the general to the specific. Because the group acts as an anchor or catalyst during this process, its members try to stay connected (Gay, 2000). African American children depend on close relationships in order to learn. They prefer the teacher to express genuine emotion, even anger, and if she doesn't, they believe she doesn't care about them (Delpit, 2006).

- *Decontextualized learning.* Teachers in the dominant culture focus on abstract ideas and concepts, isolating problems and attributes (such as the shell, white, and yolk of an egg) and seeking technical solutions through the use of books, computers, and other materials. They emphasize words and facts (Delpit, 2006) and expect students to explain their work. But in collectivist cultures, knowledge and personal experience aren't separate; it is the context that matters most. Because the context is continually shifting, children learn to focus on the whole situation, not isolated pieces of it, and connect what's happening to their own experience by telling stories, playing with words, and drawing complex analogies (Genishi & Dyson, 2009; Heath, 1983).

- *Topic-centered narratives.* In European American culture, people tell stories based on one event or topic, arrange the facts and ideas in linear order, and explain the relationship between the ideas and the facts. Sticking to the point is vital (Gay, 2000). In the Latino, African American, and American Indian cultures, people tell episodic, anecdotal stories that shift scenes and address more than one issue at a time. Narratives unfold in overlapping loops, not in a straight line; and the relationship between ideas and facts isn't made explicit—it must be inferred (Gay, 2000).

- *"Known-answer" questions.* Mainstream middle-class teachers—and parents—instruct children by asking questions whose answers they already know ("Where's your nose?" "What are the properties of an egg?"). European American children show their intelligence by supplying the correct answer. But African American children find such questions puzzling. In their culture, adults ask questions to find out new information or to challenge them ("What's that like?"), and children demonstrate their wit and intellect by responding spontaneously and creatively (Bransford, Brown, & Cocking, 2000; Heath, 1983).

- *Implicit commands.* When they're telling children what to do, European Americans often use questions ("Rheanna, would you like to put the blocks away?"). Children of the dominant middle-class culture understand that this request is actually a command. But children from working-class homes, African American and White, are accustomed to direct, explicit commands ("Rheanna, please put the blocks away") and may not realize that the teacher isn't asking a question or offering a true choice and that there are consequences if they don't comply (Delpit, 2006).

- *Testing, tracking, and ability grouping.* Standardized tests—such as those required by No Child Left Behind—and ordinary classroom tests demand a wide range of individualistic skills. The questions are decontextualized, written in Standard English, and based on experiences familiar to mainstream children (Hilliard, 2002). Schools and teachers often use the results to create tracks or "ability" groups that reward successful students with higher level teaching. But interdependent cultures don't necessarily value or teach these skills, and once students are relegated to lower track classes or groups, they have almost no opportunity to catch up.

How does culture influence behavior?

When child care or school resembles home, a child experiences less stress, and home values are reinforced. When child care or school is different from home, there is discontinuity—hence more risk. As soon as they're born, children start to acquire the skills they need to become competent adults in their own culture, and by the time they enter child care or school, they're already well on their way. In the new setting, a lot of what they've learned so far in their home culture simply doesn't apply. They must start again from scratch.

Children who find themselves in a strange environment are likely to feel confused, isolated, alienated, conflicted, and less competent. The curriculum, instruction, and discipline may not recognize or support their culture; and their teachers may not notice or appreciate the talents, skills, and abilities they developed in their home community. As a result, they don't feel accepted, respected, or valued; their self-concept and academic achievement may suffer (Gay, 2000); and they may act out. Experts often blame discontinuity for the high rate of school failure and dropout among children from diverse cultures and poor families (Gay, 2000). The dangers of discontinuity are greater when the discrepancy is large and long lasting, especially if the child is very young or doesn't adapt easily to change.

The hardest part is that we don't really know how out of touch we are. From inside the picture frame of our own cultures, we can see only the most obvious differences, such as those in food, dress, language, and potty training. A mother doesn't think to tell you that she never puts her baby on the floor to play because in her culture historically the floor wasn't a safe place—and it doesn't occur to you to tell her that you're putting her daughter there or why you think it's good for her. Likewise, when a child is having trouble at nap, you don't explain that in your center children sleep by themselves on cots—and the mother doesn't say that her child has always slept with her, never alone, on a mat on the floor. Nor do you tell parents that you encourage children to articulate their personal rights to resolve conflicts, and they don't mention that they want their child to learn to preserve peace and harmony in the group, not to express her own personal feelings. And the child, who may not speak much English—or who may not speak at all—certainly cannot tell you.

Given such discontinuity, it is easy to see how a cultural conflict, visible or invisible, can cause or contribute to challenging behavior. What was perfectly acceptable at home may be suddenly and inexplicably inappropriate at school. If a child doesn't answer when you ask how she feels, her behavior may be culturally appropriate, not defiant or sullen. She may not know how, or wish, to answer because in her

As soon as they're born, children start to acquire the skills they need to become competent adults in their culture.

Enigma

In cross-cultural interactions, meaning is often not what it seems. In *Connections and Commitments*, Costanza Eggers-Piérola (2005) puzzles over a child's behavior:

> What does it really mean when a child refuses to put on her coat by herself . . . ? Do you assume that she won't cooperate? Or that she is too dependent on adults clothing and feeding her? Do you speak to your supervisor and explain that the child may be too immature to be in your classroom of four-year-olds? . . . The mother may have told the child not to go out, believing that the cold will expose her to the flu. Or the child may equate having the coat put on her by the adult as an act of protection, a protection much needed because she has recently been separated from her nurturing extended family. (p. 164)

culture it is considered rude for people to express their personal feelings. A 3-year-old who spills her apple juice may not be clumsy or immature; she may not know how to drink from a cup because in her culture many generations ago liquid was too precious to present to a child in a spillable form and she still drinks from a bottle at home.

When faced with culturally unfamiliar behavior, teachers frequently try to control or discipline the student involved (Gay, 2000). A teacher may see an assertive or

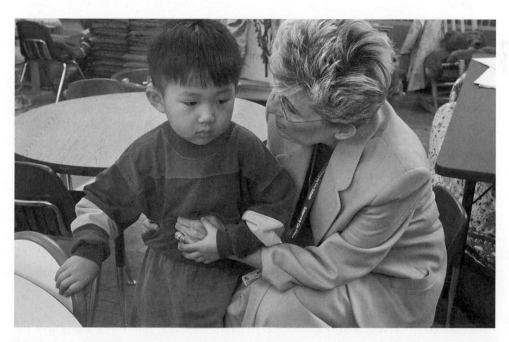

Sometimes a cultural conflict causes or contributes to challenging behavior. It is extremely important to understand both the child's cultural assumptions and your own.

emotional statement as impulsive, disruptive, or smart-alecky; and she may label fidgeting or moving around as hyperactive, off-task, or insolent. She may even regard culturally unfamiliar behavior as a problem that requires intervention or special education (García Coll & Magnuson, 2000; Kağıtçıbaşı, 1996).

It is extremely important to understand the cultural assumptions on both sides—why you expect a child to express her feelings (and to drink from a cup) as well as why for some children that is an unreasonable (or unfamiliar) demand. If you are not from the European American culture, you will have cultural expectations of your own—and you'll also encounter behavior that perplexes you. For a teacher from a Latino culture, for example, a child who requires an explanation of why she should do things the way you ask may seem rude and lacking in respect rather than assertive or logical.

How can you make your teaching more culturally responsive?

Research shows that learning how to function in more than one language and culture (often called *codeswitching*) can have decided benefits—if it's done in a way that supports the child's home language and culture.

- Children perform better academically and are clearer thinkers.
- They are less likely to drop out of school.
- They are able to keep the approval and friendship of their racial and ethnic peers.
- They have better inhibitory control.
- Their risk of emotional or psychiatric illness is lower.
- They can move easily and comfortably from one culture to the other, and they're more likely to adapt well to a new situation (Chang et al., 2007; Freire & Bernhard, 1997).

In other words, when teachers handle discontinuity in a culturally responsive way, they can make a big difference in children's lives.

Culturally responsive teaching builds connections between what children already know and what they need to know, making their learning relevant and effective (Villegas & Lucas, 2007). Compatible with best practice, it does for children of diverse cultures exactly what traditional teaching does for middle-class European Americans: "It filters curriculum content and teaching strategies through their cultural frames of reference to make the content more personally meaningful and easier to master," says Geneva Gay (2000, p. 24). Here are some essential elements of culturally responsive teaching (Howard, 2007).

Form authentic and caring relationships

For children of diverse cultures—who learn best through social interactions and are always tuned into context—caring, nurturing relationships with teachers (and with one another) are crucial to learning and behavior (Hale, 2001; Nieto, 2004).

But positive relationships between teachers and children from different cultures or socioeconomic groups may not easily come into being (Howes & Shivers, 2006; Saft & Pianta, 2001). Mainstream female teachers seem to have particular trouble forming close relationships with young, active, boisterous African American boys, whose culturally appropriate playful behavior appears to teachers to be aggressive or out of control (Hughes & Kwok, 2007). Teachers' relationships with African American parents may also be strained, making it even harder to forge close ties with their children (Hughes & Kwok, 2007).

This situation demands special effort. Talk and play with the children in your class; ask about their lives, families, interests, and concerns; show your respect by paying attention and responding to what they say, do, and write. If you teach in elementary school, invite four or five students to eat lunch with you in the classroom each week (Ladson-Billings, 1994), and dedicate regular time—perhaps at morning meeting—to discuss what they think about school, what they're learning, and the world around them (Nicolet, 2006).

Use curriculum that honors each child's culture and experience

The use of culturally relevant curricula and text materials improves children's engagement, motivation, interest, academic skills, and time on task, research shows (Gay, 2000). On the other hand, children who don't see their culture reflected in the classroom may feel alienated and conclude that no one is interested in them (Garrison-Wade & Lewis, 2006; Ladson-Billings, 1994). Instead of focusing on learning, they must use their emotional and cognitive resources to cope with unfamiliar information and surroundings (Barrera & Corso, 2003).

Tap into children's lives to build your curriculum. When you visit their homes and chat with their families, notice their *funds of knowledge*—the strengths and talents, information and strategies, that enable them to maintain their well-being. Family stories, cooking, gardening, auto mechanics, music, home remedies—knowledge of any kind can be transformed into a lesson. Research the heroes and accomplishments of children's cultures, introduce culturally relevant topics, and utilize culturally authentic books, songs, dances, and other materials. Buy fruits, vegetables, and canned goods at ethnic markets, adding the empties to the dramatic play area along with dolls, games, menus, clothes, and instruments. Make use in your displays of the pastels and ochres of the Caribbean and Latin America and the greens of Africa (Eggers-Pieróla, 2005). And invite family and community members into the classroom to share their knowledge and skills.

Shift instructional strategies to meet diverse learning needs

In collectivist, interdependent cultures, children become more engaged in learning and behave more positively when they work together as partners or small groups (Gay, 2000; Ladson-Billings, 1994). Using their well-honed group skills, they feel proud to belong and are less likely to be confused or fearful (Rothstein-Fisch & Trumbull, 2008). With their high energy and exuberance, African American children thrive when they have lots of opportunities for hands-on learning, active participation, and emotional expression—for example, in stories, role plays, drama, and movement (Gay, 2000; Landsman, 2006a). Boys in particular need to move around (Delpit, 2006).

Hold high expectations

High standards and expectations are essential: They significantly influence what teachers teach and children learn. Children understand very well—and internalize—what their teachers expect of them, and these expectations affect their self-concept, achievement, motivation, and behavior (Aronson & Steele, 2005). Too often, teachers make the stereotyped assumption that their European American and Asian American students will succeed (Gay, 2000) and their students from other cultural groups will be loud, troublesome, less intelligent, uninterested in school, or incapable of learning (Garrison-Wade & Lewis, 2006). Teachers who hold this deficit perspective water down their curriculum and instruction for children of color, fulfilling their own prophecy. They reveal their low expectations in other ways as well. By greeting failure with sympathy, teachers tell a child she can't succeed, not that she didn't try hard enough. By praising her for completing an easy task, they indicate that they think she's stupid (ASCD Advisory Panel, 1995). By giving "one more chance," they demonstrate that they don't care (Bondy & Ross, 2008).

For teachers to put forward their best efforts, they must believe children can learn (ASCD Advisory Panel, 1995). When teachers provide appropriate instruction, expect children to try hard, and do well—and push them to ensure that they do—students are likely to deliver and reward these teachers with their respect and affection. Such "warm demanders," who combine a loving manner with tough and rigorous expectations, are particularly successful with children from diverse cultures (Kleinfeld, 1975).

Make the implicit explicit

Whenever you know you're teaching in an individualistic way that's different from your students' ways—for example, when they're taking a test and aren't permitted to help one another—say so explicitly, and try to figure out how to attack the assignment in a culturally appropriate manner. (For example, they could study in a group but take the test alone.) The idea is to facilitate, and make conscious, their movement between home and school cultures (Rothstein-Fisch & Trumbull, 2008).

LANGUAGE AND CULTURE

How important is home language?

Like her culture, a child's home language is a critical part of her identity (Genesee, Paradis, & Crago, 2004). It is through her home language—the language she speaks with her family—that development and learning take place; it is through her home language that she constructs a framework for perceiving the world and functioning in it (Garcia, 2005; Genishi & Dyson, 2009).

Because young children are still learning their first language when they start to learn their second, they are called *dual-language learners* (or sometimes *English-language learners*). More than 20 percent of school-aged children speak a language other than English at home (U.S. Census Bureau, 2006). Most speak Spanish, and their numbers are rapidly rising (Hernandez, Denton, & Macartney, 2008).

Language and Love

In *Hunger of Memory*, Richard Rodriguez (1982) describes what happened when the nuns at his school asked his Spanish-speaking parents to speak to their children in English:

> As we children learned more and more English, we shared fewer and fewer words with our parents. Sentences needed to be spoken slowly when a child addressed his mother or father. (Often the parent wouldn't understand.) The child would need to repeat himself. (Still the parent misunderstood.) The young voice, frustrated, would end up saying "Never mind!"—the subject was closed.
>
> . . . . I no longer knew what words to use in addressing my parents. The old Spanish words (those tender accents of sound!) I had used earlier—*mamá* and *papá*—I couldn't use anymore. They would have been too painful reminders of how much had changed in my life. (p. 22)

Source: From *Hunger of Memory: The Education of Richard Rodriguez* by Richard Rodriguez. Reprinted by permission of David R. Godine, Publisher, Inc. Copyright © 1983 by Richard Rodriguez.

In 1968 Congress passed the Bilingual Education Act to assist children with limited English proficiency (Walsh, 2009), and subsequent Supreme Court decisions have strengthened their rights (Garcia, 2005). But it has taken decades for researchers to figure out the best way for children to learn a second language well enough to succeed in school. In the meantime, *immersion*—full-time instruction in an English-only classroom—has taken root, and many states and cities have banned or restricted the use of any language other than English (Viadero, 2009).

Now, however, there is consensus in the research community that the English-only method does not produce the best results. The data show that children taught in both their home language and English do better academically than children taught entirely in English (August & Shanahan, 2006). Whether they speak Spanish, Chinese, Black English, or any of the other 400 languages found among children across the country (Goldenberg, 2008), the concepts and skills they learn in their home language transfer to and enhance their Standard English (August & Shanahan, 2006). In a high-quality bilingual environment, it takes 5 to 6 years to become proficient in a second language (Thomas & Collier, 2003). Children aren't confused; their English doesn't suffer; and they can't afford to wait until they've learned English to start learning content.

In a classroom where the language and culture are different from her own, a child's language, cognitive development, and academic achievement are put at risk (Garcia, 2005). This is especially true for young children, who are constantly using their home language to improve their thinking skills and control their thoughts and actions. It is therefore crucial to support a child's home language while she is learning English.

Without home language support, within 2 or 3 years children may lose their ability to speak their native language, and with it the capacity to communicate with their families and benefit from their guidance (Cummins, 1999–2003; Genesee, 2008; Wong Fillmore, 1991). Children can all too easily come to believe their teachers are right and their families are wrong and ignorant (Rothstein-Fisch & Trumbull, 2008).

Teachers who speak her home language ease a child's transition into a new school environment and boost her chances of success (Pianta & Stuhlman, 2004). In one study (Chang et al., 2007), Spanish-speaking 4- and 5-year-olds had significantly more interaction and closer relationships—hence more sensitive, individualized attention—with their Spanish-speaking teachers than they did with their teachers who spoke English. By acknowledging their home language, the Spanish-speaking teachers also raised the children's status in the classroom, which in turn increased both their peer interactions and their learning opportunities. When a teacher values a child's home language and culture, the other children follow her lead and adopt her positive approach (Rueda, August, & Goldenberg, 2006). In contrast, Spanish-speaking children had troubled relationships with their English-speaking teachers, who judged them to have more behavior and learning problems. Spanish speakers in these classrooms had less status and were more likely to be teased, bullied, and socially isolated (Chang et al., 2007).

Many African American children also speak a different home language: *African American Vernacular English*, often called *Black English* or *Ebonics* (from "ebony" and "phonics"). Although the dominant culture assumes Standard English is the only correct way to speak and write English, linguists agree that Ebonics is equally legitimate. Spoken by 60 to 70 percent of African Americans (Garcia, 2005), Black English is neither broken nor slang but stems from the Bantu languages of West Africa and the African oral tradition. Although it often sounds like Standard English, it has different syntax, grammar, meanings, and usage (Smitherman, 1998).

For young African Americans, speaking Black English promotes cultural solidarity, authenticity, and legitimacy (Carter, 2005). But it also puts them at risk in school. Mainstream teachers often lower their expectations of children who speak Ebonics, view them as wrong or ignorant, and fail to offer them appropriately engaging, challenging instruction (Pranksy, 2009). In addition, the suggestion that

The Power of Language

In *Children, Language, and Literacy*, Celia Genishi and Anne Haas Dyson (2009) consider Black English a source of pride for African Americans. It "is a testament to the language-generating power of human beings, given its roots in the intermingling of languages during slavery. Ripped from their home countries, isolated from other slaves who spoke their mother tongues, denied instruction in language and literacy, still, Africans used humanity's linguistic powers in those inhumane conditions to adapt, synthesize, and stretch old ways with words to new ways that evolved over the generations" (p. 23).

something is wrong with the child and her family takes a psychological and academic toll. Children rely on their speech to decode the written symbol system—they listen to what sounds right as they work at reading and writing. Devaluing their African American English makes them doubt their own language sense and interferes with learning (Genishi & Dyson, 2009)—as well as creating resistance to mainstream teachers (Delpit, 2002).

How do children learn a second language?

Children beginning a new language face what language and literacy expert Patton O. Tabors (2008) calls a double bind: They can't make friends because they can't talk with their peers; and they can't learn to talk with their peers unless they have friends.

Children learn language at different rates, but they go through the following stages (Tabors, 2008):

- *Home language use.* They continue to speak their home language as if everyone understands it.
- *Nonverbal or silent period.* Children watch and listen to others as they gather information about the new language.
- *Telegraphic speech and experimentation.* Children try out the new language using individual words and phrases.
- *Productive use.* Once they've acquired enough vocabulary, children can build sentences, although they still make mistakes and mix languages together.

Because learning a new language is stressful and because teachers may not understand children's needs and ways of learning, children's behavior is sometimes challenging. Although children may point, gesture, and make noises to communicate, they are ignored or treated like babies by their peers (Tabors, 2008). Later they may have trouble following directions, responding to questions, and expressing their ideas and feelings, especially if they're from a collectivist culture where such behavior is unacceptable. Although they may act as if they know what's going on, they may be pretending, and they may understand the words but not the meaning of the words within the cultural context—a meaning that could be quite different in their own culture. Along with the words, children must learn when it's appropriate to speak, to whom, and in what manner—which is every bit as subtle and difficult as the language itself.

What we interpret as boredom, laziness, or inattention may also be a lack of comprehension. Children may move around the room and talk in their own language in order to help one another understand—as their culture requires—but if the teacher doesn't tolerate this behavior they may become angry or frustrated. If they're ignored or forgotten in the classroom, they may simply make trouble (Curran, 2003).

How can you support language learning?

In an ideal world, all children would have a teacher who speaks their home language. But the reality is quite different. Too few teachers are fluent in languages other than English, and schools often resemble the United Nations, with children from all over the globe. In this situation, teachers must do their best to welcome children, educate themselves about language learning, and remember that most communication is nonverbal!

Encourage children to use their home language

When you're welcoming a dual-language learner into your classroom, the first rule is to allow her—indeed, encourage her—to use her own language. Memorize a few key phrases ("Hello," "Do you need to use the toilet?") (Hickman-Davis, 2002), and make a survival chart with photos of basic needs and the daily routine (Macrina, Hoover, & Becker, 2009). Label objects in the room with different colors for different languages and phonetic spelling so that you can use the children's home languages, too (Nemeth, 2009).

Make songs, rhymes, and counting in the languages of the classroom a part of the curriculum, and recruit paraprofessionals, volunteers, older children, and family members to help and read to children in their own language (Espinosa, 2010). Be sure families understand that the best way to support their children at school is to continue to use their language at home (Goldenberg, Rueda, & August, 2006).

Interact with children as much as possible

Children learn language through countless interactions with others (Genishi & Dyson, 2009), so interact with each dual-language learner as much as you can (Saunders & O'Brien, 2006). As you get to know her, you can calibrate your exchanges to meet her particular language level. Speak slowly, use simple words and messages based in the here and now, avoid idioms, and repeat words and directions frequently (Buteau & True, 2009). Back up your language with gestures and visual clues—facial expressions, photos, pictures, and objects (Espinosa, 2010). Read books with familiar content, and act out the characters. Be sure to give children extra time to process what's been said and prepare an answer (Curran, 2003).

Create opportunities for peer interaction

You also support language learning when you provide children with opportunities to interact in pairs and small groups. Peers who speak the same language can help one another feel comfortable as well as understand the assignment, stay on task, and participate more fully (Curran, 2003). Peers who speak English can act as a resource—but wait until the dual-language learners know enough English to participate (Goldenberg, 2008). Then design meaningful and doable tasks, and teach the children how to work together.

Develop predictable routines and activities that use language

To help children feel secure, create consistent routines and safe havens (such as the puzzle, Lego, and water tables) where a child can play alone and listen to English speakers without responding (Tabors, 2008). Morning meetings offer children a chance to extend their language use and tell stories about their lives, a familiar activity for Latino and African American families (Genishi & Dyson, 2009). Children can also bring in a daily or weekly word in their home language for the class to learn and discuss (Cummins, 1999–2003).

Teachers should model Standard English and read it aloud, but it's important not to correct children's words or pronunciation while they're reading or speaking. Instead, focus on meaning and understanding (Miner, 1998) so children get the message that reading is actually about meaning. Help them study the characteristics of their home language—including Black English—and compare it to Standard English (Baker, 2002). You could even ask them to translate their work into and out of their home language (Delpit, 2006). "By asking students to translate their work," says Julie Landsman (2002b), "you are putting a name to what they do without detracting from their home [or] how their grandmother . . . speaks" (p. 226).

Ways with Words

In the 1970s, in the early days of desegregation, ethnographer Shirley Brice Heath lived and worked in the Carolinas recording how the children in three neighboring communities learned to use language. The resulting study, *Ways with Words: Language, Life, and Work in Communities and Classrooms* (1983), is recognized as "one of the most important language research projects of all time" (Power, 2002, p. 81).

Although clustered geographically, the three communities had radically different ways of using language, Heath (1983, 2002) found. Because cultures evolve extremely slowly, they still apply today.

In the White working-class community of "Roadville," parents believe they must teach their children to speak, and from infancy onwards they talk with them in full sentences. Parents label items in the environment, ask questions such as "Where's your nose?", read to them, and expect them to sit quietly while listening to a story. Roadville children start out doing well in school but run into trouble at about grade 4.

In "Trackton," an African American working-class community, children are immersed from birth "in an ongoing stream of talk from extended family members and a wide circle of friends and neighbors" (Heath, 2002, p. 76), but adults rarely speak to them directly. As they grow, children learn to tell stories, enter adult conversations, respond to teasing games and questions adults don't know the answer to, and adjust their behavior and speech to their audience. Their method of learning—watching, listening, and trying— doesn't mesh with the school's method of teaching, and their teachers report that they talk too much and work too little. They are often failing by grade 3.

Heath found that the townspeople, middle-class citizens both White and Black, differ from their working-class neighbors in one very significant respect: The adults talk endlessly to their children about what they're doing. They keep up a running narrative on surrounding events and items ("Mummy's going to get her purse and then we're going for a ride"), and as soon as children begin to talk, they ask them to construct narratives, too

("What did you do at Zoe's house?"). With their parents' help, children rack up thousands of hours of practice telling and replaying stories with different actors and settings and linking events to past and future.

These children succeed in school because, as Heath discovered, school's major activity is producing a narrative ("What did the boy in the story find on his walk?"). Parents' narratives hold the key. Heath (2002) writes, "It is as though, in the drama of life, these parents freeze scenes and parts of scenes repeatedly throughout the day . . . . They focus the child's attention, sort out labels to name, and give the child ordered turns for sharing talk about these labels and the properties of the objects or events to which they refer . . . . [Children] are not left on their own to see the relation between two events or to explore ways of integrating something in a new context to its old context" (p. 78).

Much of this talk is about talk—names, ways of retelling information, ways of linking past, present, and future. The teacher-researchers working with Heath realized that their students from Roadville and Trackton needed "intense and frequent occasions to learn and practice those language uses they had not acquired at home," and they created classrooms focused on talk. Their students "labeled, learned to name the features of everyday items and events, told stories, described their own and others' experiences, and narrated skits, puppet shows, and slide exhibits" (Heath, 2002, p. 78). They became "language detectives," studying their own language as well as the language of their families and others—how they asked questions, showed politeness, got what they wanted, settled arguments, and told funny stories.

The crash course worked: These students achieved academic success.

SOME CULTURAL CHARACTERISTICS

Does each culture has its own special characteristics?

When a child from a different culture disrupts the class or behaves unexpectedly, it's a good idea to try to figure out whether culture is responsible. One way to do this is to learn as much as you can about that particular culture. Find out about its customs and values, study its history, read its literature. Best of all, get to know the child and her family. As you converse, confer, and collaborate, you will come to understand them and their culture better, and they will shed considerable light on the challenging behavior.

Researchers have identified some cultural traits that can help to explain different behavioral expectations and outcomes. The brief cultural profiles that follow are intended to illuminate areas where cultural confusion about challenging behavior may arise. Please note, however, that they are generalizations about characteristics that are often, but not always, found, and we present them as a way to help you to think about and understand the behavior you're observing. Bear in mind, too, that people from different places with similar educational and socioeconomic backgrounds may have more in common with each other than with some members of their own culture. Ultimately, each child is unique.

Latino culture

In 2003, the number of Latinos in the United States surpassed the number of African Americans to become the largest community of color in the country (U.S. Census Bureau, 2003). Latinos, who are also known as Hispanics, come from several different Spanish-speaking areas—most notably Mexico, Puerto Rico, Cuba, the Dominican Republic, and South and Central America (Guzman, 2001). These groups have a lot in common and—depending on the country of origin, education, and socioeconomic status of the family—a lot of differences.

In the collectivist Latino culture, respect and group harmony are important values (Espinosa, 2010). Children are expected to respect and obey their elders (including their teachers), and it is considered rude to question adults, argue, or express negative feelings. There may be cultural conflict for children with Latino values in European American schools where they are supposed to ask and answer questions and speak up for their rights. Children may participate more actively and function better when their culture and language are valued in the classroom, they are allowed to work collaboratively with their peers, and their relationship with their teachers is warm and informal (Gay, 2000; Greenfield & Suzuki, 1998).

Family comes first in the Latino culture, and everyone has strong ties to both the immediate and the extended family (Espinosa, 2010). Children remain dependent as long as possible, and it's common for 3- and 4-year-olds to drink from bottles and be spoon-fed. A child who's expected to fend for herself in child care may cry and be unable to comfort herself, and a school-aged child whose mother always makes sure she has everything she needs may feel unsure of herself when she's asked to do something she's never done before. In both cases, adult soothing, close physical contact, and an offer of assistance will help to calm her. As they grow older, children may be accountable to many adults and carry family responsibilities, such as caring for younger siblings, making meals, and working after school.

Courtesy indicates caring, and discipline at home is strict but polite and affectionate (Delgado-Gaitan, 1994). Children are sensitive to social cues and the nonverbal expression of emotion (Zuniga, 2004), but parents may also use physical guidance, which is another way to demonstrate caring (Halgunseth, Ipsa, & Rudy, 2006). Because direct criticism is a sign of disrespect, it's important for discipline in school to be indirect and polite, too. When a teacher reprimands or corrects her, a young child may cry and an older one may become upset, and although they won't respond, they may lower their eyes as their culture dictates. Because belonging to the group is so vital, being singled out in any way—positive or negative—is hurtful. Time-out is especially humiliating and may even have a shaming effect (Gonzalez-Mena, 2008). Indirect guidance methods may be more effective. For example, a child who hears she's going sledding will be more likely to put on her hat than a child who's told it's cold outside. Seeing the matter from the child's perspective is very important! Humor, jokes, and verbal play are useful because they help to relieve tension and avoid disagreement.

Education in the Latino culture emphasizes the development of the whole child—the goal is to produce a good person as well as a knowledgeable one. At parent–teacher conferences parents will ask, "How is my child behaving?" and it's wise to comment on her behavior before addressing her academics (Rothstein-Fisch & Trumbull, 2008).

Because they're often in a large group, Latino children are accustomed to noise and may speak loudly without realizing it. To indicate affection, they may touch each other and sit and stand close together. Children of other cultures may feel uncomfortable and push them away when they get too near. On the other hand, a teacher who keeps her distance may lead children to think she isn't sincere, and they may withdraw or be less likely to cooperate.

African American culture

For African Americans, family (which may include kin who aren't blood relations but feel they belong to one another) is extremely important and a source of strength and resilience (Willis, 2004). One of the family's primary jobs is to instill a sense of racial identity—to make children proud of their heritage and conscious of being a Black person in a White society (Willis, 2004). Such pride boosts cognitive competence, particularly in boys (Caughy, Nettles, O'Campo, & Lohrfink, 2006).

Parents are often strict. They use directives and commands and expect obedience and respect (Greenfield & Suzuki, 1998). Discipline may be direct and physical, and it is administered as a way to teach, with love and concern rather than anger. Research has found that higher levels of physical punishment lead to higher rates of aggressive behavior in European American children—but not in African American children (Deater-Deckard, Bates, Dodge, & Pettit, 1996). Strict discipline is an adaptive response to a reality African Americans have faced since the days of slavery, and it is intended to keep children, especially boys, out of danger (Willis, 2004). Parents may chaperone their offspring wherever they go, which in turn may limit their opportunities to have friends and practice social skills (Kupersmidt, Griesler, DeRosier, Patterson, & Davis, 1995).

Although perhaps less now than in the past, every responsible adult in the African American community takes part in raising children (Hale, 1986). This provides youngsters with the assurance that an adult will correct their unacceptable behavior, and they feel free to move, explore, and assert themselves as their culture demands. In school they may be surprised when a teacher expects them to control their behavior from within, and may interpret her soft commands, chummy manner, and relatively flat emotional style as a lack of caring, authority, and control in the classroom, leading them to test her limits (Delpit, 2006). As Delpit (2006) notes, "Black children expect an authority figure to act with authority" (p. 35). They may respond more readily to an intense, stern look and clear commands like they hear at home (Gonzalez-Mena, 2008). But beware: Fairness is extremely important, and even the slightest perception of injustice can leave a child feeling hurt for a long time (Ritchie, 2009). Children learn to be extra sensitive to emotional cues, which is an important survival technique for those who don't belong to the dominant culture (Hale, 2001).

African American culture places a high value on oral expression, and children learn to express themselves openly and frankly, playing with words and trading witty insults from an early age, often in Black English. This verbal expressiveness—along with expressive clothing, hairstyles, and movement—also helps them to establish unique identities, which are vital in a culture that stresses both individuality and interdependence (Peters, 1988; Trumbull et al., 2001).

African American children also have a quality that developmental psychologist A. Wade Boykin (1986) of Howard University calls "verve," a propensity for high levels of stimulation and energetic action and interaction. Although children with verve sometimes trouble teachers, who may see them as impulsive, overemotional, and out of control, their behavior is culturally appropriate in homes where there is constant stimulation and variety—lots of people, music, and activity—and a strong emphasis on emotional expression. Children accustomed to such an environment are more likely to thrive when teachers use vigorous, variable teaching strategies that permit plenty of movement and emotion, incorporate many media, and utilize small groups to nurture interaction with both teacher and peers (Hale, 2001). However, to equip their children for the real world of school, parents may prefer didactic teaching in reading and math (Howes, 2010).

Asian American and Pacific Island culture

Asian Americans and Pacific Islanders are often dubbed the "model minority" because of their extraordinary educational and financial success in North America. But not all members of this cultural group are doing well, and like other people of color they often encounter discrimination and racism (Tatum, 1997). Speakers of Asian languages make up about 8 percent of dual-language learners (Goldenberg, 2008) and come from a number of different countries and cultures—among them Chinese, Japanese, Korean, South Asian, Vietnamese, Thai, Filipino, and Pacific Island. Whether they embrace Buddhism, Christianity, Hinduism, or another religion, they share certain values (Chao, 1994; Ho, 1994).

The Asian American and Pacific Island cultures are highly interdependent. Family is central, and individuals garner self-esteem by contributing to the success and happiness of the group (Kim & Choi, 1994). Parents are prepared to make great personal sacrifices for their children, whom they see as extensions of themselves, and they expect loyalty, respect, obedience, and high academic achievement in return (Chan & Lee, 2004).

Because an individual's behavior and achievement reflect on the honor of the family and its ancestors, parents emphasize good conduct, even in play. They are careful to model appropriate behavior, instill an ethic of hard work, help children to succeed in school, and teach empathy and concern for others (Chao, 1994). Such parenting may be strict, but it clearly indicates warmth and caring (Chao, 1994; Lebra, 1994).

Social harmony is another key value. It is essential to attend to the needs of others, pay them proper respect, and avoid confrontation, criticism, and embarrassment (Chan & Lee, 2004; Greenfield & Suzuki, 1998). Communication is indirect—a person does not express his or her own needs but expects others to understand the context, use empathy, and read body language and other signs to formulate a response (Greenfield & Suzuki, 1998). (A young child who uses her body, not her words, to let you know that she needs to go to the bathroom may be extremely frustrated, and wet, if you don't read her signals correctly; a child who's struggling with an assignment may start moving around in her seat and become frustrated if you don't read her signals correctly and ask if she needs help.) It is also important to be modest, polite, and self-restrained rather than assertive—qualities that people from an individualistic culture may mistake for lack of interest or drive (Greenfield & Suzuki, 1998).

Children prefer to learn in a group, seeking out one another's opinions and eventually reaching a solution that suits everyone (Gay, 2000). The Asian American and Pacific Island culture has great respect for teachers, who are considered authorities. A child who asks questions is challenging their competence or admitting her own failure to understand, so she will wait for the teacher's invitation to participate. (Be sure to call on her often.) She may laugh when she's confused, behavior that is also easily misunderstood (Gay, 2000).

American Indian culture

There are over 550 American Indian tribes, each with its own history, culture, and/or language. European Americans know little about the injustices the Indian people endured during the 19th and 20th centuries when the U.S. government set out to "Americanize" them, removing them from their lands, forcing their children into Christian boarding schools where they were forbidden to speak their language, and withholding citizenship from them (Doble & Yarrow, 2007). These decades of maltreatment have affected the daily lives of American Indians, who today often live away from reservations and experience poverty and discrimination.

Nonetheless, American Indians strive to retain their traditional values. Their culture is interdependent and collectivist, and they believe all living things are related and property is communal, not personal (Trumbull et al., 2001). Individuals cooperate, share, achieve, and excel for the good of the group (Suina & Smolkin, 1994). Being singled out for either praise or criticism will make a child feel uneasy and may lead to misbehavior or noncompliance, especially at the beginning of the year before she has established a comfortable relationship with the teacher. Group recognition and activities—for example, murals, choral reading, and cooperative learning groups—are far more appropriate.

Traditionally American Indian children learn by careful observation, by listening to respected adults (who are regarded as keepers of knowledge) (Williams, 1994), and by practicing in private (Tharp, 1994). Although someone unskilled in their culture may be unable to read their body language and conclude that they aren't listening or interested, they are actually taking everything in, a fact that will become apparent when they have an opportunity to demonstrate their knowledge in a group setting.

Children are not brought up to "comply." They don't do things simply because you ask but are expected to make their own interpretation of a situation. They need a reason that stems from respecting the rules or from respecting others. For example, they will put things away in their proper place if told, "We need to put the puzzles away so we can find all the pieces next time."

Direct eye contact, interrupting, and following another's words too closely are considered rude and disrespectful, and it's important to consider issues carefully

A Mother Speaks

I n *To Teach* (2001), Ayers published the following letter from an American Indian mother. The author is unknown, but the letter has been widely circulated among teachers.

> Before you take charge of the classroom that contains my child, please ask yourself why you are going to teach Indian children. What are your expectations? What are the stereotypes and untested assumptions that you bring with you into the classroom?
>
> ... My child has a culture, probably older than yours; he has meaningful values and a rich and varied experiential background. However strange or incomprehensible it may seem to you, you have no right to do or say anything that implies to him that it is less than satisfactory ....
>
> Like most Indian children his age, he is competent. He can dress himself, prepare a meal for himself, clean up afterwards, care for a younger child. He knows his Reserve, all of which is his home, like the back of his hand.
>
> He is not accustomed to having to ask permission to do the ordinary things that are part of normal living. He is seldom forbidden to do anything; more usually the consequences of an action are explained to him, and he is allowed to decide for himself whether or not to act. His entire existence ... has been an experiential learning situation, arranged to provide him with the opportunity to develop his skills and confidence in his own capacities. Didactic teaching will be an alien experience for him ....
>
> He has been taught, by precept, that courtesy is an essential part of human conduct and rudeness is any action that makes another person feel stupid or foolish. Do not mistake his patient courtesy for indifference or passivity.
>
> ... You will be well advised to remember that our children are skillful interpreters of the silent language. They will know your feelings and attitudes with unerring precision, no matter how carefully you arrange your smile or modulate your voice ....
>
> Will [my child] learn that his sense of his own value and dignity is valid, or will he learn that he must forever be apologetic and "trying harder" because he isn't white? Can you help him to acquire the intellectual skills he needs without ... imposing your values on top of those he already has?
>
> Respect my child. He is a person. He has a right to be himself. (pp. 40–41)

(Tharp, 1994), which means that conversations may contain long pauses. American Indians are very comfortable with silences (Williams, 1994).

Children care for themselves at an early age and exercise a great deal of autonomy, usually deciding what they want to do without asking for adult permission. In fact, it is impolite to tell others what to do; adults provide suggestions and guidance and show they care by respecting the child's independence (for example, by not restricting visits to the bathroom or water fountain). They also leave children to work out their own conflicts. In addition, children learn to speak for themselves, relating their own opinions, not those of other people (Delpit, 2006). As Chud and Fahlman (1985) point out, a child who is used to this much freedom of choice and action may find the routines of a school environment very limiting.

Middle Eastern and Arab American culture

The Middle Eastern and Arab American communities have their roots not only in the areas in Asia and Africa we usually consider the Middle East but also in neighboring countries such as Afghanistan and Pakistan that share their religions, languages, and values (Sharifzadeh, 2004). Middle Eastern Americans are an enormously diverse group—Christian, Muslim, or Druze, rural or urban, affluent or poor, 19th-century settlers or brand-new immigrants. Most are born in the United States and are well educated (Adeed & Smith, 1997).

Middle Eastern Americans have a collectivist, interdependent culture, where the group takes precedence over the individual and the family is paramount. An individual's identity comes from her family's name, honor, reputation, and achievements more than from her own, but at the same time she represents the family in everything she does (Ajrouch, 1999). Family members take responsibility for one another and provide each other with guidance, support, and a social life (Sharifzadeh, 2004).

Children are extremely important, and everyone fusses over them. Although childrearing is changing among the new generation, in some parents' eyes a child's independence may indicate a failure of parental love and duty (Sharifzadeh, 2004). Children learn to respect and obey their parents more by observing others than by asking questions or listening to explanations (Sharifzadeh, 2004), although this, too, is changing. Once children reach 4 or 5 years of age, fathers may take more direct responsibility for discipline (Sharifzadeh, 2004), and boys in particular may have trouble listening to women—like their teachers—in positions of authority (Adeed & Smith, 1997). Education is highly valued and children of both genders are expected to do well at school—although they're occasionally tired from staying up late to spend time with their parents (Sharifzadeh, 2004).

In this culture, harmony is important, communication is indirect, and it's essential to pay attention to nonverbal cues. When there's a problem with a child's behavior, be careful to share concerns so that no one loses face (Adeed & Smith, 1997). Virginia-Shirin Sharifzadeh (2004) points out that it's impolite to say "no" and hurt another's feelings, so a person may say "maybe" or "yes" weakly instead. It is up to the listener to infer that the speaker means "no." Likewise, the listener must understand that "thank you" or "don't trouble yourself" means "yes."

People of the Middle Eastern American culture are comfortable standing and sitting close to one another, and friends of the same sex often hug and hold hands (Adeed & Smith, 1997). This close personal space isn't meant to intimidate, and discussing this fact will enable the children of other cultures to respond appropriately.

The Middle Eastern cultures and religions are patriarchal and patrilineal, with sharply defined gender roles. Men have power and status. They earn and control the money, deal with the outside world, make decisions, and act as the moral and disciplinary authority within the family (Sharifzadeh, 2004). Women take charge of child bearing, childrearing, and homemaking, and girls start to learn these roles early (Seikaly, 1999). To preserve their modesty, Muslim girls and women wear clothing that covers their heads, and even less devout families may warn girls not to have physical contact with boys starting at about the age of 7 or 8. It's important to be sensitive to their needs and keep them with other girls as much as possible.

As women join the workforce, these divisions begin to break down, and both parents will probably want to take part in any discussion of a problem with their child. However, men in very traditional Muslim families may not allow their wives to talk to strangers; and if they're acting as interpreters they may say or report only what they deem appropriate. In this case, Sharifzadeh (2004) suggests communicating via a trusted friend or relative instead of talking directly with the mother, who is a child's primary caregiver. But, she warns, never discount the father or his role. If you're using an interpreter, be sure to choose a man to talk with a man and a woman to talk with a woman.

Why all this matters

Delpit (2006) writes, "In any discussion of education and culture, it is important to remember that children are individuals and cannot be made to fit into any preconceived mold of how they are 'supposed' to act. The question is not necessarily how to create the perfect 'culturally matched' learning situation for each ethnic group, but rather how to recognize when there is a problem for a particular child and how to seek its cause in the most broadly conceived fashion. Knowledge about culture is but one tool that educators may make use of when devising solutions for a [teacher's] difficulty in educating diverse children" (p. 167).

All too often, unexamined attitudes and assumptions influence the way we interact with children. When we work to understand them and ourselves, we have a far better chance of seeing children clearly, establishing warm and trusting relationships with them, maintaining self-control, and identifying alternate solutions to problems.

W HAT DO YOU THINK?

1. When you look at your family history, you may also get some insight into your culture. Have you ever talked with your family about coming to North America? When did they immigrate? Why? Where did they come from? What language did they speak? Where did they settle? How were they

treated when they arrived? Did their relationship with their family change when they went to school?

2. Page 97 contains some questions about understanding your own cultural beliefs and experiences that you might like to discuss.

3. Many schools have a prepackaged curriculum that teachers are expected to use in their classroom. Under these circumstances, how will you go about making your teaching relevant and culturally responsive for the children you teach?

4. People who belong to the same culture or ethnic group often like to be together. Why do you think this might be? Have you ever tried explaining your family's culture to someone else? How did it feel to you?

5. What cultural assumptions underlie your discipline practices? Divide the class in half and debate the pros and cons of adapting your practice to take account of a child's cultural values.

6. Do you think it's possible for children to learn the skills necessary to succeed in the future and at the same time honor and value their cultural heritage? How will you go about balancing these goals in your classroom?

SUGGESTED READING

Children's Book Press. *Multicultural and bilingual books for children.* http://www.childrensbookpress.org/.

Delpit, L. D. (2006). *Other people's children: Cultural conflict in the classroom* (updated ed.). New York: New Press.

Derman-Sparks, L., & Edwards, J. O. (2010). *Anti-bias education for young children and ourselves.* Washington, DC: National Association for the Education of Young Children.

Espinosa, L. M. (2010). *Getting it right for young children from diverse backgrounds: Applying research to improve practice.* Upper Saddle River, NJ: Pearson.

Fadiman, A. (1998). *The spirit catches you and you fall down.* New York: Farrar Straus & Giroux.

Gay, G. (2010). *Culturally responsive teaching: Theory, research, and practice* (2nd ed.). New York: Teachers College Press.

Gonzalez-Mena, J. (2008). *Diversity in early care and education: Honoring differences* (5th ed.). New York: McGraw-Hill.

Lynch, E., & Hanson, M. J. (Eds.). (2004). *Developing cross-cultural competence: A guide for working with children and their families* (3rd ed.). Baltimore: Brookes.

Rothstein-Fisch, C., & Trumbull, E. (2008). *Managing diverse classrooms: How to build on students' cultural strengths.* Alexandria, VA: Association for Supervision and Curriculum Development.

Tabors, Patton O. (2008). *One child, two languages: A guide for early childhood educators of children learning English as a second language* (2nd ed.). Baltimore: Brookes.

CHAPTER 7

Preventing Challenging Behavior: The Social Context

Challenging behavior is troubling and puzzling, and teachers naturally want to know how to respond to it. What do you do when Jazmine kicks you in the stomach or Andrew throws a chair across the room? We will deal with these difficult questions in later chapters. But first consider this: Wouldn't it be wonderful if you never needed that information? Wouldn't you prefer it if challenging behavior never entered your classroom door?

This is a fantasy, of course. It is probably impossible to eliminate challenging behavior entirely. But it isn't a fantasy that a lot of challenging behavior can be prevented. Prevention isn't a sexy topic because it often involves small things, such as making transitions more fun or creating class rules; and it works quietly, without flash or drama. But it can be enormously effective, and for that reason it's very important.

Prevention is also important because it can stop a child from accumulating risk factors. If he continues to behave aggressively, he can easily ride a downward spiral leading to rejection by peers and teachers, school failure, gang membership, substance abuse, or delinquency. Preventing challenging behavior early can head off the development of more serious behaviors later (Gatti & Tremblay, 2005).

The longer a child uses inappropriate behavior, the harder it is to change. Many children use the same challenging behavior for years because they don't know any

120
....

CHAPTER 7

Preventing
Challenging
Behavior: The
Social Context

other way to behave, and that behavior becomes firmly entrenched. But the more frequently that teachers help children refrain from challenging behavior, the less they're learning to use it—and the less likely it is to embed itself in their brains (National Scientific Council on the Developing Child, 2004). If you can anticipate when and where a child will have trouble, prevent the situation from occurring, and remind him of what to do instead of waiting for him to make a mistake, you can build a new pattern: The child begins to reap the rewards of appropriate behavior, feels good about himself, and yearns to have that feeling again.

How does prevention work?

Prevention is the best form of intervention. When the environment meets their physical, cognitive, emotional, and social needs, children feel competent and capable of success and have less need of challenging behavior. This is one of the basic ideas behind prevention, and it means that every aspect of the environment—the social context, the physical space, the program, and your teaching style—must take each child's needs into account. This is also one of the basic ideas behind *positive behavior support (PBS)*, a model for preventing challenging behavior adopted by schools and child care centers across the country.

Research tells us that prevention is more likely to be effective when it

- starts early (Reiss & Roth, 1993)
- continues over a long time (Reiss & Roth, 1993)
- is developmentally appropriate (Gagnon, 1991)
- works on several fronts simultaneously—at home as well as school (Reiss & Roth, 1993)
- takes place in a real-life setting instead of a psychologist's office or a special program (Guerra, 1997b)

This last point is critical because it's hard for children to use a new skill outside of the context where they learn it (Mize & Ladd, 1990).

We're all the same, yet we're all different

Some children need more individualized support than others in order to learn and behave appropriately. In fact, write Lilian G. Katz and Diane E. McClellan (1997), "Because children's needs, feelings, dispositions, and behavior vary, it would be unfair to treat them all alike" (p. 73). Fair is when every child has the opportunity to participate, learn, and flourish.

This idea of flexibility—changing your discipline or management style or altering lessons to suit the needs of one child—shocks many teachers. They think it's unfair. Some say the child needs to learn to get along in the real world. Others think they're giving one child more than they're giving the others if they always become his partner during transitions or let him deliver a note to the office while everyone else is listening to a story.

121

CHAPTER 7

*Preventing
Challenging
Behavior: The
Social Context*

It's easy to confuse being fair with being consistent. The same rules apply to all the children, so any child who hurts another will be reminded that he is breaking a rule. But every child has different needs and different reasons for his behavior, and every child deserves the treatment that is appropriate for him—which means you might respond one way to Andrew and another to Jazmine. It's a good idea to give Jazmine a head start when the class is getting ready to go outside, because she likes to do everything herself and it takes her a bit longer. But it's better for Andrew to sit beside you in his cubby space so you can remind him about what comes next. Neither child is getting anything extra; they're just getting what they need. That is fair—both for them and for the other children.

If a child with challenging behavior can't function, he may keep other children from functioning by distracting them, frightening them, destroying their work, even hurting them. In addition, he may monopolize your time, deplete your resources, and prevent you from teaching. If you can meet his needs before this happens, you will have more to give to all the children, and the classroom can become a place that's pleasant, relaxed, and conducive to learning.

The children usually understand this. They know Jazmine takes longer to dress, so they don't mind if she starts before they do. They know Andrew loses control when he's frustrated, so they don't mind if you sit beside him. If they don't understand, it's easy to explain. In *The Explosive Child* (2010), Ross W. Greene puts it this way: "Everyone in our classroom gets what he or she needs. If someone needs help with something, we all try to help him or her. And everyone in our class needs something special" (p. 276).

Greene goes further. He suggests that when children get what they need, no one is stigmatized, and they learn to help one another. They recognize each other's

Glory in the Flower

Sixteen 4-year-olds were running to the far end of the field with one teacher at the front and the other at the rear. Everyone but Michael, that is. He ran off to the right. Instead of yelling at him to join the others, the second teacher followed him. When she reached him, he was smelling some small purple flowers. The snow had finally melted, and he wanted to investigate that glimpse of purple.

The teacher called the other children to see what Michael had found. Everyone started to talk about the flowers, their color, and the coming of spring. They decided to continue their outing looking for signs of spring. The other children asked for Michael's help, and he had a great time playing outside.

Had the teacher insisted he join the others without showing any interest in his find, his self-esteem would have been bruised, and he would have been frustrated. To get acknowledgment, he probably would have behaved inappropriately. Instead, the teacher recognized his needs, turning this event into a wonderful science lesson and enabling Michael to feel accepted by the group and very proud of himself.

122

CHAPTER 7

*Preventing
Challenging
Behavior: The
Social Context*

strengths and weaknesses, and they are quick to encourage and reinforce their class-mates' positive efforts. They become part of the solution instead of part of the problem.

The social context of the classroom has an enormous impact on the way children behave. This chapter will discuss two aspects of the social context: First we'll talk about how to create a social context that's positive and supportive; then we'll focus on teaching the social and emotional skills that are so essential to maintaining it.

CREATING THE SOCIAL CONTEXT

Although you can't see or touch it, the social context is everywhere, affecting everything you do, whether you're in a supermarket, an elevator, or a classroom. The social context is a framework that tells us what attitudes and behaviors are expected, accepted, and valued in a group or setting, and it has amazing power to influence what happens there. The social context creates the social climate—the spirit of the group and the ambience of the place. In the classroom, the program and physical space help to form and reinforce the social context, but in the end, the social context really grows out of the words, actions, and body language of the people inside it.

How does the social context affect aggressive behavior?

Not surprisingly, the social context influences the appearance and spread of aggressive behavior. In a key study, Sheppard G. Kellam and his colleagues (Kellam, Long, Merisca, Brown, & Ialongo, 1998) followed more than 1,000 children from their random assignment to first-grade classrooms into middle school. In grade 1 classrooms where the level of aggression was high, boys who were already at risk for aggressive behavior acted more aggressively and continued to be at high risk for aggression into grade 6. That is, the aggressive social context of the grade 1 classroom socialized them to become more aggressive. But boys who were in first-grade classrooms with a low level of aggression avoided this outcome and were at far less risk, even if their initial aggression matched that of their peers. The nonviolent social context—established by more skillful teachers—protected them. Children at high risk were far more susceptible to the effects of the classroom's social context than children at low risk (Kellam et al., 1998).

While they're learning self-control, young children rely heavily on the external environment—including their teachers and peers—to help them. Some researchers have even suggested that the years up to grade 3 constitute a kind of sensitive period that sets patterns for future behavior (Buyse, Verschueren, Verachtert, & Van Damme, 2009; Pianta, Steinberg, & Rollins, 1995). Teachers can support children with challenging behavior as they work to develop their internal controls—and at the same time direct them onto a more positive emotional and educational trajectory—by surrounding them with a positive, prosocial, predictable, caring social context (Hamre & Pianta, 2005; Raver, Garner, & Smith-Donald, 2007; Rimm-Kaufman, Curby, Grimm, Nathanson, & Brock, 2009).

A caring community

Such a social context is often called a *community*, and its importance to learning and social and emotional development is now widely recognized (Watson & Battistich, 2006). At its heart lie caring relationships between teacher and child, between the children themselves, between the teacher and the group as a whole, and between teachers and families (Watson & Battistich, 2006). Katz and McClellan (1997) define community as "a group of individuals who have a serious stake in each other's well-being and who can accomplish together that which they could not do alone" (p. 17). A community is like a family: People have a sense of belonging; they nurture, respect, and support one another; and they work together toward common goals. Children connected to a community enjoy school and learning more and have better attendance, grades, standardized test scores, and graduation rates (Wilson, Gottfredson, & Najaka, 2001). Their social and emotional skills, relationships with teachers and peers, and prosocial behavior all improve, while their behavior problems diminish (Schaps, Battistich, & Solomon, 2004; Wilson et al., 2001).

What characterizes a caring community? To begin with, it meets children's basic psychological needs, which psychologist Edward L. Deci postulates as *belonging*,

Children connected to a community enjoy school more and have better attendance and grades. Their social and emotional skills, relationships with teachers and peers, and prosocial behavior all improve, while their behavior problems diminish.

Photograph by Rachel at Rachel B. Photo Studio, LLC.

124

CHAPTER 7

*Preventing
Challenging
Behavior: The
Social Context*

autonomy, and *competence* (Deci & Ryan, 1985). A caring community provides these essentials:

- Children feel physically and emotionally safe (Blum, 2005).
- Relationships are caring, respectful, and supportive—children, teachers, and parents work at getting along together (Blum, 2005).
- Children have many opportunities to participate, help, and collaborate with others (Schaps et al., 2004).
- Children have many chances to make choices and decisions (Schaps et al., 2004).
- Teachers proactively teach expectations, routines, and procedures to prevent challenging behavior (Hawkins, Guo, Hill, Battin-Pearson, & Abbott, 2001).
- Teachers promote cooperation and cooperative learning (Solomon, Watson, Delucci, Schaps, & Battistich, 1988).
- Teachers actively teach social and emotional skills (Watson & Battistich, 2006).
- Teachers set high academic standards and provide the support necessary for children to meet them (Blum, 2005).
- Everyone in the community shares common purposes and ideals and is committed to them (Schaps et al., 2004).

Why should we include children with challenging behavior?

If children are going to learn to function in society, they must be in society. A child who interacts everyday with his socially competent peers has many opportunities to learn appropriate ways to behave; and being accepted in a caring, nonviolent classroom community where everyone supports his attempts to act appropriately increases the chance that he'll meet those expectations. At the same time, belonging to the community strengthens his bonds to the group's prosocial norms and values (Guerra, 1997a). Including children with challenging behavior is the right thing to do, and it is also the law: The Individuals with Disabilities Education Act (IDEA) protects the rights of both children with disabilities and children with challenging behavior.

What is the teacher's role in the social context?

When it comes to establishing the social context, teachers set the stage and play the lead. They are the primary role models, teaching by everything they say and do. As Daniel Goleman (1997) writes in *Emotional Intelligence*, "Whenever a teacher responds to one student, 20 or 30 others learn a lesson" (p. 279). Her words, actions, and body language inevitably tell each child about the power, ability, and worth of everyone in the classroom.

A teacher's consistent awareness of children's needs and feelings, her caring, helpful behavior, and her high expectations—that a child has, or can develop, the skills to make a friend or understand the math concept—set a powerful example and build a positive social climate. Children also notice how their teachers behave with colleagues, administrators, bus drivers, janitors, and parents. When the adults work as a team, share resources, and help each other, the children soak up their cooperative spirit; when there's tension and acrimony, that's contagious, too. Research-based programs such as positive behavior support, Response to Intervention, and Second Step advocate a whole-school approach for exactly this reason. Although an intervention in a single classroom can be effective, its impact increases when children see that the entire community values prosocial, nonviolent, cooperative interaction and problem solving (Thornton, Craft, Dahlberg, Lynch, & Baer, 2000).

In addition to being a role model, the teacher is the group's leader. In *The Nurture Assumption*, Judith Rich Harris (1999) describes a leader's power this way:

> First, a leader can influence the group's norms—the attitudes its members adopt and the behaviors they consider appropriate . . . .
>
> Second, a leader can define the boundaries of the group: who is *us* and who is *them*. . . .
>
> Third, a leader can define the image—the stereotype—a group has of itself.
>
> A truly gifted teacher can exert leadership in all three of these ways. A truly gifted teacher can prevent a classroom of diverse students from falling apart into separate groups and can turn the entire class into an *us*—an *us* that sees itself as scholars. An *us* that sees itself as capable and hard-working. (p. 245)

Us is a community, of course. In a class like this, Harris points out, the children cheer on their classmates who have learning and behavior difficulties and encourage one another's efforts to solve problems. Just as they can offer a round of applause to an emerging reader, so they can enthusiastically support a child who is beginning to ask instead of push. Once again, the children can become part of the solution instead of part of the problem.

Getting There

Michael's behavior was very challenging. He seemed to look for every opportunity to test the limits and bug his classmates, and he often made it impossible to complete a lesson. Our center was already using a proactive social skills program that encourages caring and community among the children, and we decided to step up our efforts with Michael at the same time. We made a seating plan for snack and lunch to be sure he wasn't left out or seated beside a classmate who would provoke him; and to help him control his behavior I kept him near me in the classroom and made him my partner when the group went anywhere together.

One day when we were getting ready to go skating, Sam asked, "Can Michael be my partner? I know we'll still get to the rink." I knew then that we were on the right track. Sam cared about Michael; we had made him a member of our community.

126

CHAPTER 7

*Preventing
Challenging
Behavior: The
Social Context*

How can you create a cooperative and inclusive community?

The very beginning of the year is the best time to start making your classroom into a community and helping all the children find a place in the inclusive "us." For children from collectivist cultures, who naturally put the group first, share, and help one another, the idea of community will no doubt feel very comfortable.

Community-building activities

Psychologist Robert B. Brooks (1999) suggests that children and teachers spend the first few days getting to know one another and helping everyone feel welcome and safe. Games and activities that involve all members of the group can reduce anxiety, break the ice, and bring people together. It's especially important for the children—and you!—to learn everyone's name. Address each child by name, and organize songs and noncompetitive games that incorporate names into the fun.

People who belong to a community often share a common history. You can create a history—and happy memories—for your class by organizing activities for the whole group, taking photos, and cultivating class customs and rituals, such as a secret class handshake. To generate a history for her primary class, teacher Laura Ecken regularly eats lunch in the classroom with a small group of students, rotating them so that she spends intimate time with everyone (Watson, 2003). Children establish rituals, too—particular ways of doing things, scripts they follow in a particular place. This repetition of gestures, words, and actions binds the group together and makes the environment feel consistent and safe (Raikes & Edwards, 2009).

When they participate in structured cooperative activities or work together toward a common goal, children come to know and like each other and have a better chance to become friends. Planting a class garden, for example—planning what to plant and where to plant it, preparing the ground, going to buy the seeds and plants, putting them into the earth, watering, weeding, and harvesting the bounty—requires children to see things from another's point of view, listen to others' ideas, negotiate, problem solve, share, and help each other. Singing and other music, dance, and drama activities are a great way to create unity; and reading aloud to the whole group every day gives children an important shared interest to discuss (Watson, 2003). Noncompetitive games, cooking, murals, and large construction projects also lend themselves well to cooperative social interaction, prosocial behavior, and acceptance of others (Eisenberg & Fabes, 1998; Slaby, Roedell, Arezzo, & Hendrix, 1995). Children who participate in cooperative activities behave less aggressively and are more likely to cooperate during unstructured times, even when they're frustrated.

Research shows that programs with less structure, where children have a lot of freedom to choose and use open-ended materials and activities in their own way, engender more social interaction and prosocial behavior (Quay, Weaver, & Neel, 1986; Slaby et al., 1995). (Think of the dramatic play area, the block corner, and the sand and water tables.)

Affect and language

127

CHAPTER 7

*Preventing
Challenging
Behavior: The
Social Context*

Children are quick to observe their teacher's affect and body language, which communicate much more than her words. When you smile and show your affection for the children and your enthusiasm for whatever you're teaching, that's catching, and it sets a positive tone for the whole class.

The language you use—what you say and how you say it—also plays a vital part in establishing the social context. Your tone of voice; the volume, speed, and intensity of your speech; and your choice of vocabulary all set an example. Greeting individuals every day, addressing them by name, saying "please" and "thank you," expressing your feelings, being sensitive to others' feelings, offering your help, and accepting the help of others all show the children you respect and value them—and demonstrate how they can respect and value each other.

Using inclusive language and pointing out the shared values and characteristics of the class also build community and a positive social context (Watson, 2003). For example, you can explain why it's important for the children to treat one another well, encourage them to help each other, and remind them of how they've solved problems in the past.

When you want to talk with a child, walk over to him so that you can communicate in a normal tone of voice. Without realizing it, a teacher can create an unfriendly environment by yelling or filling the air with negative commands. If you're constantly raising your voice, the children tune you out and shout more often themselves, and no one can hear or concentrate.

Choose positive, direct language that tells children what to do, not what not to do. "Stop running!" is negative, doesn't give the child any instruction, and opens the door for trouble: Should he hop, skip, jump? "Please walk in the hallway," stated clearly, calmly, and respectfully, informs him of the expected behavior. It also de-emphasizes the messages hidden in "Don't," "Stop," and "No" sentences, such as "Don't spill the juice." Positive, direct language allows you to avoid destructive comparisons as well. Although the other children may mimic Madeleine after you've said, "I like the way Madeleine is sitting quietly," they may be feeling manipulated rather than learning to exercise self-control (Denton, 2008).

When challenging behavior is involved, it's a good idea to avoid *why* questions. Andrew may not know why he spit at his neighbor, and if you ask, he's likely to fabricate a reason. He may even come to believe that a good explanation will make the behavior acceptable. But the bottom line is that unacceptable behavior is always unacceptable, whatever the reason for it. *Why* also puts some children on the defensive, making it harder for them to calm down. Although it's difficult, eliminating these little words is worth the effort.

Rules and policies

Rules and policies (sometimes called *behavior standards* or *norms*) teach children about expectations, set boundaries for behavior, and make a substantial contribution to the social context. They also have a symbolic value: They tell children you care about their behavior (Carter & Doyle, 2006).

Rules are the cornerstone of schoolwide positive behavior support, but whether or not your school or program has a PBS system in place, it's important to develop rules for your classroom. It's common to begin with the primary need of everyone in

128

CHAPTER 7

*Preventing
Challenging
Behavior: The
Social Context*

the room—to be safe. The rules are easier to remember when they aren't too numerous—3 to 5 are enough. They should be clear, explicit, and stated in the positive (what to do, not what not to do), general enough to cover almost any situation, and important enough so that there can be no exceptions to them.

Children and teachers have proposed:

- Respect yourself.
- Respect others.
- Respect the environment.

The class will understand and respect the rules more readily if they create them themselves. You will have to determine how much support and guidance they need. Giving this responsibility to the children shows you consider them capable and allows them to practice using their reason and judgment (Katz & McClellan, 1997). It also provides them with a sense of ownership and makes the rules seem fair and relevant, strong incentives to follow them (Elias & Schwab, 2006).

Help the children understand that rules aren't arbitrary but are actually tools that make it possible for people to treat one another fairly, kindly, and respectfully (Watson, 2003). This is a difficult concept to comprehend, so plan to work on it over time, using activities and class meetings that raise their awareness of the way they want their classroom to be and how they want others to behave toward them (Watson, 2003). Include lots of examples to render the abstract concrete, and facilitate the discussion so that the children themselves make up the rules and come to a common understanding of what they mean. For instance, "respect others" may mean "listen when other people are talking" or "use an inside voice in the hallway."

Figure 7.1 shows an example of a chart that can help you with this process. Make it on a large sheet of Bristol board and post it in a prominent spot in the

Rule	Expectations	Setting				
		All Settings	Circle/ Meeting	Choice/ Centers	Hallway	Recess/ Outside
Respect yourself						
Respect others						
Respect the environment						

FIGURE 7.1 Children need to know how to follow the rules throughout the day. Discuss what each rule means in each setting, and note the meaning in words or pictures on a chart on a large piece of Bristol board. Post the chart where everyone can see it, and use it to point out the correct behavior just before you start an activity.

Source: National Center on Positive Behavioral Interventions and Supports (www.pbis.org).

classroom. Encourage the children to illustrate the rules, and post their work, too. In addition, each child should have a copy to take home.

Throughout the year, use natural opportunities and activities such as storytelling and role playing to reinforce the rules, reminding students about them whenever they need an extra nudge. Children tend to forget, especially when they're used to acting in a different way, and practice helps them to remember. From time to time, put the rules on the agenda for a class meeting, assess how well they're working, and modify them if necessary. Parents and other adults who come into your classroom should also know and understand them.

Class meetings

A basic strategy of developmental discipline, the Responsive Classroom, and other educational approaches, class meetings are a powerful instrument for turning a collection of individuals into a community and creating an inclusive social context. Meetings give children a chance to "gather—psychologically and physically—and experience themselves as a group," writes Marilyn Watson in *Learning to Trust* (2003, p. 81). Having a sense of belonging and a say about what goes on in the classroom helps children meet their need for autonomy, tells them their ideas matter, builds relationships, and fosters empathy and responsibility (Leachman & Victor, 2003). Being able to discuss concerns in a safe and open environment is a key to learning.

What happens in a class meeting? Children and teachers gather in a circle, sing songs or do a short group activity, share experiences and ideas, acknowledge one another's kind actions, talk about the day's schedule, solve problems, and set class goals. According to Alfie Kohn (1996), meetings are for questions that affect

You Can't Say You Can't Play

Vivian Paley, a kindergarten teacher at the University of Chicago Laboratory Schools and the recipient of a prestigious MacArthur Foundation award, was disturbed by exclusion in her classroom. She couldn't accept that some children had the right to limit the social experiences of their classmates, and after extensive consultation with the children from kindergarten through grade 5, she brought in a new rule: You can't say you can't play.

"In general," Paley writes, "the approach has been to help the outsiders develop the characteristics that will make them more acceptable to the insiders. I am suggesting something different: the *group* must change its attitudes and expectations toward those who, for whatever reason, are not yet part of the system" (1992, p. 33).

Though it took time to institute, this straightforward assault on the social climate was a resounding success. The most popular girl in the class invited two girls who'd been on her worst-friend list to play, no one was left out, everyone had more turns, the children were nicer to one another, and they were far more willing to try out new roles and new ideas.

130

CHAPTER 7

*Preventing
Challenging
Behavior: The
Social Context*

most of the class; sharing (what you did over the weekend); deciding (how to deal with teasing; whether to go over the homework as a class or in small groups); planning (a field trip); and reflecting (on values, learning). Other educators believe the group can discuss issues involving just a few people and anyone can bring a problem to the meeting. Emily Vance and Patricia Jiménez Weaver (2002) suggest teachers keep a list of topics to discuss: Do you clean up a place where you didn't play? Do you always do what your friends tell you to do?

Help the children understand how the class rules apply to class meetings—for example, what does it mean to treat everyone with respect? As children listen and participate, they become more sensitive and responsive, and they begin to learn basic problem-solving skills, such as sorting through different points of view, options, and outcomes to come up with a solution that works for everyone. Keep in mind that reaching a consensus or a compromise is preferable to voting, which divides the group into winners and losers and leaves some members with little commitment to the solution (Kohn, 1996).

You can meet once, twice, or three times a week for 10 to 30 minutes (10 to 15 minutes for preschoolers), but many teachers hold meetings everyday, and sometimes more often. For maximum benefit, Vance and Weaver (2002) suggest you meet daily for at least 3 months.

Peer partners

When children choose peers to play or work with, the same child often finds himself alone. Children need to feel accepted by their classmates, and when others reject them on a regular basis they may turn to inappropriate means of getting attention. Although your goal is for children to form friendships and solve problems on their own, it's important to anticipate that some will have a particularly tough time. By selecting partners for the children yourself, you can avoid these opportunities for exclusion. Try to match classmates with similar interests and bring them together in nonthreatening situations. Pairing a more socially skilled child with one who is less skillful can be particularly effective (Hymel, Wagner, & Butler, 1990). Whether you ask them to water the plants or carry the books back to the library together, the more expert child is always modeling social skills—and in this one-on-one situation may discover a more likeable side to his awkward peer and offer him a path into the group.

Rolling the Dice

To assign partners so that no one feels left out, divide the class into two groups: children who may need support, and children who can be good role models. For example, if there are 16 children in the class, build an eight-sided pair of dice out of heavy cardboard. Put photos of the supportive children on one dice and the remaining eight children on the other. When you roll the dice to form partnerships, the selection seems random (Bruce, 2007).

TEACHING SOCIAL AND EMOTIONAL SKILLS

In addition to creating an inclusive, prosocial environment, you can tackle the social context head-on by teaching social and emotional skills—the behaviors, attitudes, gestures, and words that enable us to initiate and maintain positive social relationships (Rubin, Bukowski, & Parker, 1998). In fact, social and emotional learning and a positive, cooperative social context go together: Each enhances the power of the other (Hawkins, Smith, & Catalano, 2004).

There is no doubt children learn social and emotional skills simply by being in a group, but they learn much more when you teach these skills proactively. Giving them formal status in the program makes your teaching intentional rather than hidden (Elias & Schwab, 2006), highlights their value, and amplifies the classroom's prosocial ambience. Furthermore, a social and emotional learning program offers children with challenging behavior a chance to learn skills they might not learn otherwise.

Why are social skills important?

Besides helping children make friends and get along with others, social and emotional skills enable them to

- recognize and manage their emotions (Fabes & Eisenberg, 1992)
- gain self-confidence and self-esteem (Michelson & Mannarino, 1986)
- resolve conflicts more readily and less aggressively (Fabes & Eisenberg, 1992)
- avoid peer rejection and victimization (Perry, Kusel, & Perry, 1988)
- perform better at school (Elias & Schwab, 2006)
- lower their risk for later delinquency and violence (Nagin & Tremblay, 2001)

These skills are especially important in assisting children in low-income families to manage the stress in their lives and succeed academically (Raver, 2002).

Children with challenging behavior have great difficulty in the social and emotional realm (Bierman & Erath, 2006). Rejected by their peers and often without friends, they have few opportunities to learn and practice these skills or build self-confidence. As they become more isolated, they also become more angry and insecure, and their aggressive and disruptive behavior may increase (Fabes, Gaertner, & Popp, 2006; Raver et al., 2007). Because emotional development is related to cognitive development, children's thinking may be impaired as well, jeopardizing their school success (National Scientific Council on the Developing Child, 2004).

Children who behave aggressively may also have difficulty with social information processing. They may fail to understand social cues and assume others have hostile intentions; they may not look around for additional information or think of alternative solutions to problems; and they may not consider what will happen if they respond aggressively (see Chapter 1). Other students (and teachers) are afraid of them and often see their behavior in a negative light. Even when children with

132
....

CHAPTER 7

Preventing
Challenging
Behavior: The
Social Context

challenging behavior begin to learn social and emotional skills, their reputation makes it hard for them to be accepted (Coie & Koeppl, 1990). These are the children who need social and emotional skills the most.

How do children learn social and emotional skills?

Adults model, teach, reinforce, and provide feedback about social and emotional skills, but during early childhood children increasingly learn these skills through interaction with their peers (Fabes et al., 2006). With their social equals (who are less forgiving than their families), they play roles and face dilemmas they don't encounter with adults, so if they're socially skilled and the interaction is positive, they learn to lead, follow, contribute ideas, communicate, respond assertively to threats and demands, negotiate, compromise, defer, problem solve, see multiple perspectives, work through issues of power, persuade, take turns, reason, cooperate, share, give and accept support, experience intimacy, and learn the rules and subtleties that make interactions run smoothly. Socially skilled children prefer to be together, and the more time they spend interacting, the more socially competent they become. For them even conflict is useful: It helps them develop all of these skills and understand other people's feelings as well (Fabes et al., 2006).

However, children at risk may have an entirely different experience with their peers. Because they lack social and emotional skills and have difficulty regulating their feelings, their social interactions are often short, negative, and disruptive. Rejected and excluded by the more socially competent children, they are denied the chance to learn the skills they need (Fabes et al., 2006).

Nonetheless, a child can have a friend after the group has rejected him (Katz & McClellan, 1997), and that friendship will insulate him from some of the pernicious effects of rejection (Andrews & Trawick-Smith, 1996). On the other hand, children who've been rejected because of their aggressive behavior often hang out together, reinforcing one another's antisocial tendencies (Bagwell, 2004).

Peers are extremely important role models: Children tend to imitate those most like themselves (Michelson & Mannarino, 1986). When socially skilled peers are involved in an intervention, children with challenging behavior are more likely to become both less aggressive and more accepted (Bierman, 1986). In a study of children who'd been abused and neglected, teachers' reinforcement of desirable behavior worked only 12 percent of the time. But when peers paid attention, the children responded positively 53 percent of the time (Strayhorn & Strain, 1986). Socially competent peers who can model and reinforce appropriate behavior every day are the best possible teachers for children with challenging behavior (Slaby et al., 1995; Vitaro & Tremblay, 1994).

How do you teach social and emotional skills?

Because children with challenging behavior learn best when they're with their socially skilled peers, it's a good idea to teach social and emotional skills to the whole class—or the whole school, as the positive behavior support system suggests. All of the children benefit; no one is singled out or stigmatized; and everyone learns the same concepts and vocabulary, making it much easier to model, use, and reinforce the skills during the day (Elias & Schwab, 2006). This kind of *universal intervention* works well with approximately 80 to 90 percent of children (Sugai, Horner, & Gresham, 2002). A few children may require more *intensive intervention*, which can either be *targeted* to a small group or *individualized* for a child who has particularly persistent problems. See Figure 7.2 below.

Some experts consider the preschool years the optimal time to begin (Bierman & Erath, 2006; Mize & Ladd, 1990). Children who don't learn social and emotional skills before they start school are likely to suffer from peer rejection and its consequences, and it's easier to change a child's social status when he's young. But later training in social competence is also beneficial and should continue for several years (Mize & Ladd, 1990).

Social and emotional learning programs are often based on Bandura's social cognitive learning theory, and they use a variety of methods, including didactic instruction, modeling, role playing, feedback, and group discussion. When a child is under stress, it's difficult for him to access a new skill (Elias & Butler, 1999),

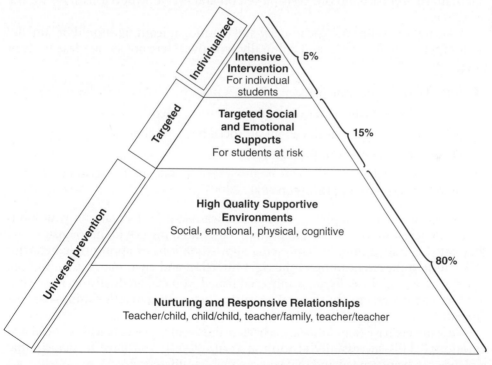

FIGURE 7.2 The Pyramid model demonstrates how the promotion of social and emotional competence can prevent and reduce challenging behavior. Nurturing and responsive relationships form the foundation for social and emotional competence for all young children. As the Pyramid shows, they also need a high-quality supportive environment. For some children, extra support may be necessary to prevent challenging behavior; and a small percentage with especially difficult problems require intensive individualized intervention.

Source: Adapted from Fox, L., Dunlap, G., Hemmeter, M. L., Joseph, G., & Strain, P. (2003). The teaching pyramid: A model for supporting social emotional competence and preventing challenging behavior in young children. *Young Children, 58*(4), 48–52.

134

CHAPTER 7

*Preventing
Challenging
Behavior: The
Social Context*

so regular, plentiful rehearsal and practice in a calm, safe atmosphere are essential. To help children transfer these skills, be sure to reinforce them in real-life interactions in the classroom and schoolyard (Mize & Ladd, 1990).

Integrating social and emotional learning into the curriculum makes it especially effective (Elias & Schwab, 2006). For example, children can practice taking another's perspective by talking or writing about how fictional characters feel, discussing the impact of their actions on others, and speculating about what might have happened if they'd made different choices.

When you're presenting a social skills activity, remember that you're a role model, and concentrate on being your prosocial best. It is also extremely important to be aware of the needs of individual children. Often, the child who stands to gain the most may be the least interested in taking part. Perhaps the ideas threaten a pattern of behavior he relies on, or he lacks the self-esteem to believe that anything can change his status in the group. If he doesn't want to participate, he can listen from elsewhere in the room. Disguise and recycle real incidents using puppets, photographs, drawings, books, role playing, and discussion. With this impersonal, externalized approach, no one feels picked on and everyone develops skills for the next time.

Like anything else you teach, social and emotional learning should be fun, developmentally appropriate, and culturally sensitive. Here are some ideas to liven things up:

- Include games and role plays.
- Make a video of what you're doing and discuss it afterwards.
- Ask children to share stories about prosocial behavior they see.
- Publicly celebrate accomplishments.
- Connect activities to children's goals—more friends, better academic performance, a safer school (Thornton et al., 2000).

When children are applying what they've learned in real situations, your job is to stay closely attuned and coach, prompt, cue, and reinforce them to ensure that they get the desired results. Reinforcing approximations of appropriate behavior tells children they're heading in the right direction and encourages them to keep trying. Once a child's skills are firmly established, you can gradually decrease your reinforcement because the natural rewards—better peer relationships—will be enough.

Researchers have found that a teacher's enthusiasm is key in teaching social and emotional skills successfully (Thornton et al., 2000). You have to believe that violence can be prevented and that you can make a difference!

What skills should children learn?

To promote peer acceptance and a positive, inclusive social context, social and emotional learning programs usually focus on emotional regulation and empathy, impulse control, entering groups, anger management, social problem solving, and assertiveness.

Emotional regulation and empathy

135

CHAPTER 7
*Preventing
Challenging
Behavior: The
Social Context*

Acquiring the foundations of social competence is a complicated process that begins in the first 5 years (National Scientific Council on the Developing Child, 2004). Infants can't regulate their own internal states and emotions; they depend on their caregivers to decipher the clues they provide and respond with the help they need (Cicchetti, Ganiban, & Barnett, 1991). That is, caregivers act as a kind of external arm of the baby's own internal regulatory system, gradually handing over control as the baby internalizes what they've taught him and can manage his emotions himself. Temperament definitely plays a role here—a child who feels everything intensely may find this much more difficult (Vandell, Nenide, & Van Winkle, 2006).

According to attachment theory, the more sensitive and responsive the caregiver is to the baby's signals, the better at regulating his own emotions the child will eventually become. On the other hand, if his primary caregiver is unpredictable, unavailable, or rejecting, the child learns to manage his feelings in ways that may be inappropriate in the classroom (Greenberg, DeKlyen, Speltz, & Endriga, 1997). His relationship with his primary caregiver also becomes a working model for future relationships and the basis of his feelings of self-worth (Bowlby, 1969/1982).

Talking about feelings—acknowledging, validating, labeling, and mirroring them—helps children learn to differentiate and label their emotions for themselves (Dunn & Brown, 1991). This emotional understanding is fundamental to social competence and emotional regulation, and at the same time it provides children with a powerful tool: It permits them to use words rather than acting out their feelings (Raver, 2002).

Whenever emotions arise in the classroom, it's a good idea to label and discuss them. Ask a child how he feels and make a suggestion or two ("Are you angry because Jeffrey took the racing car?"). You can also point out positive feelings ("You and Leo seem very excited about that book"); help children figure out which situations provoke which feelings ("You feel sad when Noah won't let you play"); and talk about how different people can have different feelings about the same situation (Juan may be thrilled at the top of the big slide, but Inès is terrified). Engaging in pretend play, observing others, looking in a mirror, looking at pictures of people in different emotional states, asking questions, being coached through difficult situations, and using strategies such as self-talk also help children learn about their feelings (Dunn & Brown, 1991). Children who are prone to anger and aggression may find it harder to identify the causes of emotion (Raver et al., 2007).

Perhaps the best tool you have for helping a child regulate his emotions is your relationship. When you listen and respond empathically, you not only provide comfort but also help him to deal with his feelings and give him the sense they can be controlled (Karen, 1998). You convey this message again by expressing your own feelings (both positive and negative): He learns it's all right to have and express emotions and that emotions are manageable. If he knows you'll be there when he needs you, he may eventually feel secure and confident enough to handle his own difficult feelings and even have sufficient control to consider the emotions of others (Karen, 1998).

Empathy, which is the ability to understand what others are feeling and to put oneself in their shoes, begins to develop before the age of 2, when a child is likely

136
....

CHAPTER 7

*Preventing
Challenging
Behavior: The
Social Context*

to try to console his crying sister by patting her or bringing her a blanket—whatever he associates with relieving his own pain (Dunn & Brown, 1991). As children realize that not everyone feels what they feel and that different people can have different feelings, they can learn to anticipate how others might feel and to respond appropriately.

Being able to look at a situation from another's perspective makes a considerable difference in the way children perceive the world, and it's crucial when it comes to controlling aggressive behavior (Beland, 1996; Cartledge & Milburn, 1995; Slaby et al., 1995). Children with challenging behavior find it hard to see things from someone else's point of view. They may feel so threatened by a classmate's anger or distress that they protect themselves by ignoring or hurting him (Thompson & Lagattuta, 2006). Children who've experienced or witnessed abuse also close down their empathic responses in order to cope (Beland, 1996).

Conversely, children who can imagine another's feelings are less inclined to act aggressively. When they can identify and sympathize with a peer, they're more likely to help him and less likely to become angry or misinterpret events and intentions (Eisenberg & Fabes, 1998). They can anticipate the effect of their words and actions and understand that if they push or tease, someone will get hurt. They make better decisions, and they'll probably try to take others' feelings into account when they're solving problems, increasing the chances they'll find satisfying solutions (Ianotti, 1985).

You can teach empathy by employing exactly the same tactics you use to help children recognize and label their own emotions. Be sure to explain the connection between a provocative act and an emotional consequence ("It makes Hannah feel sad when you leave her out"), encourage and reinforce signs of empathy in the classroom, and organize activities that help children to take someone else's perspective. Like other social and emotional skills, becoming empathetic takes practice.

When it comes to regulating and displaying emotion, different cultures have different beliefs and values. In the individualistic European American culture, children are encouraged to express their feelings. But in collectivist cultures, such as Japan, Korea, and China, where the harmony of the group takes precedence, people keep their feelings to themselves so that they won't hurt others (Chan & Lee, 2004).

Children crossing from one culture to another may find these different emotional modes disturbing (Gonzalez-Mena, 2008). It's important for teachers to teach and respond in a culturally sensitive way. For example, try not to put children from a collectivist culture into situations where they have to disagree with a classmate. (See Chapter 6.)

Impulse control

Impulse control has nothing to do with knowing the rules or the consequences of breaking them. Many children with challenging behavior—especially those who interrupt and talk over others, blurt out answers without raising their hands, and have difficulty taking turns—can tell you all about the rules and why their behavior was inappropriate, but this knowledge doesn't help them. Although most children gradually learn to control their impulses, some, including those with ADHD and FASD, whose problems have a biological origin, find the process much more difficult.

How Does Randy Feel?

The Second Step Violence Prevention Curriculum (Committee for Children, 2002) uses photos and text to teach social and emotional skills. Teachers hold up the large photos, ask the class the questions suggested on the back, and draw on the ideas for integrating the concepts into social studies, language arts, and science.

Here are Randy and his grandfather. Randy is sharing what happened at school today. Randy's friend, Derek, invited Sonji to play a special recess game, but he didn't invite Randy to join in. Randy tried not to show that he was upset, but his tummy hurt and he couldn't finish his lunch. He was quiet the rest of the day. On the way home from school his stomach still hurt. He wanted to cry.

1. How do you think Randy feels?
2. How can you tell Randy feels sad?
   He wants to tell someone what happened and how he felt. When we have feelings that keep bothering us, sharing our feelings with grown-ups we trust can make us feel better.
3. How does it feel to talk with someone you trust? When we trust someone we feel safe and comfortable with that person.
4. Randy wants to tell his grandfather how he feels. It helps to name the feeling. What could Randy say?
5. What makes Randy's grandfather a good person to talk to?
6. Who are some grown-ups you trust at school?

Source: From Lesson 5, Unit 1, Grade 1, of *Second Step: A Violence Prevention Curriculum*, 3rd edition, 2002. Copyright © 2002 by Committee for Children. Reprinted with permission from Committee for Children, Seattle, WA. www.cfchildren.org

138

CHAPTER 7

*Preventing
Challenging
Behavior: The
Social Context*

"There is perhaps no psychological skill more fundamental than resisting impulse," Goleman (1997) writes. "It is the root of all emotional self-control, since all emotions, by their very nature, lead to one or another impulse to act" (p. 81). Teaching impulse control helps to prevent challenging behavior because it gives children the opportunity to slow down and notice what they—and others—are feeling.

Children usually learn self-control skills—which are also crucial to thinking—between the ages of 2 and 5. Besides the ability to delay gratification (if you can wait, you can have two marshmallows), these include

- *tolerating frustration* (not hitting when you don't get what you want)
- *effortful control* (inhibiting action in order to do something else, even when you don't want to, such as not grabbing a toy you want from another child or asking for help rather than tearing up your math paper)
- *adapting behavior to the context* (talking quietly in the library)

In the hurly-burly of classroom give-and-take, children often go on automatic pilot and act impulsively. They do what they've always done, and if they've behaved aggressively in the past, then aggressive behavior just reappears. According to Ronald G. Slaby and his colleagues (1995), children act impulsively for several reasons:

- They have trouble regulating their emotions.
- They don't listen carefully.

The Marshmallow Test

In the 1960s, psychologist Walter Mischel began an extraordinary study. He and his researchers told 4-year-olds they could have two marshmallows if they could wait about 15 minutes while the researcher ran an errand. If they couldn't wait, they could have a marshmallow right away—but just one.

About two-thirds of the children earned both marshmallows. They covered their eyes, sang, talked to themselves, and played games with their hands and feet to fend off temptation.

The researchers sought out these children again when they were graduating from high school. They discovered that the double-marshmallow children were extremely socially competent—"personally effective, self-assertive, and better able to cope with the frustrations of life" (Goleman, 1997, p. 81). In addition, they were superior students, with SAT scores 210 points higher, on average, than the single-marshmallow children.

The impulsive children's inability to delay gratification had them cost dearly. As adolescents, they were more likely to be seen as stubborn, indecisive, easily upset by frustration, mistrustful, jealous, and prone to fights and arguments.

- If they have verbal skills that could help them to stop and think, they may not use them.
- It doesn't occur to them to consider what else they could do or what will happen if they respond aggressively. Passive or aggressive solutions seem perfectly all right.

One of the secrets to impulse control is learning the difference between feelings and actions, Goleman (1997) says. When a child learns to recognize that he's feeling angry or frustrated, he can also learn that having that feeling is a signal to stop and think—not a signal to act. Part of learning to identify the feeling is learning that it's all right to feel whatever he's feeling and he can express those feelings nonviolently.

Remaining calm is also central. The two-marshmallow 4-year-olds on page 138 employed a strategy that works: *self-speak*, also called *self-talk* or *verbal mediation*. The child thinks out loud (or to himself) to guide his own actions. Self-talk enables children to realize they're in charge of their own behavior (Watson, 2003).

Several social and emotional skills programs teach children to remind themselves aloud to "Stop, look, and listen" when they realize they're becoming angry or frustrated. Teachers can model this method by talking out loud and making the usually hidden process of reasoning more apparent. Children can also learn to take deep breaths, count to five, or do relaxation exercises. When they're composed, they should rehearse these techniques in role plays of potentially provocative situations with puppets, teachers, and peers before trying them in real life. Be sure to provide them with lots of cues, prompts, and reinforcement.

Prevention is extremely important when you're teaching impulse control. As always, knowing the child is key: Then you can predict when and where he might explode. If you monitor closely, remind him of the rules and expected behavior, help him identify his feelings, and give him a script of what to say before he loses control, you are providing cues and information that will eventually enable him to control himself. Give him as much help and encouragement as he needs to succeed.

Entering groups

Children must enter groups again and again each day. But entering a group is not an easy task. In studies, preschoolers who knew each other rejected more than half of all initial entry attempts by their peers, and even popular second and third graders were rejected or ignored 26 percent of the time (Putallaz & Wasserman, 1990).

Impulse control is essential to success. Children who can wait have more opportunity to figure out what the group is doing and how they can fit in, and when they try again their peers are more receptive. Children who make at least three attempts generally make it, so persistence pays off, too (Putallaz & Wasserman, 1990).

The sequence of tactics also matters. The following seems to be the most successful route (Putallaz & Wasserman, 1990; Walker, Ramsey, & Gresham, 2004):

- Knowing the rules of the game or activity
- Hovering on the outskirts of the group without speaking
- Mimicking what the children in the group are doing (parallel play is a useful bridge)

140

....

CHAPTER 7

Preventing
Challenging
Behavior: The
Social Context

- When a natural break appears, saying something positive that relates to the group's activity
- Promptly accepting any offer, even for partial involvement (e.g., to become the referee)

Asking to join usually works, but children hesitate to try this direct approach, probably because it's harder for them to try again if they're rejected (Putallaz & Wasserman, 1990). It is most effective to focus on the social interaction and show understanding of what the group is doing (Putallaz & Sheppard, 1992).

Disrupting play or talk by bulldozing one's way in, introducing new topics, directing the conversation to oneself, asking questions that require an answer, giving instructions, or disagreeing will almost certainly lead to failure (Walker et al., 2004). Boys are more likely to adopt these strategies, which enable them to save face after they've been rejected (Putallaz & Wasserman, 1990). For them, saving face and preserving status are more important than actually entering the group.

Teachers can facilitate the process by designing whole-group activities geared to the needs and interests of a specific child. If you know that Luke, who's often left out because of his aggressive behavior, loves trains and knows all about them, create a train project. Because of his expertise, Luke will become an attractive member of the group and enter the play with relative ease (Carr, Kikais, Smith, & Littmann, n.d.). Again, teach these skills with discussion, role playing, rehearsal, prompting, and reinforcement.

Anger management

When psychologist Diane Tice asked 400 people how they manage their moods, she discovered they had the most trouble with anger (Goleman, 1997).

Anger in both children and adults comes from a feeling of being in danger—either physical or emotional. When you're insulted, treated unfairly, or thwarted in reaching an important goal, your self-esteem or dignity feels threatened (Goleman, 1997), and the body's first response is to gear up for fight or flight. Then, thanks to the adrenocortical system, the body remains in a state of arousal, ready to convert any new offense into more anger. Even mulling over the original provocative incident—for instance, thinking "That makes me so mad!"—has the effect of escalating anger (Goleman, 1997; Novaco, 1975). This is why venting anger or hitting a pillow doesn't calm a child down or teach him to regulate his feelings. On the contrary, it can actually increase aggression (Berkowitz, 1993).

To a child with challenging behavior, the world seems filled with threats and potential sources of anger. Because he can't process social information correctly, he misunderstands others' actions, and he is frequently rejected by his peers, excluded from activities, or frustrated by the task at hand. When he has a math problem that's too difficult, he will probably get angry—angry at his parents for making him go to school, angry at the teacher for giving him such a hard problem, angry at his classmates for being able to solve it. To keep this anger from blowing up, it's important to intervene early in the anger cycle, while it's still possible to interrupt it. That is precisely what anger management programs teach children to do.

Children learn best when they're calm. When they're in the middle of an angry outburst they aren't listening, and talking actually escalates their behavior. Instead, map out a strategy ahead of time for situations where tempers flare, such as when a child doesn't get what he wants, he's hurt or frustrated, or the other children try to provoke him.

The first step is to learn to recognize and label anger by becoming sensitive to its body cues: a hot face, clenched fists, a frowning mouth, a wrinkled forehead, crossed arms (Elias & Schwab, 2006). Children also need to learn that it's all right to feel angry, that feelings—even feelings that make them uncomfortable—are natural responses to events, and that learning to label, understand, and accept feelings is crucial to managing them.

Children must also learn that feelings are signals, and feeling angry is a signal to stop and consider what to do next. Anger management programs teach direct techniques, such as those used for impulse control—self-speak ("stop," "calm down," "I'm getting angry; I'm not going to lose my temper"), slow breathing, relaxation, and counting slowly to five (Coie & Koeppl, 1990; Kreidler & Whittall, 1999). One preschool teacher asks children to put their hands over their hearts to check out how they feel. "I point out that a wildly beating heart is a sign of being out of control," he says (Bauer & Sheerer, 1997). The Turtle Technique (Robin, Schneider, & Dolnick, 1976), which teaches children to go inside their "shell" by bringing arms and hands toward the body when they feel upset, also inhibits physical action and allows them to calm down.

Reframing is another effective technique for dealing with anger. You can use empathy to see the situation from a different point of view ("Emma wasn't trying to hurt you; she was trying to help"); or you can suggest explanations for the event ("Emma banged into you because she was carrying so many things she couldn't see where she was going"). You can also reframe anger by externalizing it, perhaps with humor (but avoiding sarcasm) ("The computer seems to be in a bad mood today"), perhaps by stopping the "temper monster," perhaps by explaining that when a child loses his temper, the other party in the dispute comes out on top (Coie, Underwood, & Lochman, 1991).

Once the child's anger is under control, it's time to apply problem solving to the original situation. At that point the child can say, "I'm angry because the math is too hard and I don't know what to do," and with the teacher's help, he can brainstorm ideas to solve the problem. Throughout this process, ensure that the child understands it's all right to feel angry but not to throw a chair.

Social problem solving or conflict resolution

Good problem-solving skills enable children to avoid aggression, stand up for themselves, build competence and self-esteem, and have friends (Slaby et al., 1995; Spivack & Shure, 1974). They will need your help as a facilitator, and you will need enough time and energy to carry through from beginning to end. There's no point in starting if everyone is exhausted or you'll have to stop for snack or recess in the middle. It's useful to remember that conflicts are normal events that provide excellent teaching and learning opportunities and children are more likely to honor solutions they've thought up themselves.

142
....

CHAPTER 7

Preventing
Challenging
Behavior: The
Social Context

A feeling—anger, sadness, anxiety—is usually the first indication that there's a problem (Elias & Schwab, 2006), so help children tune into that feeling and acknowledge it. When everyone involved is calm and able to listen, you can begin. Most experts agree there are five basic steps (Committee for Children, 2002):

- *Identify the problem.* Each participant in the dispute must have a chance to give his point of view and define the problem as he sees it. In the end the children must frame the problem as a shared one where there are competing perspectives and a possible solution. "Cesar pushed me" and "DeShawn won't let me use the computer" lay out the facts, but they don't describe the problem. When DeShawn and Cesar can agree that the problem is "We both want to use the computer," they can begin to find solutions.

- *Brainstorm solutions.* It's good to have a selection to choose from. When you treat every suggestion nonjudgmentally, you empower the children and improve their thinking skills. Using a phrase like, "That's one idea. What's another?" will help ideas to appear: "De Shawn can go first and we each have 10 minutes," "We can find a computer game to play together," "Maybe Ms. Rodriguez will let one of us use her computer." Remind children of satisfactory ways they've handled similar problems in the past and urge them to think about their goals as they propose (and select) solutions.

- *Evaluate solutions.* This is the time to examine what might work and why. The Second Step program calls this step "What might happen if . . . ?" to help students learn to think about the possible consequences of a proposed action. The children should agree on the solution, which should take the perspectives of all participants into account.

- *Choose a solution and try it.*

- *Evaluate the outcome.* If the first solution doesn't work, go through the steps once more.

Although young children can't learn all of this at once, they can begin to learn and use one skill at a time.

It's especially important for children who have difficulty processing social information to learn and practice these skills. If they believe their failures are their own fault while their successes are due to luck—as many children with social information processing problems do—they may give up too easily (Rubin et al., 1998). Learning to problem solve may empower them at the same time that it boosts their skills. It can help them to distinguish accidents from intentional acts, be less suspicious of their peers' intentions, and come up with nonviolent alternatives (Price & Dodge, 1989). Remember, however, that in some environments attributing hostile intent to others is adaptive—and can be a matter of life and death (Guerra, 1997b).

Assertiveness

Children with assertiveness skills—who know how to express their feelings, needs, and opinions and stand up for themselves without violating the rights of others—are less likely to be harassed and more likely to have friends who protect them (Hodges, Boivin, Vitaro, & Bukowski, 1999). (See Chapter 13.)

143

CHAPTER 7

Preventing
Challenging
Behavior: The
Social Context

The European American school day is constantly presenting situations that call for assertive behavior—a child wants to enter a group or have a turn on the swing; another child bosses, intrudes, or calls him names. Knowing how to approach or respond assertively offers children a means to achieve their goals without aggression. An assertive response can protect a child from being victimized, and an assertive overture can enable a child who behaves aggressively to get what he wants without resorting to aggression. When all the children learn these skills, they help one another, reinforce each other's assertive behavior, and avoid blaming or stigmatizing anyone.

Assertive behavior lies on a continuum about halfway between passive behavior (when an individual disregards his own needs in favor of another's) and aggressive behavior (when a person denies other people's rights altogether) (Bedell & Lennox, 1997). Children need a wide range of responses along this continuum in order to choose the one that best fits a particular situation (Rotheram-Borus, 1988).

Slaby and his colleagues (1995) describe two types of assertive behavior. We use *reactive assertive behavior* to respond to someone else, express a different opinion, ask a person to change his behavior, or refuse an unreasonable request. *Proactive assertive behavior* helps us to initiate and maintain interactions, express positive feelings, give and receive compliments, make requests and suggestions, and offer thoughts and ideas in a polite open-ended manner (Hargie, Saunders, & Dickson, 1994). This style of assertiveness comes with a smile and is softer, friendlier, and quieter than the reactive version.

Assertiveness is culture bound. In cultures where modesty and group harmony are important values, it may even be frowned upon (Bedell & Lennox, 1997; Hargie et al., 1994). In the European American culture, assertive responses usually involve these behaviors:

- Facing and looking at the other person without staring
- Speaking loudly, clearly, and directly to the other person in a firm voice
- Using I-messages to tell the other person how his actions make you feel
- Having a facial expression and body language that match the verbal message
- Standing straight, 1½ to 3 feet from the other person
- Replying promptly (Bedell & Lennox, 1997; Weist & Ollendick, 1991)

Taking a Stand

To avoid being victimized, children should learn to use the following assertive responses—immediately, directly, and firmly (Slaby et al., 1995):

- To physical attack, "I don't like it when you hit," "Stop kicking me; that hurts."
- To a seizure of objects or territory, "I'm not done with that," "I'm staying here."
- To verbal abuse or discrimination, "I don't like it when you say that," "Everyone is allowed to play here."
- To unfair treatment, "It's my turn now."

144
....

CHAPTER 7

*Preventing
Challenging
Behavior: The
Social Context*

Assertiveness requires several skills. Besides impulse control, perhaps the most important is for a child to recognize his own thoughts and feelings, both positive and negative, so that he can figure out what he wants to say and do. Researchers who looked at the assertive responses of popular children noticed they gave reasons for their requests and refusals (Weist & Ollendick, 1991).

Like other social and emotional skills, assertiveness should be taught away from the heat of the moment. Coaching and reinforcement are especially important, both in practice sessions and when children are putting their new skills to use in the classroom. Some children may never have heard an effective assertive response and need a script.

Once again we repeat our mantra: It's essential to present, rehearse, and role play social and emotional skills when children are calm. As they put them into practice, they'll need plenty of prompting, coaching, cuing, and reinforcement from you. Although social and emotional learning won't solve all the problems they face, it can go a long way toward creating a positive social climate and helping them feel comfortable and safe.

In Appendix A you'll find a reflective checklist to help you think about the ideas in this chapter and actually put them into practice in your own classroom.

W HAT DO YOU THINK?

1. The professor who assigned this text plays a major role in developing and supporting the social context in your classroom. Describe the social context and the methods he or she has used to create it.

2. You often hear children say, "That's not fair!" What does being fair mean to you? How would you explain to parents that you do not teach all children the same way?

3. Vivian Paley instituted the rule "You can't say you can't play" in her kindergarten classroom. Why did she do this? Do you think she was right? Could she have handled the problem another way?

4. Think about times when you were trying to enter a group. What did you feel? Do you remember what you did? Do you remember what worked and what didn't?

5. How do you know you're angry? What are your personal cues? How does knowing you feel angry help you to manage your anger?

6. Behavior that's adaptive in one context (school, for example) may not be adaptive in another (a child's home neighborhood). What do you think about teaching nonaggressive strategies to children who live in dangerous neighborhoods where problems may not be solved with words?

S UGGESTED READING AND RESOURCES

Apacki, C. (1991). *Energize! Energizers and other great cooperative activities for all ages.* Newark, OH: Quest Books.

Children's book list. (n.d.). www.vanderbilt.edu/cse-fel/documents/booklist.pdf

Collaborative for Academic, Social, and Emotional Learning (CASEL). http://casel.org/

Goleman, D. (1997). *Emotional intelligence.* New York: Bantam.

Joseph, G. E., & Strain, P. S. (2003). Comprehensive evidence-based social-emotional curricula for young children: An analysis of efficacious adoption potential. *Topics in Early Childhood Special Education, 23(2)*, 65–76.

Katz, L. G., & McClellan, D. E. (1997). *Fostering children's social competence: The teacher's role*. Washington, DC: National Association for the Education of Young Children.

Paley, V. (1993). *You can't say you can't play*. Cambridge, MA: Harvard University Press.

Responsive Classroom. www.responsiveclassroom.org/index.html

Slaby, R. G., Roedell, W., Arezzo, D., & Hendrix, K. (1995). *Early violence prevention: Tools for teachers of young children*. Washington, DC: National Association for the Education of Young Children.

Technical Assistance Center on Social Emotional Intervention for Young Children (TACSEI). www.challengingbehavior.org/

Vance, E., & Weaver, P. J. (2002). *Class meetings: Young children solving problems together*. Washington, DC: National Association for the Education of Young Children.

Note: In the last few years, a virtual library of user-friendly social and emotional skills programs has appeared on the market.

Incredible Years, Dina Dinosaur Curriculum, 1411 8th Avenue West, Seattle, WA 98119; phone 888-506-3562 or 206-285-7565; www.incredibleyears.com/program/child.asp

PATHS, Promoting Alternative Thinking Strategies, Channing Bete Company, 1 Community Place, South Deerfield, MA 01373-0200; phone 1-800-477-4776; www.channing-bete.com/prevention-programs/paths-preschool/; www.channing-bete.com/prevention-programs/paths/

RCCP, Resolving Conflict Creatively Program, Educators for Social Responsibility, 23 Garden Street, Cambridge, MA 02138; phone 1-800-370-2515; http://esrnational.org/professional-services/elementary-school/prevention/resolving-conflict-creatively-program-rccp/

Second Step: A violence prevention curriculum, Committee for Children, 568 First Avenue South, Suite 600, Seattle, WA 98104; phone 800-634-4449; www.cfchildren.org/programs/ssp/overview

Preventing Challenging Behavior: Physical Space, Routines and Transitions, and Teaching Strategies

Like the previous chapter, this chapter focuses on preventing challenging behavior, but its approach is probably more familiar: It describes tried-and-true methods to minimize behavior problems in the classroom. We've divided the chapter into three parts. The first covers the classroom's physical space; the second is about routines and transitions; and the third describes a variety of teaching strategies.

THE PHYSICAL SPACE

"Space speaks to each of us," the late Jim Greenman (2005) wrote in *Caring Spaces, Learning Places* (p. 13). Think of a library, a restaurant, a swimming pool—each lets you know exactly what behavior is expected there. So does a classroom.

As we've seen, the social context delivers most of the message, but the relationship between the social context and the physical space is reciprocal. Because each influences the other, the physical environment provides important clues for the people within the space. That is, the way you set up your classroom can help to prevent challenging behavior (Katz & McClellan, 1997). The overall plan of the area, the arrangement of furniture and equipment, and the use of wall space will invite children to be comfortable or uneasy, inclusive or elitist, orderly or out of control, prosocial or aggressive. It is certainly easier to change a space than to change behavior, but paradoxically, changing the physical space *can* change behavior. This is why property owners rush to scrub off graffiti and repair broken windows: They want people to know that their buildings are cared for and deserve respect.

Sharing space, toys, and the teacher's attention all day long is stressful for children. School boards and states regulate teacher–child ratio, group size, and classroom space per child (Pianta, 2006), and the National Association for the Education of Young Children (2007) has recommended standards as well. But even when standards are followed, many children end up in classrooms where the conditions are less than optimal. This makes it difficult for those who require more space or adult attention to have their needs met.

How can your space help you to create a caring, cooperative, and inclusive community that encourages learning and fosters appropriate, prosocial behavior? How can the surroundings help you to meet the children's needs for belonging, autonomy, and competence (Deci & Ryan, 1985)? Here are some ideas.

Welcome

First impressions are crucial. As you ready your space for the first day of school, take a look at the children's files and talk with their previous teachers to find out more about their lives and interests. When children and their families see themselves and their culture reflected in the classroom, they are more likely to feel that they belong and become engaged in what's going on. Prepare a place for each child to store her belongings; and to help families feel at home, outfit an area with at least one piece of adult-size furniture. Then you, too, can sit comfortably, and there will be laps where children can cuddle. Add a carpet, a lamp, some plants, books for parents and toys for younger siblings, photos of families and staff, and a sign welcoming everyone in all the languages of the classroom (Gonzalez-Mena, 2010).

Arranging the furniture

You will no doubt reconfigure your space many times over the course of the year as you come to know the children better, hold class meetings, and teach groups of varying sizes. But the basic arrangement—home base—should indicate your top priorities and facilitate the behavior you're trying to nurture. In an early childhood or kindergarten classroom, the dramatic play area inspires the most complex social interaction, followed by blocks, games, woodworking, sand, and manipulatives (Quay, Weaver, & Neel, 1986), so it's important to create spaces that can accommodate these small-group activities and encourage children to play together. Even the computer can have seating for more than one child, and if the sand table is accessible on all four sides, four children can each have their own space, yet share the sand toys. The result is likely to be more friendships and better social and negotiating skills.

148

CHAPTER 8

Preventing
Challenging
Behavior:
Physical Space,
Routines and
Transitions, and
Teaching
Strategies

Dramatic play, woodworking, and blocks present more opportunities for social interaction—and also
for aggression.

Children with challenging behaviors will probably have trouble functioning
in a physical space filled with lots of rules and restrictions. Of course, all children need some limits, and we will talk more about that later. But too many imposed limits may make matters worse (Kritchevsky & Prescott, 1977). At a
certain point children stop listening—which is dangerous in an emergency. It is
therefore wise to set up the room so that children can move about without constant warnings.

To cultivate independence and autonomy, make sure the activity centers and
shelves are well organized, inviting, easily accessible to the children, and strategically located. If the blocks are next to a high traffic area, sooner or later someone
will knock over a construction masterpiece, causing anger and frustration. Place
sand, water, and art activities near the sink so children don't have to walk across
the room carrying containers of water or paint-laden brushes; and put quiet
activities—reading, writing, and art—close together and far away from noise. When
toys, supplies, and materials reside in clearly defined and well marked areas and
containers, the children know where each item belongs, simplifying cleanup.
Be sure to close or cover the shelves during circle and story time. Otherwise, they're
just too tempting.

Because children sometimes need peace and quiet, it's important to have a place
where they can shut out the world. Construct an area where primary school children
can study, take a break, meet in a small group, or recover from a meltdown. You'll

help them to calm themselves if you provide a rug, comfy cushions, an armchair, or bean bags. Younger children also need a private retreat with soft furniture and pillows. Note, however, that a quiet space in a noisy room may not be quiet enough for very distractible and easily stimulated children, who may unconsciously use challenging behavior to take refuge in the office.

As you position things, remember the empty space. One study found that large numbers of children need "no less than one-third to no more than one-half uncovered surface" (Kritchevsky & Prescott, 1977, p. 19), but too much open space inspires running, chasing, and chaos. Use low shelves and furniture to divide large spaces into uncluttered, well-organized areas. If you mark the boundaries clearly and lay out well-defined pathways from one area to another by putting masking tape or cut-out footprints on the floor, the children will feel more comfortable and their behavior will be more cooperative and less disruptive. To prevent possible invasions of personal space, construct an entrance and an exit to each area.

And don't forget to designate a place where the whole community can come together—preferably on a carpet.

In the primary school classroom, the configuration of desks and tables should reflect your goals and philosophy. Small tables or desks pushed together to form clusters of three to six students let everyone know that cooperation and collaboration are expected. In this position the children can work together, share materials, and help each other. If you create clear pathways between desk clusters, small groups can collaborate without distracting one another, and you'll have enough space to walk around facilitating—moving from group to group listening, helping, taking part in discussions.

Desks in rows tell the children the classroom is teacher-centered. In this formation, it's harder for children to talk to one another, and teachers interact more with children in the "action zone"—the front row and the middle of the class (Adams & Biddle, 1970). If you choose this arrangement, be sure to seat some of the struggling students and dual-language learners near the front, sprinkle others throughout the class, and make a point of walking around and paying attention to children all over the room. Later in the year you may feel relaxed enough to try other floor plans.

Whatever arrangement you select, prepare seat assignments for the first day of school (Wong & Wong, 2001). Although it's often good practice to let children make their own decisions, this is one time when you must take charge. If children sit where they please, they're more likely to form cliques, whereas mixing them up creates new ties, promotes social skills, and enables diverse talents and intelligences to emerge. Again, reading students' files and talking with colleagues will help you decide who to put where.

Children who are easily distracted may need help to focus. Cut down on the stimulation around them by seating them near the front of the room and away from windows and high traffic areas such as doors, the pencil sharpener, and your desk (Epstein, Atkins, Cullinan, Kutash, & Weaver, 2008). If you place them beside children who find it easy to concentrate, they'll have good role models and partners for collaboration (U.S. Department of Education, Office of Special Education Programs [OSEP], 2004).

In a conventional classroom, the teacher's desk stands at the front. But a desk in this position can create a barrier between you and the children, so think about placing it at the back or side of the room, where you won't have to stand behind it to

150

CHAPTER 8

*Preventing
Challenging
Behavior:
Physical Space,
Routines and
Transitions, and
Teaching
Strategies*

use the white board or projector. Locate it where you can see the whole class and where you can meet with individuals or small groups without disturbing the other children.

Choosing materials

The materials, toys, games, and books you select also have an impact on children's behavior. To be engaging they must match the children's interests, abilities, cultures, temperaments, and developmental levels. If a construction toy is too difficult, it may become a simple shape—such as a gun. Competitive games incite aggressive behavior (Slaby, Roedell, Arezzo, & Hendrix, 1995; Sobel, 1983), and so do superheroes, soldiers, games that require a lot of waiting, and toys based on violent television shows (National Association for the Education of Young Children, 1990, 1994). Tactile experiences such as play dough, sand, or water play help the children relax and ride over difficult patches; and parachutes and tire swings call out for cooperation.

War on Violence

The children born since 9/11 have always lived in a nation at war, and they seem increasingly obsessed with war play (Levin & Carlsson-Paige, 2006). Children need to work on the issue of violence in their lives in order to make sense of what they've seen, and *creative play*—where they're actively in control and determine the script themselves—enables them to do this.

But highly realistic toys linked to increasingly violent television shows and video and computer games have changed the nature of children's play (Levin & Carlsson-Paige, 2006). It has often become, in Piaget's term, *imitative*. Narrow and repetitive, it merely replicates television scripts and characters without giving children the chance to gain mastery over their experience and meet their developmental needs. Instead, more children are getting hurt and learning harmful lessons about violence.

In *The War Play Dilemma* (2006), Diane E. Levin and Nancy Carlsson-Paige conclude that the best approach to war play is to facilitate it actively. In this way, teachers can help children learn to gain control of their aggressive impulses, take another's point of view, understand what they've heard about the world, and experience a sense of their own power. Levin and Carlsson-Paige (2006) make these suggestions:

- Try to figure out how children are using play to work out their feelings and ideas.
- Help them expand their play by suggesting new roles, offering new materials, and temporarily assuming a role in the play (without taking control of it).
- When children aren't playing, talk with them about their play and its content, and work on their concerns through art, books, storytelling, and building.

*Preventing
Challenging
Behavior:
Physical Space,
Routines and
Transitions, and
Teaching
Strategies*

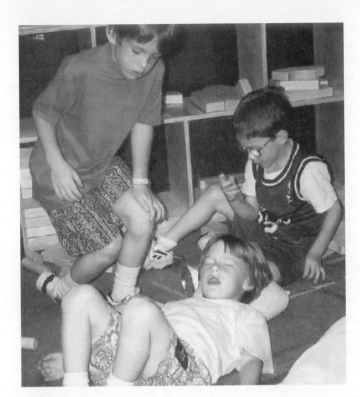

*After the 1995 bombing of the federal building in Oklahoma City, which killed 168 people, including 19
preschoolers, children at the Early Childhood Learning Center in Kingsport, Tennessee, "bombed" the structures they'd built in the block area. They also remembered those who'd helped, and in response to a 9-1-1
call, rescue workers (including rescue dogs) came from the dramatic play area to care for the injured. The
children replayed this scenario for several days. Later, with their teachers, they talked about and visited the
town's services that would keep them safe in an emergency.*

Photo by Betty Jane Adams

Although toys and objects from home may supplement your supply and ease
the transition to child care or school, they create a whole new set of problems. Some
children appear with inappropriate toys (such as guns or swords), and others spend
the day protecting their property. Parents also become embroiled. When they're running late, they may decline to fight over an action-hero toy, and it ends up at child
care or school despite the rules. It's important to negotiate the solution to this problem with the parents. One center reached this compromise: Unsuitable toys such as
weapons went straight into the director's office for the day; other toys were allowed
until 9:30 a.m., when they had to be placed in the children's cubbies. Do encourage
the children to bring things from home that they can share—books or tapes of music from their own culture that the class can listen or dance to.

What about personal space?

All children need personal space as they move around the room and interact with
their peers. How much depends on their culture and temperament.

CHAPTER 8

*Preventing
Challenging
Behavior:
Physical Space,
Routines and
Transitions, and
Teaching
Strategies*

Children with challenging behavior often have a definite idea of how much personal space they should have, and an invasion can easily set off pushing and shoving. Help Andrew understand that Eva didn't mean to come so near and give him a script to tell her to move back: "Say, 'I don't like it when you come so close.'" These discussions alert Andrew to his own and others' space requirements and help him extend his tolerance of another person's proximity.

When they're crowded together, children accidentally bump into each other, ruin one another's work, and have lots of misunderstandings, all of which can lead to frustration and aggression. It therefore makes sense to control the number who can play in each area. The size of the space, the activity, the availability of materials, and the chemistry of the participating children are all part of the equation. With the children's collaboration, figure out how many fit comfortably into an area and set up a method to regulate it. For example, at the entrance to each learning center, place hooks where the children can hang name cards to claim a play spot.

The numbers in an area can change. After a few days you may discover that Andrew can't function with five children in the block area—but he's fine when there are four. The solution is to reduce the number permitted and explain the change to the children without pointing at a particular child: "I notice that people are having more fun when there are four instead of five children in the block area. What do you say we change the number to four and see how it goes?" Alternately, you could expand and enrich the area with extra materials to make the play more complex—for example, by adding Legos to the block area or popsicle sticks to the play dough (Curtis & Carter, 2003).

Boys often need to move around more than the usual classroom permits. Dan Gartrell and Margaret King (2003) suggest that planned outdoor playtime and large motor equipment indoors—a climbing apparatus, a wrestling mat, a physical fitness center, a woodworking area with real wood, nails, and hammers—can meet boys' need for physical play and prevent them from using their energy in inappropriate ways. But physical activities (along with blocks and dramatic play) also present more opportunities for conflict (Quay et al., 1986), and you must supervise closely with so many potential weapons at hand. Trust your knowledge of the children, even if that means replacing the woodworking tools with their plastic counterparts and Styrofoam or plastic "wood."

Culture also has an impact on the way people use space. An environment that seems warm and exciting to one child may appear cold and uninteresting to another. Sybil Kritchevsky and Elizabeth Prescott (1977) found that Mexican American preschoolers played and socialized comfortably in a space that seemed cramped by middle-class European American norms. Though the researchers believed the conditions were conducive to aggressive behavior, there was no hint of conflict.

Does the level of stimulation make a difference?

Classroom noise and hubbub make it hard to hear, hard to focus, hard to talk quietly, and hard to settle disputes peacefully (Slaby et al., 1995). Children with fetal alcohol spectrum disorder (FASD), hearing loss, sensory integration disorder, or sensitive temperaments may be particularly affected. Pay attention to the buzz as you move through the day, and reduce the level of stimulation by turning off the music, leaving some of the wall space blank, organizing children's artwork by color, putting away some of the toys, reducing clutter, and installing a dimmer switch for the lights.

One solution is to think about quiet times. You don't have to schedule these moments; if you watch the children carefully, you'll know when to say, "Okay, everyone, stop everything, lie down on your back, and look at the ceiling. Think about how you're breathing." (School-aged children can put their heads on their desks.) Ask them to think about their toes and each individual body part in turn. By the time you've reached the tops of their heads, the atmosphere will be completely altered.

Deck the walls

Your classroom walls also send a message about what matters: The décor should show that the classroom belongs to the children, so put up photos and pictures that reflect their interests, families, and cultural heritage, past and present (but be careful to avoid a tourist approach). The displays should also support what you're teaching and show the children's work. Be sure everyone in the class is represented. As H. Jerome Freiberg (1999) puts it, "Selecting the work of a few . . . sends a message that 'only the best need apply'" (p. 167).

Dedicate some space to the classroom rules and their accompanying illustrations and chart, and leave room for the emergency procedures, lunch menu, daily assignment, and schedule.

Consider the results

When you've finished arranging everything, you should be able to survey the whole room from anywhere you stand. If all the children can see you, your very visibility will deter challenging behavior; if you can see all the children, you'll be well situated to detect early triggers and head off challenging behavior before it starts.

Try looking at the space from the child's perspective, too. By getting down on your knees you'll see how inviting and accessible it is. Is there too much visual clutter? Or does it look cold and empty? Are there corridors that invite running? Are the learning centers visible, clearly defined, large enough, and welcoming? Is the artwork on the walls at the children's eye level? Is the space confusing? From this angle, the world shouldn't look like a maze.

Taking responsibility in the classroom

Even young children can take on the responsibility of looking after the classroom by doing many of the jobs you might do yourself. They can collect recyclables, bring in snack, carry messages to the office, water the plants, lead lines, set the tables, sweep, tape ripped books—the list goes on and on. Just ask them what else needs to be done (Bovey & Strain, n.d.; Curtis & Carter, 2003). They can work in pairs (a good arrangement for children from collectivist cultures) (Trumbull,

154

CHAPTER 8

*Preventing
Challenging
Behavior:
Physical Space,
Routines and
Transitions, and
Teaching
Strategies*

Rothstein-Fisch, & Greenfield, 2000); each child can have a job of her own; or you can rotate the jobs every week or two. Post a job chart so everyone knows what to do. Taking responsibility allows children to feel they're making a contribution and gives them ownership of the classroom—as well as legitimate reasons for moving around.

ROUTINES AND TRANSITIONS

Teachers do many things to establish and maintain order in the classroom at the same time that they strive to create an inclusive, caring environment that fosters children's self-regulation and academic, social, and emotional skills (Elias & Schwab, 2006; Weinstein, 2003). In such a community, teachers and children collaborate, children want to learn and behave ethically, and they respond in kind to respectful treatment (Watson & Battistich, 2006).

There is always a tension between providing opportunities for children to develop self-control, autonomy, initiative, and competence while simultaneously sustaining an orderly, productive learning environment (Watson & Battistich, 2006). The key is to let the children know your expectations. They find it easier to function and behave appropriately when they know what to do, when and how to do it, and what is coming next. Tell them what you expect on the very first day, and remind them before they begin each activity. Children forget, but when the environment is predictable and they have the necessary support, there is little need for challenging behavior and more freedom to explore and socialize.

There are several ways to create a predictable classroom where children know what to do. We discussed one way in Chapter 7: *Classroom rules* clarify expectations and prevent problem behavior, especially when children understand why rules are needed and formulate them themselves (see pages 127–129). Other techniques are developing a daily schedule, teaching procedures, and using thoughtful transitions.

A daily schedule

In general, children enjoy a varied and balanced day with quiet and active, indoor and outdoor time, small- and large-group, teacher- and child-directed activities (Harms, Clifford, & Cryer, 2005). Predictability and consistent expectations are especially important at the beginning of the day. To help your students settle into learning and remind them they belong to a group, start with a regular class meeting or circle time. While you're all together, go over the schedule and point out anything unusual, such as a field trip. Post a picture schedule to help the children remember.

Teaching procedures

Teachers use another method to establish a predictable environment: They develop and teach *procedures*, which specify how to carry out certain activities. The grease that makes the classroom run smoothly, procedures tell the children exactly what

155

CHAPTER 8

*Preventing
Challenging
Behavior:
Physical Space,
Routines and
Transitions, and
Teaching
Strategies*

Picture This

ith the children's help, you can make an engaging picture schedule.

- Brainstorm: How do the children see the day? Begin with drop-off time or school bus arrival.
- Take photographs of every facet of the daily routine—snack, bathroom, dressing for outdoors, recess, nap, and so on.
- Print and laminate the photos in 8" X 10" format.
- With the children, arrange the photos in the proper order and put them into an album or on a ring or post them at eye level with Velcro strips.
- Take new pictures throughout the year to update the schedule and give every child a chance to appear in it.
- Save the old photos. You can use them for events that haven't occurred yet.

you expect them to do. They can cover virtually everything from entering in the morning to leaving at day's end—personal needs, transitions, participation in teacher-led activities, working in small groups and centers, getting help, handling materials and equipment. Such routines, taught step by step and practiced assiduously in the early days of the year, contribute substantially to children's success. The procedures should fit easily within your classroom rules.

Each procedure should have a clear rationale. Rules and procedures aren't ends in themselves but a means of creating a positive and relaxed learning environment that supports the social context as well (Brophy, 1999; Emmer, Evertson, & Anderson, 1980).

It's wise to introduce just a few procedures at a time. On the opening day of school, start with those the children need first—putting away their belongings, entering and leaving the classroom, going to the bathroom, getting help, and asking questions. Over the next few days you can add other procedures, such as that all-important beginning-of-the-day routine. Before you start a new activity, teach any procedures that go with it.

Carefully explain the reasoning behind the procedures, and describe and demonstrate each one, breaking it into simple steps. Then practice, practice, practice until the children can follow the whole procedure quickly and automatically. Provide them with plenty of prompts and cues, supervise closely, and encourage them with immediate corrective feedback and positive reinforcement (Brophy, 2000; Evertson, Emmer, & Worsham, 2003; Smith, 2004).

Review the procedures regularly (especially during the first few weeks), and solicit the children's feedback. Their ideas are usually helpful and innovative, and when they contribute to developing or fixing a procedure, they're more committed to following it. Be sure to post the procedures—along with visual cues—wherever they're used.

156

CHAPTER 8

*Preventing
Challenging
Behavior:
Physical Space,
Routines and
Transitions, and
Teaching
Strategies*

It may encourage appropriate behavior if children with challenging behavior—who often have trouble sitting still—have acceptable reasons to move around. It legitimizes activity and builds trust and responsibility when they can sharpen a pencil, move to a comfy seat in the back of the room, go to the bathroom, or dispose of their recycling without asking permission. But you still need a procedure—they must know they can go one at a time, quietly, after the first 20 minutes, or whatever you decide.

Getting from A to B

Transitions present a special challenge for children with challenging behavior, especially when the entire group is involved. Ideally, the day should contain as few transitions as possible, but even after you've examined your program with a magnifying glass there will be some you can't eliminate. In fact, elementary school classes spend about 15 percent of their day in transitions (Carter & Doyle, 2006).

Whatever the procedure or transition, children like Andrew—those with a persistent and negative temperament, those with ADHD or FASD—need extra help from the very beginning. It is imperative not to wait for them to use their behavior to demand your assistance. Keep a plan geared to their particular needs in your mind at all times. For example, to ensure that Andrew will make it to the next activity without incident, ask him to be your partner and label his feelings: "I know it's frustrating when you have to stop reading before you're ready, but let's be partners and we can talk about the story on the way to the park." This is not a punishment but a way to help him succeed, and he should be your partner as often as necessary. By furnishing him with the support he needs to act appropriately, you preserve his self-esteem and enable the whole group to move from one activity to another.

The number one strategy for managing transitions is to give a warning. Tell the whole group, "When I finish reading this story, we will be going outside," or deliver the message by visiting each small group individually. You can also alert the children by flashing the lights, but remember that in some cultures, such signals seem arbitrary, so if you have a diverse group give the children a proper reason to finish what they're doing. Another way to warn the children of an upcoming transition is to sing or put on music. If you always use the same song in the same circumstances, the children will soon know what it means and how much time they have to get ready. Alternately, you could sing or play music during the transition itself, lending a positive, energizing air to the proceedings.

Transitions can be fun.

157

CHAPTER 8

Preventing
Challenging
Behavior:
Physical Space,
Routines and
Transitions, and
Teaching
Strategies

When the class leaves the room for recess, lunch, the bathroom, or anywhere else, it's important to have everyone together and focused, but is a straight line necessary? By the time all the children get into place, Andrew will probably have kicked someone, been sent to the back of the line, or been told to sit down—none of which will prepare him to behave appropriately during the next activity or be accepted by his peers. A key strategy here is to divide the group into smaller units. You can do this in several ways. One is to create a teaching opportunity: For example, children wearing brown socks can go first to the door on one day; on the next, those whose names start with the letter "J" can lead off. Match the divisions you make to the content you're teaching: If you're studying the calendar, the children can line up according to the month of their birth (Jones, 2008).

Another way to segment the group is to have the children stand on shapes you've put on the floor near the door. Arranged singly or in pairs, the shapes should be a reasonable distance apart to respect each child's personal space and discourage pushing. You can choose footprints, geometric shapes, or letters of the alphabet, group them by color, or write a child's name on each shape.

Before lunch or after a messy activity, all the children will need the classroom sink at the same time. Most can handle the crowding and waiting, but Andrew will be convinced the other children are pushing him on purpose, and he'll probably push back. Once again, send the children to wash up in small groups, and to expedite the process, assign one child to distribute the soap from the soap pump and another to hand out the towels.

If you're lucky enough to have a bathroom in your classroom, the children can use it whenever they need to. But too often the bathroom is down the hall, and there's no way to avoid this harrowing and potentially dangerous time of the day. If it's safe for children to use the bathroom on their own, create a procedure where they go one at a time. For example, hang a pass next to the door, and when it's not in its place, the children will know they must wait for its return. If you have to escort the entire group to the bathroom, you will need a different procedure. By standing at the entrance, you can keep an eye on the bathroom and oversee the children in the hallway. Bring along a box of books and have the children sit quietly before and after they use the facilities. To keep peace inside the bathroom, ask permission to install hooks on the cubicle doors to prevent them from slamming.

Another approach—especially effective for cleanup—is to assign everyone her own specific, achievable task. This extra direction ("You are responsible for putting away the costumes") gives children a goal and a clear responsibility. It also allows you to provide a rationale for the children who need one ("You are responsible for putting the trucks on the shelf. Then we'll know where they are when you want to play with them again."). When children finish their own task, they can help someone else ("We're not done until everyone is done") (Rothstein-Fisch & Trumbull, 2008). You can also make cleanup easier by thinking ahead about the number of objects you make available!

Here are some additional techniques to ease transitions:

- Give students who are slow to adapt more time to make a change.
- Some children feel more comfortable when they know all the concrete details: Tell them where they're going, who will be with them, who will be in charge, how long the activity will last.

158
....

CHAPTER 8

Preventing
Challenging
Behavior:
Physical Space,
Routines and
Transitions, and
Teaching
Strategies

- Some children do better if they have a job to perform during a transition: Let them lead the line, hold the door, take a note to the Spanish teacher.
- Allow some children to use a peer buddy to guide them.
- Prepare all your materials before an activity begins. The children can help set up before and clean up afterwards.
- After a noisy, active period such as recess or lunch, move the children to quieter learning by reading them a story.
- Make transitions fun and educational. Float down the hall like astronauts; sing the song about the five little ducks following their mother; count steps; follow the leader's motions; or take a theme from a story you read recently. Many songs and games adapt well to this purpose.

The hardest transitions of all

Some changes are particularly difficult. Naptime, for example, is a potential minefield. Many children, including some with specific behavioral disorders, don't need to sleep or even rest. Others who glide through the rest of the day without difficulty glow with the effort of staying awake and entertaining their classmates during nap. All of this can transform you into a dictator or turn nap into a nightmare. The physical facilities, your philosophy, and the group itself will all play a role in the solution you devise. To begin with, everyone benefits if you send the most tired children to nap first. Next, to allay anxiety, allocate separate areas for sleepers, resters, and those who can play quietly. Nonsleepers will tolerate naptime better if you put on some music, allow them to look at a book, and assure them they must stay on their cots only until the sleepers actually fall asleep. Then they can get up and play quietly with puzzles, markers, and books.

Arrival is the hardest time of day for many children with challenging behavior. They are bringing emotional baggage from home—they're mad because they had to wear their rain boots or upset because their parents were fighting last night—but you may not be available or tuned into their needs. Everyone is arriving at once, parents want to talk to you, and someone left her lunch box on the bus. If a child has trouble almost every morning, it's sensible to talk with the family. It may help if they bring her directly to you—thereby giving her a signal that they trust you and she should trust you as well. But if she's happier joining a friend in the playroom, that's all right, too. Ask the family to alert you if the day's start has been a disaster, and let them know there may be times when you need their assistance.

Communicating openly with families is also important at the end of the day, when children with challenging behavior often revert to old patterns. Encourage parents to give their child a few minutes to adjust to the idea that she's going home. If they sit beside her, help her finish what she's doing, talk with her and her friends, or look at something she worked on that day, she can prepare herself to leave. Tactfully remind families about the classroom rules. Just because their parents are present doesn't mean children can run in the hall or jump on the trikes.

Eyes in the back of your head

In the 1970s, educational psychologist Jacob S. Kounin (1970) noticed that reprimanding one student altered the attention level of his entire class, and he decided to videotape and examine the behavior of teachers and children in elementary classrooms. He discovered that proactively preventing challenging behavior is far more important than responding to it afterwards.

To work effectively with a group, teachers use techniques that elicit student cooperation and involvement in academic activities, keep the classroom running smoothly, and head off behavior problems (Good & Brophy, 2008; Kounin, 1970). These methods are especially critical at the beginning of the school year, when you're setting the tone for everything that follows (Emmer et al., 1980):

- *Withitness*, or having eyes in the back of your head. Without question, this is the most important strategy Kounin discovered. Thomas L. Good and Jere E. Brophy (2008) describe teachers who are "with it" in this way:

  They "regularly monitored their classroom. They positioned themselves so that they could see all students and continuously scanned the room, no matter what else they were doing at the time. They let their students know that they were 'with it'—aware of what was happening and likely to detect misbehavior early and accurately." (p. 112)

- *Overlapping*, or the ability to seamlessly do several things at once. It's important to continue an ongoing activity while acknowledging an interruption, such as a child who needs help.

- *Momentum*, or keeping the activity or lesson moving along at a reasonable clip. This requires good organization and preparation as well as unobtrusive, nonverbal strategies (spending time in all sections of the room, and at the first sign of a possible problem making eye contact or moving closer). These techniques check potential misbehavior in its earliest stages while allowing activities to continue uninterrupted.

- *Smoothness*, or keeping the lesson on track. An effective teacher doesn't lose focus, become distracted, or go off on a tangent.

- *Maintaining group focus*, or engaging the attention of the whole class. You can sustain student interest by using suspense, eliciting active participation, and giving frequent feedback (Evertson et al., 2003).

Brophy (1996) found another important feature of effective teachers: They respond to individual needs and approach each child differently, whereas ineffective teachers use the same strategies with all their students. Teachers must develop a wide repertoire of skills, Brophy suggests. A solid relationship with a child makes it easier to anticipate difficult situations, remind her of appropriate behavior in advance, think about what you'll do to minimize problems, and expect her to succeed (Marzano, 2003).

TEACHING STRATEGIES

CHAPTER 8

*Preventing
Challenging
Behavior:
Physical Space,
Routines and
Transitions, and
Teaching
Strategies*

A child with challenging behavior dares you to examine your teaching strategies—to consider not only the content and skills you want to teach but also the behavior you're trying to encourage. If a task is too difficult, a student will do whatever is necessary to avoid failing. Whether it's a puzzle with 40 pieces for a child who can manage 25 pieces, a circle that requires an American Indian child to respond individually, or a math project that demands a lot of sitting from a very active child, the result will be frustration, and she will probably find a challenging way to escape. Instead of forcing students to fit into the program, you can help them to learn—and behave appropriately—by designing and bending the program to meet their needs.

Don't forget that children have different needs on different days. On Monday, after an unstructured weekend at home or time spent with a noncustodial parent, many children have trouble returning to group activities and a completely different set of expectations. They are usually back in the groove by midweek, but when Friday rolls around they're tired and wondering who will pick them up. Certain times of the year—Christmas, Halloween, flu season, to name a few—are also unsettling. All of this means you must reconsider your expectations and rejig the program, perhaps offering fewer and less challenging options, to coincide with their ability to succeed.

Ultimately, how much the children learn and how much fun they'll have learning will depend on how well your curriculum and teaching strategies reflect the interests, abilities, cultures, temperaments, learning profiles, and readiness of the children in your class. As you plan, think of the child with challenging behavior. If you can make things work for Andrew, they'll work for everyone.

Providing choice

Since Friedrich Froebel founded the first kindergarten, European American theorists have maintained that children are motivated and empowered when they can make meaningful choices about the way they spend their time (Hewes, 2001). If you build choice into your program and give children the opportunity to make their own decisions, they don't need inappropriate ways to seek power and independence.

But unstructured choice time, especially outdoors, may bring out aggressive behavior if there isn't enough to do, if the children don't know how to play or choose, or if the choices don't meet their needs (Slaby et al., 1995). The room will get noisier and messier; the dramatic play area will suddenly become too small for cooperative play; and children will wander around looking for something to do. Be sure to end the activity and offer new options before they reach this point. You can gradually extend free choice time as their social, emotional, and play skills improve.

Some children need extra structure and guidance during free play. Those with limited play skills are easily frustrated or bored and need help while they're finding something to do or learning something new. (There is more about play skills on pages 150 and 163–166.) Children who feel anxious when no one is directing them will manage better if you reduce their choices and remind them to ask for help. Still others know exactly what they want to do and with whom, and if their plans are thwarted they respond with frustration, anxiety, even anger. Jazmine expected to draw with Jenny when she came to school, but Jenny was in the dramatic play area. Jazmine felt lost, unable to connect with any child or activity, afraid no one would play with her. To support Jazmine, assist her in choosing an activity she enjoys or accompany her as she approaches a peer she can play with successfully. Help her to engage, and stay as long as necessary. With your guidance, she won't need to get Jenny's attention (or yours) by throwing a block across the room.

Close supervision will help you figure out which choices to offer. Too many toys and activities breed confusion, but too few create conflict. Providing duplicates of popular toys and materials is a solution for very young children. Older children can share—within reason. You might try doubles at the beginning of the year and gradually replace them with materials that extend the use of your toys. In the block corner, for example, you could add animals, trees, cars, trucks, and people so that the children can make a total environment.

You can also use choice to avert challenging behavior. If you've tried everything possible to help Andrew sit in circle—including a variety of supports for him and the rest of the group and changing circle itself—and he still can't sit through it, you might offer the children the choice of quietly leaving the circle and reading a book, drawing, or doing a puzzle instead. They should also be able to choose to return if they want to. (Be sure to create a procedure for leaving and returning.)

Differentiated instruction

In *The Differentiated Classroom*, Carol Ann Tomlinson (1999) writes, "Differentiated instruction isn't an instructional strategy or a teaching mode. It's a way of thinking about teaching and learning that advocates beginning where individuals are rather than with a prescribed plan of action" (p. 106). You don't have to spend blocks of time with a child to differentiate instruction for her, but you do have to know her well enough to respond to her particular needs and interests. This requires careful planning.

Differentiated teaching recognizes that children have different ways of acquiring information, processing what they're absorbing, and demonstrating what they've learned (Tomlinson, 2001). It works best when teachers assume from the outset that their students have diverse needs and offer them many routes to learning (Tomlinson, 2001).

Ongoing assessment—which Tomlinson (1999) describes as "today's means of understanding how to modify tomorrow's instruction" (p. 10)—is essential to planning. It should begin at the start of a term or unit and continue throughout, examining three student characteristics (Tomlinson, 2001).

The first is *readiness*. Learning is easier and more natural when children are cognitively and developmentally ready. When the work is too hard, they get frustrated; when it's too easy, they're bored. The tasks and materials available for each child should match her knowledge, skills, and understanding and present a moderate challenge as well (Tomlinson, 2005). Because Andrew has poor fine motor skills, he can't cut on a line; he needs opportunities to practice cutting on a blank sheet of paper.

The second characteristic is the student's *interests*. Children who do what interests them are more likely to be engaged in their learning. If you ask them what they'd like to learn and offer them choices, the result is more satisfaction, creativity, and autonomy (Tomlinson, 2001).

CHAPTER 8

*Preventing
Challenging
Behavior:
Physical Space,
Routines and
Transitions, and
Teaching
Strategies*

Differentiated teaching works best when teachers assume from the outset that their students have diverse needs and offer them many routes to learning.

The third characteristic to assess is the student's *learning profile*. Each of us has our own particular approach to learning that is a mix of four different components (Tomlinson, 2001):

• *Learning preferences* are the environmental and personal factors that children favor when they're studying or processing information—bright or soft light, quiet or noisy surroundings, moving around or sitting still, working alone or in a small group, and using sight, hearing, or touch to understand material. However, be warned: A new study has found that matching instruction with children's preferences doesn't necessarily produce more effective learning (Pashler, McDaniel, Rohrer, & Bjork, 2009), so it is probably wise to use a variety of approaches.

• *Intelligence preferences* shape learning, too. According to Howard Gardner (1983), different minds work in different ways. Some talents, such as those with a linguistic or logical-mathematical bent, fit right into conventional methods of teaching and learning; but others—musical, spatial, bodily-kinesthetic, naturalistic, interpersonal, intrapersonal, and existential—show up in classrooms less often. You'll have to think outside the box to tap into this potential (Moran, Kornhaber, & Gardner, 2006).

• *Culture* also influences learning. For example, in individualistic cultures, students understand concepts and facts as things that stand alone, decontextualized; but for children in collectivist cultures, concepts and facts draw their meaning from their context (Trumbull et al., 2000). Do you remember the story of the egg on page 94?

• Last but not least, *gender* affects learning. Boys' strengths are often in abstract and spatial-mechanical areas, whereas girls' brains, which develop more quickly, tend to devote more space to verbal and emotional matters (Tyre, 2008).

Effective differentiation uses *multiple teaching strategies and materials* that encompass a range of reading levels and learning modalities. It also uses *flexible grouping*, which allows the teacher to help different children to explore different skills and subject matter in different ways, at different rates, depending on their needs (Good & Brophy, 2008; Tomlinson, 2005). And differentiated instruction *focuses on the big ideas*, concepts, and principles that give meaning to a topic. The teacher bases her lesson on what she believes is essential in a unit—what all children must learn—and figures out different ways for them to go about understanding it and to be evaluated (Scherer, 2006; Tomlinson, 2005). Everyone's work has to be equally engaging, appealing, and important (Rebora, 2008). Teaching that's based on such careful assessment also prevents frustration—and challenging behavior.

The importance of play

With the introduction of No Child Left Behind and the increase in testing, playtime is disappearing. Recent studies found that kindergarten children spend 2 to 3 hours a day being instructed and tested in literacy and math but just 30 minutes in free play or choice time (Miller & Almon, 2009). Blocks, sand and water tables, and dramatic play props have almost vanished.

But play is fundamental to learning and essential to children's cognitive, physical, social, and emotional well-being (Ginsburg, 2007; Hirsh-Pasek & Golinkoff, 2008). The *Tools of the Mind* curriculum, developed by Elena Bodrova and Deborah J. Leong (2007) and based on the work of Russian psychologist Lev Vygotsky, places play at its center. According to *Tools*, mature, multidimensional, sustained pretend play is the key to developing self-regulation. When children engage in make-believe, they plan an imaginary scenario, act out the various roles, and follow the rules of the characters they've chosen to become—for example, a server in a restaurant must take care of the customers. If she forgets who she is and tries to make the pizza, her peers will correct her, helping her to regulate herself (Bodrova & Leong, 2007). While pretending, children act in a more socially mature fashion, pay attention and remember more deliberately and consistently, and in general show better self-regulation of behavior, emotion, and cognition. At the same time, they are practicing symbolic thinking.

Tools of the Mind has sailed through evaluations by both educators and neuroscientists, providing evidence that the executive functions involved in self-regulation can indeed be taught (Barnett et al., 2008; Diamond, Barnett, Thomas, & Munro, 2007). Children in *Tools* classes significantly outperformed children using another curriculum on tests of inhibitory control, working memory, and cognitive flexibility, all critical for success in school and life (Diamond et al., 2007). In addition, *Tools* children showed substantially lower levels of problem behavior (Barnett et al., 2008).

164

CHAPTER 8

*Preventing
Challenging
Behavior:
Physical Space,
Routines and
Transitions, and
Teaching
Strategies*

FIGURE 8.1 Just before children start to play, help them make a plan of who they'll be, where they'll go, and what they'll do. After they discuss these questions, they should draw, dictate, or write down the plan to shore up their memory.

Source: Tools of the Mind: The Vygotskian Approach to Early Childhood Education by Elena Bodrova & Deborah J. Leong (2007). Used with permission of Deborah Leong.

Because children today may not learn to play, teachers must help. Experts (Bodrova & Leong, 2003, 2007; Levin & Carlsson-Paige, 2006) make these suggestions:

• Set aside enough time. To develop rich themes and characters, children need 20 minutes of uninterrupted play every day to begin with, and they can work up to 40 to 60 minutes (Bodrova & Leong, 2007).

• Provide ideas for themes that extend the content of play. Children can use their own experiences, such as attending a birthday party or visiting relatives; and you can introduce new experiences through books and field trips. In the new situation, point out the people and the roles they play.

• Choose props and toys—such as blocks, paper towel rolls, and cardboard boxes—that can be used in multiple ways, and encourage children to make their own props. For children who insist on using realistic props, sprinkle in a few generic and open-ended items. In a grocery store you might have a real shopping cart to load up with generic boxes and a real cash register to fill with slips of paper. Props help children to remember their roles.

• Just before children start to play, help them make a plan of who they'll be, where they'll go, and what they'll do. After they discuss these questions, they should draw, dictate, or write down the plan to shore up their memory. (See Figure 8.1.)

- Monitor children's progress, and think about how you can boost their play skills. Comment occasionally on what you see, ask open-ended questions, and actively introduce a new character or action when play seems stuck for a long time.

Bodrova and Leong (2007) point out that other playlike activities also promote self-regulation:

- *Games with rules* complement make-believe play by teaching children to conform their actions to mandatory rules.
- *Dramatizations* of familiar stories allow children to act out roles and may provide a bridge to pretend play.
- *Motor activities*, especially those requiring children to start and stop on cue (Freeze, Statues, Follow the Leader, Duck, Duck, Goose, jump rope, hopscotch, clapping to a beat) develop attention and motor control, which are related to later control of mental processes.
- *Art and drawing* activities aid memory. Children can record stories, recipes, field trips, and visits by special guests.

Teachers can also provide children with *mediators*—physical objects that remind them about their role in a particular task. (In *buddy reading*, one preschooler holds a

Time and Patience

Teachers can help children perform a task such as sitting still in circle by supporting them with mediators. Bodrova and Leong (2007) point out you can use more than one:

Lani is very distractable during group meeting time and requires maximum mediation before he is able to attend through a story. He does best when he sits on a carpet square with his name on it, with a stuffed animal on his lap, between two children who hold his hands during the story, and in front of the teacher (four mediators!). With this much mediation, he is able to sit through the story. After [he has done this] successfully for a week, the teacher begins to remove the mediators one by one. First, Lani sits alone in front of the teacher on his carpet square with the stuffed animal. The next week he sits on his carpet square alone. Then 4 weeks later, the teacher takes a name tag off the carpet square and Lani puts it on his arm; he no longer needs the physical reminder of the carpet square. Finally in 5 weeks he no longer needs the name tag. The teacher carefully plans how she will take the scaffolding away. (p. 58)

Source: Elena Bodrova & Deborah J. Leong, *Tools of the Mind*, p. 58, © 2007. Reproduced by permission of Pearson Education, Inc.

166

....

CHAPTER 8

*Preventing
Challenging
Behavior:
Physical Space,
Routines and
Transitions, and
Teaching
Strategies*

picture of an ear, which prompts her to listen. The other holds a picture of a mouth and "reads" a book aloud. When she finishes, they switch roles.)

Working in groups

In small groups, ranging from two to six members, children work together to achieve a common goal. This arrangement yields many benefits: high motivation, engagement, and academic achievement (especially for children from diverse families and those at risk); an understanding of others' perspectives; more interaction and prosocial behavior; and more acceptance of fellow classmates (Ormrod, 2008).

Peer tutoring

Older students can help younger ones, or children the same age can take turns tutoring each other. Besides gaining a deeper understanding of academic content, both children feel needed and empowered and come away with a more positive attitude toward themselves and one another (Haager & Klingner, 2005). This technique works best when they meet regularly and receive training in such subjects as problem solving, sensitivity to others' feelings, and giving clear instructions (Walther-Thomas, Korinek, McLaughlin, & Williams, 2000). For example, PALS (Peer-Assisted Learning Strategies), a structured peer-tutoring program in reading and math, is effective with all kinds of students, including dual-language learners and children with learning disabilities (Peer-Assisted Learning Strategies, 2005).

Partner learning

Children work in pairs to practice skills, do academic tasks, follow routines, and participate in social interaction (Walther-Thomas et al., 2000). In Think-Pair-Share, for instance, students think about a topic, pair with a partner to discuss it, and share their ideas with the whole group (Slavin, 1995).

Cooperative learning groups

Children working in small, heterogeneous groups are responsible for the learning of every group member. The teacher acts as a facilitator, training children in the skills they need to cooperate successfully, planning the academic content, structuring the group's tasks and evaluation criteria, selecting its participants, and monitoring progress. Cooperative learning groups decrease challenging behavior (Johnson & Johnson, 2004), improve academic achievement and social skills, and promote perspective-taking and acceptance of diversity (Slavin, 1995). Cooperative learning groups work for any subject and any age (Johnson & Johnson, 2004). Making them heterogeneous is crucial to their success.

Rachel A. Lotan (2003) outlines five features of "group-worthy tasks" for cooperative learning:

- The task creates and supports interdependence. Everyone is a valuable member of the group because everyone needs everyone else's contribution to complete the assignment. Each member must also be accountable for her own share of the work.

- The subject matter is significant, interesting, and relevant to children's lives.
- The task is multidimensional, making use of the children's diverse talents, competencies, knowledge, and problem-solving strategies.
- The task is open-ended—it doesn't have a pat answer but contains real-life uncertainties and ambiguities that require analysis, synthesis, and evaluation.
- It has clear evaluation criteria that apply to all facets of the task.

A child with challenging behavior can participate successfully in these activities if you remind her and the group that everyone can make a valuable contribution and that she has the ability to succeed. Be sure there's a role that will allow her to use her particular talents, and give her positive reinforcement when she's helping the group reach its goal (Lotan, 2006). It's also wise to place her with a supportive peer and ensure that she has enough personal space.

A compendium of teaching strategies

Children learn better—and behave more appropriately—when they're engaged in what they're doing, and they're more engaged when their teacher is positive, enthusiastic, caring, and sensitive to their needs (Rimm-Kaufman, Curby, Grimm, Nathanson, & Brock, 2009). Some children need your attention more frequently than others. Instead of waiting until they demand it, schedule regular check-in times for them to ask questions, show you what they're doing, or simply touch base. Here is a compendium of strategies that can help make your teaching better.

Get them going

Motivation is crucial—the motivated brain operates better and signals faster (Bronson & Merryman, 2009). Children are more motivated when they have some choice in what they do and the task is challenging, achievable, interesting, and connected to their lives. The more actively they can participate and share their learning with their peers, the better. You can support their engagement by scaffolding, arousing curiosity, offering encouragement, giving specific feedback, and creating opportunities for self-expression (Rimm-Kaufman et al., 2009).

Children's prior knowledge—what they already know—is the starting point for all new learning (Zull, 2002). It is therefore essential to activate and work with that knowledge. Many teachers use a technique called *K-W-L*—first asking the children what they already *Know* about a topic, then *What* they'd like to know, and finally, what they actually *Learned*. All of this helps to make learning deeper—as well as more interesting and enjoyable (Hodges, 2001).

Expect the best

Having high expectations for your students is imperative, because your expectations for each child guide what and how you teach her; and your behavior in the classroom quickly reveals your feelings. Your students internalize your expectations and comply with them. One student puts it this way: "It's okay for your teachers to push you—it just shows they care and they want to see you succeed in life" (Cushman et al., 2003, p. 64).

168

CHAPTER 8

*Preventing
Challenging
Behavior:
Physical Space,
Routines and
Transitions, and
Teaching
Strategies*

Give it over

Just as children can shoulder some responsibility for maintaining the classroom, so they can take on responsibility for their own learning. Give them a say in what they'll learn, and let them set learning goals for themselves at the beginning of a unit (Marzano, 2003). They can also select activities, design their own tasks, and keep a record of their own work, comparing their accomplishments with established goals (Tomlinson, 2001). Along the way they can choose their own materials and learning media, select the order in which they'll do things, lead class meetings, and act as expert of the day or the resource person for a group or project.

Break it up

It's easier to remember one thing at a time, especially for children with memory and information processing problems. They can succeed when they get their instruction in small, manageable pieces. Analyze the content and skills you're teaching, and break them into small segments and steps. Provide concrete examples, visual cues, demonstrations, and sequence cards that list or illustrate each step (Cook, Klein, & Tessier, 2004), and teach one step at a time in logical sequence, beginning with the most basic. Give your instructions in clear, direct, positive language, keep asking for feedback to be sure the child understands, and review the main points at the end (Brophy, 2000). Moving ahead before she has learned a step will lead to frustration, low self-esteem, and challenging behavior.

This technique works for long activities as well as for complex ones, and for the whole class as well as for individuals. If the children can't handle a 30-minute meeting or a 15-minute circle, hold two shorter ones instead; and divide lessons into short segments to give children a break in the middle.

Mix it up

No matter what the activity or lesson, variety will give it some spice. Young children can pay attention for just 5 to 8 minutes, so plan to switch gears frequently (Jensen, 2005). Schedule the most demanding lessons during the time of day when engagement is highest, and put preferred activities (such as recess) after demanding ones (such as math) to act as an incentive (Epstein et al., 2008). Slow down when you're teaching harder concepts, and speed up when they're easier (Yehle & Wambold, 1998); alternate tedious tasks with more exciting ones, and make a few simple demands before you make a difficult one (Yehle & Wambold, 1998). Highlight important ideas by changing your tone of voice and using colored chalk or ink.

To capture the interest of students with different learning preferences and types of intelligence, use different media, including videos, audiotapes, computers, live demonstrations, manipulatives, and assistive technology. Children with challenging behavior and children with disabilities may have strengths in more neglected intelligences—music, art, physical movement, computers, for example. This approach allows them to develop and showcase their unique abilities.

Shake it up

Push your tolerance for the wiggles as high as you can, resist using whole-class instruction and long periods of independent seat work, and make movement and active participation an integral part of your program. During small-group learning, movement is natural and acceptable—by following procedures, children can move furniture, join and leave groups, and confer while they're together. Setting up centers in the classroom builds movement into the day, too. When children come to a center, they have official approval to use their bodies as well as their heads.

In addition to using centers, partners, or small groups regularly, involve the children in acting out stories, historical events, and concepts; turn lessons into games; ask lots of questions and expect lots of answers, alone or in chorus; and let students check each other's work. They retain more and disrupt less when learning is hands-on and physical.

Permit children to work standing up and to use the board as a work area. You can even appoint scribes to write key ideas on the board. Teach relaxation, and when the occupational therapist comes into the classroom to help a child with a disability, the whole class can accompany her as she does her therapy exercises. Take regular breaks to enable the children to stretch, get a drink, stand, cheer, stomp their feet, clap in patterns, sing, or go to the bathroom (Emmer et al., 1980; Jensen, 2005); and allow students to hold objects that they can quietly manipulate to give themselves sensory input (U.S. Department of Education, OSEP, 2004).

Children work at different speeds. If you open quiet activities—the computer area, the reference and reading center, for example—those who finish quickly won't need inappropriate behavior to occupy themselves. This is especially important for students with ADHD and those who lack impulse control.

During art, try taking away the chairs, covering the table with a large piece of paper, and arranging the activity to give each child enough space and ready access to

A Horse of His Own

Four-year-old Noah was prone to meltdowns when he didn't get his way. I worked hard to get to know him, and in November his mother told me that he talked about school and his teacher all the time.

During free play one day in early December, Noah started to gallop around the room. His gallop, like everything about him, was very creative and required both hands and feet. As he jumped around on all fours, the other children scurried away to avoid injury. I told him this play wasn't safe in the classroom, but he said he "needed to gallop."

I thought about this and realized there might be a safe way to meet his needs. I asked him to tell me the next time he needed to gallop and I would see if galloping was safe in the hallway outside the classroom. This turned out to be a successful strategy, and Noah galloped in the hallway at least once a day.

After about 3 months, a day came when the hallway wasn't safe. I held my breath, anticipating a meltdown, but Noah smiled and went back to playing. He trusted me and knew he could gallop again soon.

170

CHAPTER 8

*Preventing
Challenging
Behavior:
Physical Space,
Routines and
Transitions, and
Teaching
Strategies*

the supplies. This will make it easier for children with challenging behavior, who because they often lack fine motor control may become frustrated and dislike art. Select tools and materials that are easy to handle—large brushes, toothbrushes, and popsicle sticks; fabric, cotton balls, and wallpaper scraps; feathers, cellophane, magazine photos, and pieces of colored paper. If you make the project open-ended rather than creating a model for the children to follow, those who have trouble won't feel they've failed.

Wait it out

Although it may drive you crazy when a student with ADHD calls out an answer, remember that although she knows she's supposed to raise her hand, this is very hard for her. To assist her in gaining control, ignore the answer she shouts out, and when her hand goes up, call on her at once. You can help children learn to wait by using a timer that ticks or an egg timer that shows time passing; by teaching deep breathing and self-talk ("I can wait"); and by bookending your activities with clear beginnings and endings (Kostelnik, Onaga, Rohde, & Whiren, 2002).

Ask complex questions and give the children plenty of time to answer: Research shows that waiting at least 3 seconds for a reply will elicit longer answers, more unsolicited and appropriate answers, more questions, and more participation from students who are struggling (Rowe, 1986). As you teach, model cognitive strategies—for example, thinking aloud—that help guide behavior and foster concentration. Anticipate frustration and offer encouragement: "I know this is going to be tough, but you can do it. I'll go slowly" (Kostelnik et al., 2002).

Out in the open

Recess is fast becoming an endangered species. A recent study found that 30 percent of 8- and 9-year-olds have little or no recess—and more trouble paying attention than their peers who enjoy at least 15 minutes of recess a day (Barros, Silver, & Stein, 2009). By allowing the brain to relax, recess enhances learning and helps children handle stress and conflict (Jensen, 2005), so if your school has jettisoned recess, it's important to beef up both movement and break time in your classroom.

However, recess and lunch are mixed blessings. Because they're often boring and poorly supervised, they can spawn aggressive behavior, bullying, and exclusion of children who are different. Work with the whole class to think up methods for making the playground and cafeteria safer and more pleasant. One possibility is to pair a child who has difficulty with a socially skilled buddy who is willing to help on the playground. Another is to talk with the child about her plans for recess and lunch. Help her organize a specific activity with a classmate; later ask about what happened and help prepare a strategy for the next day. You could also recruit adult volunteers to stay in the classroom with anyone who needs a peaceful option, or invite older children to supervise noncompetitive games and activities, a tactic that can ward off both isolation and disruption (Litner, 2000). Some schools have instituted recess programs supervised by a "recess coach" (Hu, 2009), but it's important for children to have some down time to daydream, imagine, and solve their own problems, says Dr. Romina Barros, author of the recess study (Hu, 2009).

Homework or not?

When a child doesn't—or can't—do her homework, she enters the classroom filled with anxiety, fear, anger, or frustration. Escape may be foremost in her mind, and challenging behavior will provide it.

Homework for elementary students continues to spark controversy. Some experts believe children need homework to practice what the teacher has already taught and master the content of the curriculum; develop the skills necessary to complete homework successfully later; give teachers information about who needs extra help and which learning objectives to revisit; or provide an important link between school and home.

On the other hand, homework expert Harris Cooper (2001) has concluded there is little correlation between students' academic achievement and the amount of homework teachers assign in elementary school. And according to Alfie Kohn (2006a), homework doesn't help children who don't listen or understand or who have trouble following directions. In fact, it may make them feel stupid and accustom them to doing things the wrong way.

Homework also widens the gap between rich and poor (Kralovec & Buell, 2001). Middle- and upper-class children can count on home computers and well-educated parents for assistance. But the parents of children on the bottom of the economic ladder may work at night or speak little English, their home may lack a computer or quiet space to work, and the child may have family responsibilities such as looking after siblings and cooking dinner.

If there must be homework, many experts oppose grading it. Cooper (2001) advocates evaluating it only to identify and remediate skill deficits. Here are some suggestions for making it more palatable (Bennett & Kalish, 2006; Darling-Hammond & Hill-Lynch, 2006; Kohn, 2006a):

* Give no more than 10 minutes per night per grade.

* Differentiate assignments to meet children's needs and available resources.

* Assign work that's doable and worthy of effort. When it's authentic and relevant, children have a reason to do it.

* Make reading paramount. But, adds Kohn (2006a), don't assign a specific number of pages or a specific number of minutes.

* Provide opportunities for children to do their homework at school if they choose. Get them started in class to be sure they understand the assignment (Brophy, 2000). When they work in small groups, they can help each other come up with problem-solving strategies (Trumbull et al., 2000); and the next day they can check their homework the same way (Evertson et al., 2003).

In Appendix A you will find several reflective checklists based on the material in this chapter. By facilitating reflection, they will help you to intentionally utilize all that you've learned here about physical space, routines and transitions, and teaching strategies.

WHAT DO YOU THINK?

1. Go to a restaurant, store, or library, or if you're teaching or student teaching, look around your classroom. What are the messages you get from the physical environment? Why? What are the clues?

2. Think of times of the day when defined expectations and procedures would make things run more smoothly in the classroom. Then select one, develop a procedure, and teach it to the class (or if you're teaching, teach it to your students).

3. Create five ways to make transitions fun. Describe where the children are coming from, where they're going, and how you'll get them there.

4. Write a lesson plan for an activity or lesson on a subject of your choice that will enable everyone—the child with challenging behavior, children from diverse cultures, children with varying abilities—to participate and benefit.

5. Divide the class into two groups and debate the pros and cons of giving children the choice of leaving an activity such as circle or story time.

SUGGESTED READING

Bodrova, E., & Leong, D. J. (2007). *Tools of the mind: The Vygotskian approach to early childhood education* (2nd ed.). Upper Saddle River, NJ: Pearson.

Feldman, J., & Jones, R. (1995). *Transition time: Let's do something different!* Beltsville, MD: Gryphon House.

Greenman, J. (2005). *Caring spaces, learning places: Children's environments that work.* Redmond, WA: Exchange Press.

Hemmeter, M. L., Ostrosky, M. M., Artman, K. M., & Kinder, K. A. (2008). Moving right along . . . Planning transitions to prevent challenging behavior. *Young Children, 63*(3), 18–25.

Levin, D. E., & Carlsson-Paige, N. (2006). *The war play dilemma.* New York: Teachers College Press.

Smith, R. (2004). *Conscious classroom management: Unlocking the secrets of great teaching.* San Rafael, CA: Conscious Teaching Publications.

Tomlinson, C. A. (2001). *How to differentiate instruction in mixed-ability classrooms* (2nd ed.). Alexandria, VA: Association for Supervision and Curriculum Development.

Tomlinson, C. A. (2007-2008). Learning to love assessment. *Educational Leadership, 65*(4), 8–13.

CHAPTER 9

Guidance

This chapter describes several strategies for working directly with children with challenging behavior.

We offer you more than one strategy for three reasons. First, people have different styles, values, and life experiences, and what suits the teacher down the hall might not suit you at all. It's important to believe in the strategy you're using; if you don't feel comfortable with it or understand the philosophy behind it, it probably won't work for you. Second, every child is unique, and each requires an approach that fits his state of mind, to say nothing of his temperament, age, stage of development, and culture. When you know how to use several strategies, possibilities open up, and you can choose the one that's most appropriate for the circumstances. As Abraham Maslow once said, "If the only tool you have is a hammer, you tend to see every problem as a nail." Third, if a child's challenging behavior doesn't change over time, what you're doing isn't working, and you will need to try a different tactic—an excellent motive for having many tools in your toolbox.

Because they aren't recipes or formulas, you can use these strategies one at a time or mix and match them.

How do strategies differ?

The process of addressing behavior problems and teaching children to behave in socially acceptable ways has several different names. Some people refer to it as *guidance*; others use the word *discipline*; and still others prefer to call it *behavior*

173

management. The name you choose and the method you employ probably depend on your background and philosophy. In this book we use the word *guidance*.

Strategies vary along a continuum in the degree of teacher control they require (Wolfgang, 2001). *Guidance* usually refers to low-control methods advocated by Haim Ginott, Thomas Gordon, Alfie Kohn, and Marilyn Watson. Their approach is based on attachment theory, constructivism, and the humanistic psychology of Carl Rogers. They believe children are active participants in their own learning and flourish in a supportive and democratic classroom where they can make their own choices and construct their own values and knowledge. The teacher's role is to facilitate their development by attending to their feelings, thoughts, and ideas. Children misbehave because their needs aren't being met or because they lack the skills to solve their problems (Burden, 2003; Greene, 2008; Watson, 2003).

Educators who believe in using more control (Rudolf Dreikurs, William Glasser, Richard Curwin and Allen Mendler, Linda Albert, Jane Nelsen, Forrest Gathercoal) frequently use the term *discipline*. Inspired by the theory of Alfred Adler, they take the position that a combination of internal and external forces governs children's development and a child misbehaves because he has mistaken ideas about how to belong to the group. Children learn to behave appropriately by understanding the consequences of their decisions. Teachers who take this stance tend to place the needs of the group before the needs of the individual child (Burden, 2003; Wolfgang, 2001).

Teachers who use the techniques of Lee and Marlene Canter, Fredric Jones, Paul A. Alberto, and Ann C. Troutman usually call their approach *behavior management*. Drawing on the behavior modification theory of B. F. Skinner and the social learning theory of Albert Bandura, they ascribe children's development to external conditions. According to social learning theory, children learn by observing and imitating the people around them. Because they aren't able to monitor and control their own behavior effectively, it is the teacher's responsibility to take charge and assist them by making and enforcing rules, reinforcing appropriate behavior, and applying consequences for inappropriate behavior (Burden, 2003; Wolfgang, 2001).

This chapter is divided into two parts. Part 1 begins with an overview of what makes a strategy effective, and then describes some specific strategies. Part 2 discusses what to do when a child loses control.

RESPONDING TO INAPPROPRIATE BEHAVIOR

What makes a strategy work?

Although the experts have their philosophical differences, they agree that several factors increase the effectiveness of any strategy. These are the keys to success.

Build a positive, responsive teacher–child relationship. Such a relationship may be difficult and time consuming to establish, but it is vital to guiding behavior successfully. (See Chapter 5.)

Structure the classroom environment to prevent challenging behavior. Since no behavior exists in a vacuum, it's essential to create a safe, caring, cooperative, inclusive social context and physical space; clear rules, routines, and procedures; and interesting, relevant, differentiated instruction, all of which maximize learning, minimize behavior problems, and lay a solid foundation for any guidance strategy. (See Chapters 7 and 8.)

Have high expectations when it comes to appropriate behavior. Believe in a child's capacity to learn, and demand his best efforts.

Spend time working with children on behavior problems, rather than removing them from the group or referring them to the office. The Classroom Strategy Study (Brophy, 1996; Brophy & McCaslin, 1992) found that effective teachers aim for long-term solutions, not quick fixes.

Act intentionally and stay in control of your emotions. Any strategy's effectiveness depends on your behavior during a challenging situation. *Remaining calm* makes it easier to think clearly, solve problems, and prevent the situation from escalating. It's preferable to *keep your voice low and steady, your body language relaxed and non-confrontational* with your arms at your sides (Kottler, 2002), and *your distance from the child carefully calculated* for his sense of safety and cultural comfort. (See Circles of Comfort, page 94.) By refusing to let a child push your buttons, you model emotional regulation, a skill that many children with challenging behavior lack.

Address the behavior, not the person. Make it clear you like and value the child; the problem is not with him but with what he did (Kohn, 1996; Kottler, 2002).

Talk with the child privately. An audience heightens embarrassment and often results in grandstanding, which inflames the situation and makes it nearly impossible for anyone to disengage without losing face.

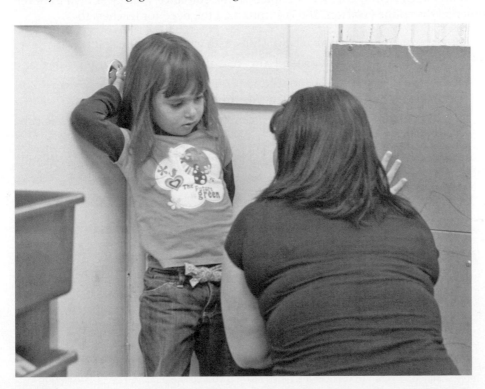

When there is a problem, talk with the child privately. An audience heightens embarrassment and results in grandstanding, which inflames the situation.

Use humor to defuse a tense situation and allow everyone to maintain self-respect (Curwin, Mendler, & Mendler, 2008). Be sure to avoid sarcasm and putdowns.

Be reflective. At the end of the day, revisit incidents of challenging behavior and try to *figure out the message the behavior was communicating* (Kottler, 2002). What thoughts, feelings, or needs were behind it (Kohn, 2006b)? Was the child saying he was embarrassed and frustrated because he didn't understand the directions? Was he afraid no one would choose him as a partner? (For more about behavior as communication, see Chapter 10.)

Start fresh every day. Whatever happened yesterday, let it go (Curwin et al., 2008).

Be patient and flexible. The child has been using this behavior for a long time, and it's hard to change a habit. A new strategy can take several weeks to work, and the behavior often gets worse before it gets better. However, once it becomes clear that nothing is changing, discard the strategy and try another.

Remember that challenging behavior is an opportunity to teach (Kohn, 1996). When a child engages in challenging behavior, he is usually telling you he must learn new skills to meet his needs and behave appropriately. But remember, too, that teachable moments never occur when a child is angry and out of control.

What is developmental discipline?

Based on attachment theory (see Chapter 5), the guidance strategy known as developmental discipline (Watson, 2003) emphasizes the need for teachers to

- Form warm and supportive relationships with and among their students
- Help their students understand the reasons behind classroom rules and expectations
- Teach any relevant skills the students might be lacking
- Engage students in a collaborative, problem-solving process aimed at stopping misbehavior
- Use nonpunitive ways to externally control student behavior when necessary (p. 4).

Brain to Brain

"Emotional states are contagious, brain to brain," writes Daniel Goleman (2006b, p. 77). Whenever we interact with someone, the *mirror neurons* in our brain automatically adjust our feelings to synchronize with his.

The most powerful person in a group—usually the teacher—has the strongest concentration of emotions and is most able to influence others (Barsade, 2002). This state of affairs implies that when you like a child, he'll feel more inclined to like you and more inclined to listen to you. On the other hand, if you dislike him, he'll be less willing to cooperate.

This approach takes time and effort, and at first a teacher may question whether it's worth it. But when you persevere and the class becomes more proficient at both talking and listening, everything will begin to fall into place. The children will care about you, each other, and learning, and you will get your time back.

Developmental discipline assumes that a child's relationship with his care-givers, including his teachers, provides the basis for his development. When those relationships are sensitive and responsive from the start, the child becomes securely attached and learns to regulate his emotions, have confidence in himself, trust other people, and accept support and guidance.

Children with challenging behavior often have insecure relationships (Fearon, Bakermans-Kranenburg, van IJzendoorn, Lapsley, & Roisman, 2010) and may not be easy to like. Like other children, they need and desire caring, trusting relationships with adults, but they often use inappropriate means to make these connections and will test a teacher's caring again and again. In fact, they may regard a teacher's efforts to teach and guide them as a way to control them (Watson, 2003). But developmental discipline stresses the importance of liking a child and accepting him uncondi-tionally. A teacher must therefore strive to overcome this resistance and, without diminishing the child's autonomy, establish a caring and trusting relationship. Rewards and punishment won't work—they just confirm his view that relationships are about manipulation (Watson, 2003).

So how do you help children who need adult intervention but fight it in any form? Furthermore, how do you provide it respectfully and without punishment? Because developmental discipline sees challenging behavior as the result of mistrust and missing skills, a teacher's first response is to figure out why the child couldn't do what was asked. As Alfie Kohn (1996) puts it: "Our point of departure should al-ways be this: *How can we work with students to solve this problem? How can we turn this into a chance to help them learn?*" (p. 121). This process involves lots of talking, rea-soning, and negotiating, with children fully engaged in both problem solving and

Unconditional Liking

In *Learning to Trust* (Watson, 2003), teacher Laura Ecken describes one method she used to convince Danny, who had disrupted her class for months, that she liked him.

I just sat down with him, and I said, "You know what, I really, really like you. You can keep doing all this stuff and it's not going to change my mind. It seems to me that you are trying to get me to dislike you, but it's not going to work. I'm not ever going to do that. If you really need to do this stuff all the time, I can deal with it. I'm going to stop you. I'm going to talk to you about it and explain to you why you need to stop it, but it's never going to change the way I feel about you. I'm just letting you know."

It was after that, and I'm not saying immediately, that his disruptive behaviors started to decrease. (pp. 2–3)

planning to prevent the reappearance of challenging behavior. Once the teacher has discovered what the child needs, she knows what and how to provide help—that is, to teach.

Just as you can use *scaffolding*—assistance that enables children to learn skills and concepts that are slightly out of reach—to teach academic subjects, so you can use it to teach social, emotional, and behavior skills. A caring, cooperative social context, where children know what's expected, supplies the foundation for all scaffolding, and teachers can supplement it with support that meets individual needs.

After a child and his teacher have resolved a conflict and created a plan together, they often use *reminders* or *private signs*—a glance, a few words, hand movements—that redirect the child to the task at hand, remind him of an agreement they've reached, or signal that he needs help. These gestures aren't threats; on the contrary, they confirm that teacher and child understand one another. Owen bumps into Andrew as the class is gathering to go to the gym. Andrew raises his hand as if to push Owen back, but the teacher catches his eye and touches her ear, using their special signal to remind him to use words rather than physical force. Andrew puts down his arm and speaks to Owen.

Occasionally children with challenging behavior construe a reminder as a menace to their autonomy, and in that case it may be wise to avoid confrontation. Instead, make a clear request, ignore the child's defiant attitude, and withdraw, implying you believe that he will choose to do what you've asked. When you give him *time and space*, he may well repay your trust by complying, but if you stand over him, waiting for him to obey, he may see you as a threat, interpret the situation as a win-lose proposition, and act out to save face. You can also literally give children time and space, for example, by sending them to run an errand or get a drink of water, to help them compose themselves.

Developmental discipline also suggests encouraging children to use *self-talk* to take charge of their behavior. When they can analyze a situation and give themselves instructions in their minds, they can choose what to do, rather than act on impulse (Watson, 2003). (For more about self-talk, see pages 139 and 141.)

Your relationship with a child with problem behavior is tested each time he behaves inappropriately. You can protect this relationship by softening the use of power as much as possible, preserving the child's sense that he is competent, cared for, and autonomous (Watson, Solomon, Battistich, Schaps, & Solomon, n.d.). It is also helpful to show empathy for his situation ("Josh, I know it makes you angry and it's hard to react calmly when someone insults you, but it's not okay to ruin his work"); to attribute the best possible motives to him ("Ryan, I'm sure you and Patrick were talking about the story, but when you and I are talking at the same time no one can hear"); and to offer the child a choice ("Andrew, you have a choice to make. Would you rather look at a book or join Darryl at the sand table?").

How does teacher effectiveness training work?

Like developmental discipline, teacher effectiveness training (Gordon, 2003) springs from the humanistic psychology of Carl Rogers, who believed an individual's behavior is primarily determined by his perception of the world around him. Developed by clinical psychologist Thomas Gordon, this approach also emphasizes the importance of the teacher–student relationship, which for Gordon has far more power to influence children's behavior than rewards and punishments.

When a problem arises, Gordon (2003) asks teachers to figure out who owns it. If the problem doesn't have any real effect on the teacher but disturbs the child—and his emotions interfere with his ability to learn—the child owns the problem. For example, on a morning when Andrew spills his cereal, he feels anxious at school and has fewer reserves. He may be unable to wait his turn or sit still at morning meeting. This behavior, whether he's more fidgety or quieter than usual, is easy to miss; but if you don't respond to it, his anxiety may turn into more disruptive behavior, hampering your ability to teach and making the problem yours as well as his.

Open Communication

If you respond quickly to a child who's feeling on edge, you can help him regain control and prevent his behavior from escalating. According to WEVAS (Working Effectively with Violent and Aggressive States), developed by psychologists Neil Butchard and Robert Spencler (2000), the following techniques facilitate this process (Carkhuff, 1987; Gibb, 1961; Gordon, 2000):

- *Using door openers.* Gentle comments or questions ("Can I help?" "Do you want to sit with me for a while?") tell the child you care and are ready to listen.
- *Asking open-ended questions.* Genuine requests for information can reduce a child's anxiety by giving him a voice and a sense of control. *Who, what, when, where,* and *how* questions (which aren't judgmental) facilitate problem solving by helping a child think about what happened and what he feels.
- *Validating and paraphrasing.* It is the child's perceptions that matter here (Gordon, 2000). Let him know you understand his message by restating it in your own words. To a child who says, "I hate Gavin," you might answer, "You're feeling left out." Respond to the need within the message, not to his words. Is he asking for assistance? An offer to support him when he tries to enter the group may relieve his anxiety.
- *Reframing.* Help the child see the event in a more positive light if you can do this honestly. ("Making mistakes isn't stupid; it's how we learn.")
- *Noticing the child's tone of voice.* When he's anxious, his speech may go to extremes and become fast or slow, high or low, loud or soft. If you match his voice pattern, then slowly make your own more normal, you can lead him into speaking more normally and feeling more relaxed.

Teachers can help children resolve their problems. The key lies in listening, which conveys that you accept the child just as he is, "troubles and all" (Gordon, 2003, p. 59). First, you must find a private moment to show you're available—for example, by saying to Andrew, "You look worried. Would it help to talk?" Then you can listen passively, showing interest with verbal or nonverbal cues, such as "I see," a nod, a smile, a frown. But, depending on your comfort level, *active listening* may be even better. As you listen, try to discover the feelings and message that lie under Andrew's words. Then you can restate the message to confirm that you've understood him ("You're upset because you think your mother may still be angry with you"). A series of these exchanges encourages Andrew to delve deeper into his problem, helping him to clarify what's bothering him, express his feelings, and start working out a solution.

When the problem belongs to the teacher—hinders your ability to meet your needs or upsets you in some way—Gordon (2003) counsels the use of *I-messages*. A nonjudgmental way of communicating your feelings, I-messages (which begin with "I") allow you to show your human side and promote change more readily than messages that blame the child or tell him what to do. I-messages let the child know how his behavior affects you and permit you to take ownership of your feelings instead of hiding them. Whenever you use an I-message, you are modeling how to identify and express feelings and helping the child develop empathy. Most of all, I-messages place responsibility for changing the behavior squarely on the child, trusting him to respond in a way that takes all parties into account (Ginott, 1956; Gordon, 2000).

Because they require honesty and openness, I-messages foster strong and close relationships. But their effectiveness also depends upon these relationships—a child who doesn't care what you feel will probably ignore an I-message.

If you're feeling anger, beware. Receiving an I-message that expresses anger makes a child feel you're blaming him or putting him down.

Feelings First

I-messages tell children how their behavior affects others and invite them to find solutions to problems (Gordon, 2000). When you're describing unacceptable behavior in an I-message, it is important to avoid labeling and judgmental statements. This is how to construct an I-message:

- *Describe the behavior.* "When you talk while I'm reading a book to the class . . ." (Note that this statement doesn't judge or blame.)
- *Describe the tangible effect the child's behavior has on you.* "I lose my place . . ."
- *Describe your feelings.* "And I get frustrated because the other children can't hear the story."

The three statements can appear in any order. Don't forget that you can use I-messages to convey positive feelings, too.

After you've sent an I-message, you may have to switch to active listening. Even a carefully worded message that helps the child to empathize could leave him with negative emotions that prevent him from concentrating, and it's important to stay with him until the problem is resolved and he's feeling better.

When I-messages don't work, or when the child's needs come into conflict with yours, the problem belongs to both of you. Solving it requires what Gordon (2003) calls a "no-lose method" of resolving conflicts (p. 220). The steps of the process are similar to those used for problem solving, described on pages 141–142. The idea is to resolve the issue in a way that satisfies everyone, and you will probably need both I-messages and active listening.

Gordon (2003) doesn't believe in using power to solve problems. Power creates its own opposition and reduces a teacher's influence because it doesn't teach or persuade children to change their behavior but simply forces them to obey temporarily. They will return to their previous behavior as soon as the teacher turns her back. In addition, the use of power imperils the teacher–child relationship. Very occasionally, you may have to use power—for example, in a dangerous situation. But afterwards you can repair the damage to the relationship by apologizing, explaining why you used power, actively listening to the child's feelings, or collaborating on a plan to prevent a recurrence.

Using collaborative problem solving

Collaborative problem solving (CPS), developed by psychiatrist Ross W. Greene (2008), resembles both developmental discipline and teacher effectiveness training: All three rely on a positive teacher–child relationship, and all believe teacher and child can find and remedy the causes of challenging behavior by talking together.

According to Greene (2008), a child with challenging behavior knows how we want him to behave and wants to behave well, but he doesn't have the cognitive skills to do so. If he lacks flexibility, frustration tolerance, or the ability to problem solve, his difficult behavior will let you know he's facing a task he can't do or a problem he can't unravel. A teacher's job is to ferret out the reasons for this behavior and teach the child the skills he's missing. She can do this with collaborative problem solving.

Straight Talk

When a child's behavior disrupts both teaching and learning—he is throwing sand around the room, bugging his neighbor, or constantly rocking on his chair—WEVAS (Butchard & Spencler, 2000) suggests using a "teaching response." Instead of telling the child to stop his disruptive behavior, you can tell him what he should be doing. Staying in control of your tone of voice, body language, and affect, calmly walk over to him and say, "Andrew, sand stays in the sandbox." What makes this technique effective without being punitive is the fact that you haven't said "No," "Stop," or "Don't," words that children who consistently engage in inappropriate behavior have learned to tune out.

CPS works best when you use it not in the heat of the moment but proactively, when the child is calm. Before you approach him, meet with the other adults who work with him to figure out exactly which problems he's having, which skills he's lacking, and which situations trigger his challenging behavior. If you observe him carefully, you will be able to predict them. (You can find an assessment form on the Internet at www.lostatschool.org.) Once you've decided on the problems to tackle first, you can involve the child in the three CPS steps:

- *Use empathy.* The goal here is to understand the child's concerns and see things from his perspective. He should know you're not angry with him and you're not going to tell him what to do. Greene (2008) advises starting with a neutral statement about the problem: "I've noticed that you've been getting pretty mad at some of the other kids lately. What's up?" (p. 75). It's important not to rush this step, because if you don't understand the child's concerns it will be hard to find a solution that lasts. To clarify what he's thinking, use active listening and ask him to tell you more. The process may take a number of exchanges. If he has trouble explaining what's wrong—and many children with challenging behavior can't find the right words or organize their thoughts—you can help him by making an educated guess based on your observations. "Ah, they won't let you play with them and that makes you mad" (Greene, 2008, p. 76).

- *Define the problem.* Now you can bring up your own concerns. They will probably be that his behavior is hurting others or others' feelings or interfering with learning, or that it's your job to keep everyone safe. "I'm not saying you shouldn't get mad when they won't let you play with them. The thing is, we want everyone to feel safe in our classroom and to let one another know how we're feeling with our words. When you hit the other kids, I think they get hurt and don't feel safe . . . and they may not even know why you're mad" (Greene, 2008, p. 79).

- *Invite collaboration.* When both perspectives are on the table, you can look for solutions. Invite the child to collaborate with you by restating the concerns: "I wonder if there's a way for you to let me know you're mad that the other kids won't let you play with them without you hitting them. Do you have any ideas?" (Greene, 2008, p. 81). Let him offer the first solution, and if this doesn't satisfy you, offer an idea of your own. Continue to brainstorm until you can agree on a plan that's realistic and mutually satisfactory. You should believe that both of you can follow through. Agree to talk again if the solution doesn't work.

Every time you use collaborative problem solving, you're not only solving a problem but also teaching skills as the child learns to identify and articulate his concerns, think about the perspectives of others, and generate and evaluate alternative solutions. The eventual result is to significantly reduce challenging behavior.

How useful is positive reinforcement?

Positive reinforcement is perhaps the most basic of all guidance strategies—so prevalent that we use it almost without noticing. It draws its inspiration from social learning theory and behaviorism and is, of course, a reward, a pleasant response that follows a behavior and usually increases its frequency or intensity.

A staple of positive behavior support, positive reinforcement is actually feedback. It provides information about the behavior you accept and value in your classroom, and it supports children while they're trying it out, making mistakes, and trying again. It can be verbal or physical, social or tangible (such as an encouraging phrase, a pat on the back, a smile, or a sticker).

Although research shows this technique can be an effective way to influence behavior (Marzano, 2003), its use is controversial. Many educators (Fields & Boesser, 1998; Gordon, 2003; Kohn, 1996) believe that praise, the traditional positive reinforcer, is coercive or manipulative—that it motivates children to do things for extrinsic reasons (to please others) and not for intrinsic reasons (to please themselves or because the task is inherently worth doing), and that once the rewards stop, the motivation will stop, too. In addition, in giving praise, a teacher is passing judgment on a child's performance and teaching him to rely on the views of others instead of evaluating his own effort and satisfaction. According to its opponents, praise also hurts relationships, tells children what to feel, and has a dampening effect on their autonomy, creativity, self-control, self-esteem, and pleasure. The critics reserve special scorn for evaluative praise, which expresses the teacher's approval, compares children with one another, or is very general. Meta-analyses of research (Deci, Koestner, & Ryan, 1999, 2001) report that tangible rewards undermine intrinsic motivation, but verbal rewards can have a positive effect when they're used to give information, not as a control mechanism.

How can you make positive reinforcement effective?

When you offer a child *encouragement*, you can avoid the pitfalls of praise. Encouragement is not judgmental, but places the emphasis on behavior and process rather than person and product. By recognizing effort, improvement, and mastery of skills as well as real accomplishment, encouragement expresses trust and confidence in the child and nourishes intrinsic motivation, autonomy, and self-esteem.

"Our students look to us to learn the standards for success and to know if they are meeting those standards," says Marilyn Watson (2003). They "need expressions of our genuine delight and interest in what they have done and honest feedback about their efforts" (p. 47). "Genuine delight and interest" and "honest feedback" probably won't seem coercive to children with challenging behavior and can help to build a relationship.

It's also useful to *recognize approximations* of desired behavior—effort, progress, and even pauses in challenging behavior—rather than demanding perfection (Barton, 1986). If Ryan, who has ADHD, raises his hand at the same time that he shouts out an answer, that's progress that deserves recognition, so call on him and look for a private chance to thank him for raising his hand. This positive reinforcement must be unequivocal, with no condescension, sarcasm, implied criticism of past performance, or reminders about the future (Webster-Stratton & Herbert, 1994).

If a child can capture your attention with positive behavior and learn to accept your encouragement, he will probably have less need for challenging behavior. And if you look for and acknowledge his strengths, chances are you'll feel more positive, understanding, and empathetic toward him—which may improve your relationship and allow him to behave more appropriately.

Accentuate the Positive

Studies by Carol S. Dweck (2007), who's been researching motivation for decades, show that "process praise"—given for engagement, perseverance, strategies, and improvement—fosters motivation by telling children what they've done to be successful and what they need to do to be successful in the future.

Children who receive such positive reinforcement care about learning and are willing to take on challenges, keep working on a hard problem, look for ways to correct mistakes, and rebound from failure (Dweck, 2007).

To make your encouragement more meaningful, try the following:

- Focus on specific attributes of a child's work or behavior rather than on generalities. ("You felt angry when Michael bumped into you, but you remembered to use your words instead of kicking.")
- Emphasize the process, and let the child know mistakes are part of learning. ("The first few times you couldn't get the bridge to stay up, but you kept at it and figured out how to do it!")
- Point out how a child's positive action affects his peers, the same way you point out how a hurtful action impacts them. ("Look at Caitlin's smile! You really made her happy when you said she could be a firefighter!")
- Be honest, sincere, and direct. Children can spot a phony a mile away.
- Deliver your encouragement privately.
- Use your natural voice, but be aware that some children prefer enthusiastic, intense interaction, and others need their positive attention in small, low-key doses.
- Avoid comparisons between children.
- Help children appreciate their own behavior and achievements. ("You must feel proud of the way you shared the markers with Lan Ying," rather than "Good job" or "I like the way you . . . ." (Dweck, 2007; Kohn, 2001).

What if positive reinforcement provokes challenging behavior?

With some children, positive reinforcement seems to have exactly the wrong effect. At the first kind word, they throw books on the floor or kick the nearest person.

Why does a child react this way? The most likely explanation is that positive attention is a rare commodity in his life, and it scares him. Because he doesn't succeed frequently, he doesn't experience the good feelings and natural reinforcements that come along with success. If his teachers notice he's acting appropriately, they are so reluctant to rock the boat that they withdraw from the scene. On the other hand, they have eyes in the back of their heads when it comes to inappropriate behavior. The result is that most of their interactions with him are negative, and he and his classmates learn that the best way to get attention is to make the teacher angry.

A child with challenging behavior knows exactly what to expect if he punches someone—criticism from adults and rejection from his peers. He has become comfortable with this response and believes he deserves it. Convinced he's unworthy of positive attention, he dedicates himself to the motto, "If you think I'm bad, why should I be good?"

When a child has so much trouble with positive reinforcement, it is tempting to conclude it's the last thing he needs. But such children need *more* encouragement, not less. So what can you do? Combating the child's negative view of himself takes commitment, patience, and perseverance. It requires you to trust, respect, and care for him so that he can learn to trust, respect, and care for himself. It's important to believe in his ability to succeed and look for what he can do instead of what he can't do. If you expect him to disrupt the class or hurt others, that's what he will do. But if you believe he can wait his turn and share the trucks, his potential for success will increase.

Every child does things right some of the time. If you can catch him being good, as the expression goes, and support his efforts at those moments, you will build his strengths, help him replace inappropriate behavior with appropriate behavior, and make him feel good about himself. To avoid overwhelming him, start out with nonverbal positive reinforcement—a smile, a high five, a wink, a nod, a thumbs up. Because each child is different, you must watch carefully to see what he likes, what he's good at, what works as a reinforcer for him, then offer him activities you know he enjoys, books and materials that interest him, assignments he can complete if he tries. Create positive moments with him, doing something he chooses himself,

When children have trouble with positive reinforcement, they need more encouragement, not less.

A Penny for Your Thoughts

When Angela wasn't interrupting me, she was talking loudly or poking the child next to her. When I tried to talk with her about this behavior, she flipped over her chair or demonstrated her mastery of four-letter words. I became so anxious about having her in the classroom that I couldn't find anything to like about her. I kept hoping she'd be absent.

I knew I had to break this pattern somehow. A colleague reminded me that teachers are more effective when their positive interactions with their students outnumber their negative ones—some advise as many as five positive comments for each criticism. My colleague suggested a simple strategy. In the morning I could place 10 pennies in my right-hand pocket, and every time I found a way to recognize Angela's efforts to behave appropriately I could move a penny from my right pocket to my left. My goal was to have all the pennies in my left pocket by the end of the day. Using the pennies reminded me to look at Angela in a more positive way, and eventually our relationship and her behavior both improved.

letting him be in charge, and telling him that you like talking and being with him. Sit beside him or join his activity, share jokes, ask questions about his family, his pet, his culture, and what he likes to do outside of school. Ask him to help you or another child with a task, offer to help him with one, teach him a new skill. Show appreciation for his contributions to the group, his sense of humor, or his sensitivity. Include other children when you can. Gradually you will increase his comfort zone and accustom him to feeling better about himself and less anxious when he is behaving appropriately.

What about natural and logical consequences?

In addition to being a strategy in its own right, positive reinforcement is one-half of another well-known guidance technique: natural and logical consequences. In fact, positive reinforcement *is* a consequence, and as you've just seen, it can be an effective motivating force. Often, however, teachers focus on the other kind of consequence, one that's a response to inappropriate behavior.

According to Rudolf Dreikurs (1964), who developed this technique based on the work of Alfred Adler, the most meaningful consequences flow from the natural or social order of the real world (Coloroso, 1995; Dreikurs, 1964). The child does something, and something happens as a result of his action. The consequence helps him to reflect on the action he's chosen.

Some consequences occur *naturally*: If the child goes without mittens when it's freezing outside, his hands will be cold; if he doesn't listen to the explanation of a math concept, he will have trouble doing the problems. In a situation where natural consequences are too remote or dangerous, teachers often create *logical* consequences instead: After hitting Paolo, Andrew helps the teacher get some ice to make Paolo's bruise feel better. Whether they're natural or logical, positive or negative, consequences are a teaching tool, because the child learns from experiencing the consequences of his own behavior (Dreikurs, 1964). The consequences tell him he has control over his life and responsibility for what he does (Coloroso, 1995; Dreikurs, 1964). They help him learn to make decisions, profit from his mistakes (Webster-Stratton & Herbert, 1994), and express his feelings appropriately (Curwin et al., 2008).

To be effective, logical consequences should be

- *related to the child's actions*
- *fair and reasonable* (Asking Andrew to mop up the mess he made spraying water all over the floor near the water fountain is logical; making him stay in for recess is not.)
- *respectful* (A calm, matter-of-fact manner, a firm but friendly tone of voice, words free of judgment and criticism, and a culturally appropriate and comfortable distance between you and the child make him more receptive to your message.)
- *enforceable* (Think about what will work for both you and the child—consequences should be *simple and practical*, such as asking a child to get ice for an injury he inflicted.) (Coloroso, 1995)
- *enforced* (A consequence that isn't implemented doesn't teach what it's supposed to; instead, the children learn there are no consequences.)
- *instructive* (The consequences should teach the child something useful about his behavior, not that the teacher is mean.)

Be careful, too, that the consequence doesn't reinforce inappropriate behavior—for example, being sent to the principal's office may help a child achieve his goal of avoiding an activity he dislikes or finds too difficult. (For more about the purpose of behavior, see Chapter 10.)

If you have a range of consequences available, you can choose the one that will help the child the most and is the most appropriate for the situation (Curwin et al., 2008). Rick Smith (2004) recommends leaving "wiggle room." "My job," he says, "is to do what will most help each student learn. Period. Sometimes that differs from student to student and situation to situation. It's our call. Therefore allowing for a range of consequences . . . will give us the leeway to make judgment calls, while at the same time being consistent. A simple way to do this is to designate as one of our consequences, 'Student meets privately with teacher after class.' In that meeting we can determine what, if anything, has to happen next" (pp. 173–174). By giving both teacher and child an opportunity to calm down and think about what to do, this consequence prevents them from saying things they might regret, enables them to save face, and avoids a confrontation in which the child refuses to comply with a consequence. It also allows the other children to return to work.

Consequences seem threatening and punitive when they're arbitrary (such as missing recess for spraying water on the floor), or when you're feeling angry or vengeful at the time you're creating them. Your attitude and delivery can actually determine whether the child perceives your action as a consequence or a punishment.

Surprise

W EVAS suggests another technique that gives a child a chance to change his behavior without losing face or feeling powerless (Butchard & Spencler, 2000). The *interrupt* is an unpredictable response that fits neither his past experience nor his present expectations. Because it surprises and confuses him, it stops him in his tracks and helps him to think about what he's doing.

Michael was running all around the room bopping other children on the head with a truck. To stop him, the teacher stood in front of him, but instead of demanding he give her the truck, she folded her legs and sat down on the floor right at his feet. The astonished Michael sat down beside her. Although he continued to need the teacher nearby, he began to calm down as they played with his truck. Soon after another child joined the play, it was clear that the challenging behavior had run its course.

If you elect to establish consequences for breaking class rules, it's a good idea for the children to participate in creating them. (See pages 127–129.) They will know which consequences can help them control their behavior (Curwin et al., 2008), and having a say will enable them to understand and accept both the rules and the consequences.

The WEVAS strategy suggests an alternative form of consequences called an *options statement* (Butchard & Spencler, 2000). Although it offers an explicit choice, its intent isn't to teach a child to make good choices but to get him to stop and think when his behavior is driven by intense feelings, negative thoughts, and previous experiences. Because at this point he is usually looking for a challenge, not a choice, options may surprise him. To make a decision, he has to weigh the choices, and the act of weighing them may dislodge him from his negative behavior cycle and jolt him into thinking and acting rationally.

Because offering choices makes you seem less threatening, you're less likely to push his behavior over the edge (Butchard & Spencler, 2000). It also gives the child some control. When you pose options, use his name to capture his attention, followed by, "You decide" or "You have a decision to make," which hooks him into thinking about his options: "Andrew, you have a choice. Either you can be Ben's partner, or you can walk to the park with me." Again, your demeanor is contagious, so be aware of your body language and tone of voice.

Let the child take his time considering his options. He should feel this is a chance to make a choice, not a power struggle. You could even proceed with other activities, which may make it easier for him to collect himself. If he behaves appropriately, it doesn't matter if he complains. Saying "This is stupid!" allows him to save face and preserve his reputation and self-esteem. By ignoring his remarks and recognizing his appropriate behavior, you give all the children the message that they can comply and still be safe.

If the child doesn't act right away, don't repeat the choices. His actions will tell you what he's decided to do (Butchard & Spencler, 2000). After a reasonable amount of time, remind him of what the choice entails: "It appears you have made a choice, so I guess you and I are going to be partners." If he changes his mind and says he'll go with Ben, respond in a positive way that resolves the situation ("That's great. I'm glad you decided"), rather than in a negative one ("No, you've had your chance") that will escalate it. Otherwise be sure to follow through.

Time-out and punishment

Like positive reinforcement, time-out—which actually means time-out from positive reinforcement—stems from social learning theory and behaviorism. Although there are many variations, time-out usually involves requiring a child to leave the group and go to a remote area of the room, perhaps to a specified chair, for one minute for each year of his age, to think about what he's done. If a child's behavior continues, he may be sent to the principal's office. Time-out reaches its extreme forms in suspension and expulsion.

Misused and overused, the practice has been debated in the education community for years. Adherents maintain time-out tells the child you care and want to help him keep himself in control. If it's used sensitively and correctly, they say, it assists in maintaining a respectful, trusting relationship. They also believe that time-out interrupts and prevents aggressive behavior, protects the rights and safety of the other children, and keeps them from turning into an encouraging audience (Rodd, 1996). It allows the child who behaves aggressively, the child who is victimized, and the adult enough time to compose themselves without giving undue attention to the child who acted aggressively. The National Association for the Education of Young Children (1996) considers the use of time-out appropriate as a method of last resort for a child who's harming another or is in danger of harming himself. It shouldn't be humiliating, make him feel threatened or afraid, last longer than it takes for him to calm down, or leave him by himself unless he wants to be.

Opponents argue time-out is a form of punishment—a penalty for wrongdoing, imposed by someone in power who intends it to be disagreeable in order to decrease inappropriate behavior (Quinn et al., 2000). Does it work? In the short term, yes. But to remain effective, it has to become stronger and stronger, and because the punishment suppresses the undesirable behavior only in the presence of the person who administers it, it can reappear as soon as she departs.

A punishment that requires a child to move to a designated spot creates another problem. Why do teachers expect a child whose behavior is defiant and

---

Outcast

A mother who was searching for child care visited a center in her neighborhood, where a friendly 4-year-old helped the director show her around. He saved his own group's room for last. "This is the science corner where we're weighing different stones," he said. Then he showed her the block corner, the dramatic play area, the art area, and the quiet space where children could curl up with music or a book.

"And that," he said, pointing to a chair in a corner, "is Gary's chair. He's not my friend."

noncompliant to be agreeable about going to the back of the room or the princi-pal's office? Do you raise your voice? Wait until he changes his mind? Or just give up? If you make a fuss, you may be placing everyone in danger and once again demonstrating that the more challenging his behavior, the more attention you and his classmates will award him. Because this spectacle is more exciting than your les-son, the other children may even egg him on. On the other hand, if you decide not to follow through with your original request, he learns he's in control. All of this scares the rest of the class, who see that you can't cope and begin to doubt you can keep them safe.

There are several other powerful arguments against time-out and punishment:

- They make children angry, resentful, and defiant and lead to more aggressive or devious behavior. Some educators suggest a child in time-out is thinking about how mean the teacher is and plotting his revenge (Katz & McClellan, 1997) rather than thinking about his own behavior.

- They teach children it's acceptable to use power to control other people.

- They frighten, embarrass, and humiliate children in front of their peers. Preschoolers report feeling alone, sad, scared, and disliked by their teacher and classmates (Readdick & Chapman, 2000).

- They damage self-esteem by saying, in effect, "You are bad, and I don't want you here." For children from cultures where being part of the group is important, time-out is experienced as shunning and is especially dire punishment (Gonzalez-Mena, 2008).

- They don't address the causes of challenging behavior and fail to teach appro-priate behavior (Katz & McClellan, 1997). The proof is that the same children find themselves in time-out again and again. Indeed, time-out may uninten-tionally increase behaviors you're trying to eliminate.

- They undermine a child's sense of safety and interfere with learning and the de-velopment of initiative and autonomy (Hay, 1994–1995).

- They increase distrust and harm the relationship between adult and child. Kohn (1996) writes, "To help an impulsive, aggressive, or insensitive student become more responsible, we have to gain some insight into why she is acting that way. That, in turn, is most likely to happen when the student feels close enough to us (and safe enough with us) to explain how things look from her point of view. The more students see us as punishers, the less likely it is that we can create the sort of environment where things can change" (p. 27).

Time-away as an alternative

Interestingly enough, some of the staunchest foes of punishment and time-out be-lieve in "time-away," "cool down," "take a break," "private time" or "sit and watch." The two sides agree time-away should have these goals:

- To give everyone a chance to regain control in a safe place so that the child is ca-pable of success when he re-enters the group

- To teach children to recognize when their emotions are building to a dangerous level and to know when they're ready to function again

- To allow the rest of the group to continue its activities

Calm Opportunity

The other children in the block corner were coming too close, and Tyrone was feeling very nervous. He began to knock over all the structures, including his own.

His teacher realized he needed time away. In a matter-of-fact voice she said, "Tyrone, being in the block area just isn't working for you right now. You can try again later. In the meantime, would you like to draw at the art table or pick a book we can read together?" She selected the words and choices carefully. She wasn't punishing or threatening him; she was offering him an opportunity to regain control of himself. She knew he enjoyed both activities and they usually had a calming effect.

Tyrone chose to look at a book with the teacher. When she finished reading, she felt he was calm enough to go back to the blocks if he wanted to. "Tyrone," she said, "I need to help Megan now. Would you like to look at another book or try playing in the block corner again?"

Advocates for both positions also agree that to be effective the adult must be calm and respectful, not angry or threatening (Slaby, Roedell, Arezzo, & Hendrix, 1995).

Unlike time-out, time-away is used proactively. Rather than isolating the child, it offers a kind of redirection, a way to teach impulse control and anger management. You can suggest he take time-away to begin with, but the idea is for him to figure out how to do this for himself. When he feels himself becoming anxious or agitated, he can learn to take some deep breaths, count to 10, or move to a less stimulating activity, such as the sand table. This self-directed change in locale, activity, or stimulation level allows him to settle his feelings, just as jogging or having a cup of tea calms and restores us when we're struggling with a problem. He can return to the group whenever he's ready, knowing you'll welcome him warmly.

Diversity in discipline

Physical punishment is never appropriate in a child care setting. And using emotion as a weapon—threatening, scaring, humiliating, yelling, embarrassing, teasing, intimidating, shaming, insulting, or putting someone down—is also considered damaging, punitive, and unacceptable in the European American culture (Hay, 1994–1995).

But other cultures may consider some of these practices—used in a way that is appropriate in that culture—both reasonable and normal. For example, in the Haitian culture, teachers help children behave appropriately by asking, "Do you want your parents to be ashamed of you?" emphasizing the values and responsibilities of family membership (Ballenger, 1992).

After a year of teaching Haitian children, Cynthia Ballenger (1992) wrote: "The process of gaining multicultural understanding in education must, in my opinion, be a dual one. On the one hand, cultural behavior that at first seems strange and inexplicable should become familiar; on the other hand, one's own familiar values and practices should become at least temporarily strange, subject to examination" (p. 297).

In the mainstream North American culture, adults use guidance to help young children learn to exercise self-control, and by the time they reach child care and school they are expected to control themselves with very little help from their teachers (Gonzalez-Mena, 2008). In many other cultures, however, adults—not children—take charge of controlling children's behavior. Because they rely on adults to correct them, children behave more freely and with less inhibition. If they go too far, the adults use their personal power to stop them—clearly, sharply, authoritatively. This action demonstrates caring (Delpit, 2006).

Children brought up in such a culture may be confused or unresponsive when their teachers speak softly and make their demands indirectly. Janet Gonzalez-Mena (2008) writes:

> It's not too hard to see what kinds of problems might arise for children who are disciplined one way at home and another way in child care. When no one gives children directions . . . do they wonder if no one cares what they do? That would be a strange feeling indeed. If teachers become dedicated to the idea that being fair doesn't mean treating all children the same, they will be able to expand their notions of guidance. Once they know that a child is more used to external control messages, teachers can pay attention to what those messages are and learn to watch closely, use eye contact, and send various signals more like the kind of authority the child is used to. (p. 135)

When families use a different kind of discipline at home than you use at school or child care, you have a lot of learning and thinking to do. What cultural assumptions underlie your own practices? Do you know how adults in the child's culture teach and guide their children? Would you feel comfortable adopting any of their methods? (For more about culture, see Chapter 6.)

WHEN A CHILD LOSES CONTROL

A child who is behaving aggressively is out of control and doesn't hear anything you say. Whether the aggression is verbal or physical, reasoning no longer works: He is driven by emotions and behavior patterns that worked for him in the past. This is not a time to teach. As WEVAS puts it, a fire is burning inside him and it will burn anyone who comes too close (Butchard & Spencler, 2000). Your goal is to put out that fire—or let it extinguish itself. To accomplish this feat you need to know what to do, and you have to remain calm enough to do it. Then you can provide the child with the support he needs to return to a competent state. The better your relationship with the child, the more successful you will be.

You can't focus on a child who's lost control if you're worried about the other children. The most effective way to keep them safe is to take them out of the room. This not only protects them but also removes the audience—and enables the child who is out of control to calm down more rapidly. It's important to organize this

The WEVAS concepts and models are presented in this book with the written permission of WEVAS Inc., 778 Ibister Street, Winnipeg, MB R2Y 1R4, Canada. Email: neil@WEVAS.net or bob@WEVAS.net.

emergency response well before you need it (Butchard & Spencler, 2000). With your colleagues, work out where the children will go, how you will alert one another that you need help (including a signal like "Code Red"), who will take responsibility for the other children, who will remove the chairs (or other dangerous objects), and who will talk to arriving parents.

Like gasoline on a fire, words seem to fuel the emotions of a child who's acting aggressively (Butchard & Spencler, 2000). Until he's calm, talking is out of the question, and you must use your nonverbal skills to communicate with him and deescalate the aggression. The child is acutely aware of your physical presence, and your body is your most useful tool. If you confront him, put your hands on your hips, or use your body language and size to exert your power and intimidate or threaten him, you will make him feel more defensive and increase the possibility things will get worse. Without giving up your authority, you can communicate your openness, caring, and confidence through your relaxed posture, facial expression, and behavior.

The key to this Houdini act is in your head: You have to distance yourself psychologically (Butchard & Spencler, 2000). Whatever the child says or does, don't take it personally. Your emotions can draw you into the struggle, impede your ability to focus on him, and make you less effective. To keep your cool, imagine yourself by the sea, concentrate on the bottom of your feet, or utilize breathing and self-talk.

This doesn't mean you ignore the child or cut off contact. You can remain neutrally involved, giving him attention with your presence, carefully observing his behavior and adjusting your actions. Your message is that you're not going to engage in battle, but when he's ready to make other choices, you'll be there.

To ensure your own safety and allow the child to feel safe, you must also distance yourself physically. Because he's responding to your physical presence and isn't rational, he may need more space than usual. WEVAS suggests a relaxed and flexible standing posture called the centered *L-stance* (Butchard & Spencler, 2000). In the L-stance you don't face the child directly; instead, you stand sideways so you don't seem so threatening. What's most important is the position of your shoulders. If they're at right angles to the shoulders of the child (forming an L), you appear less menacing. Your feet are more or less facing in the same direction as your body, although the front one should be turned slightly toward the child at about a 45-degree angle. Keep your feet 12 to 18 inches apart, more if you think there's some danger. Your head is up but not rigidly high, your mouth and eyes are relaxed, your shoulders are dropped but not hunched, your spine is straight, and your knees are slightly bent. For safety's sake, place your weight on the front foot so that you can move out of the way quickly by shifting your weight to your back foot. (See Figure 9.1.)

FIGURE 9.1 The L-stance sends a message of safety to children who are afraid and a message of stability to children who are out of control.

In the European American culture it's natural to make eye contact, but with a child who's lost control, eye contact can ignite the situation, intensify a power struggle, or reinforce a child whose goal is to get your attention (Butchard & Spencler, 2000). Therefore avoid eye contact when you first enter the L-stance. If you gaze over the child's shoulder or at the middle of his body, you remove the eye contact without sending a message of fear.

Even a child who's acting aggressively has to breathe from time to time. During these lulls it's important to figure out whether he's actually calming down or simply out of fuel (Butchard & Spencler, 2000). Slowly bring your eyes to his to see if he's ready to begin interaction with you again, and try to gauge whether eye contact increases or decreases the aggressive behavior. If it increases or maintains the aggression, look away once more. In this context, eye contact should become a reward reinforcing calmer behavior and telling the child you're there for him.

If you feel his behavior is deescalating, you can attempt to reason with him (Butchard & Spencler, 2000). Smile and try a few well-chosen words that match his new emotional state: "Andrew, I know this is hard for you." Acknowledge his feelings. If you can show you care, his need to confront you may diminish. At this stage the words you use are critical, even the small ones. Instead of *but*, use *and* (which doesn't discount the previous statement); in place of *you*, use *we* (which suggests support); and instead of *should*, use *can* (which implies personal choice). Avoid anything that makes him think you're challenging or devaluing him. "Andrew, I realize you're angry and feeling everyone is against you, and I think we can figure out some ways to deal with the situation." During an aggressive outburst your role is to help the child deescalate and stabilize as quickly as possible. A bonus of this approach is that he learns he can calm himself down.

If Andrew's target is another child and the other child is looking for your help, catch his eye and slowly move in to replace him so that you're in Andrew's line of vision instead. This will allow him to leave and make it easier for Andrew to deescalate. When there are two children fighting, you may have to separate them to keep someone from getting hurt. If they are both assaultive and neither looks your way, try hockey referee tactics. Be very careful, wait for a lull in the action, then step in and pull them apart. Without facing either child, stand between them and wait for them to calm down. Neither will want to lose face, so it may be better to remove the other children from the room. You can also learn specific strategies and releases to respond to strikes, grabs, chokes, bites, and hair pulling. The best way to learn these techniques is in a course or workshop where you can try them out for yourself and benefit from the expertise of a qualified instructor.

After a child has returned to a competent state, it's important to debrief. Find a private, safe place to sit down and talk about what happened, what he was feeling, and what he can do the next time. You may have to follow through with consequences as well. If possible, make this an opportunity for him to collect himself and to rebuild your relationship. For example, if he trashed the room, you could clean up together.

What about using restraint?

When a child is dangerously out of control, your instinct may be to restrain him to keep him from hurting himself and others. There are compelling reasons not to do so. In many places, you must get permission from the parents, a physician, or the

Picking Up the Pieces

After a serious altercation, you need to debrief as much as the child does. Within a day or two, get the team together to discuss what happened. Was your response quick and effective? Did everyone understand what to do? What should you do differently the next time? Note what went right as well as what went wrong.

Be sure to leave enough time to talk about what you felt—frustration, powerlessness, anger, sadness, fear. Acknowledging your feelings in a safe place makes it easier to move on.

school or child care authorities before you can restrain a child. You must also have proper training—used incorrectly, restraint can injure both the child and the adult. Restraint is intrusive and punitive and doesn't teach a child to calm himself or meet his own needs. Some children, particularly those who have been abused, may have extreme escalations in behavior or may suddenly become limp and unresponsive when they're restrained. Others actually seek out the feeling of deep pressure restraint gives them. It is obviously better to teach children to ask for a hug and to hold them when they're behaving appropriately. The use of restraint should be part of a comprehensive behavior intervention plan developed by a multidisciplinary team that includes a mental health professional and administered by a teacher trained in restraint techniques.

What do you think?

1. Now that you've read this chapter, which guidance strategies do you feel most comfortable with? Why?
2. How does your relationship with a child affect your choice of strategy? How does the relationship help or hinder you when challenging behavior is involved?
3. With a partner, role play a situation that includes a child whose behavior is interfering with your ability to teach. Develop a response using an I-message. If the situation calls for it, follow through using active listening and more I-messages. When you're finished, switch roles and repeat the exercise.
4. What is the difference between a consequence and punishment? Create a scenario and respond using first one and then the other. If you like, you can role play this with a partner to see how it feels to be on the receiving end of both.
5. In pairs, do the L-stance. Look at the illustration on page 193 to check your position. Every detail is important. The person playing the child's role should help you to stand so that you give a message safety and stability. Practice in front of a mirror at home.

Suggested reading

Curwin, R. L., Mendler, A. N., & Mendler, B. D. (2008). *Discipline with dignity: New challenges, new solutions* (3rd ed.). Alexandria, VA: ASCD.

Dweck, C. S. (2007). The perils and promises of praise. *Educational Leadership, 65*(2), 34–39.

Gordon, T. (with Burch, N.). (2003). *Teacher effectiveness training*. New York: Three Rivers Press.

Greene, R. W. (2008). *Lost at school: Why our kids with behavioral challenges are falling through the cracks and how we can help them*. New York: Scribner.

Kohn, A. (1996). *Beyond discipline: From compliance to community*. Upper Saddle River, NJ: Merrill Prentice-Hall.

Watson, M. (with Ecken, L.). (2003). *Learning to trust: Transforming difficult elementary classrooms through developmental discipline*. San Francisco: Jossey-Bass.

CHAPTER 10

Functional Assessment and Positive Behavior Support

Every challenging behavior can be thought of as a child's solution to a problem and a form of communication. These ideas go back to Plato, who said that a crying baby's behavior serves a function: She is trying to get someone to care for her (Durand, 1990).

This is the underlying principle of *functional assessment* (*FA*, sometimes called *functional behavioral assessment*) and *positive behavior support* (*PBS*), two linked strategies developed by behavioral psychologists for understanding a child's challenging behavior. Their goal is to figure out what is triggering the behavior and what the child is getting from it—and to teach her a more acceptable way to fulfill those needs (O'Neill et al., 1997; Repp, Karsh, Munk, & Dahlquist, 1995). Together, they enable you to look at the world through the child's eyes.

Challenging behavior isn't really as random and unpredictable as it sometimes seems. By focusing on the child's immediate environment, you can understand where her behavior is coming from, why it's happening at a particular time in a particular place (Durand, 1990), the logic behind it, and the function or purpose it serves for the child (Dunlap & Kern, 1993; Iwata, Dorsey, Slifer, Bauman, & Richman, 1982; O'Neill et al., 1997). Even if the behavior is inappropriate, the function seldom is. Once you understand the function, you can design a *positive behavior support plan*, sometimes called a *behavior intervention plan* or *BIP*, to help the child

198

....

CHAPTER 10

*Functional
Assessment and
Positive Behavior
Support*

achieve her purpose in an appropriate way and render the challenging behavior "irrelevant, ineffective, and inefficient" (O'Neill et al., 1997, p. 8).

Of course, all the causes of challenging behavior aren't in the immediate environment, but viewing it from this angle can be extremely helpful. Functional assessment and positive behavior support are powerful strategies to add to your toolbox, especially when you have already built a positive, responsive relationship with the child and created an inclusive, supportive learning environment (see Chapters 5–8 and 11). Although it takes time and effort to do a functional assessment and develop a positive behavior support plan, it's a sound investment. In the end, you'll spend less time addressing behavior problems and more time teaching.

This chapter is divided into two main sections. The first describes the functional assessment process; the second is about creating a positive behavior support plan. Five-year-old Jazmine, who attends kindergarten, appears throughout. Because of her consistently challenging behavior, her teachers have decided to develop a behavior support plan for her, based on a functional assessment.

PERFORMING A FUNCTIONAL ASSESSMENT

When do you use functional assessment and positive behavior support?

Most children respond well to the universal strategies we've described in previous chapters, but not all. Approximately 5 to 15 percent need extra help, often called a *secondary intervention* (Sugai & Horner, 2002; Walker, Ramsey, & Gresham, 2004). And an additional 1 to 7 percent—more in some inner-city schools—require an intensive, individualized intervention, termed a *tertiary intervention* (Warren et al., 2003; Clonan, Lopez, Rymarchyk, & Davison, 2004). (A diagram of this intervention model appears on page 133.)

Functional assessment and positive behavior support are tertiary interventions; and serious, frequent, and intense behavior problems clearly qualify for their use (Gable, Quinn, Rutherford, Howell, & Hoffman, 1998). More moderate behaviors—especially those that occur often or over a long period and affect learning and social relationships—may be candidates as well (Chandler & Dahlquist, 2005).

It may feel to you as though Jazmine kicks and hits dozens of times a day, but before you undertake a functional assessment and develop a positive behavior support plan, you need to know just how serious this behavior really is. An *informal observation* will provide a reality check by helping you figure out exactly how frequently the behavior takes place—how many times a day, how many times a week—and whether it appears at specific times—for example, only during free play, only during teacher-directed activities, or only at the end of the day when she is tired.

Record your observations on a simple chart with the days of the week across the top and the times of the day along the side. Choose one or two of the most challenging behaviors to observe (kicking or hitting, for example), and put a mark in the appropriate spot each time you see the behavior. If the behavior goes on for a long time, it may be more useful to note its duration. Does it last for 10 minutes or

Power Plus

Although functional assessment and positive behavior support were originally developed to help individuals with developmental disabilities, schools across the country have adapted and adopted PBS as a systemic, whole-school approach for preventing and addressing challenging behavior (Fox, Dunlap, & Cushing, 2002; Sugai et al., 2000). Schoolwide PBS serves as a foundation and support system for both classroom and individual strategies, enhancing their power (Sugai, Horner, & Gresham, 2002).

Because functional assessment and positive behavior support are so effective, the Individuals with Disabilities Education Act (IDEA) of 1997 and 2004 counsels their use whenever behavior interferes with learning or requires disciplinary action (Quinn, Gable, Rutherford, Nelson, & Howell, 1998; Mandlawitz, 2005). The National Association of School Psychologists considers them best professional practice (Miller, Tansy, & Hughes, 1998).

Recently educators and researchers have begun to apply the *Response to Intervention (RTI)* method to behavior. A kind of differentiated instruction most often used to teach reading (Sandomierski, Kincaid, & Algozzine, n.d.), RTI aims to prevent school failure and special education referrals by providing all children with effective evidence-based teaching strategies and curricula and by adding early and quick intervention for those who need more support (Fox, Carta, Strain, Dunlap, & Hemmeter, 2009).

With its proactive, three-tiered approach, RTI seems a natural partner for both schoolwide positive behavior support and the early childhood pyramid model (see page 133). In all three systems, the tiers represent a continuum of increasingly intensive evidence-based interventions (Fox et al., 2009; Sugai, n.d.). Using data gleaned from frequent screening and monitoring of children's progress, a team matches interventions to each child's requirements. Children with the most persistent behavior problems usually receive individualized support in the form of a functional assessment and positive behavior support plan (Fox et al., 2009).

Because challenging behavior is often related to academic difficulties, some schools are integrating academic and behavior RTI into one system, with encouraging results in both areas (McIntosh, Chard, Boland, & Horner, 2006; Stewart, Benner, Martella, & Marchand-Martella, 2007).

10 seconds? (A watch that shows the seconds is helpful here.) Although a behavior's intensity is difficult to measure, it may also be helpful to create a scale of 1 to 5 to figure out how serious or destructive it is.

At the end of the day, you'll know how many times the behavior occurred, and after a week or two you can make a bar or line graph that will enable you to visualize exactly what's happening. Put the dates or days of the week along the bottom axis,

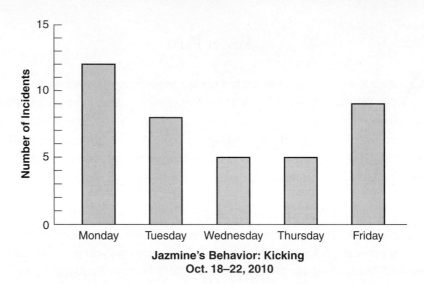

FIGURE 10.1   It's easier to see a pattern in a child's behavior when you make a bar graph with your data.

and the frequencies along the side. You can make a separate graph that shows the times or activities (such as free play or math) when the challenging behavior occurs. For future reference, don't forget to label the graph with the child's name, the behavior you've observed, and the dates. The frequency of Jazmine's kicking shows clearly on the bar graph in Figure 10.1.

If your results show that the behavior is truly challenging, the next step is a functional assessment, which will provide the basis for a positive behavior support plan.

Enter the teacher as detective. When you perform a functional assessment, you and everyone else who works with the child become a team of sleuths searching together to discover the function of the challenging behavior and solve this case.

A functional assessment lies at the heart of positive behavior support. This process allows you to figure out the function or purpose of the challenging behavior and to identify events in the environment that trigger and maintain it. With this information in hand, you will be ready to develop an effective behavior support plan.

Create and convene a team

It takes a team to make functional assessment and positive behavior support work well. Everyone who comes into contact with the child—family, teachers, directors or principals, psychologists, social workers, paraprofessionals, bus drivers—has something to contribute, and when you pool information and ideas, you are more likely to make connections, see patterns, and come up with an effective plan that everyone can implement (Gable et al., 1998). If you have access to an *intervention assistance team* (see page 221), which may include people trained in functional assessment, they should certainly join you.

201

CHAPTER 10

*Functional
Assessment and
Positive Behavior
Support*

Steps for Success

E xperts outline these steps for performing a functional assessment and creating an individualized positive behavior support plan for a child with challenging behavior.

- Create and convene a team.
- Identify the problem behavior(s).
- Identify the function(s) of the behavior(s).
- Design a behavior support plan.
- Implement and monitor the plan.
- Evaluate the outcomes.

To be as effective as possible, the plan must be *comprehensive*—that is, it should cover all aspects of the child's day at home, at school, and in the community. The family has great strengths, knowledge, and expertise to bring to the table, and when they participate in developing the plan they will be more likely to understand the logic behind it, believe in it, and implement it faithfully. As always, a sensitive and respectful relationship is crucial. Work to gain the family's trust and cooperation by learning about their daily lives, culture, interests, and resources; understanding the roles of each family member (who is the caregiver; who is the disciplinarian); and helping them to recognize you're on their side. With their good will, problem solving and implementation of the plan will become easier and more consistent.

When the team meets for the first time, your tasks are to identify the problem behavior clearly and set goals for your intervention. What do you want to achieve? With Jazmine, your overarching long-term goal will probably be to reduce her disruptive behavior so that she can learn and function in class. You can also begin to think about the purpose of the challenging behavior and the conditions that precipitate it. Brainstorming will prod memories and stimulate thoughts and ideas. You may feel certain you know why Jazmine behaves inappropriately, but the situation is probably more complicated than you think. Maybe she wants to get out of cleaning up as you suspect, but it's also possible she wants more attention or she finds cleanup time noisy and overwhelming. Try to keep all the possibilities in mind as you gather information. Eventually a hypothesis—a tentative theory or best guess—about the purpose of the behavior will emerge.

How do you figure out the function of a behavior?

The functional assessment reveals the purpose of the challenging behavior by focusing on the environment immediately surrounding it (Carr, 1994). Because the classroom is such a complex place—comprised not only of physical space,

202
....

CHAPTER 10

*Functional
Assessment and
Positive Behavior
Support*

curriculum, and routines but also of a social context and the many behaviors of both teachers and children—functional assessment asks teachers to look at it in a special way called an *A-B-C analysis* (Bijou, Peterson, & Ault, 1968; O'Neill et al., 1997).

A stands for *antecedents*—events that take place right before the challenging behavior and seem to trigger it. The research mentions demands, requests, difficult tasks, transitions, interruptions, and being left alone (O'Neill et al., 1997). Peers' actions can be antecedents, too—think of teasing, bullying, showing off, coming too close, and exclusion. When you flash the lights and start to sing the cleanup song (which signal it's time to clean up), Jazmine kicks or hits Liane. The flashing lights and the cleanup song are the antecedents.

It is often hard to distinguish between antecedents and their more distant relations—known as *setting events*—that occur before or around the antecedents. Setting events make the child more vulnerable to the antecedents and the challenging behavior more likely (Durand, 1990; Repp et al., 1995). The adults who are present or absent (a substitute teacher often inspires challenging behavior), changes in routine, the number of children in the group, the setup of the room, the noise level, the lighting, the type of activity, the sequence of activities, and the time of day can all act as setting events. Setting events also include the child's physical or emotional state—being hungry, tired, or sick; being on medication (or not); spending the weekend with the noncustodial parent; having a parent deployed; being forbidden to bring a favorite toy to school; being pushed on the bus; and so on. Even the child's culture can be a setting event if behavior that's appropriate or encouraged at home is unacceptable at school (Sheridan, 2000). Setting events are hard to pin down, often depend on information supplied by someone else, or are just plain unknowable (you probably won't know that Jazmine's mother had an important meeting at 8 A.M. and rushed Jazmine through her morning routine). Setting events may be difficult or impossible to alter, but sometimes they are easy to identify and amenable to change, so it's important to look for them.

B stands for *behavior*, which you must describe so clearly and specifically that anyone who's observing can recognize and measure it (not "Jazmine is aggressive" but "Jazmine kicks and hits other children") (Durand, 1990; Gable et al., 1998). If the child has several challenging behaviors, describe them all, because you will need to find out if they serve the same or different functions ("Jazmine also swears, and sometimes she spits"). Of course you can't observe or

Difficult tasks, demands, requests, transitions, and interruptions often trigger challenging behavior.

measure thoughts or feelings such as sadness or anger—but you can observe and measure crying, yelling, or throwing chairs.

C stands for *consequences*—that is, What happens after the challenging behavior? Here you must look at your own actions as well as the response of Jazmine's peers. Did you pretend not to see her kick Liane? Did you reprimand her sternly, take her aside for a private conversation, or change her seat? Did you redirect her to another activity or send her to the office? Did the other children laugh, join in, move away, or tell her to stop? Any of these responses, positive or negative, may have an effect on Jazmine's behavior and serve to reinforce and maintain it.

What functions can behavior serve?

Taken together, the A-B-C analysis and the setting events form a pattern that points you toward the function or purpose of the challenging behavior. Functional assessment postulates three possible functions:

• *The child gets something* (attention from an adult or a peer, access to an object or an activity, and so on). When Jazmine kicks Liane, she gets attention in the form of a yelp from her classmate and a reprimand or private conversation with you. Because she's obtaining something she wants, her behavior is being positively reinforced, and it will probably continue.

• *The child avoids or escapes from something* (unwelcome requests, difficult tasks or activities, contacts with particular peers or adults, and the like). Ronnie, who is clumsy at gross motor activities, pushes his classmates in the gym. You remove him to the sidelines—and he doesn't have to participate. This response strengthens his behavior and increases the likelihood it will persist.

• *The child changes the level of stimulation.* All people try to maintain their own comfortable level of stimulation, and when they get too much or too little, they act to change it (Karsh, Repp, Dahlquist, & Munk, 1995; Repp et al., 1995). When Jamal has to sit in circle for more than 8 minutes or wait in line to go to the bathroom, he pokes and pushes the children around him, and the world instantly becomes more stimulating. Because he is changing the level of stimulation in the environment, his behavior is creating its own reinforcement (Iwata, Vollmer, & Zarcone, 1990).

What about appropriate behavior?

It may seem as if the child never behaves appropriately, but when you keep your eyes and mind open you will discover this is by no means the case. Appropriate behavior also has antecedents, consequences, and setting events (O'Neill et al., 1997). Because part of planning an effective intervention is knowing how to increase the child's appropriate behaviors, you'll need to know what engages her, where her talents lie, which peers and teachers she's comfortable with, whether she likes being in structured or unstructured settings, in a small group, with a partner, or on her own. Tuning into Jazmine's preferences and strengths—her energy, her persistence, her intelligence, her love of drawing—will enable you to provide her with new acceptable behaviors and potent reinforcers for them.

204
....

CHAPTER 10

*Functional
Assessment and
Positive Behavior
Support*

What will help you understand the function of the behavior?

Reviewing records

To figure out the function of Jazmine's behavior and develop a hypothesis, you will need current and accurate data, and the more sources you have, the more accurate the information is likely to be (Dunlap & Kern, 1993; Durand, 1990). Official records are an obvious starting point. Although schools and centers often have policies about opening their files, they should make information available when the challenging behavior is serious. Medical forms, incident reports, grades, children's personal files, and your own daily logs may be hiding valuable nuggets. It's especially important to read the notes on any previous behavior management plans. Have any strategies worked with this child, even for a while? Which didn't? You don't want to repeat them!

Perusing Jazmine's file, you see she has attended three child care centers. One center suggested testing for ADHD, but her family hasn't followed up.

Conducting interviews

Once again, it's tempting to assume you already know all there is to know, but a formal interview helps to put the information into a structured format—and may surprise you (Durand, 1990). You can begin by interviewing members of the team, starting with the family, who can add important background information and insights. This is a good opportunity to ask about setting events: Sleeping and eating habits, allergies, medical conditions, medications, events in the community, or family problems may all be influencing Jazmine's behavior. Her mother tells you she comes home late from work, and because her daughter waits up for her Jazmine often goes to school tired.

A family from a diverse culture may find the functional assessment process inappropriate, intrusive, or just plain strange (Sheridan, 2000), so be sure to seek their permission to ask questions before you start. Remember to take your own cultural bias into account as well. Because the family may see both the problem and the solution quite differently than you do, it's a good idea to emphasize solutions (Sheridan, 2000). Their participation and belief in the process are crucial to successful implementation of the plan.

You can also interview other members of your team, including Jazmine's teachers, past and present (O'Neill et al., 1997). The teacher at the after-school program tells you Jazmine enjoys art and gym—not a surprise—and she gets along well with some of the older children. The bus driver mentions Jazmine is frequently in a bad mood when she boards the bus in the morning, and she swaggers down the aisle bugging the other children until she finds a seat alone at the back.

Don't overlook the most obvious source of all: the child herself. Even a 5-year-old can shed light on what causes her reactions. Talk with her in a quiet place when she's feeling calm and good about herself. Stay away from *why* questions, which make some children feel defensive, and zero in on her preferences and pleasures as well as her complaints. If your manner, voice, and body language are open, warm, and unthreatening, some very useful information may emerge.

You can take questions from existing questionnaires (see the box below) or make them up yourself. Include some queries about the A-B-Cs. Which circumstances almost always surround this child's challenging behavior and which never do (Dunlap & Kern, 1993; O'Neill et al., 1997)? Does the interviewee have a theory about why the child is behaving this way? Interviews also help you to fill in the particulars about previous interventions, especially if you're talking to someone who took part in them.

Collecting Clues

When you're interviewing people who know the child well, experts (Durand, 1990; Gable et al., 1998; Iwata et al., 1990; O'Neill et al., 1997; Quinn et al., 1998) suggest you ask such questions as these:

- Which of the child's behaviors do you consider challenging, and what do they look like?
- When and where does this behavior occur?
- When and where does the child behave appropriately? Which activities does she enjoy?
- Who is present when the challenging behavior occurs? Who is present when the child is behaving appropriately?
- What activities, events, and interactions take place just before the challenging behavior? How predictable is the child's daily schedule? How much waiting is there? How much choice does she have? When the routine changes, does her behavior change?
- What happens after the challenging behavior? How do you react? How do the other children react? Does the child get something from the behavior, such as your attention or a favorite snack? Does she avoid something, such as cleaning up or wearing her rain boots? According to Brian Iwata (1994), one of the pioneers of functional assessment, "Parents, teachers, and other caregivers sometimes can describe the functional characteristics of a [child's] behavior problem with uncanny accuracy" (p. 414).
- Can you think of a more acceptable behavior that might replace the challenging behavior?
- What activities does the child find difficult?
- Which approaches work well with her, and which don't? Does she prefer her interaction with you to be loud or soft, fast or slow? How much personal space does she need? If a particular family member or staff is especially successful with her, what does she do?
- If the child is from a different culture, this behavior may not have the same meaning for the family as it does for you. Does it trouble them? Why or why not? How would they like you to respond to it?

206

CHAPTER 10

*Functional
Assessment and
Positive Behavior
Support*

Observing the child and the environment

By far the best way to learn about a child's behavior is to observe and collect data about it (O'Neill et al., 1997). As the great New York Yankee catcher Yogi Berra once said, "You can observe a lot just by watching."

There are two major reasons to observe a child's challenging behavior. The first is that it gives your assessment a scientific base. Collecting data before, during, and after an intervention allows you to find out precisely what you're dealing with and reliably measure any change that occurs. The second reason is to enable you to see the relationship between the immediate environment and the challenging behavior more directly (Dunlap & Kern, 1993; Repp et al., 1995)—in other words, to pinpoint what triggers the behavior, what consequences are maintaining it, and what the child is getting or avoiding as a result.

If your team includes a special education teacher or someone else trained in functional assessment, he or she should observe the child; and the principal or the school psychologist might also lend a hand. You can even do an observation yourself—you may be able to collect some very good data without outsiders around to make you nervous, distract the children, and change the environment (Durand, 1990; O'Neill et al., 1997). In fact, anyone who spends time with the child should participate.

Although teachers recognize that observing behavior is crucial to intentional teaching, observation isn't often a priority. Teaching and observing at the same time takes willpower, a quick and perceptive eye, and a good memory. One of the most daunting aspects of this process is watching yourself: You are observing not only the child's behavior but also your own. Fortunately, it's like any other skill, and the more you practice, the easier it will become.

Your own previous experience with a child—or a reputation that precedes her—can make it difficult to observe objectively. Teachers tend to see what they expect to see—especially if they're expecting challenging behavior. Self-reflection can help. Try to identify your biases so that you can observe what's actually happening.

This is where the A-B-C analysis comes in. Using the data the team has gathered so far as a guide, select two or three behaviors to observe more closely. Plan to observe during a variety of activities, routines, times, and days so that you'll see when and where the behavior occurs—and doesn't. Pay close attention to what happened just before the challenging behavior, who was involved, and what happened afterwards.

There are many ways to record your observations. One is to make a basic *A-B-C chart*. (Don't forget to put in the child's name, the date, the time, and the subject and/or teacher.) Or you can use a special *functional assessment observation form* developed by O'Neill and his colleagues (1997). (For examples and explanations of how to use both charts, see Appendices B and C.) If you stash the chart on a clipboard in a convenient spot in the classroom, you can fill it in as you watch. Sometimes it isn't possible to do this, so wear an apron or clothing with pockets and carry a pen, pad, note cards, or sticky notes. Write down what you see and when you have a moment (at lunch, naptime, the end of the day), transcribe the information onto the chart. It may be easier to begin with an A-B-C chart and transfer the information to a functional assessment form later. Everyone who observes should record and initial her impressions.

Collect data until a clear pattern emerges. This usually takes at least 15 to 20 incidents over 2 to 5 days (O'Neill et al., 1997). Be careful not to jump to conclusions or interpret the data prematurely. If you've made a substantial effort and things still

207
....

CHAPTER 10

*Functional
Assessment and
Positive Behavior
Support*

One for All and All for One
....

In a study in Illinois, researchers trained teams working with preschool children in special education and at-risk classes in the use of functional assessment and positive behavior support (Chandler, Dahlquist, Repp, & Feltz, 1999). The result? Addressing the behavior of one child substantially lowered the challenging behavior of the whole class. At the same time, both active engagement and peer interaction rose, creating a better learning environment for everyone.

aren't clear, perhaps your description of the target behavior isn't specific enough or your personal biases are getting in the way. You may need to bring in additional help.

How do you develop a hypothesis?

When you have enough information, call the team together for another brainstorming session. It's time to create a hypothesis and a hypothesis statement. To do this, you must analyze your data and come to a conclusion about what it shows. What triggers the challenging behavior? What are the consequences that maintain it? And what purpose or function does it serve for the child?

Looking at the functional assessment observation form on page 280, you can see that Jazmine's problem behavior is tied to certain transitions. When you ask her to clean up or get ready for lunch, she responds by kicking or hitting. But you notice she rarely kicks or hits during the afternoon cleanup and other transitions when she is with Grace. What is Grace doing differently, and what does that tell you about the function of the behavior?

The data show that you flick the lights and sing the cleanup song to signal a transition—and Jazmine often kicks or hits another child. But in the team meeting Grace says that when she is in charge of the cleanup transition, she speaks to every child individually and gives each of them specific tasks to complete before she flicks the lights and sings. Then she gets Jazmine started on her assigned task and stays with her until it's clear she knows exactly what to do. Jazmine doesn't kick or hit. This gives a hint about the function: Before and during cleanup, Grace spends time with Jazmine and makes sure she knows what she's supposed to do. Perhaps Jazmine is looking for attention and direction.

Because consequences often reinforce and maintain challenging behavior, your observation will help to clarify this hypothesis. What you see is that when Jazmine kicks, you always give her attention by sternly reminding her of the rules and keeping her at your side until the next activity is under way. Suddenly you realize that by giving Jazmine attention you have inadvertently reinforced the kicking! As is often the case with children with challenging behavior, Jazmine doesn't care whether the attention she gets is positive or negative, as long as she gets attention.

Now you can make a hypothesis statement: When Jazmine doesn't know what to do, she kicks and hits in order to get attention and assistance. The maintaining consequence is that you reprimand her and help her move into the next activity. Be sure your hypothesis statement describes the trigger event or antecedent, the behavior, the function, and the maintaining consequences.

208

CHAPTER 10

*Functional
Assessment and
Positive Behavior
Support*

CREATING A POSITIVE BEHAVIOR SUPPORT PLAN

How do you develop a positive behavior support plan?

With a clear hypothesis statement to guide you, you can create a behavior support plan that teaches the child how to get what she wants through appropriate means and lays out what you and the other adults must do to sustain that behavior (Quinn et al., 1998). In addition to identifying the behavior with its antecedents and consequences, a positive behavior support plan for the child includes

- developing long- and short-term goals for the child
- identifying changes to be made in the child's environment to prevent the challenging behavior
- identifying and teaching skills to replace the challenging behavior
- specifying how everyone will respond when the child uses the new appropriate skills and when she uses challenging behavior
- an evaluation framework

Trigger	Behavior	Maintaining Consequence
	Function	
Preventions	**Goals/Skills**	**New Responses**
		To challenging behavior: To use of new skill:

FIGURE 10.2 A Behavior Support Planning Chart displays the plan in a clear form.

Source: Adapted from *Positive Behavior Support* by Lise Fox and Michelle A. Duda. Reproduced with permission. www.challengingbehavior.org

At this point you're ready to set long- and short-term goals for Jazmine. The positive behavior support team believes that their original long-term goal—to reduce her disruptive behavior so that she can learn and function in class—is still correct. The members decide that a short-term objective should be for her to learn to ask for help when she's confused or doesn't understand a request.

The next step is to figure out the strategies that will teach her how to get what she wants through appropriate means (O'Neill et al., 1997). There are four ways to accomplish this, and you should probably use them all (Dunlap et al., 2006): *prevention* (changing the environment so she won't need the challenging behavior); *teaching replacement skills* (replacing the challenging behavior with appropriate behavior that achieves the same purpose); *recognizing appropriate behavior*; and *responding to inappropriate behavior in a manner that doesn't reinforce it*.

Prevention

This is perhaps the easiest way to address challenging behavior. Rather than trying to change the child, you can change the environment, including your own behavior. As psychologist Kevin Leman (1992) points out, there is no way to change anyone else's behavior. You can only change your own, and when you do, the strangest thing happens: Other people make the behavior changes you've been hoping for.

Begin with the setting events if you can. Jazmine's mother has mentioned that Jazmine isn't hungry at 6:30 A.M., which is the last chance she has to eat before they leave home in the morning. You realize that Jazmine will probably have more self-control if she eats something, and you decide to offer her a breakfast snack as soon as she arrives. You also decide to teach her to request a snack if she is hungry.

The next step is to change the antecedents. This usually involves changing the physical setup, routines, curriculum, your expectations, and your approach to the child to eliminate opportunities for the challenging behavior to arise. Sometimes this is as simple as reminding her of what is appropriate before the activity begins, reassuring her that you'll provide any assistance she needs, or changing your tone of voice or body language when you're making a request or giving directions.

Because you've hypothesized that Jazmine needs more attention during cleanup and other difficult transitions, you and the rest of the team decide to change your routine. Just before cleanup, you will warn all the children individually and assign each of them a specific achievable task, giving Jazmine a job she likes. Then you can give the cleanup signal—flicking the lights and singing the cleanup song—and help Jazmine get started. You will reinforce her efforts to put things away even if they're only close approximations. That way, she'll achieve her goal of having your attention without kicking or hitting. Better still, you will reinforce her appropriate behavior so that she realizes she can get your attention and assistance by behaving appropriately. (For more about how to prevent challenging behavior, see Chapters 7 and 8.)

In the case of Ronnie, whom the behavior support team hypothesized was pushing his classmates in the gym to avoid doing the planned physical activities, you decide to change your program completely. Instead of taking your class to the gym, you will do some gentler physical activities in the classroom—games with scarves and music and daily yoga poses, which you will connect with a story (turtle,

210

CHAPTER 10

*Functional
Assessment and
Positive Behavior
Support*

tree, etc.) to keep the group interested. The easy movement will reduce Ronnie's anxiety and help him gain body awareness, strength, and coordination.

Interestingly, the team's observations show that Jamal, who poked his neighbors while he was standing in line and sitting in circle, stays on task in art and gym, activities that require active physical participation. This leads to the conclusion that he needs more stimulation, as the team had hypothesized. You decide to get the whole class up and moving more often. You will make the transitions more active, eliminate lines entirely, and add some small-group and partner activities. To enable Jamal to leave circle and other whole-group activities without using challenging behavior, you will create procedures that allow children to leave, join, or rejoin an activity appropriately. (With older children you might decide to make it easier to get a drink, sharpen a pencil, and go to the bathroom.)

Depending on the results you get with these tactics, perhaps later the team will try the *Tools of the Mind* (Bodrova & Leong, 2007) approach and give Jamal more help staying in circle—something to hold, something to sit on, friends beside him. In addition, Jamal's teacher decides she will try to increase her own tolerance of his movement around the classroom by regarding it as a physical need, not a desire to disrupt learning. Her colleagues suggest using the impulse control techniques she teaches the children—breathing slowly, counting to 10 backwards—to help her stay calm. If she can resist responding to his perambulations, she can reduce the stimulation she provides and concentrate instead on making the environment more stimulating in legitimate ways.

Teaching appropriate replacement skills

It is not enough to decide what the child must stop doing. You must also know what you want her to do instead—and what will enable her to achieve the same results she got with her challenging behavior just as efficiently and effectively. If possible, choose a replacement behavior that utilizes strengths and skills she already has. You can prompt her to use it at times when the problem behavior usually occurs, and teach and reinforce it throughout the day.

Different children lack different skills, so in addition to teaching them how to ask for help or take a break, you could teach virtually anything, be it physical, social, emotional, or cognitive— how to hold a pencil or cut with scissors, how to join in or wait for a turn, how to control anger or use words to express it. "Remember that teaching is among the most powerful behavior management tools at our disposal," O'Neill and his colleagues write (1997, p. 74). Plan to start with skills the child can learn quickly and easily—it's important for her to experience success as soon as possible. Sometimes we think that if we wait the child will learn the skill when she's ready, but in reality she often becomes convinced that her classmates don't like her or she's incapable of learning.

Teaching new skills is one of the best ways to prevent problem behaviors.

Give the child plenty of opportunities to use the new skill and give yourself plenty of opportunities to reinforce it with words, body language, and activities she enjoys. Remember to respond to every attempt and every close approximation, stressing effort and improvement, especially in the beginning. To get rid of the old behavior, the new one has to be very successful indeed (Durand, 1990). It's also a good idea to teach new skills as part of the daily routine—children will learn and generalize them more readily if they learn them where they use them (Durand, 1990; Gable et al., 2000).

Jazmine's team decides to teach her an unobtrusive way to ask for assistance when she's confused so that she doesn't have to advertise that she needs help. Together you will arrange a private signal, and whenever she asks appropriately by touching her nose, you will promptly provide positive reinforcement by giving her the help and attention she needs.

Although you are already teaching social and emotional skills to the entire class, you think that Jazmine may need extra help. Improving these skills is a long-term goal, and you will start by helping her recognize when she's feeling confused or uncertain as well as other emotions. Any time she identifies her feelings, you will give her lots of positive reinforcement.

The team plans to teach Ronnie an appropriate way to ask for a break from physical activity, but because he has difficulty in this area, they realize they can't allow him to avoid it entirely: They must actively teach him some physical skills. In addition to the daily yoga in the classroom, in a few weeks you will try some games in the gym using colored shapes on the floor. You will also try a small-group activity where the children sit on the floor and roll a large ball. You will encourage all Ronnie's attempts, no matter how feeble or wild. If he feels overwhelmed, he can use his new skill to ask for a break appropriately. At the same time, you decide to motivate and reinforce him by letting him choose a favorite activity when gym time is over (Repp et al., 1995). By improving Ronnie's competence and self-esteem, you hope to increase both his fun and his willingness to try. You know that gym is going to be hard for him for a long time, and you must continue to support him. (This is what positive behavior support is all about!) Then you resolve to take a fitness class yourself—if you join in more, maybe Ronnie will, too.

For Jamal, the team needs to find replacement behaviors that will raise his stimulation level—that is, appropriate ways for him to move around the classroom and engage his peers. You will teach him to ask for a break when he can't sit still or stay focused, and together you'll work out a list of things he can do when he needs to move—work at the board, sit on a ball, set the tables, water the plants, take books back to the library, take notes to the office.

Responding to appropriate and challenging behavior

Your individualized behavior support plan depends heavily on your prompt and positive recognition of appropriate replacement behavior that meets the child's needs. Be sure to choose a method that's appropriate for the function of the behavior. It will take time for her to realize you are serious, but if you hold steady she will figure out that her appropriate behavior and replacement skills are working better than her challenging behavior, and it will diminish in force and frequency. You discover that Jazmine loves to have her back rubbed. When she's behaving appropriately, you will

212

CHAPTER 10

*Functional
Assessment and
Positive Behavior
Support*

Prep Time

Children often use challenging behavior to escape from situations they don't have the skills to handle. They may want to avoid feeling frustrated, stupid, or confused, and they may worry that their peers (or the teacher) will make fun of them. In *Beyond Functional Assessment*, Joseph S. Kaplan (2000) suggests these questions to ponder as you and the rest of the team decide what to teach and how to teach it:

- Does the child know what's expected in this situation? Does she understand it? Are your expectations different from what's required at home?
- Does she know how to do what's expected?
- Does she know when to do what's expected?
- Does she have the self-control to do what's expected?
- Is she aware of her own behavior?
- Seen from the child's point of view, is there more to gain from the challenging behavior or from the appropriate behavior? (It's essential to make the appropriate behavior more rewarding!)
- Are the child's beliefs compatible with the appropriate behavior? Does she believe she's capable of learning and performing the appropriate behavior? Does she believe she can exert any influence on the situation? Does she believe the new behavior will get her what she wants? Some children may not even try to behave appropriately because they think they have no control over what happens to them.

provide her with the gentle touch she enjoys, and you will stop if her behavior changes in the hope she will associate the good feeling with appropriate behavior.

Your plan should also help you to respond to inappropriate behavior without rewarding it. If the functional assessment indicates that the child is trying to obtain your attention, you can use *planned ignoring*. This means you must plan not to respond to the child's challenging behavior—not to come to her side, speak to her, or look at her when she behaves inappropriately—but instead provide attention when she's behaving in an acceptable manner (or a close approximation thereof). This action shows the child that the challenging behavior will not serve the function or purpose it has served up until now—it will no longer get her what she wants (Durand, 1990; O'Neill et al., 1997). Warning: Any time you stop reinforcing challenging behavior, there will probably be an "extinction burst" (Durand, 1990, p. 152)—that is, the behavior will get worse before it gets better. This is a well-known phenomenon, so be prepared, and wait for it to pass.

Ignoring challenging behavior is not easy, and it could be dangerous. The well-being of the children must always come first; planned ignoring therefore takes a back seat in hazardous situations. To deal with either physical or emotional aggression, intervene to protect the child being victimized if you can do so safely. Stand between the two children so that the child who's been attacked can move away. Maintaining a safe distance, use the L-stance and wait until the child who acted aggressively has calmed down (Butchard & Spencler, 2000). Once she is calm you can talk about what happened and what she could have done instead (see page 194). If you don't actually see the aggression, first tend to the child who was hurt, then ask the child responsible for the aggression to help make the other child feel better by getting some ice or finding a book or activity she likes.

If the function of the challenging behavior is to avoid an activity or task, you cannot ignore the behavior. When Ronnie is screaming because he doesn't want to roll the ball with his group today, plan to hang in there and watch carefully for a pause, an action, or even a breath you can interpret as a tiny effort or a remote close approximation of appropriate behavior. When you see it, provide some positive reinforcement that is meaningful to him, and as he regains control, offer your help or a choice: "You choose. You can roll the ball or you can give it to me. Then you can take a break." When he chooses, no matter how badly or angrily he behaves, reinforce the behavior you want to encourage: "Terrific, you rolled the ball. Now you can take a break" (Chandler & Dahlquist, 1997).

Such situations can be tricky, and they require you to think on your feet and use all the flexibility and ingenuity at your command. The solution may seem silly—Ronnie isn't really calm when he takes a breath—but it's close enough, and it works. He stops screaming, he doesn't avoid the task, and he doesn't lose face. Furthermore, neither do you. Needless to say, in order to perform such a maneuver you must stay calm and collected yourself!

Remember, when the function of the challenging behavior is to avoid the activity, removing the child is not an option, even if she hurts someone. She must begin to recognize that the challenging behavior doesn't work and she can get help with a difficult task or leave an activity she dislikes if she makes an effort or asks appropriately. The appropriate replacement skills need to be as efficient and effective as her challenging behavior or she will not use them.

If you follow your plan and implement your interventions consistently, you should soon see changes. Bear in mind that the child's history will play a role here: The longer she's used her challenging behavior and the more successful it's been for her, the harder it will be to change or eradicate it. Patience is therefore essential (O'Neill et al., 1997).

How does the plan look?

When you've figured out the function and carefully considered all four methods for helping the child fulfill her needs appropriately—preventing the behavior by changing the environment, successfully teaching replacement skills, and finding meaningful ways to respond to both appropriate behavior and challenging behavior—you are well on your way. Write down exactly what you want to achieve—your goals and objectives—in measurable terms (Jazmine will clean up without hitting; Ronnie will try new skills in the gym; Jamal will learn to request a break), a time frame for reaching them, the methods you've decided to use, and who will be responsible for implementing each intervention. Figure out all the details—what you'll say and do, what materials you'll need, and so on. O'Neill and his colleagues (1997) also recommend including a description of a typical routine and a description of how you'll handle the most difficult situations. Even when you're well prepared, the problem behavior can still occur, and clearly defined procedures ensure that everyone knows what to do and

214
....

CHAPTER 10

*Functional
Assessment and
Positive Behavior
Support*

everyone does the same thing. Make sure family and staff agree and are ready to do their part. To succeed in the long run, an intervention has to be acceptable to all the people who will implement it and live with it. It has to be consistent with your values, skills, and resources. (For a summary of this entire process, see Figure 10.3.)

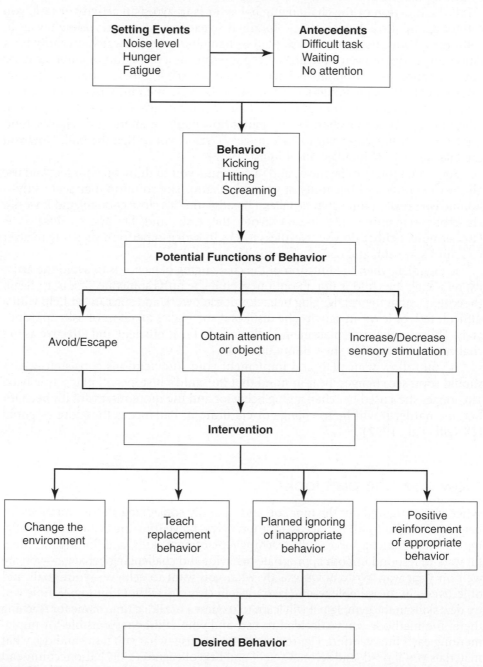

FIGURE 10.3 This diagram illustrates the process involved in using functional assessment to create a positive behavior support plan.

How do you evaluate the plan?

Decide how you'll measure your progress and set a date to review it. After the behavior plan is in place, it's important to continue observing and recording the child's behavior, using the A-B-C chart, the functional assessment observation form, or the simpler method you used before you began the functional assessment (remember the bar graph on page 200). Depending on the nature of the challenging behavior, you can count the frequency or the duration (both of which should have diminished). You can also note and record increases in positive behavior, such as when the child

- initiates private time
- allows another child to play with her
- participates in small groups
- needs the staff less
- has a friend
- uses words to ask for help or breaks more often
- copes better with transitions
- doesn't hit when she could have (Meyer & Evans, 1993)

It can take up to 6 weeks to change a behavior that has worked for a child for years. Even very small improvements indicate you're on the right track.

If you notice no progress at all, you may need to go back to your data to look for a new hypothesis, new strategies, or a totally different slant. Dust off and reconsider your earlier hypotheses (perhaps Jazmine wanted to avoid cleanup; or perhaps she was overstimulated after all). You might try to manipulate the antecedents in another way—for example, change your approach to transitions—to see whether that changes the behavior. Look at how closely the team is following the behavior support plan. It probably won't work if you aren't implementing it correctly. Positive behavior support is an ongoing, cyclical process in which you're constantly trying things out, getting new information, and revising your strategies in order to give the child a better quality of life.

What do you think?

1. "Every challenging behavior can be thought of as a child's solution to a problem and a form of communication." What does this mean to you? Can you remember a time when you or someone you know used challenging behavior to communicate or to solve a problem? Why did you use this method?

2. How does understanding the function of the behavior affect your attitude toward the child and the child's behavior? In what way does your attitude affect your ability to use an appropriate intervention?

3. In small groups, think of an experience you've had with a child with challenging behavior. If you haven't yet had this experience, team up with someone who has or make up a scenario. Try to figure out the function of the challenging behavior. Using one of the forms on pages 281 and 282, formulate a hypothesis, and make a positive behavior support plan.

Suggested Reading and Resources

Artesani, J. (2000). *Understanding the purpose of challenging behavior: A guide to conducting functional assessments.* Upper Saddle River, NJ: Prentice-Hall.

Center for the Social Emotional Foundations for Early Learning (CSEFEL). www.vanderbilt.edu/csefel/briefs/wwb10.pdf

Chandler, L., & Dahlquist, C. M. (2010). *Functional assessment: Strategies to prevent and remediate challenging behavior in school settings* (3rd ed.). Upper Saddle River, NJ: Pearson.

Kaplan, J. S. (2000). *Beyond functional assessment: A social-cognitive approach to the evaluation of behavior problems in children and youth.* Austin: Pro-Ed.

O'Neill, R. E., Horner, R. H., Albin, R. W., Sprague, J. R., Storey, K., & Newton, J. S. (1997). *Functional assessment and program development for problem behavior: A practical handbook* (2nd ed.). Pacific Grove, CA: Brooks/Cole.

OSEP Center on Positive Behavioral Interventions and Supports. www.pbis.org/

Technical Assistance Center on Social Emotional Intervention (TACSEI). www.challengingbehavior.org/

CHAPTER 11

The Inclusive Classroom

These days you can take it for granted you will have at least one child with a disability in your classroom. The odds are he'll have a learning disability—because about half of the children who receive special education services in the United States have learning disabilities (U.S. Department of Education, Office of Special Education Programs [OSEP], 2008b)—but it's also possible that his condition will be a rare one. The disability may be mild or severe, visible or invisible; and the child may spend all, most, or part of the school or child care day with you and the other children. But even if he receives special instruction in a resource room or elsewhere several hours a week, this child is entitled to full membership in your classroom community, with all the rights and opportunities that entails.

This chapter is divided into two parts. The first presents the philosophy and basic facts of inclusion; the second contains information about preventing and addressing challenging behavior in children with disabilities.

ABOUT INCLUSION

Ever since the early 1970s, when Congress passed the original version of what is now the *Individuals with Disabilities Education Act (IDEA)* and other civil rights legislation, children with disabilities have been taking their places alongside children without disabilities in classrooms across the nation. Reauthorized in 2004, the law views *inclusion* as the norm and gives all children, regardless of abilities, the right to participate actively in regular public and private schools, preschools, Head Start programs, and child care centers in the community—the *natural environments* they would attend if they were developing typically. These educational institutions have the obligation to provide all children with educational opportunities geared to their capabilities and needs, as well as the supports and services necessary for their success (Stainback & Stainback, 1996).

Why is inclusion important?

Inclusion represents a basic American and human ethical value: equality. It is the same value the Supreme Court upheld in Brown v. Board of Education in 1954 when it threw out segregation in the schools and made integration the law of the land. Separate is not equal, the high court said; it is a form of discrimination with noxious effects, including isolation, a sense of inferiority, and slowed educational and mental development (Karagammis, Stainback, & Stainback, 1996).

Inclusion, on the other hand, "is about embracing everyone and making a commitment to provide each student in the community, each citizen in a democracy, with the inalienable right to belong," write Mary A. Falvey and Christine C. Givner (2005). "Inclusion is a belief system, not just a set of strategies; it is about an attitude and a disposition that a school intentionally teaches by example" (p. 5).

Inclusion enables children with disabilities to become part of the fabric of society and promotes appreciation and understanding of diversity among children without disabilities. Both groups acquire better academic and social skills and better preparation for living in the community (Holahan, 2000; Karagammis et al., 1996). The benefits of an accepting inclusive setting are greater when children are very young. Those who are

A child with disabilities is entitled to full membership in your classroom community, with all the rights and opportunities that entails.

typically developing are less likely to tease or reject their classmates with disabilities and more likely to accept and include individuals with disabilities as they grow up. Those with disabilities function better in a typical environment and are more likely to move on to—and succeed in—inclusive schools and later life (Holahan, 2000).

How does IDEA work?

IDEA specifies that all children with disabilities have the right to a *free appropriate public education* (*FAPE*) starting at the age of 3, and its 1997 amendments make it clear that children with and without disabilities must be educated together in a regular, general education class—the *least restrictive environment* (*LRE*). The school must provide whatever special education supports and related services a child needs to succeed, and it is only when—despite those full supports and services—the child is still unable to succeed that another placement can be considered (Individuals with Disabilities Education Act, 1997).

IDEA describes categories of disability that give children access to special education. These are

- learning disabilities
- speech or language impairments
- mental retardation (cognitive disabilities)
- emotional disturbance (emotional and behavior disorders)
- deafness-blindness (i.e., students who have both)
- visual impairments
- hearing impairments
- orthopedic (physical) impairments
- other health impairments
- autism (autistic spectrum disorders or ASD)
- traumatic brain injury
- multiple disabilities
- developmental delays

In 2007, about 6.6 million school-age children, 700,000 preschoolers, and 300,000 infants and toddlers received special education or early intervention services under IDEA (U.S. Department of Education, OSEP, 2008a, 2008e).

What services does IDEA offer young children?

Young children are entitled to *early intervention* services under IDEA from birth to their third birthday. Rather than being classified with a specific disability, infants and toddlers are often designated as developmentally delayed or at risk of developmental delay. Because most of their learning takes place through interactions with their caregivers, IDEA emphasizes the family's crucial role and calls for an *individualized family service plan* (*IFSP*) that sets goals and provides services to the family and child based

It's How You Play the Game

At the age of 5, Martin could draw a perfect map of the route from his house to the child care center. He had autistic spectrum disorder and juvenile-onset diabetes, and his teachers modified the program to make sure he participated in every activity even though they had no paraprofessional to help in the classroom. In the winter, Martin went skating with his group and walked back from the rink repeating the advertising slogan, "It doesn't matter if you win or lose; it's how you play the game. Nestle's hot chocolate." In the summer when the children went to the pool, he learned how to swim.

The teachers enjoyed and valued Martin's presence and modeled acceptance throughout the day. Because the teachers accepted him, the children accepted him, too. Liz was his special pal, and when she entered the room his eyes sparkled and he greeted her by name. She sat with him, reacted with delight when he showed her his amazing drawings, and worried about him on the days when he didn't come to the center.

on their particular resources, concerns, priorities, and needs. Along with specialists—including public health nurses, occupational and physical therapists, speech and language pathologists, and nutritionists—the family takes part in planning the IFSP, which is intended to enhance their capacity to meet the child's needs. Specialists visit the child in his natural daily settings—at home, child care, or elsewhere. The IFSP must be reviewed every 6 months (Turnbull, Turnbull, Erwin, & Soodak, 2006).

An agency such as the state board of health or local school board has responsibility for organizing assessments and coordinating and monitoring services through a *family service coordinator*, who also works with the family to ensure a smooth transition into IDEA's preschool division when the child turns 3 years old and becomes eligible for his own individual education plan (Cook, Klein, & Tessier, 2004). A written transition plan should include strategies to help him behave appropriately in the new setting (Fox, Dunlap, & Cushing, 2002). In states where children can continue to have an IFSP until they enter kindergarten, the IFSP must promote school readiness (Council for Exceptional Children, n.d.a).

What's happening on the front lines?

Federal legislation mandates inclusion, along with regulations for putting it into effect, and Congress allocates a percentage of the money to pay for it. But every community implements inclusion differently. Each state and school district has policies, regulations, and resources of its own, and everything varies—funding, eligibility for services, the proportion of children with and without disabilities in the classroom, the amount of time they spend together, training for teachers, the supports and services children and teachers receive. Specialists are in short supply, and some communities offer special education services in all schools and child care centers, some in a few, and some in none (Klass & Costello, 2003). A special education teacher may act as a full-time co-teacher in a general education classroom, a resource teacher who

Help Appreciated

Although Ms. Price had taught for 25 years, she worried about what her first graders were learning this year. Out of 26 children, 7 had been identified with disabilities ranging from ASD to ADHD, and some had behavior issues. In her inner-city school, where resources were limited, she was grateful to have the support of a paraprofessional every afternoon and a special education teacher three mornings a week. The children looked forward to the days when Ms. Hernandez came. She radiated calm and never got rattled when Ivan screamed or Zoe tried to leave the room.

Although Ms. Price knew she lacked the special educator's skills, she tried hard to follow Ms. Hernandez's example. Little by little, as she watched her colleague at work and attended professional development workshops on inclusion, she found herself learning what to do and gaining confidence in her ability to do it.

instructs children with disabilities directly, or an itinerant teacher who appears at regular intervals and concentrates on teaching the early childhood or general education teacher what she needs to know when she's alone in the classroom (Odom, 2000).

How is a child who needs special education identified?

As a teacher who meets hundreds of children and knows about child development, you may be the first to notice that a child requires extra help. In a national survey of families of children with disabilities, 40 percent credited a teacher with jump-starting their child's evaluation for special education (Johnson & Duffett, 2002).

When you have concerns, it's important to observe the child carefully, record what you see, compare his capabilities with those of his peers, and discuss the problem with the family and your colleagues. Broach the subject with the family sensitively. Because a teacher isn't a doctor, you aren't trained to make a medical diagnosis. You can suggest a medical evaluation, but take care not to share your suspicions about what's causing the difficulty (Friend, 2005). Think about the child's needs and look hard at what you're doing in class. Would it help if you revamped the schedule or worked on your relationship with the child? As you try out possible solutions, monitor his response. If your interventions don't work, the next step is to alert the center's director or the school's principal, psychologist, or *prereferral team* (also called a *screening committee*, a *child study*, *teacher assistance*, *intervention assistance*, or *instructional consultation team*). They will observe in the classroom, make recommendations, and help implement strategies, supports, and services to address any academic or behavior problems.

A formal special education assessment under IDEA is in order only when these interventions fail. An interdisciplinary team (which must include the child's teacher, a special education teacher, and a representative of the school district) will carry out the IDEA evaluation, taking into consideration the child's history, observations by the family and professionals who've worked with him, and several types of measurements in the language the child knows best (Friend, 2005). This process often includes a functional assessment (see Chapter 10). To preserve everyone's rights, the evaluation must be culturally appropriate and follow the rules of *due process*. Parents are full members of the team (U.S. Department of Education, Office of Special Education and Rehabilitative Services [OSERS], 2000). If they don't want their child to receive special education services, they can refuse to have him evaluated, but you will continue to have responsibility for helping him succeed.

If the team concludes that the child is eligible, the evaluation will become the basis for an *individual education program (IEP)* setting out measurable goals for the child for the next year and stipulating all the special education, related services, and supports he must have to accomplish them. The IEP will also indicate how to measure his progress in the general education curriculum and how he will participate in state or district testing (U.S. Department of Education, OSERS, 2000). In some states the IEP may also provide short-term objectives or benchmarks, but they are no longer required except for a child taking *alternate assessments* (Turnbull et al., 2006). The team must review the IEP annually, even in states trying out multiyear IEPs that run for up to 3 years (Council for Exceptional Children, n.d.a).

Built-in Bias?

A disproportionate number of African American children wind up in special education: Despite being about 15 percent of the school-age population in 2007, they made up more than 20 percent of children served under IDEA (U.S. Department of Education, OSEP, 2008c, 2008f). Especially high proportions were identified in the categories of emotional disturbance, cognitive disability, and developmental delay, which have the most subjective criteria for eligibility (U.S. Department of Education, OSEP, 2008d). In some states, the learning disabilities group also contains a disproportionate number of African American and Latino American students (Donovan & Cross, 2002). In addition, African American children spend less of their school day in regular classrooms than European American children. Too often the result is negative labeling (National Alliance of Black School Educators, 2002) and lower expectations (Delpit, 1992).

These figures have provoked a great deal of controversy—and soul-searching—in the special education community. Is bias built into the IDEA identification process and the education system itself? Are teachers' attitudes to blame as well?

High poverty among African Americans contributes to the problem by increasing risk factors for disability, such as tobacco and alcohol use during pregnancy, poor nutrition and prenatal care, and lead exposure. But the disproportion remains even when these factors are taken into account (Oswald, Coutinho, & Best, 2002).

To correct this imbalance, IDEA 2004 requires the states to keep track of how many children from diverse cultural groups are identified for special education and provide them with early intervention (U.S. Department of Education, OSERS, n.d.).

Does IDEA include all disabilities?

IDEA doesn't cover every disability. A notable exception is attention deficit hyper-activity disorder (ADHD), which may qualify in some states but usually falls under the wider umbrella of civil rights law. *Section 504* of the *Vocational Rehabilitation Act* of 1973 defines disability more broadly than IDEA and offers support and protection from discrimination to children with ADHD or any other disability, impairment, or social maladjustment that limits their ability to learn in school (Hayes, 2000).

The federal government doesn't help fund services for these children, and re-sponsibility for determining eligibility falls on the school district. Teachers often make the initial referral; and a multidisciplinary committee that includes teachers who know the child will draw on a variety of sources to do the evaluation. Parents must give their consent and may participate in decision making. The team then de-velops a *Section 504* or *individual accommodation plan (IAP)* (U.S. Department of Education, Office for Civil Rights, 2009), which, like an IEP under IDEA, must be reviewed periodically and can require a wide range of *accommodations*, including changes in the physical environment, schedule, and instruction. However, because there are fewer regulations governing a 504 plan, students may receive less assis-tance and monitoring than they would under IDEA.

Can an IEP address behavior?

When a child with a disability has serious behavior problems, IDEA requires the IEP team to create a *behavior intervention plan*, or *BIP*, which immediately becomes part of the IEP. IDEA places clear limits on the use of punishments and intends the BIP to prevent behavior problems or catch them at an early stage. Like a positive behav-ior support plan (described in Chapter 10), the BIP is based on a functional assess-ment and outlines individualized positive behavior supports and strategies for replacing inappropriate behavior with appropriate behavior (U.S. Department of Education, OSEP, 2006).

Any child with both a disability and challenging behavior can have a BIP; but children with *emotional and behavior disorders* (called *emotional disturbance* by IDEA) are more likely to need one. Although their behavior probably isn't so different from the behavior of other children, it tends to be more intense, frequent, and long lasting (Friend, 2005). IDEA specifically excludes students who are *socially malad-justed* from qualifying for special education in this category, and as a result many children with emotional and behavior disorders aren't eligible. A child may qualify under Section 504 (Friend, 2005), but even if he doesn't, a team can still do a func-tional assessment and create a positive behavior support plan for him.

Who is responsible for implementing an IEP?

When it comes to implementing an IEP, Section 504 plan, or BIP, you are in com-mand. Rather than mere pieces of paper, these plans are legally binding—but they should also be living documents you refer to on a daily basis. If they aren't working, you can request a special review (U.S. Department of Education, OSERS, 2000).

This whole process—from the day you first notice a child needs extra help until you hold his individualized plan in your hand—may take some time. Be prepared to wait.

PREVENTING AND ADDRESSING CHALLENGING BEHAVIOR IN CHILDREN WITH DISABILITIES

Successful inclusion relies on good teaching, and good teaching begins with the understanding that all children are special and every child learns in his own unique fashion. When you consider the needs, abilities, interests, preferences, cultures, and learning styles of each child and make the program fit the child rather than the child fit the program, you will find ways for all children—with and without disabilities—to participate and succeed.

As you face an inclusive class for the first time, it's natural to feel nervous. You may wonder whether you have the skills and knowledge necessary for this job; and if there haven't been many individuals with disability in your life, you may feel uneasy about what to say and do. Because the children will take their cues from you, it's important to come to terms with those feelings. The self-reflection strategies in Chapter 5 will help. Talk with your family, friends, and colleagues; write in a journal; read up on the disabilities of the children in your class; and learn as much as you can from their families. The bottom line is not to let the negative take over. Concentrate on thinking of each child as a child first, search out his strengths—what he can do, not what he can't do—and build a relationship.

As you strive to create an environment that is highly accepting of differences, your attitude is crucial. If you feel that every child belongs in your classroom, that each has a valuable contribution to make—and your words and actions explicitly foster that acceptance of diversity—you will create a caring community where all children feel connected and all can learn (Haager & Klingner, 2005).

Does disability play a role in challenging behavior?

Children with disabilities frequently exhibit more behavior and social problems and are more likely to be rejected than their peers who do not have disabilities (Haager & Vaughn, 1995; Odom, Zercher, Marquart, Sandall, & Wolfberg, 2002). Children with common or *high-incidence disabilities*—learning disabilities, speech or language impairments, mild cognitive disabilities, and emotional disturbance, as well as those with ADHD—are at particular risk.

Children's challenging behavior is often their in disability talking. For example, a child with a speech or language impairment who has trouble expressing his needs in words may express them with inappropriate behavior instead. But it is important to remember that virtually all children with challenging behavior—including those with disabilities—communicate through their behavior. For this reason, when a child with a disability is involved, everything you know about addressing challenging

Double Disability

High-incidence disorders—which often come with behavior problems attached—tend to overlap, so children may wind up with more than one. You may encounter these combinations:

- Learning disabilities and ADHD (Willicutt & Pennington, 2000)
- Emotional disturbance and ADHD (Handwerk & Marshall, 1998)
- Emotional disturbance and language disorders (Benner, Nelson, & Epstein, 2002)

behavior applies. All the tools at your disposal—a warm relationship with the child and family; an inclusive social context and physical space; classroom procedures and teaching strategies that prevent challenging behavior; and effective techniques for responding to it—become indispensable.

Who can help?

You have some important allies in this venture, and families are number one. Families play a central role in the lives of children—children with disabilities above all. Perhaps this is because a child with disabilities depends on his family far more than a child without disabilities; and family members, in turn, are asked to give much more of themselves—in time, money, physical and emotional energy—to help their child succeed. When it comes to education, the stakes for them and the child are sky high.

If they aren't already experts on their child's disability, they soon will be; and they are certainly experts on the child himself. Many families can tell you what works and what doesn't, put you in touch with specialized resources, and raise awareness of disability by sharing information about their child's condition with you and your class (Grigal, 1998).

Most parents of children in special education award high marks to schools and teachers, but about 40 percent say they have to "stay on top and fight to get the services their child needs" (Johnson & Duffett, 2002, p. 23). Researchers Jeannie F. Lake and Bonnie S. Billingsley (2000) point out several reasons for conflict: Families and schools often hold different views of the child and his needs (e.g., the family thinks the school focuses on his weaknesses rather than seeing him as an individual with unique strengths), and they may disagree about the delivery and quality of inclusion (e.g., the time, money, or personnel available to provide services). But the most important factor, the researchers found, is trust. When parents and professionals trust one another, they manage to work through their differences. But when trust is broken, there are serious consequences for the child. Lacking confidence in the school's efforts and recommendations, parents ask for new school placements and use the mediation and due process hearings available to them under IDEA.

Because families may have been ignored, insulted, or rejected in the past, it can take a lot of effort and reassurance to establish a trusting relationship (Kluth, 2003).

It is helpful to talk with them honestly and often but keep a positive tone; explain how the system works; ask about their needs, preferences, and dreams for their child; if they're unhappy, ask why; welcome their questions and search out the answers; and listen carefully to what they have to say. If you expect parents to value and respect your concerns, you must value and respect theirs. Use your best problem-solving skills, try to match your strategies and resources to what the family desires, and follow through on anything you undertake to do. By supporting the family, you are supporting the child (see Chapters 5 and 12).

Your colleagues, including your principal or director, are also allies with invaluable assistance to offer. Historically, classroom and special education teachers come from different traditions (Friend & Bursuck, 2002), but as they have more opportunities to collaborate, expand their expertise, and share responsibility for students, the line between specialties is beginning to blur.

Good collaboration takes effort. It requires teachers to respect others' beliefs, examine their own, and treat one another as equals who are making a vital contribution to the success of all the children (not "yours" and "mine"). Teachers must plan together, clarify how they'll handle procedures and discipline, and talk about problems before they get out of hand (Friend & Bursuck, 2002). With time, determination, and conscious planning, they can become a smoothly functioning team who trust and respect each other, share goals and expectations, and communicate and solve problems effectively.

Paraprofessionals are also important members of the classroom team. Whether they're called *paraeducator, paraprofessional, teaching assistant, instructional assistant, educational assistant, one-to-one assistant, therapy assistant,* or *coach,* you are entitled to have their support when an IEP calls for it. Working under your supervision, paraprofessionals do many things to make classroom life easier, such as leading small groups and facilitating interaction between children (French, 1999).

Paraprofessionals may be assigned to one child, but they should not assume primary responsibility for teaching him—that is your job (Giangreco, 2003). What works best, researchers have found, is when a paraprofessional helps with the whole group. Then children with disabilities interact more with their peers, feel less isolated and stigmatized, and receive more competent instruction (Giangreco, Edelman, Luiselli, & MacFarland, 1997). Ideally, a stranger walking into the classroom shouldn't be able to tell which child is assigned to the teaching assistant.

Here are some tips for working with a paraprofessional (Cook et al., 2004; Giangreco, 2003; Lehmann, 2004).

- Decide what you want the paraeducator to do, and give her professional plans to follow. Meet at least once a week to discuss them and deal with any problems—people work better when they know what's expected of them.

- Get to know her—her skills, talents, interests, and knowledge of the children—and use this information to assign her appropriate tasks. Provide training if necessary.

- Supervise her work supportively, giving specific and timely feedback, asking for her ideas and comments, and letting her know you appreciate her help.

- Share your inclusion and guidance philosophy with her so that you can back each other up in the classroom. Discuss any disagreement outside of the children's hearing, and don't criticize her in front of others.

- Develop ways to communicate without speaking.
- Debrief at the end of the day. What worked, what didn't, and why?

The more planning you and your collaborators can do, the more effective your strategies are likely to be. It's best to schedule a regular time to get together, but if necessary you can meet during lunch hours, breaks, spares, or before or after school. Solid relationships with families and colleagues can make a huge difference to your success, your feelings about your work, and the children.

How can an inclusive social context prevent challenging behavior?

Once again, prevention is the best intervention (see Chapters 7 and 8). A positive, accepting climate where all the children feel they belong can go a long way to prevent challenging behavior in the inclusive classroom. Diane Haager and Janette K. Klingner (2005) observe that strong classroom communities have these characteristics:

- There are clear expectations that all children will participate, and there are natural, fluid supports to enable that to happen.
- Children appreciate diversity and understand they all differ in learning styles and abilities. There is no stigma attached to difference.
- Children help one another learn and feel accountable for both themselves and others.
- Teachers use positive behavior support and emphasize children's strengths and progress.
- Classrooms are child centered. Teachers consider children's interests in their planning and give children the opportunity to make choices and direct their own learning.

Develop sensitivity

Some children may never have met a person with a disability. Without isolating anyone in the class, explain that a disability doesn't define a person but is only a part of who he is—we are all different in some way, and differences are valuable assets (Kluth, 2003). Clarify that there are several types of disability, some visible (because the child uses a wheelchair or a hearing aid, for example) and some invisible (because you can't see a learning disability or ADHD).

As early as possible, ask the parents how they'd like you to talk about the disability with their child and the other children (Derman-Sparks & Edwards, 2010). With their permission and the permission of the child, talk with the class about what they know and think. A child with a disability may want to talk about his experiences as well. Together, create guidelines to enable the children to feel at ease and help one another—for example, remember to focus on each child's strengths, and allow each child to be the judge of his own capabilities (Karten, 2005).

Teach values directly

One way to help the children in your classroom learn to respect and care for each other is to teach this behavior explicitly. When you model it yourself, they are more likely to understand that it matters to you and follow your example. At the same time, integrate these values into the curriculum. Talk about caring and respecting differences as you and the children draw up your class rules; read and discuss books about friendship and diversity, including disability; sing songs like "That's What Friends Are For" (Salend, 1999); build a prosocial component into songs and games (Simon says, "Give your neighbor a hug") (Odom et al., 2002); use an antibias curriculum (Derman-Sparks & Edwards, 2010). Whatever you're teaching, emphasize and demonstrate inclusive values. Make it clear there are many ways to talk, play, socialize, and participate (Kluth, 2003).

Normalize and include in every possible way

William A. Corsaro (1988), a sociologist who studies children's culture, suggests that young children see themselves as members of a group because they are always doing things together. To them, those who don't participate—who leave the room for special instruction, ride a different bus, sit on a special chair—are part of an out-group (Diamond & Stacey, 2002). To minimize this effect, post pictures of people with disabilities; give everyone a special chair; turn therapy into an activity for the whole class; and alter activities so every child can take part. *Differentiated learning* and *activity-based intervention* make everyone feel part of the group by expecting each child to choose different materials and activities and by integrating special teaching seamlessly into lessons, routines, and activities.

Many children with disabilities or challenging behavior do better in a one-on-one situation with an adult (DuPaul & Stoner, 2003), but to avoid singling them out, be sure that special education teachers, therapists, paraprofessionals, and volunteers in the classroom work with many children.

Create opportunities for interaction and friendship

Children with disabilities and challenging behavior can learn appropriate behavior and social skills—and make friends—by spending time with their more socially accomplished peers. Because it's fun to be with others, this learning is self-reinforcing (Odom et al., 2002); and because peers can get children to do things that teachers can't, peer support is especially important in an inclusive classroom (Kluth, 2003).

Children with disabilities often need help getting together with other children (Odom et al., 2002). You can create opportunities for interaction by regularly placing children who are more and less socially skilled together in pairs or small groups for structured or unstructured activities (see page 166); inventing chances for them to be together, such as during transitions and classroom jobs where the skilled partner can model the appropriate behavior; assigning seats at snack and lunch; and casting children in roles during free play—for example, by turning the dramatic play area into a store and appointing shoppers, a cashier, a delivery person (Odom et al., 2002; Sandall & Schwartz, 2002).

Children learn appropriate behavior and social skills—and make friends—by spending time with more socially accomplished peers.

Teach children who are socially adept how to act as the buddy of a child who needs help getting along with others (for example, a child with ASD) and how to relate to him as a friend—to call him by name, tap him on the shoulder, invite him to join a game, give him a toy, ask for his help, or offer their own (Strain & Danko, 1995). Teach them to read his communication cues; to be persistent in engaging him in interaction (Cook et al., 2004); to use scripts (Hall, 2009); to ask if he wants help before they start to help; and to provide only as much help as he requires. Tell them a child with autism may find eye contact difficult or irritating and they should understand if he doesn't look at them (Kluth, 2003). Involve several children in these efforts, and let them know how much you appreciate their assistance.

Employ peer-teaching strategies—cooperative group learning, partner learning, peer tutoring, group projects, and cooperative activities—as often as possible; provide materials that lend themselves to interaction, such as balls, puppets, and board games; and teach children whatever skills they need to take part (Cook et al., 2004). Use their shared interests to entice them to collaborate when they're working with materials or equipment they could use alone, such as puzzles or computers (Sandall & Schwartz, 2002). And give them chances to share and pass along supplies during circle and art (Sandall & Schwartz, 2002). Be sure to positively reinforce every effort to help, share, and communicate.

These techniques improve communication and socialization, heighten respect and appreciation for children with disabilities, give children without disabilities a sense of responsibility and accomplishment, improve academic achievement—and decrease challenging behavior (Soodak & McCarthy, 2006).

Once Upon a Time

To help a child deal with a new, difficult, or upsetting situation, try creating a *social story*. Written at the child's level, from his point of view, a social story puts complex or overpowering emotion and thoughts into a brief, concrete form the child can understand and tells him what to expect or how to respond (Thompson, 2007).

A social story is composed of three types of statements:

- *Descriptive*, setting out objective information about an event
- *Perspective*, explaining the feelings of the people involved
- *Directive*, showing the desired behavior

Use three to five descriptive and perspective statements for each directive one. Here's an example from *Making Sense of Autism* by Travis Thompson (2007):

> Jamal is upset.
> Ms. Mary usually plays with Jamal in the sandbox, but she is busy today.
> Jamal is sad because Ms. Teresa is going to play in the sandbox with him.
> It's OK if Jamal is upset, but he will have fun with Ms. Teresa. (p. 123)

Illustrate the story with photos or drawings, put it into book format, and read it to the child (or let him read it to himself) until he no longer needs it. Social stories are particularly helpful for children with autism (Thompson, 2007).

Teach social and emotional skills

When children's social and emotional skills improve, their interactions improve—and vice versa. We can proactively teach children to take turns, give a compliment before they try to enter a group, and ask and answer questions as they play. We can teach them play routines, such as playing store or school or playing with dolls or trucks (Sandall & Schwartz, 2002). And we can help them develop emotional skills such as empathy, impulse control, and anger management through direct instruction, role playing, practice, prompting, and reinforcement. (For more about social skills, see pages 131–144.)

How can space, procedures, and teaching strategies prevent challenging behavior?

Make room for everyone

An inclusive class provides you with an opportunity to look at your space in a new way. Everything in the room should convey acceptance. Children with disabilities should be in the thick of things, with full access to the teacher and their peers, not off to the side with a paraprofessional (Giangreco, 2003). It's especially important to seat a child with behavior problems near where you'll be teaching—in the center of the class, in the middle row, at the center of a semicircle, at the same level as the rest of the class (Guetzloe & Johns, 2004).

Keep the aisles wide enough for traffic of all kinds (including a wheelchair) to circulate freely (Bauer & Matuszek, 2001); and remember to create a comfortable, quiet area where a child who has trouble concentrating can work without distraction (Grigal, 1998). This is especially important for children with ASD, who hear many sounds we automatically filter out, such as a pencil scratching on paper. Equip the area with earplugs, headphones, quiet music, and soft indirect lighting (Kluth, 2003).

Children sometimes need assistance staying in their own personal space. Use trays, placemats, or box lids on table surfaces and carpet squares or tape on the floor to create individual work areas and meeting-time spots (Sandall & Schwartz, 2002). You could also keep a box of stuffed toys, Koosh balls, and other small objects for children to borrow and hold when they need help sitting still (Kluth, 2003).

Make the day predictable

Structure and consistency help children feel safe: They find it easier to behave appropriately when they know what to expect and what is expected of them. The suggestions in Chapters 7 and 8 will help make your classroom predictable: Work out a daily schedule, post it in words and pictures for all to see, and every morning go over it and talk about any changes. For a child with ASD and others who need more help, create a personal picture album of the schedule so they can refer to it throughout the day.

You also give children a sense of security by creating class rules, teaching and using procedures and routines, and posting visual cues in each area to remind them of what to do. For a child who finds transitions difficult, give a personal warning of upcoming changes and use gentle physical support—tap him on the shoulder, lead him, or show him how to clean up and begin the next activity (Kostelnik, Onaga, Rohde, & Whiren, 2002). If there is a child with ASD in your class, do not flash the lights or use loud noises to signal a transition—he may find this sensory input overwhelming. Use a song or soft chimes instead (Willis, 2009). Whenever you do anything new, rehearse the activity and go over unfamiliar materials with him ahead of time (Koegel & Koegel, 1995).

Develop a schedule and regular routines, and post the schedule prominently in words and pictures for all to see.

Implement the IEP

An IEP is mostly about instruction. It describes (and at the same time prescribes) specific ways to help a particular child learn the core general education curriculum (National Dissemination Center for Children with Disabilities [NICHCY], n.d.b) by providing for

- *special education*, that is, instruction designed especially to address the child's unique needs; and special education teachers, who are, of course, the experts in this area

- *related services*, such as speech-language pathologists or psychologists

- *supplementary aids and services*, including equipment such as special computers, communication boards, and books on tape; staff such as paraprofessionals; and teaching strategies such as cooperative learning

- *accommodations and modifications* to enable the child to participate in state and local assessments

Among the many ways the IEP specifies to enable a child to meet his annual goals perhaps the most important is *differentiated instruction*. Children come to child care and school with radically different abilities, outlooks, and skills and learn in different ways. With differentiated instruction, the teacher tailors her curriculum and teaching to suit the child. Experienced inclusion teachers (Horn, Lieber, Sandall, Schwartz, & Wolery, 2002) have collected 529 ways to differentiate learning and adapt curriculum, classified as follows:

- *Environmental supports* alter the physical, social, or temporal environment. The children are the best thermometer when it comes to the temporal environment. If they start to fidget, it's time to cut the activity short. Temporal support for a school-age child may mean providing extra time on a test (U.S. Department of Education, OSEP, 2004).

- *Adapting materials* helps a child participate more independently. For example, you can provide contact paper for collages when pasting is too hard or suggest children tear paper instead of cutting it.

- *Special equipment* can be commercial, such as software, or homemade, such as a picture board with familiar objects and activities to help a child who doesn't talk make his wishes known.

- *Using children's preferences, interests, strengths, preferred objects, and expertise* encourages them to take part in activities. For example, for an outer space enthusiast you could transform the dramatic play area into a space station. Plan backwards: Start with what works for the child and build an activity from there (Kluth, 2003).

- *Simplifying an activity* reduces frustration. Use prompts, break tasks into steps (hand the child one puzzle piece at a time), reduce the number of steps, create a photo sequence to guide him through the activity.

- *Adult support* takes many forms—for instance, you can model appropriate behavior, join the child in play, and scaffold learning for him.

- *Peer support*, which encourages interaction, is important because children learn so well from one another.

- *Invisible support* means subtly rearranging activities to give a child a better chance to succeed. For example, make sure a child with ADHD is near the front of the line so he won't have to wait too long.

Although schools tend to focus on verbal and mathematical intelligences, children with disabilities may have great strengths in other intelligences—music, art, physical movement, computers, for example—and can excel when they have the chance to learn and express what they know in different ways.

When a child needs more focused teaching and practice to meet his IEP goals, *activity-based intervention* (Pretti-Frontczak & Bricker, 2004) or *embedded learning opportunities* are very effective. In both of these strategies, teachers intentionally teach specific skills during the course of ordinary classroom routines and activities. For instance, if you're working on one child's gross motor skills, you could have all the children take giant steps or tiptoe from activity to activity (Pretti-Frontczak & Bricker, 2004); if you're helping a child with ASD improve his communication skills, you could focus on how he greets you at arrival time. Regularly collect data on the child's progress toward each IEP goal so that your strategies stay attuned to the child's needs (Hall, 2009).

Adapt assessment

All of these strategies are adaptations, and although you can use them all in your classroom, they don't necessarily qualify for use in state- and districtwide testing, which is now required for students with disabilities.

Adaptations approved by the state are called *accommodations*, and they must appear in the child's IEP. According to Douglas Fisher and Craig H. Kennedy (2001), an *accommodation* is "a change made to the teaching or testing procedures to provide a student with access to information and to create an equal opportunity to demonstrate knowledge and skills" (p. 54). An accommodation can allow changes in timing (giving extra time), setting (providing a quiet room or study carrel), scheduling (permitting frequent breaks), presentation (furnishing an audiotape or reader), and/or response (allowing answers to be dictated or typed) on an assignment or test, but it doesn't alter what it's measuring in any significant way (Luke & Schwartz, 2007). When a student listens to a book on tape, that is an accommodation. Remember what you're measuring. If it's the understanding of a concept and not the child's reading skill, accommodation can be easy.

Note that when his IEP requires it, a child who can't participate in standard testing, even with accommodations, can take an *alternate assessment* (NICHCY, n.d.a). Under this arrangement there is a change in what the child is supposed to learn or demonstrate.

During the ordinary school day, it's important to use a child's IEP accommodations so that he'll be familiar with them and can experience success in the testing situation. If he can't perform at assessment time, everything you've done to help him feel valued and capable can fall apart. His self-esteem will drop, his level of frustration will rise, and he will lose interest in the class, confidence in himself, and trust in you. All of this may lead to challenging behavior. Children with invisible disabilities may be more embarrassed about using accommodations than children

Measure for Measure

....

Increasingly, schools are demanding measurement of student progress that's based on evidence, not impressions. In *curriculum-based assessment (CBA)* and *curriculum-based measurement (CBM)*, teachers use brief, frequent, standard tests to measure how well students are learning. The results help teachers make informed decisions about instruction (Friend & Bursuck, 2002; Haager & Klingner, 2005) and show whether accommodations are working.

Schools are also adopting *Response to Intervention (RTI)* to screen and prevent students from falling behind. An alternative means of identifying children who may have learning disabilities (Council for Exceptional Children, n.d.b), RTI uses short, periodic assessments and provides extra intervention for those who need more help. If they don't respond adequately to supplemental instruction, they can be referred for an evaluation under IDEA (Council for Exceptional Children, n.d.b).

with visible disabilities. A caring classroom community will help them feel comfortable enough to use the supports they need.

Because assessment provides information about what and how to teach, it's important to assess learning throughout a unit in many ways—class discussions, oral quizzes, quick reviews at the beginning or end of a lesson, to name a few. Portfolios of work are an excellent way to observe progress.

How can you respond effectively to challenging behavior?

When it comes to challenging behavior, almost everything you know about children without disabilities applies to children with disabilities. The basis for all effective guidance is a caring relationship. When you understand a child's feelings, preferences, and triggers, you can help him learn appropriate behaviors that allow him to do his best; and if he knows you care about him and support him, he'll come to trust you and respond more positively to whatever you're teaching.

A variety of theoretical perspectives, including humanistic and psychoanalytic thought, social learning theory, and behaviorist theory, underlie the most widely used guidance strategies. If you have several to draw on, you can choose one or a combination that suits the circumstances. You can find some of these approaches in Chapters 9 and 10.

What is ASD?

Autism spectrum disorder (ASD) is on the rise—nearly 1 in 100 eight-year-olds (four times as many boys as girls) were diagnosed with the neurodevelopmental disorder in 2006, compared to 1 in 300 in the early 2000s (Rice, 2009). This growth spurt—the result of heightened awareness, broader criteria for diagnosis, and the availability of services (Rice, 2009)—has brought more children with autism into inclusive classrooms, often perplexing their teachers (National Comprehensive Center for Teacher Quality, 2008; National Professional Development Center, 2009).

ASD is a *spectrum disorder*, meaning its symptoms occur in many varieties and intensities, and no two children experience it the same way (Kluth, 2003). Its most common forms, autism disorder, Asperger's syndrome, and pervasive development disorder (not otherwise specified) (PDD-NOS), share the following characteristics (Kluth, 2003):

- *Communication differences.* Children with autism may speak very little or not at all, and those who do may have difficulties with language, expression, and the rules of conversation. They must work hard to process language and often need extra time to respond. To comprehend what's been said, they may involve the visual part of the brain and think in pictures (Williams, 2008). They find visual cues extremely helpful.

- *Interaction differences.* Although it's often thought that children with autism aren't interested in relationships, they probably wish to have friends—they just don't know how to go about it. When they look at familiar faces, the brain region that normally registers faces doesn't light up; instead, this area turns on when they see objects that fascinate them (Goleman, 2006a). Because children with autism pay little attention to faces, they don't learn to understand facial expressions, the subtleties of social interaction, or others' mental states (Thompson, 2007). A possible reason for this avoidance is that eye contact can create intense anxiety or fear (Goleman, 2006a).

- *Special absorbing interests.* Although their passionate interests are sometimes dangerous or embarrassing, they may help children with autism to focus, stay calm, listen more carefully, or connect with others. Disrupting them may provoke tantrums.

- *Sensory differences.* The extremely sensitive sensory system of a child with autism can be easily overwhelmed, leading to meltdowns. Touch, hearing, sight, and smell may all be affected.

- *Movement differences.* Occurring in multiple areas, the movement problems of children with autism may interfere with action, speech, thoughts, emotions, and memories (Donnellan & Leary, 1995; Leary & Hill, 1996).

Each child is different, but certain circumstances often predict challenging behavior in children with autism: They are vulnerable when there is a change in routine, when a child's preferred repetitive activity is thwarted, when he can't communicate his wants or needs, and when he's feeling sensory overload (Thompson, 2007). Strange social situations also provoke anxiety and problem behavior. Children can react by hurting themselves, acting aggressively, running around flapping their hands, and crying.

When you understand the behavior better, it may easier to accept it or teach new skills to replace it (Kluth, 2003). Is it really a problem, and for whom? How does the family see it? Is it hard or easy for the child to control, and does he want it in his life?

Swing Dancing

....

Special educator and author Paula Kluth (2003) describes this ingenious solution to a difficult inclusion problem:

> Matt . . . would frequently run out of his classroom and into the schoolyard. Once there, he would jump on the swing. . . . [He] repeated this behavior approximately five times each day. When we tried to lock the door near his classroom . . . , he would make a break for the library and jump on the hammock hanging in the corner.
>
> Everyone felt that Matt must need the input the swing could provide, but none of us wanted him to . . . miss out on the . . . opportunities provided in his general education classroom. My boss . . . piped up . . . , "Matt shouldn't have to go to the swing, the swing should go to Matt," and proceeded to draw out plans for installing a hanging basket swing in the back of the first-grade classroom. All of us—the first-grade teacher, Matt's mother, my boss, the school principal— got excited . . . and began planning. . . . We decided that the swing would become part of a reading corner and . . . all children would have opportunities to use it when Matt was taking a break from it. . . . (p. 171)

Source: "You're Going to Love This Kid!" Teaching Students with Autism in the Inclusive Classroom by Paula Kluth, p. 171, © 2003. Baltimore: Paul H. Brookes Publishing Co., Inc. Reprinted by permission.

To enhance a child's ability to meet his needs, work on communication. An *augmentative alternative communication (AAC) system* (whether it's a homemade picture board or a sophisticated talking computer), pointing, gesturing, writing, and sign language all boost communication, lessen frustration, and reduce challenging behavior (Hall, 2009). Teach the rest of the class to use these devices, too (Kluth, 2003). You can also structure the environment to increase a child's verbal proficiency—put the markers where he must ask for them, pair him with a helpful peer, encourage him with puppets, songs, rhymes, and animated gestures (Hall, 2009). Then make a continuing effort to observe, listen, and respond to whatever he's trying to tell you.

Stay calm in a crisis. To help the child feel safe, talk slowly and softly, offer comfort, and convey that you care (Kluth, 2003). Sending him out of the room is not helpful—it's important for him to feel he belongs to the classroom community.

Using the tools in your toolbox

Do you remember these ideas for addressing challenging behavior?

- Know what the child does well and build on his strengths—they offer opportunities for him to succeed.

- Be aware of your buttons, and don't let children push them. When you get angry, raise your voice, or lose control, you are modeling the very behavior you're trying to eliminate.

- When you want to redirect a child's inappropriate behavior, call him by name to capture his attention.

- Tell students what to do, not what not to do—"Please walk," not "Don't run." This information will help them know what's appropriate.

- When you're working with a child who loses control easily, establish simple visual cues to remind him of what to do. Before he gets too wound up, move close, make eye contact, and use your prearranged signal—nod, wink, scratch your head (Cook et al., 2004).

- Children need the opportunity to choose, but you also need to know how many choices each child can handle.

- Children with memory and information processing problems can't handle a lot of information at once, but they can succeed when you break content and procedures into small segments and teach one step at a time, moving forward only when a child has learned the previous step.

- After an outburst or when children are stressed, they sometimes find it calming to do "order tasks" requiring eye–hand coordination, such as stringing beads, doing puzzles, or working on pegboard designs (Cook et al., 2004). This tactic won't work with children who have weak eye–hand coordination!

- Teach children to reward themselves with self-talk (e.g., "You finished writing your story today. How do you feel about that?"). This encourages them to think positively about themselves (ERIC Clearinghouse on Disabilities and Gifted Education, 1998).

- Be patient. Look for small changes—they tell you whether you're heading in the right direction and keep you from getting discouraged.

W HAT DO YOU THINK?

1. What do you think are the benefits of inclusion? How will you help children with and without disabilities take advantage of being together in your class?

2. To understand what the world is like for a person with a disability, try using your nondominant hand to do your written work, getting your point across without using words, doing something in 3 minutes that normally takes 10. Would this be a good exercise to do with the children in your classroom?

3. Once you realize there is a child with a possible learning disability in your class, what steps will you follow? What is the role of parents as IDEA sees it, and how will you get them involved? What if there is resistance?

4. Should your response to challenging behavior in a child with a disability be different from your response to challenging behavior in a child without a disability? Why or why not?

5. Imagine you have a child with ADHD in your class. What strategies would you use to prevent challenging behavior? Chapter 8 may help you answer this question.

Suggested Reading

Karten, T. J. (2005). *Inclusion strategies that work: Research-based methods for the classroom.* Thousand Oaks, CA: Sage.

Kluth, P. (2010). *"You're going to love this kid!" Teaching students with autism in the inclusive classroom* (2nd ed.) Baltimore: Brookes.

Paley, V. G. (1991). *The boy who would be a helicopter.* Cambridge: Harvard University Press.

Rief, S. F. (2005). *How to reach and teach children with ADD/ADHD: Practical techniques, strategies, and interventions.* New York: Wiley.

Sandall, S. R., & Schwartz, I. S. (with Joseph, G. E., Chou, H.-Y., Horn, E. M., Lieber, J., Odom, S. L., & Wolery, R.). (2002). *Building blocks for preschoolers with special needs.* Baltimore: Brookes.

U.S. Department of Education, Office for Civil Rights. (2009). *Protecting students with disabilities: Frequently asked questions about Section 504 and the education of children with disabilities.* www2.ed. gov/about/offices/list/ocr/504faq.html

CHAPTER 12

Working with Families and Other Experts

Even when you know the causes of challenging behavior are complex, it's sometimes tempting to put all the blame on a child's family. But families are not the enemy. On the contrary: They are on your side. They love their child and want to help her, and creating a partnership with them is definitely the best strategy. It's important to make this connection early, before difficulties arise, especially when you know a child has struggled in the past. If your first contact with the family is to report a problem, finding a solution will be harder.

In Chapter 5 we discussed how to build a relationship with a family; in this chapter we consider how to work with families after challenging behavior appears. The chapter has three main sections: preparing to meet the family, meeting with the family, and working with other experts.

PREPARING TO MEET THE FAMILY

As you prepare to approach a family about a child's challenging behavior, it's important to consult your colleagues. Part of the job of the director, principal, school counselor, or special education teacher is to furnish information, support, and resources when you're having difficulty: Talking with them can only enhance your ability to understand and help the child and family. You could also turn to more experienced classroom teachers, who have met many a child with challenging behavior and may even have worked with this particular child or family before. Raising the subject at a center staff meeting is another possibility.

Anything you feel (from bewilderment to anger) or anything the child does (from not sitting at class meeting to hitting someone over the head with a book) can be reason enough to seek out a sympathetic ear. If you put off looking for help until you can't face the classroom another day, you've waited too long. Sometimes teachers don't ask for assistance because they fear they'll be judged incompetent or because they think they're supposed to fix any problem by themselves. This is a mistake. Some children are harder to teach, and everyone needs an outlet, peer support, and advice from time to time. Teams are especially important when you're dealing with challenging behavior: People who have different perspectives and skills can help one another come up with creative and effective solutions.

(As you talk with your colleagues, be sure to safeguard the confidentiality of the child and the family. It is your ethical obligation to be discreet in both your professional and private life. Don't talk in public places or mention last names. You never know who will be sitting behind you in a crowded restaurant or movie theater.)

Once it's clear there's a problem, the family needs to know about it. It is their right to know, and it's easier to deal with problems sooner rather than later. By contacting the family immediately, you're telling them you care about their child. This gives you a better chance of enlisting their support (Walker, Ramsey, & Gresham, 2004).

More to the point, families can help. They know their child best, and they can tell you about their lives, their culture (family roles, origin, support network, patterns of authority) and their stresses (illness, divorce, financial problems). They can fill you in on the child's developmental milestones and offer information about the nature, frequency, and severity of the challenging behavior at home and in the past as well as how they deal with it. The better you understand where the child is coming from, the better equipped you will be to respond to her effectively.

As you and the family interact, try to see things from their point of view and look for their strengths, competencies, and resources. If you can make the assumption that they're capable people, they're likely to fulfill your expectations, and together you'll come up with a variety of possible solutions.

How do families react to news of challenging behavior?

Families have a strong emotional investment in their children, and they're never really ready to hear about problems, although they're often acutely aware of them. They may struggle with their child over meals, bath, and bedtime every day; regard a trip to the supermarket as a nightmare; and dread taking her to the playground for fear she will hurt another child—but that doesn't mean they're prepared to hear someone else call her difficult. In *Troubled Families—Problem Children*, psychologists Carolyn Webster-Stratton and Martin Herbert (1994) write, "It is not easy for parents to admit that they have a child with behavior problems, a child who is different from other children" (p. 201).

Chances are that a family living with a child with challenging behavior is also living with enormous stress (Fox, Vaughn, Wyatte, & Dunlap, 2002). Parents may blame one another for the child's behavior and feel isolated, victimized, insecure, angry, out of control, guilty, depressed, and/or utterly powerless (Webster-Stratton & Herbert, 1994). In their own minds, having a child with behavior problems is a sign they're bad parents, who are judged and rejected not only by other parents (whose children seem perfect) but also by their own extended family. As you talk with them, you may be talking with years of self-blame, disappointment, and defensiveness.

Although this may be the first time you've broached this subject with the family, it probably isn't the first time someone has informed them about their child's problems. If the previous encounters were less than ideal, any new discussion may seem threatening. On the other hand, if they're hearing about the child's difficulties for the first time, they may be devastated and even consider you the cause of her problems.

As a result, not all families will be willing to collaborate on a strategy for addressing challenging behavior. Some will quickly join you in trying new tactics, but others will be disinclined—for example, families who distrust or fear teachers and schools because of their own school experiences or who believe in a clear separation between home and school or child care (Lareau & Shumar, 1996). Still others, who can't face any more conversations about their child's problems, may seem disinterested or belligerent (Martin & Hagan-Burke, 2002). And many others just won't have the time, energy, or money to work with you because a child with challenging behavior devours a family's reserves.

Lost at Sea

Parents who are living with a child with challenging behavior may feel abandoned by the child's school or child care setting. One mother told Webster-Stratton and Herbert (1994) about her experience with her son's kindergarten:

> The principal came up to me and said, "Your boy is a very sick boy and is going to need many years of psychoanalytic counseling."—I feel all the teachers knew this and set us up in the school so we couldn't win. I felt everyone else in the kindergarten was on this raft while we were swimming around trying to clutch to get on . . . .
>
> By the end of the school year we started realizing that the kindergarten raft was sailing away, and when they told us not to come back we felt we were left drowning in the water. (p. 59)

Source: Carolyn Webster-Stratton and Martin Herbert, *Troubled Families—Problem Children: Working with Parents: A Collaborative Process* (Chichester, England: Wiley, 1994). Copyright John Wiley & Sons Limited. Reproduced by permission.

An immigrant family may also be struggling with the language and mores of the dominant culture. They may believe it's inappropriate to discuss family problems with a teacher or to ask questions when they don't understand. They may see you as the expert, while you are trying to form a partnership. Or they may believe it's impolite to disagree with you and therefore seem willing to go along with your suggestions when they actually see the situation in an entirely different way. Respecting their beliefs is the first step toward communication, but at the same time it's important to remind them of their own expertise where their child is concerned.

Regardless of how the family responds, you cannot allow yourself to become defensive. If they resent you or think you don't like their child, they may not want to listen to you or share their thoughts with you, and collaboration will be next to impossible. The bottom line is clear: Responsibility for the success of this venture lies with you, the teacher.

How do you feel?

There may be some anxiety on your side, too. You aren't sure how the family will react to what you have to say, and you might fear they'll hold you responsible for the child's difficulties or simply refuse to believe you. Families who use very strict or physical discipline at home may think you haven't been strict or direct enough—and they may be correct, depending on the child's culture (Delpit, 2006) (see Chapters 6 and 9). If you feel angry and upset with the child, these feelings may spill over into your relationship with the family (Kay, Fitzgerald, & McConaughy, 2002). It is therefore important to become aware of your emotions and keep them under control.

You probably bring some biases to the table as well. According to a Public Agenda (2004) survey, 82 percent of teachers blame parents for not teaching discipline to their children. And researchers have found that teachers often judge marginalized families—who are different because of their race, class, sexual orientation, disability, or immigrant status—as uninvolved and uncaring, when in fact they are involved in ways the mainstream culture doesn't recognize (Lopez, 2001). To battle these views, get to know these families and learn about their lives and culture, particularly the way they raise their children and communicate with others.

If you don't have any children of your own, it may be hard for you to imagine how the family feels. Nonetheless, you share a commitment with them to help their child succeed. When you are open to seeing the child from the family's point of view, when you can recognize that different settings elicit different behaviors and different solutions, you've begun to collaborate.

MEETING WITH THE FAMILY

Arranging a meeting

Your first meeting about a child's challenging behavior will establish a new tone for your relationship with the family. What happens there will classify you as either ally or adversary, and that label will influence all your future contacts. It is important to avoid an expert or authoritarian approach. When you and the family regard each other as equals, recognize one another's expertise, and acknowledge that differences in opinion are normal, you can use your combined strengths to set goals, make plans, and solve problems.

In different cultures, different people are responsible for making decisions about the children. In some cultures, men have the say; in others it is the oldest family member who is in charge; in still others, mothers are responsible. Before you contact the family, research whom to approach first and whom else should be present. With all families, find out what names they use and address them as Mr. and Ms. on the phone and in person.

If the parents are separated or divorced but live in the same city, invite them both to participate. Especially in cases of joint custody, it's better for both parties to get the same information at the same time, preferably directly from you. Be sure to give them plenty of advance warning of their ex's appearance!

The best way to make the first contact is by telephone. Because calling parents at work induces panic, phone them at home where you can set a friendlier tone and take the time you need to choose your words carefully. Since several family members will probably be around, it will also be easier to schedule a time that suits everyone.

It is imperative to begin with a positive statement about the child. Go over the days in your mind and take notes so that you have a few encouraging comments prepared. If you're drawing a blank, do an observation where you look exclusively for appropriate behavior. When parents know that you appreciate their child's assets, they're more likely to approach you and the problem constructively.

Begin by introducing yourself, then state the purpose of the call clearly. It's better not to say vaguely, "I want to talk with you about Jazmine," because parents immediately assume the worst. Instead, stick to the facts and describe exactly what you've noticed: that she's hitting other children and destroying their work. Tell them you want to talk with them about what you're doing at school and ask for their advice. Be careful not to accuse or judge them (Dunst, 2002).

Some parents have been anxiously awaiting this call, and others may be caught totally off guard. Feelings—of guilt, anger, disappointment, embarrassment—inevitably surge up, coloring their reaction. They may deny, justify, rationalize, minimize, or even abdicate responsibility: "She's not like that at home," "Maybe she's bored," "She has lots of friends in the neighborhood," "We've just gone through a divorce," "She never listens to us, even when we spank her." Even parents who sound like partners may feel helpless and defensive (Losen & Diament, 1978). Show your concern, and listen carefully.

Talk with them long enough to make it clear you care about their child and want to work with them. Some parents continue to talk, then decide there's no reason to meet. Try not to let things reach this point. Be polite, but point out that it's better to discuss these matters in person. When everyone has time to reflect, the conversation will be more fruitful.

Plan to meet as soon as possible. To enable everyone to attend, you may have to get together in the evening in a neutral setting, such as a community center or coffee shop. While you're making arrangements, also schedule a time to end the meeting. Knowing the stopping point helps everyone stay on topic and keeps parents from being insulted when the meeting concludes. Be sure to set aside enough time

Where They're Coming From

Parents often become defensive when a teacher invites them to discuss their child's challenging behavior. Such a reaction may come from

- feeling they should have been told about the problem before it became so severe
- thinking this must be the fault of the teacher or the other children
- having previous negative experiences with the school or center
- living with a lot of stress (Losen & Diament, 1978)

so that you won't be rushed. In some cultures the family will notice you're in a hurry and defer to your needs, but they may also believe you don't respect them and feel offended or hurt, which will not help the child.

If you don't speak the same language, ask if they would like an interpreter and decide who will be responsible for finding one. It's better not to press an older sibling into service (Lynch, 2004a). Family members may not want to discuss delicate issues in the sibling's presence, and the child-interpreter may not wish an outsider to know about sensitive family matters. In addition, being in this position alters the sibling's relationship to her elders and causes problems for both child and parents. On the other hand, the family may not feel comfortable talking with a stranger, and even a member of the same cultural community may pose problems of privacy and confidentiality (Lynch, 2004a). If you have taken on the task of selecting the interpreter, double-check with the family to be sure they're satisfied with your choice (Joe & Malach, 2004). It's a good idea to use a skillful professional who can interpret cultural cues as well as language and let you know what isn't said as well as what is.

What should happen in a meeting?

First, prepare. Decide what you're going to say, and make an agenda with the objectives and main points you want to cover. Organize your reports, notes, and observation charts so you don't have to search for things during the meeting.

Plan to go to the first meeting by yourself. Involving other staff intimidates the family and looks as if you've been discussing the child behind their back. If it seems useful, you can agree to invite another person to a future meeting.

If you're getting together at the school or center, choose a private space and put a "meeting in progress" sign on the door to forestall interruptions. Collect adult-size chairs for everyone, and place them where they convey partnership—with no physical barriers (such as your desk) between you and the family. If the child comes along, arrange child care for her.

Remember that in many cultures communication is indirect and courtesy is highly valued. Meeting a family calls for more formal clothing than sitting on the floor with the children, so indicate your respect by dressing in businesslike attire. Lynch and Hanson (2004) also suggest using culturally comfortable practices such

Team Building

When researchers (Blue-Banning, Summers, Frankland, Nelson, & Beegle, 2004) asked parents and professionals what they valued in a partnership, six themes emerged:

- *Communication.* Parents want their communication with professionals to be frequent, open, and honest, with no sugar coating or hidden information. At the same time, they like two-way communication and tact—professionals who respect their privacy, don't judge them, and find positive things to say.

- *Commitment.* Professionals who regard their work as more than just a job win parents' approval. They demonstrate dedication in gestures such as meeting outside of regular working hours or remembering a child's birthday.

- *Equality.* Parents want professionals to acknowledge the validity of their point of view, and they appreciate a sense of harmony and empowerment in the relationship.

- *Skills.* Parents admire professionals who can make things happen for their child and praise those who admit to not knowing something but are willing to find out.

- *Trust.* First, trust for parents means *reliability*, a professional doing what she says she will do. Second, it means providing *safety*, ensuring that the child is treated with dignity and protected from hurt. Finally, it means *discretion*, keeping personal information confidential.

- *Respect.* Professionals show respect by valuing the child as a person and acting courteously—calling family members by their last names, arriving on time for meetings, and acknowledging parents' efforts and contributions on behalf of their child.

as serving tea or coffee, spending a few minutes in polite general conversation before launching into the subject of the meeting, and conducting the meeting in a formal way, depending on the family's culture (Joe & Malach, 2004). If you're using an interpreter, bear in mind that he or she is a go-between. Talk directly to the family— they are the ones you're addressing.

When you meet with the family, you'll need great sensitivity and your very best listening skills. Take some deep breaths to calm your butterflies, and remember that you have important contributions to make: expertise about children, a nonjudgmental ear, and respect for the family's opinions and feelings.

Greet them with a smile, and before you talk about problems, once again let them know where their child is succeeding: what she does well, who her friends are, what she enjoys. Then you can talk about the challenging behavior you're observing and the things you need their help with. Be calm, factual, and specific as you describe the child's behavior, your expectations, and the strategies you've tried. Tell the family what you see rather than what you think.

Invite parents to share their experience and ideas and work with you to develop a plan.

Invite them to share their thoughts and concerns as well as their past successes with their child and any information they have regarding her behavior or diagnosis. Why might this be happening? Have there been any new stresses or changes in routine? How does she behave at home? Has she behaved this way before and how have they responded? What works for them now? What are their goals for their child? Do these goals suggest any solutions to the problem? Some parents may already be working with specialists or parent groups and know about appropriate methods for managing their child's problems. Do they have any advice to offer?

If they indicate that their child's behavior is no problem at home, believe them: They may not perceive the behavior as a problem, and not every child with challenging behavior has difficulty outside of a group setting, especially an only child. But it's important to say politely that her behavior is a problem in your class, where she must share space, toys, and attention. Gently remind them that if the child is having trouble in a child care center, she will have a harder time at school, where there are fewer teachers, more children, and many more demands.

Any remarks that sound like criticism of their child may cut them deeply. They are doing their best for her, and they may feel upset, defensive, or angry. These are all normal coping mechanisms. Let them vent their feelings, and give them time to come to terms with the situation. Listen carefully to what they have to say. Active listening will enable you to understand them and demonstrate your respect and empathy. Pay attention to both the surface and the underlying message, and comment on the feelings with phrases such as "That's hard, isn't it?" Paraphrase what they have said to clarify the meaning and verify you've understood their message (see pages 180–181).

As you talk, be aware of your body language. Keep your arms open, and mirror their message. If they are engaged and leaning forward, you should also be engaged and leaning forward. Be conscious of your eye contact, as well. Remember that this can be a cultural issue, and it is important to communicate respect on their terms. Pay attention to the pace, cadence, and tone of their speech, and decide whether it's better to mirror or lead their actions. Their speech, facial expressions, and gestures will also give you clues about their emotions.

Sometimes teachers are afraid the family will punish the child at home. Although it is in the child's best interests for you and the family to coordinate your strategies, it isn't your job to tell parents how to parent, and unsolicited advice (no matter how useful) can make them feel they're under attack. Instead, tell them how you handled the situation, and if they bring up the subject, talk with them about what they feel should happen at home. Perhaps they'll recognize that you've dealt with the matter already or be willing to work out a related consequence. You could point out that the most effective consequences are those that follow immediately.

Brainstorm as many ideas as possible and work out a plan. Then schedule another conference to assess the child's progress, and wrap things up so the parents don't feel cut off: "Our time is almost up. I just want to be sure we're all clear about what was said and what we've agreed to do next." Thank the family for their input and their contribution to the problem-solving process; it's important for them to have a sense of ownership not only of the child and her problems but also of the solutions and the child's potential for success.

After the parents leave, make notes of the discussion and evaluate how the meeting went. Did you say what you needed to say? How did the family react? What commitments did everyone make? Is the follow-up clear? Write a brief note to the family, thanking them again and reiterating the decisions you've made together. If you agreed to send information or call someone, do it as quickly as possible.

Family Social Skills

Problem solving with families is just like problem solving with children. Ellen Galinsky (1988) suggests using these six steps:

- Describe the situation as a problem out front. Avoid accusations or the implication that the source of the problem resides in the personality of the parent or the child.
- Generate multiple solutions. Parents and professionals should both contribute, and no one's suggestions should be ignored, put down, or denounced.
- Discuss the pros and cons of each suggestion.
- Come to a consensus about which solutions to try.
- Discuss how you will implement these solutions.
- Agree to meet again to evaluate how these solutions are working so that you can change your approach, if necessary. (p. 11)

What if you and the family disagree?

Things won't always run smoothly. When a conflict arises, first pay attention to what you're feeling (which helps defuse those feelings) and then lock the feelings in a drawer, where you can find them later. If you're going to come out of this situation with a solution everyone can live with, you need an open mind, your reason, and your best eyes and ears. This means staying calm and professional. Perhaps your most important goal is to keep the discussion going; resolving differences takes time and communication.

Once again, the best thing to do is listen. Even when you don't agree with what the family is saying, it's important to accept what they feel. This shows respect. Again, active listening will help. If they say, "Jazmine says you're always picking on her," stifle your impulse to say Jazmine has it all wrong. It's normal for them to stand up for their child. Try to hear their feelings and reply, "You're worried that I'm not being fair to Jazmine."

When you and the family come from different cultures, it's easy to misunderstand and be misunderstood. As people come to know and understand one another and their cultures, the chances of resolution improve. Or at least everyone's ability to handle disagreement gets better.

Some values are nonnegotiable, such as those enshrined in the United Nations Convention on the Rights of the Child (United Nations Office of the High Commission on Human Rights, 1989). You would never agree, for example, to hit a child, no matter how passionately parents argue their case. Nor would you compromise on a matter of racial or gender equality. But other situations aren't so clear. You may think you could never change your practice and later realize that some changes would make the child much happier. Routines such as eating, sleeping, and toileting might fall into this category—think of how a Japanese child like Aki, who sleeps with his parents at home, would feel if you lay down beside him at naptime. It's also worth looking seriously at a parent's request for more holding and nurturing for a child (Chud & Fahlman, 1995). From there, it's a matter of dialogue, negotiation, problem solving, and compromise, always keeping the best interests of the child in mind.

An Open Mind

In *The Essential Conversation*, her exploration of parent–teacher relationships, Sara Lawrence-Lightfoot (2003) writes:

> We must . . . admit that conflict is endemic to parent-teacher dialogues, that it is not to be ignored or avoided. Rather it must be met with open minds and open hearts, made visible and named, and worked with over time. (p. 73)

This section has been adapted from *Partners in Quality, vol. 2/Relationships* © CCCF 1999, written by Barbara Kaiser and Judy Sklar Rasminsky, based on the research papers of the Partners in Quality Project. With permission from Canadian Child Care Federation, 201–383 Parkdale Avenue, Ottawa, ON, K1Y 4R4.

You may reach a solution; you may agree to disagree. Either way is all right if you keep communication open and treat one another with respect.

If you're worrying that your next meeting will become confrontational, consider asking a third person to join you. Choose someone with a legitimate reason to come—another teacher or the director, for example—and make sure you let the family know who will be there.

How do you handle challenging behavior when the parent is present?

When parents and teachers are in the same room—as in a cooperative preschool, at arrival and departure time, and during field trips and special events—everyone gets slightly confused about who's in charge, and problem behaviors may reemerge. If the parents don't act, use the chance to model an appropriate response. If they do act, you have a golden opportunity to watch them interact with their child—and no matter what you think of their behavior, you'll have to let it go.

What if a child is hurt?

Whenever a child requires first aid for an injury caused by another child, you must tell your supervisor or principal and complete an incident report right away.

As soon as the parents of the injured child arrive, let them know exactly what happened without mentioning the name of the child who was responsible. (Although the children may tell their families what's going on, it is important for you to protect everyone's privacy.) Be prepared for an angry reaction, either on the spot or after they've seen the bruise. They may accuse you of failing to pay attention or demand that the other child leave the program, and they may not hear any explanation you offer. Stay as calm as you can. In a day or two, you, the director, or the principal can talk with them privately about plans for handling the situation.

Even the families of children who aren't directly involved may become upset, protest, gossip, or contact the program's board of directors or the principal. Some may instruct their children not to play with the child who behaves aggressively. Explain that you are watching carefully, keeping everyone safe, and teaching the children to defend themselves with words—a skill they need on the playground and in life. If families want more information or wish to discuss a child who isn't theirs, refer them to the administration.

WORKING WITH OTHER EXPERTS

What about getting expert advice?

At a certain point it's time to call in the experts. Remember that asking for help is not a sign of weakness; rather it's a sign of wisdom. You are trying to solve your problem by thinking creatively and acquiring new skills. You have to trust your professional judgment—your knowledge of child development, the instinct you've developed by working with children, your awareness of how a child is pushing your buttons. The crucial thing is to act *long* before you feel yourself approaching the breaking point. A burned-out adult is incapable of dealing with the child, the challenging behavior, or a consultant's recommendations.

Together with your supervisor or principal, consider the available services. There may be a psychologist or social worker who works with the center or school from time to time, or your school may have a counselor or a prereferral support team to help you out. If you've been working with them for a while, they may now suggest a functional assessment and positive behavior support plan (see Chapter 10) or an evaluation for special education under IDEA (see Chapter 11). In either case, the family must be involved and give their formal consent. Because you've been collaborating all along, this shouldn't be a problem, but be sure to mention how useful it is to have a fresh point of view. Make it clear that the consultant can observe not only their child but also you and the other children. Having this information should make it easier for the parents to agree.

When you meet with the consultant or prereferral team who will be observing your classroom, explain what you've been seeing, the strategies you've tried, and what you know about the family's point of view. When the observations are concluded, get together with the full team—including the parents—to work out an intervention plan that includes a time frame and an evaluation method. The consultant or a member of the prereferral team should be available to provide support as you implement the plan.

The consultant or the team may suggest some kind of therapy. Because a family is more likely to accept suggestions from someone they have a relationship with— and who knows their child (Koplow, 2002)—it's a good idea for you to participate when a referral is discussed. Timing is also critical. If you and the family haven't been talking about the child's behavior or you haven't tried solutions within your classroom, it will be difficult to get their support. They may not believe extra help is necessary, and they probably won't follow through. If they fear the involvement of a social services agency, they may look for another school where the teachers "care more" about the children—or even move.

Because in most cases the family will have to make their own decisions and appointments, tell them as much as you can about the system and resources in your community. Your director or principal can help you compile an up-to-date list of hospital services, clinics, private practitioners, alternative schools and programs, social service organizations, resource and referral agencies. Schools and Head Start programs may have staff social workers who can help. To minimize the family's frustration, find out about waiting lists, too.

Raising this matter with the family will require extraordinary delicacy. Even though you've had several difficult talks with them, this will probably be the hardest. Don't try to impose your values, and be sure to separate the child from the behavior. Be specific about why you still have strong concerns. Remind them of strategies you've tried, and explain that you think it's important for the child's long-term development to get help for her. Tell them again how much you appreciate their collaboration.

This is serious stuff, and it is much harder to accept than merely "having trouble" in school. The family may not hear what you have to say, so be sure to impress on them that they can call you with their questions. Some families may find the idea of a specialist or special education totally alien and see it as a rejection or a form of stigmatization. They may have fears about what this might mean for their child and themselves and need emotional support. They may also be worrying about the cost and length of the treatment and wondering how they can fit it into their already overburdened lives. In addition, their culture may consider it inappropriate to discuss family problems with a stranger. If the family has had a previous negative experience with an outside professional, they may be reluctant to try again. Ask them about what problems they had, and try to match them with a service or personality that will best meet their needs.

Getting an assessment for a preschool-age child can be difficult. Because she is growing so quickly and the range of normal is so wide, some problems, such as attention deficit hyperactivity disorder, may be hard to diagnose and professionals are reluctant to give her a label she may keep for years. A letter from you with a detailed description of the behavior will help. Ask the family's permission to write it, and put the original and a copy for them into an unsealed envelope so that they can read it and decide whether they want to deliver it. If you would like feedback from the specialist, ask the family to authorize him or her to release information to you—although they may prefer to keep the findings to themselves.

It is possible that the family will reject the idea of outside intervention. This is their right, and their decision doesn't imply that they don't love their child—only that they aren't ready or that their view of the situation is different from yours.

Can you ask a child with challenging behavior to leave?

If you're really at the end of your rope, you could ask your administrator to pull out her bag of tricks and pitch in at critical times, give you a couple of hours (or days) of leave, hire additional staff for part of the day, or set up training or support sessions. If you've already discussed the situation with her and your colleagues, they will understand your request and help pick up the slack. They, too, want what's best for the child. Burnout is a legitimate complaint, and you may be eligible for short-term disability.

It is only when a child becomes a real danger to herself or others—and when you've exhausted every technique you and the experts can devise—that exclusion becomes thinkable. Sometimes asking the parents to withdraw the child from the program may spur them to get the intervention the child needs, but you should never use this possibility as a rationalization for making such a decision.

Handing the child over to another adult is rarely a viable solution. Unless the program can afford to hire an extra person, a move like this usually requires too much juggling of people and schedules. There is another important consideration: Attachment is critical in child development. You spend many hours a day with this child, and it's important for her long-term development (and particularly her ability to trust) for her to know she can trust you, that you can take care of her, and that she can't destroy you. Sending her away doesn't teach anything positive. Rather, it is the ultimate destroyer of self-esteem because it says in neon lights, "I don't want you here," confirming the child's most negative self-image.

Being asked not to return also tells a child you think she's bad—which means she must be *really* bad. When she goes to another school, she brings along that sense of who she is and feels more comfortable trying to show teachers and peers how bad she is rather than showing them (or herself) that the previous school made a mistake.

Teachers have a responsibility to teach every child in their class (and no child is truly unteachable).

W HAT DO YOU THINK?

1. Examine your own attitude. Do you think families are responsible for how their child behaves at school? How? What other factors may be involved?

2. Talk to a teacher who has a child with challenging behavior in her class about working with the parents. What are some of her attitudes? Has she been successful in creating a positive relationship? How? If she hasn't managed to develop a sense of teamwork, what might have played a part in the family's position?

3. With a classmate, role play a parent–teacher meeting with one person being the teacher and the other the parent of a child with challenging behavior. Evaluate the meeting. What were some of the difficulties for the teacher? For the parent? How did you deal with the parent's response? What would you do differently? Conduct a follow-up meeting to iron out some of the problems that arose.

4. Many organizations help children with challenging behavior and their families. Compile a list of resources in your neighborhood, describe what they do, get the contact information for someone at each place, and collect a brochure or other written information useful to a family.

S UGGESTED READING

Baker, A. C., & Manfredi/Petitt, L. A. (2004). *Relationships, the heart of quality care: Creating community among adults in early care settings.* Washington, DC: National Association for the Education of Young Children.

Blue-Banning, M., Summers, J. A., Frankland, H. C., Nelson, L. L., & Beegle, G. (2004). Dimensions of family and professional partnerships: Constructive guidelines for collaboration. *Exceptional Children, 70,* 167–184.

Lareau, A., & Shumar, W. (1996). The problem of individualism in family-school policies [Extra issue]. *Sociology of Education, 69,* 24–39.

Lawrence-Lightfoot, S. (2003). *The essential conversation: What parents and teachers can learn from each other.* New York: Ballantine.

Trumbull, E., Rothstein-Fisch, C., Greenfield, P. M., & Quiroz, B. (2001). *Bridging cultures between home and school: A guide for teachers.* Mahwah, NJ: Erlbaum.

Webster-Stratton, C., & Herbert, M. (1994). *Troubled families—Problem children: Working with parents: A collaborative process.* Chichester, England: Wiley.

CHAPTER 13

Bullying

Bullying has probably existed forever, but few researchers took it seriously until 1982, when newspapers in Norway reported that three boys had committed suicide after being bullied by their peers. The news shocked the country, and in 1983, Norway's Ministry of Education launched a nationwide program against bullying in schools (Olweus, 1991, 1993). Since then, interest in the subject has spread around the world (Smith et al., 1999).

Because bullying is such a complex topic, we have left it for last. To address it, you will need all the skills and knowledge you acquired in the previous chapters. In the three parts of this chapter, you'll learn what bullying is, how teachers can reduce and prevent it, and how to respond to it.

WHAT IS BULLYING?

Bullying is a special form of aggressive behavior. The world's leading authority on bullying, Dan Olweus, who designed the Norwegian intervention program, defines it this way: "A person is being bullied when he or she is exposed, repeatedly and over time, to negative actions on the part of one or more other persons" (Olweus, 1993, p. 9). What differentiates bullying from other aggressive acts is that the child who bullies intends to harm, there is more than one incident, and an imbalance of power makes it hard for the child who is being bullied to defend himself. This difference in power can be physical—the child who bullies can be older, bigger, stronger; or several children can gang up on a single child. It can also be psychological, which is harder to see but just as potent—the child who bullies usually has more social status.

There are several kinds of bullying:

• *Physical* bullying is the easiest to identify: Hitting, kicking, shoving, and taking or destroying property, for example. Physical bullying is more widespread among boys (Nansel et al., 2001).

• *Verbal* bullying includes name-calling, insulting, mocking, threatening, taunting, teasing, and making racist or sexist comments. When does teasing cross the line and turn into bullying? Not everyone agrees, but some researchers see teasing and bullying as points on a continuum of intentionally hurtful behavior, different only in degree (Froschl, Sprung, & Mullin-Rindler, 1998). One study (Oliver, Hoover, & Hazler, 1994) found that children are confused about teasing: They said it was done in fun, but they also ranked it as the most frequent bullying behavior. Verbal abuse is the most common form of bullying for children of both sexes, even young ones (Kochenderfer & Ladd, 1996; Nansel et al., 2001).

• *Relational or psychological* bullying, which begins as early as 3 years (Ostrov, Woods, Jansen, Casas, & Crick, 2004), uses relationships to control or harm another person (Crick, Casas, & Ku, 1999; Crick et al., 2001)—excluding him from the group or events, talking behind his back, spreading rumors, or telling lies about him. Relational bullying deprives children of the opportunity to be close to and accepted by their peers, which is important for their well-being and development (Crick et al., 2001). Girls are more likely to use, and become the targets of, relational bullying (Crick et al., 1999; Crick & Grotpeter, 1995), but both boys and girls consider it the most hurtful type of bullying (Rigby, 2002).

• *Sexual harassment*—unwanted sexual behavior that interferes with a student's life—is common among older children of both sexes (Gruber & Fineran, 2008).

• *Cyberbullying* is also growing as electronic media become omnipresent in children's lives (Hertz & David-Ferdon, 2008; Juvonen & Gross, 2008).

Although they're hard to classify, making faces and gesturing can be bullying, too.

The experts also categorize bullying as *direct* (when a child bullies openly, allowing the child under attack to identify his assailant) (Olweus, 1993), or *indirect* (when the child doing the

The difference in power can be physical—the child who bullies can be older, bigger, stronger; or several children can gang up on a single child.

Mean Girls

At 3 or 4 years of age, some children have already mastered the skill of relational bullying. In a study of 328 preschoolers, David A. Nelson, Clyde C. Robinson, and Craig H. Hart (2005) found that a substantial number of girls and some boys used fear and power to manage relationships, excluding classmates, spreading rumors, telling secrets, and threatening not to play if their demands weren't met. Nonetheless, their proficient social skills enabled them to be well liked.

bullying inflicts harm without revealing his intention) (Alsaker & Valkanover, 2001). Physical bullying is usually direct, but verbal and relational bullying can be either direct or indirect. Some preschoolers don't yet have the social skills to bully indirectly, so their bullying tends to be direct ("I'm going to cut off your mother's head") (Crick et al., 1999; Crick et al., 2001). Others—and older children—use more subtle and indirect methods, such as never finding space at the lunch table for Aisha (Ostrov et al., 2004).

By and large, bullying is a clandestine activity. The favorite venues for harassment—playgrounds, hallways, cafeterias, locker rooms, and bathrooms (Vaillancourt et al., 2010)—feature few or no adults. Children who've been victimized may find ways to stay in the classroom during recess and endure great physical discomfort to avoid using school bathrooms.

How common is bullying?

Bullying appears in all racial and ethnic groups and all socioeconomic classes (Orpinas & Horne, 2006), whether schools are large or small, urban or rural (Olweus, 1993). Although most children experience a minor and fleeting form of it at some point during their school careers (Juvonen & Graham, 2001), for a surprising number bullying is a frequent and serious event. A large-scale study of bullying in the United States revealed that almost 30 percent of children are involved in bullying either moderately ("sometimes") or frequently ("once a week or more")—13 percent bully others, 11 percent are targeted, and 6 percent both bully others and are targeted themselves (Nansel et al., 2001). Playground observations show that bullying occurs every 3 to 7 minutes (Craig & Pepler, 1997; Snyder et al., 2003).

Bullying seems to peak between 6 and 13 years (Finkelhor, Turner, Ormrod, & Hamby, 2009). In preschool, up to 18 percent of children are targets, and 17 percent bully others (Alsaker & Valkanover, 2001; Crick et al., 1999). One study that followed children from kindergarten to grade 3 determined that 4 percent were persistently victimized (Ladd & Ladd, 2001). Some children never stop bullying, though we call their handiwork by different names in adult life—such as harassment, spousal abuse, child abuse, racism, and sexism (Pepler & Craig, n.d.).

Because of the secret nature of bullying, teachers may underestimate its prevalence. When Wendy Craig and Debra J. Pepler (1997) videotaped bullying on Toronto playgrounds, they saw teachers intervene in only 4 percent of incidents, although

75 percent said they always responded. This low rate probably means the teachers didn't actually see or recognize the harassment. And children who bully make it clear that neither the onlookers nor the children who are victimized are to divulge what happened. This tactic is strikingly successful: In one study, 30 percent of children told neither their parents nor their teachers they'd been targeted (Smith & Shu, 2000).

Who are the children who bully others?

By definition, children who use bullying behavior are strong individuals who choose to dominate their more susceptible peers. They may have an impulsive temperament and a tendency to hotheadedness, and they have a positive attitude toward violence (Olweus, 1993). In school they earn below average marks (Nansel et al., 2001), don't always follow the rules, and often behave aggressively and defiantly toward adults. If they are boys, they may be physically strong and good at sports and fighting (Olweus, 1993), but girls who bully tend to use indirect methods.

Children who target others probably acquire their view of violence at home, where they see how effective it can be. They may have observed parents or siblings bullying others or have been bullied themselves (Sharp & Smith, 1994). Olweus (1993) found that the families of children who bully often use power-assertive child-drearing methods, such as physical punishment and violent emotional outbursts. They don't set clear limits or outlaw aggressive behavior, and they are usually cold and indifferent toward their child, which leads to an avoidant attachment relationship and increases the risk of aggressive behavior. A child in such a family grows up with a strong need to dominate others, get his own way, and be in control, and he isn't interested in negotiating, cooperating, or accepting anyone else's ideas (Olweus, 1993; Rigby, 1998). Pepler and Craig (n.d.) point out that he's learned some important lessons—that having power allows people to be aggressive, and that power and aggression can bring dominance and status.

Unlike children who use aggressive behavior indiscriminately, children who bully are generally popular, well liked, and surrounded by friends and supporters from an early age (Alsaker & Nagele, 2008; Olweus, 1993). It is a myth that they lack social skills and self-esteem (Olweus, 1991, 1993). In fact, they are socially skilled, outgoing, and self-confident, with little anxiety or insecurity. They often dominate their peer group and manipulate others to maintain their high status (Pepler, Jiang, Craig, & Connolly, 2008).

Researchers have suggested children who bully have a superior *theory of mind* or *social cognition*—that is, an advanced ability to understand the minds of others (Sutton, Smith, & Sweetenham, 1999). This is especially important in indirect bullying, where the child who's doing the bullying must know who will join his efforts to exclude another child and what justification the group will find acceptable. Even direct bullying takes sharp social insight: The child who's bullying must avoid detection and choose a method that leaves him unscathed while hurting the target. He may try out his tactics on several targets before settling on one who doesn't resist (Perry, Perry, & Kennedy, 1992).

Although children who are adept at bullying understand others' emotions, they have little empathy and don't worry about the pain or discomfort they cause (Olweus, 1993). On the contrary, they may even enjoy it (Rigby, 2001b).

As they grow older, children who bully are at risk for a host of difficulties, including aggressive behavior, alcohol and drug abuse, delinquency, gang involvement, sexual harassment, school dropout, and peer rejection. They may also suffer from mental health problems, such as conduct disorder, depression, anxiety, and suicidal thoughts (Olweus, 1991; Yale University Office of Public Affairs, 2008). When Olweus (1993) studied boys with a history of bullying, he found that by early adulthood about 60 percent had been convicted of a criminal offense, and about a third had three or more convictions. Children who use relational bullying also face risks: They struggle with behavior problems and self-esteem and are likely to be lonely, depressed, and rejected (Crick & Grotpeter, 1995).

Who are the targets of bullying?

It is no fun to be on the receiving end of bullying. The immediate effects—physical injury, humiliation, helplessness, rejection, unhappiness—are painful enough, but the knowledge that all this will soon be repeated multiplies the distress. Children who are harassed experience fear, anxiety, insecurity, oppression, depression, inability to concentrate in class, headaches, stomachaches, and nightmares. It is not surprising that they want to avoid school (Kochenderfer & Ladd, 1996). Being bullied has a devastating effect on self-esteem. It's hard for a child to stop thinking that he deserves whatever he gets (Boivin, Hymel, & Hodges, 2001), and the worse he feels about himself, the more susceptible he is (Swearer, Song, Cary, Eagle, & Mickelson, 2001).

How does a child become the target of bullying? Olweus (1993) terms most children who are bullied "passive victims": "cautious, sensitive, quiet, withdrawn, passive, submissive and shy . . . anxious, insecure, unhappy, and distressed" (p. 57). They may also be physically weak (Perry, Hodges, & Egan, 2001), clumsy, and afraid of being hurt. They often have a history of insecure attachment, trouble separating from their parents, and a fear of exploring their surroundings. Their families tend to overprotect them, manipulate their thoughts and feelings, and use coercive and power-assertive discipline (Card & Hodges, 2008). These tactics threaten the development of the child's sense of self, undermine confidence, and batter self-esteem (Perry et al., 2001).

Sensing a child's vulnerability, a more powerful child or group may decide to tease or ridicule him (Rigby, 2002). Instead of standing up for himself, he feels threatened and scared and cries or runs away, signaling he's an easy mark. Because a child who's targeted usually has poor social skills and few or no friends, the child doing the bullying knows no one will come to his defense (Hodges, Boivin, Vitaro, & Bukowski, 1999; Perry et al., 2001). Some children are so eager to belong to a group they'll put up with any kind of abuse (Roberts, 2006). Even in a new classroom or school, children who've been bullied communicate their insecurity and fear, setting themselves up for more victimization (Salmivalli, Kaukiainen, & Lagerspetz, 1998). They become locked into the role of victim by 8 or 9 years of age (Pepler, Smith, & Rigby, 2004).

Are children bullied because they're different in other ways? Psychologists David G. Perry, Ernest V. E. Hodges, and Susan K. Egan (2001) point out that physical differences seem to incite teasing, which can cause distress and a loss of self-esteem—and may put a child at risk of harassment. In the large American survey

Early Signs

To find out how children take on the role of victim, psychologists David Schwartz, Kenneth A. Dodge, and John D. Coie (1993) ran a series of experimental play groups of first- and third-grade boys who didn't know each other.

In the early sessions, some boys were unassertive. They started fewer conversations, spent more time in parallel play, and didn't tell their peers what to do. When others approached them aggressively and in rough-and-tumble play, they submitted, rewarding their attackers. This behavior marked them as potential targets. In later sessions, the other boys treated them more and more negatively, coercively, and aggressively.

(Nansel et al., 2001), about 20 percent of the boys and girls who were bullied most often were victimized because of their looks or speech. Children with disabilities (Whitney, Smith, & Thompson, 1994) and children who are obese (Janssen, Craig, Boyce, & Pickett, 2004) also face a higher risk of harassment.

Ethnicity or culture sometimes makes a child a target. In the large American study (Nansel et al., 2001), about 8 percent of the students who were bullied frequently reported that their race or religion was the cause. But other studies have found much higher rates. In surveys in New York and New Jersey, about 45 percent of African American, Latino, and European American students and about 65 percent of Asian American students said their peers had harassed or discriminated against them because of their race or ethnicity (Way & Hughes, 2007). Children targeted by racial harassment face profound educational, emotional, and physical consequences.

Not all children who are harassed are passive. Perhaps 10 to 20 percent fight back and even egg on their abusers. Dubbed "provocative" victims by Olweus (1993), they are also called "aggressive" or "bully-victims." New research shows that children who are the most highly and chronically victimized are themselves highly aggressive from toddlerhood onwards (Barker et al., 2008). They are bullied in preschool and continue to be victimized by both peers and teachers in primary school (Brendgen, Wanner, & Vitaro, 2006).

Like children who bully, these "bully-victims" try to dominate others, and their behavior is often antisocial, impulsive, and hyperactive (Olweus, 1993). Like children who are targeted but don't retaliate, they are anxious, depressed, rejected, lonely, and physically weak. Lacking social skills, they have few friends (Perry et al., 2001; Schwartz, Proctor, & Chen, 2001). But perhaps their most prominent quality is their volatility. They lose their tempers, overreact, argue, and fight about all kinds of things, and they almost invariably lose (Perry et al., 1992). With this provocative behavior, they elicit negative reactions from just about everyone (Olweus, 1993).

It is no surprise that such children usually come from a harsh environment where the parenting is hostile and punitive and there is lots of conflict and violence. In one study, 38 percent of "aggressive victims" had been physically abused; many had witnessed domestic violence (Schwartz, Dodge, Pettit, & Bates, 1997).

In the long run, there is risk for all children who are bullied. They lack self-esteem and are more depressed, anxious, socially dysfunctional, and physically unwell than their nonvictimized peers (Olweus, 1993, 2001; Rigby, 2001a). A Dutch study revealed that some as young as 9 years of age had suicidal thoughts (van der Wal, de Wit, & Hirasing, 2003). Children who've been the targets of relational bullying are even more depressed, lonely, anxious, and rejected in later life (Crick et al., 1999; Crick et al., 2001). "Bully-victims" are the most disturbed of all, with the most serious behavior problems and difficulties at school (Juvenon, Graham, & Schuster, 2003). An analysis of 37 school shootings disclosed that 70 percent of the shooters had been bullied by their peers (Vossekuil, Fein, Reddy, Borum, & Modzeleski, 2002).

Who are the bystanders?

Bullying is a group activity, situated in a social context that influences both the emergence of bullying and the response to it. The hard evidence of Craig and Pepler's (1997) cameras showed that peers were involved in 85 percent of bullying incidents. Bullying lasts longer when more peers are present (O'Connell, Pepler, & Craig, 1999), and when they don't intervene—sending the unmistakable message that they condone the behavior—bullying becomes increasingly acceptable. The result is a harsher, less-empathetic social climate that fosters more bullying (Salmivalli, 2010).

An audience is the lifeblood of a child who bullies. The bystanders' reactions—their active assistance, comments, and laughter—reinforce and incite his behavior (Slaby, 1997), spread word of his power, and raise his status (Sutton et al., 1999). Psychologist Christina Salmivalli (1999, 2001) has shown that during bullying episodes children take on different roles, depending on their individual dispositions and the group's expectations. In addition to bullying and being victimized, they play the following parts:

• *Assistants* help the child who is doing the bullying. In a study of 7- to 10-year-olds, about 7 percent of children acted as assistants (Sutton & Smith, 1999).

• *Reinforcers* encourage bullying behavior by laughing and commenting on the action. Almost 6 percent took on this role (Sutton & Smith, 1999).

• *Outsiders* stay away and don't take sides, but their silence permits bullying. Nearly 12 percent fit this description (Sutton & Smith, 1999). In the Toronto schoolyard study, children acted as silent witnesses 54 percent of the time (O'Connell et al., 1999).

• *Defenders* come to the defense of the child under attack. Only 17 to 20 percent of students in a Finnish study stood up for him (Salmivalli, 2010); and in the Toronto study, peers took his side just 19 percent of the time, usually bringing bullying to a halt (Hawkins, Pepler, & Craig, 2001). Defenders are more likely to be self-confident, popular, and well liked by their peers (Sutton & Smith, 1999).

Paradoxically, 83 percent of the children in a Canadian survey reported that bullying made them feel uncomfortable (O'Connell et al., 1999), and many felt they should help a child who's being bullied (Hawkins et al., 2001). Witnessing an attack can even traumatize some children (Garbarino & deLara, 2002). Clearly, there is a gap between children's attitudes and their behavior.

Why do bystanders behave the way they do?

- *Attraction to aggression.* As Pepler and Craig (2000) put it, "Peers are the audience for the theater of bullying" (p. 9), which excites and arouses them.

- *Fear.* They may be afraid of the child who bullies and realize they will put their own safety at risk if they try to defend the child who's been targeted (O'Connell et al., 1999). They also fear being excluded from the group (Garandeau & Cillessen, 2006). Behaving aggressively or being unfriendly to a child who's being harassed is a way to belong (Salmivalli, 2010).

- *Social contagion.* When children see someone acting aggressively, they tend to act more aggressively themselves. This effect increases if they think highly of the aggressor. When a popular child bullies, the assistants and reinforcers are more likely to follow his lead (Salmivalli, 2010), boosting their own social status and safety from future harassment (Olweus, 1993). Bullying is highest in classrooms where the bystanders seem to support it—everyone infers that the rest of the group accepts it (Salmivalli, 2010).

- *Weakening of the controls against aggressive behavior.* Children's inhibitions against aggressive behavior become loosened when they realize it has no negative consequences and is even rewarded. Seeing aggressive behavior pay off may also desensitize children to violence.

- *Diffusion of individual responsibility.* When several people are involved, each individual feels less empathy, guilt, and responsibility (Thompson & Grace, 2001).

- *Changes in perception of the children involved in bullying.* The child who bullies gains a reputation as a protector; but the more harassment a child endures, the more his peers regard him as weird, worthless, and deserving of abuse and rejection (Ladd & Troop-Gordon, 2003). Many children believe the child being victimized can control his own behavior and is therefore responsible for the harassment (Graham & Juvonen, 2001). They may also blame him because it's difficult to function if one believes that life is random and unfair; it's less threatening to view the world as a just place where people get what they deserve (Wilczenski et al., 1994). In general, people who blame uncontrollable circumstances are more sympathetic and willing to help.

Social Contagion

Five-year-old Vicky waited for all her friends to get their lunches and sit at the table. Then she asked them to raise their hands if they liked chocolate. She raised her hand, and everyone followed. Next she said, "Raise your hand if you like spaghetti." She raised her hand, and once again so did everyone else. Finally she said, "Raise your hand if you like Carmen." She didn't raise her hand, and neither did any of the other girls. Carmen, who was seated near the end of the table, began to cry.

- *Role stabilization.* Once a child assumes a role in a group, it's hard to change it (Salmivalli, 1999).

- *Scapegoating.* When there is bullying, all members of the group contribute by their action or inaction (Twemlow, Fonagy, & Sacco, 2004). A child who bullies operates with the support of the group and on its behalf. To feel better about themselves, the group members project their worst fears and impulses onto the child in the victim role. He becomes a scapegoat who deserves this treatment and is ostracized from the school community (Thompson & Grace, 2001).

- *Lack of understanding.* Children don't intervene in a bullying incident because they don't understand it and don't know how to counteract it (O'Connell et al., 1999).

HOW CAN TEACHERS REDUCE AND PREVENT BULLYING?

It is hard to eliminate bullying, but finding ways to cut down on its frequency or duration can make an important difference in a child's ability to cope (Ladd & Ladd, 2001).

The whole-school approach

To reduce and prevent bullying, many researchers advocate a whole-school approach, where everyone in the environment—administrators, teachers, children, parents, paraprofessionals, bus drivers, lunch supervisors, clerical staff—undertake to fight bullying. This is the method Olweus and the Norwegian government used in their successful national bullying intervention (Olweus, 1993, 2001). Although this approach is far from perfect—replications in the United States have produced much smaller effects than those in Norway—researchers have concluded it is better than anything else that's available (Farrington & Ttofi, 2009; Merrell, Gueldner, Ross, & Isasva, 2008; Smith, Schneider, Smith, & Ananiadou, 2004; Vreeman & Carroll, 2007).

The goal of the whole-school approach is to restructure the environment in order to decrease opportunities and rewards for bullying and increase reinforcement for positive behavior (Olweus, 1993). This change in the social context lets children know that bullying is not acceptable and adults will intervene to protect them. Once a school has adopted an anti-bullying policy, it must commit itself to its underlying values and implement it fully (Salmivalli, Kaukiainen, & Voeten, 2005). Otherwise it will provide little protection and even put children at risk (Sullivan, Cleary, & Sullivan, 2004). When everyone is on the same page, the anti-bullying message comes through loud and clear, and there's more backup for prevention and intervention (Sharp & Thompson, 1994).

Schoolwide positive behavior support provides a solid foundation for bullying prevention, offering an inclusive social context and clear rules about respecting everyone's rights. PBS adherents are even in the process of developing a bullying

The Lion's Many Roars

Quit It! A Teacher's Guide on Teasing and Bullying for Use with Students in Grades K–3 includes a unit on courage. Merle Froschl, Barbara Sprung, and Nancy Mullin-Rindler (1998) write:

- It takes courage not to "follow the crowd," especially at this young age when belonging is so important. If we can help students find their own inner strength in the early grades they will be better prepared to resist the peer pressure that becomes so intense in adolescence.
- It takes courage to disagree with someone and risk that they might not be your friend . . . .
- It takes courage to perform acts of kindness, especially when they involve overcoming a barrier or standing up for someone who is often a target of teasing or bullying . . . .
- It takes courage to control your own emotions and not lash out. (p. 67)

prevention program (Ross & Horner, 2009). But if your school or child care center doesn't use PBS or have an anti-bullying policy, you can introduce one in your own classroom. Be aware that the process will take time, and because the children are becoming more aware of bullying, the problem may seem to get worse before it gets better (Pepler & Craig, 2000). Much of what is suggested here has been discussed in previous chapters, so you are already well on your way.

Because of the power imbalance inherent in bullying, children cannot fight it alone, and adult inaction equals tacit approval: We have known for decades that the presence of passive adults—bystanders—increases children's aggressive behavior (Siegel & Kohn, 1959). In classrooms where teachers don't intervene to stop bullying, children don't step in either (Slee, 1993). As the leader of the class, you hold the key to the success of your anti-bullying project.

Teachers have some effective tools to bring to the anti-bullying enterprise. First and foremost, you are a role model. If you insult, bully, or put your students down, you will give them "a first-hand lesson in the use of power and aggression," write Pepler and Craig (2007). Instead, you can demonstrate the positive use of power on a daily basis and role model respectful behavior.

You will also need to develop sensitive and responsive relationships with the children in your class; build an inclusive, cooperative classroom climate; and place firm limits on unacceptable behavior (Pepler et al., 2004; Roland & Galloway, 2002). Clear rules against bullying are vital (Farrington & Ttofi, 2009), and the best way to create them is to involve the whole class (see pages 127–129). Olweus (1993) suggests three:

- We will not bully other children.
- We will try to help children who are bullied.
- We will make a point of including children who are easily left out.

As they draw up their rules, the children need to talk about what bullying is as well as why rules are important and what they can do to make the class safer.

Because the social context plays such a crucial role in encouraging or inhibiting bullying, many researchers believe that an anti-bullying program should target the group, not just the individuals involved (Salmivalli, 2010). Children often think bullying is wrong, feel sorry for the child who's been victimized, and would like to help, but they fail to act. Making them aware that others share their views could make a difference—and even a single defender can reduce the painful fallout for a child who's being harassed (Salmivalli, 2010). In fact, children are more willing to intervene in a bullying situation when they believe their friends and parents expect them to (Rigby & Johnson, 2006).

In other words, bullying issues should be an ongoing, integral part of the curriculum (Olweus, 1993; Salmivalli et al., 2005). Power, empathy, peer pressure, courage, prosocial behavior, the difference between accidental and on purpose, the difference between tattling to get someone into trouble and telling to get someone out of trouble, the line between teasing and bullying, how it feels to be unwelcome—all of these topics kindle discussion, and you can reinforce the anti-bullying message with age-appropriate books, drawings, puppets, and role plays. But be careful not to cast a child who is victimized in a role where he's harassed or a child who bullies in a bullying role—or even in the role of a target since this may provide him with greater insight into how to harass.

Be sure to sensitize the children to the role of the bystander. Explain that they probably don't realize it, but when they're present during a bullying incident, even if they're only watching, they are supporting the child who bullies. Discuss and role play what they can do instead—walk away, tell the child who's bullying to stop, tell the teacher, include the child who's left out. When they act collectively, they can change the balance of power, so give them scripts and coach them to step in together (Pepler & Craig, 2007). If they suggest fighting back, help them understand that although aggression may work in the short term, it's counterproductive in the long run—it escalates the aggression, endangers the child who's intervening, and reinforces the idea that it's an appropriate way to resolve problems (Hawkins et al., 2001).

Emphasize that secrecy enables bullying to continue and that grown-ups can help. You can encourage children to tell an adult about bullying by clarifying the difference between tattling to get someone into trouble and telling to get someone out of trouble. Let them know you will always believe them when they disclose bullying and you will try your best to keep the source of your information confidential. In the end, children will report bullying only if they feel certain you will believe them and will act discreetly and effectively to stop it.

Help children identify bullying hot spots such as bathrooms and secluded areas on the playground. If they know they're in danger, they can avoid this territory, go with a friend, or stay within a reasonable distance of a teacher's watchful eye. It's important to increase supervision in these areas, stock the playground with age-appropriate equipment (Swearer & Doll, 2001), and organize noncompetitive games, which can decrease both playground and classroom bullying (Froschl et al., 1998). In addition, you'll need a system that allows children to report bullying safely and privately.

It's also important to bring parents into the picture. The more they know about bullying and the class rules, the more support they can provide. One way to involve them is to invite them to see a video about bullying (see page 272 for suggestions). Then present your policy and the facts about bullying, and encourage them to discuss the topic. To help them talk with their children at home, be sure to explain the difference between tattling and telling to protect someone, the bystanders' role, and how children can assist a child who's being harassed or excluded (Olweus, 1993).

What helps children cope with bullying?

Researchers have pinpointed some protective factors and strategies that enable children to avoid bullying, deter future attacks, and cope without being overwhelmed. Although natural endowments such as physical strength and intelligence provide protection (Smith, Shu, & Madsen, 2001), children who are targeted need a range of responses.

- *Self-esteem.* Children who feel good about themselves put up an effective defense against bullying (Egan & Perry, 1998). To build self-esteem, search out and support children's strengths and give them lots of opportunities to feel proud of their accomplishments. It is especially important to encourage and reinforce positive interactions with peers.

- *Assertiveness skills.* When children respond assertively, the perpetrators of bullying will stop or move on. Assertiveness training helps children gain self-control, confidence, and self-esteem (Sharp & Cowie, 1994), and it isn't just for those who are harassed. Learning to act assertively can help the children who take the role of assistants and reinforcers to resist peer pressure and refrain from bullying, and it can encourage the outsiders to act as defenders (Salmivalli, 1999). Changing the attitudes and behavior of his associates may provoke change in the behavior of the child who bullies.

- *Social skills.* Social and emotional skills enable a child to become a valued member of a group and provide some immunity to bullying (Egan & Perry, 1998; Perry et al., 2001). Training in these skills can be useful for bystanders and children who are victimized (DeRosier, 2004), but it is not a panacea. For example, children who are bullied seldom possess the social competence and supportive peer group necessary to deescalate a bullying situation through problem solving (Kochenderfer-Ladd & Skinner, 2002). There is also little evidence that social skills training will work with children who bully (Rigby, Smith, & Pepler, 2004). In fact, it may be ill advised to teach them empathy, which could heighten their already acute social perception and boost their bullying skills. Several experts (Sutton et al., 1999) instead suggest focusing on moral issues and trying to change their positive attitude toward aggression (Thompson & Grace, 2001).

- *Cooperation skills.* Children who bully and children who are victimized both tend to be less cooperative—the former because they have little empathy, and the latter because they're introverted and less accepted by their peers (Rigby, 1998). Because children who cooperate with others are happier and more popular, this is a valuable skill for building friendships and preventing bullying. A cooperative, inclusive social context and techniques such as cooperative learning groups and peer tutoring can foster cooperation.

Under Cover

Rachel, an only child who spent a lot of time with adults, and Gabriella, the younger of two siblings, were best friends, or so it appeared. Rachel would seek out Gabriella as often as Gabriella looked for Rachel, but on close inspection, there seemed to be a power difference between the 4-year-olds.

The teachers never saw the conflict. They found out what was happening when Gabriella's mother told them that Gabriella had come home with soiled underpants. She was embarrassed to go to the bathroom because Rachel had said her brown skin and outy belly button were ugly.

• *A friend.* Having a friend can be a powerful buffer against harassment (Boivin et al., 2001) and cushion a child who's been bullied from emotional and behavioral problems (Hodges et al., 1999). But a friend who's too weak to furnish protection may actually increase the risk of harassment (Bollmer, Milich, Harris, & Maras, 2005; Hodges et al., 1999). Teachers can play an important role in decreasing the isolation that makes children vulnerable (Hazler & Carney, 2006). By using cooperative learning groups, organizing a buddy system or a circle of friends for a solitary child, and selecting teams, groups, and seating so that he's always included, teachers can help him make friends and surround him with peers who will stand up for him (Pepler & Craig, 2007). Be aware, however, that bullying within friendships is also common, and it's important to watch for an imbalance of power (Mishna, Scarcello, Pepler, & Wiener, 2005).

• *An internal locus of control.* When a child thinks something immutable in his character makes him a target, he may feel helpless or depressed and ready to give up. But when he believes he has some control over his life, he is more likely to look for ways to change and cope—to seek help or use positive self-talk, for example (Graham & Juvonen, 2001; Ladd & Ladd, 2001). You can nurture self-efficacy by giving children responsibility and opportunities to succeed and encouraging them to reflect on their own competence (Doll, Song, & Siemers, 2004).

• *Telling a teacher.* When 5- and 6-year-olds in a large Australian study (Rigby, 2002) told someone they'd been victimized, the bullying situation improved about half of the time. For

A friend can be a powerful buffer against harassment.

older children it is more effective to ignore bullying (Smith et al., 2001). However, it is still important for children of all ages to tell an adult about bullying.

Many of these strategies are described in more detail in Chapters 7 and 8. Role playing and rehearsal are essential for learning them all. An evidence-based anti-bullying curriculum could also help.

RESPONDING TO BULLYING

Despite your best efforts to prevent it, bullying may still arise. Before it does, take some time to understand your own feelings on the subject. If you bullied or were bullied as a child, your emotions may be surprisingly strong, and it's important to understand them and separate them from what the children are experiencing. In a bullying situation, where a clear head and a nonthreatening tone of voice and body language are essential, you must keep your cool.

What does the law say?

Federal law prohibits harassment on the basis of race, ethnicity, religion, or disability as well as sexual harassment (American Association of University Women, 2004; U.S. Department of Education, 2005a, 2005b). In addition, most states and school districts have anti-bullying legislation, policies, or procedures that compel schools to provide a safe educational environment (U.S. Department of Education, 2005a, 2005b). It is essential for you to know exactly what local laws and policies require.

How can you respond to bullying?

Acting to stop bullying is more than a legal obligation; it is a necessity. A teacher's response to bullying sends a message to every child: that you will tolerate bullying, or that you will not (Sullivan et al., 2004). Even small incidents demand a response, and handling them effectively will help to prevent an escalation. Intervene at once. Whether the attack is verbal or physical, inside or outside of the classroom, do what you'd do with any other act of aggression. Separate the children if necessary, protect the one who's being harassed, let him know you support him, and help him to respond assertively (Sharp & Cowie, 1994). ("It's my job to keep everyone safe, and it's not okay to bully. Tell him you don't like that.") This allows you to state the rules without giving attention directly to the child who's doing the bullying. You may have to clear the bystanders from the area or take along the child who's been targeted when you leave the scene.

What if you don't see the bullying?

It is more likely that a child will tell you about bullying you haven't witnessed yourself. Your instinct might be to refrain from acting until you've seen it with your own eyes, but this isn't necessary: Children do not make up tales about being harassed

Inside Out

It is hard for teachers to identify and respond to bullying. A qualitative study (Mishna et al., 2005) found that they often have no idea a child in their class is being victimized. In interviews, teachers revealed several factors that influenced their perceptions and willingness to intervene:

- *Whether the incident is considered serious.* Sometimes teachers discounted indirect bullying. One teacher disregarded complaints about name-calling because "the child has friends and is liked." Another thought boys who were repeatedly taking a girl's possessions and calling her names were merely trying to get her attention.
- *Whether the child is considered responsible.* In the mind of some teachers, if the child was at fault he didn't deserve support.
- *Whether the child matches assumptions about victimization.* Some teachers assumed a child who seemed well adjusted or assertive couldn't possibly be bullied.
- *Whether the teacher feels empathy for the child who is bullied.* Having compassion strongly affects a teacher's willingness to offer support. Those who realized the bullying might seem more painful to the child than it did to them were able to intervene.

(Pepler & Craig, 2000). Telling a teacher is difficult and risky, even for a child who isn't the target. If the child doing the bullying knows who told the teacher, the bullying may escalate and spread to the defender (Smith & Shu, 2000). Now that you know what's going on, you can take action to protect the child who's being bullied and help him protect himself.

You may never know exactly what happened. What matters is knowing bullying has occurred, where and when it is taking place, and who is involved. Then you can move to prevent it by supervising more closely and stepping up your work with the whole group.

What do you say to children involved in bullying?

Once you know about bullying, what do you do next? Here the experts disagree. Pepler and colleagues (2004) point out that the decision rests in part on your perception of the problem. If you believe bullying is a matter of one child's behavior, you'll probably want to speak with that child one-on-one and arrange consequences. If you think bullying depends on group dynamics, you'll favor a group solution. Olweus (1993) leans toward the first view. He recommends "serious talks" with both the child who's been harassed and the child who did the bullying and imposing sanctions if talks don't work. Other experts prefer "formative consequences," and still others champion a teaching approach where the group is the object of the intervention and no penalties are attached. Many researchers advise taking both actions (Farrington & Totfi, 2009; Salmivalli, 2010; Smith et al., 2004).

Talking with the child who's been targeted

No matter what your philosophical perspective, you'll need to talk with the child who's been victimized. Sit down with him as soon as possible—before you talk with the child who bullied him. Tell him he has the right to feel safe, and your job is to protect him (Pepler & Craig, 2000). Use open-ended questions and active listening to talk about what happened, taking care not to suggest the bullying is his fault or in any way deserved. The child's view of the situation may differ from yours, and his distress may be greater than you realize. Listen carefully to his concerns and feelings, and remember that empathy will help, whereas trivializing or ignoring them will make things worse (Mishna et al., 2005).

Together explore ideas for improving the situation. Remind him of assertive responses, suggest he avoid areas where bullying is likely to occur, coach him in needed social skills, and ask him to select a buddy to help him feel safer and less alone (Pepler & Craig, 2000). Reassure him that you'll assist him in putting these plans into action. If he is a "bully-victim," whose impulsive, argumentative behavior and careening emotions seem to provoke bullying, try to understand the reasons behind his behavior, and use your relationship to work on improving his self-esteem, sense of belonging, and emotional regulation.

It's also important to tell a child who's been targeted that you're going to speak to his parents. Explain that it is safer if they know what's going on and they will want to help. If he protests, encourage him to accept the idea, but eventually you will have to go ahead anyway—with his knowledge but without his permission.

Talking with the child who bullies

It is not easy to speak with the child who bullied. He is likely to push your emotional buttons and deny all wrongdoing, but if you're going to make any headway, it's essential to treat him with respect and listen to what he has to say without judging him. If a group of children is participating, plan to see them individually, one right after the other, so they won't have a chance to cook up a common response or use the group as a power source.

The goal is to convey that bullying is unacceptable and must stop. Stay away from power-assertive language and methods such as hostility, aggression, sarcasm, threats, and humiliation. They are sure to backfire, providing a justification and an inspiration

When you talk with a child who's been bullying others, stay away from power-assertive language and methods. They're sure to backfire.

for more covert ways to bully (Sharp & Cowie, 1994; Sharp, Cowie, & Smith, 1994).
Instead, meet with the child in a private spot and remind him of the rules. (Even if
you have no anti-bullying rules, you should have rules about respecting, taking care
of, or not hurting others.) Let him have his say. But tell him that it's not all right to
hurt others and you'll be contacting his parents.

Spending one-on-one time with a child who bullies is extremely important.
A positive relationship can help you understand the reasons behind the bullying,
focus on his strengths, recognize and redirect his leadership abilities, and think up
positive replacement behaviors to meet his needs. Psychologists Pamela Orpinas
and Arthur M. Horne (2006) make these suggestions:

- *Establish an invitational approach.* "I'd like to talk with you about what's going
on, to get your sense of what's behind the problems . . . " (p. 193).

- *Show respect and dignity.* Students who bully are used to being in trouble and
expect to be treated ignominiously. It is therefore doubly important to treat them
with respect.

- *Be understanding but not approving.* Make an effort to understand the child's
point of view, but avoid giving the impression you approve of inappropriate behavior. "We need to find a different way for you to manage your anger and a way for
you to tolerate other students, even if you don't like them" (p. 194).

- *Accept that the child and his parents are doing the best they can.* "I think that you
are doing the best you can right now . . . but what you've been doing isn't working. . . .
My goal is to spend some time helping you to identify new ways of getting along
with . . . other people, ways you haven't been able to use because you didn't know
about them . . . " (p. 195).

Should there be consequences for children who bully?

Many bullying experts believe that penalties don't deter children with serious bullying problems and that punishment leads to harsher attacks. Children who bully
may blame their punishment on the child they targeted, seek vengeance, and issue
new threats (Robinson & Maines, 2000). Punishment also teaches that bullying is
acceptable for people with power. Severe punishments, such as suspension or expulsion, discourage children from disclosing bullying or intervening in a bullying situation, and experts advise against using them (U.S. Department of Education, 2010).
Olweus (1993) regards a serious talk with a child who's bullying as a consequence and suggests some other conventional sanctions, such as sending him to the
principal's office. Some schools use behavior contracts where, without actually admitting to bullying, the child promises not to bully in the future and understands
the consequences of breaking the contract (O'Moore & Minton, 2004). Pepler and
Craig (2000) favor formative consequences, which teach empathy, awareness, and
social skills, at the same time that they hold children responsible for their behavior
and emphasize that bullying is unacceptable. Formative consequences help a child
who behaves in a cruel way learn to treat others with more kindness and make
amends for his behavior, for example, by asking him to repair the damage he's done,
reading stories about bullying, talking about how bullying makes people feel, and
observing and reporting on acts of kindness in the school and community. This approach enables children who bully to "turn their negative power and dominance

into positive leadership" (Pepler & Craig, 2000, p. 19). Barbara Coloroso (2002) also endorses giving children who bully the opportunity to have responsibility, make a contribution, and experience their own ability to do good.

Rigby (1998) and others advocate a respectful, humanistic approach based on the desire to understand the children involved. They propose listening carefully, establishing two-way communication, and using a technique such as the Support Group Approach developed by George Robinson and Barbara Maines (2000) in England or the Method of Shared Concern created by Anatol Pikas (1989) in Sweden.

These interventions are designed to deescalate denial and defensiveness, focus on the impact of the bullying, and redirect children who are bullying to more positive ends. To solve the problem, they call on a group that includes the children involved in the bullying as well as some supporters of the child who's been targeted. The aim is to arouse their empathic concern, help them to reflect on what can be done to resolve the problem, and assist them to move away from a bullying group (Smith, Cowie, & Sharp, 1994). The group has responsibility for finding the solution, and the process enhances the self-esteem of its members, subtly changes the group's power structure, and prods the leader to find more prosocial ways to lead and retain his status (Sullivan et al., 2004; Young, 1998).

Following up

Consult with your director or principal right away, set up appointments to meet with the parents of the children involved as soon as possible, and continue to monitor the children carefully. In your classroom, rearrange the furniture so that you can see all corners of the room, and change the schedule so that an adult can supervise children as they go to the cloakroom or bathroom. And be sure to follow up with anti-bullying activities for the whole group—they will increase the power of the intervention.

Working with parents

It's imperative to tell parents about bullying (Pepler & Craig, 2000). Olweus (1993) found that parents wanted to know when their child was involved, even if the teacher "merely suspected bullying was taking place" (p. 95). It's always best for the child when teachers and parents work together, so as soon as you have spoken with the children involved, arrange to meet separately with each set of parents (see Chapter 12). Although it's generally more productive to meet with parents by yourself, bullying is a special case. Parents of children who've endured bullying will find the presence of the director or principal reassuring; and you may feel more comfortable having backup when you talk with the parents of a child who bullies.

Because children don't reveal this information, the parents may know nothing about the bullying (Pepler & Craig, 2000). It's humiliating to tell, and a child who's being bullied is probably worried his parents will interfere and make things worse. For parents, learning about bullying may bring a surprising sense of relief and clarity about why their child doesn't want to take the school bus or go to school. But once they've processed this news, they may feel angry, embarrassed, and helpless, blaming you and the school for not providing adequate supervision. They'll want action—and possibly retribution—right away (Pepler & Craig, 2000).

Sometimes, however, an irate and worried parent will inform you about the bullying (Ziegler & Pepler, 1993). If you're just learning about the situation as you meet, you can't offer much feedback—and once again, the family will feel angry and possibly construe your ignorance as incompetence. Under these circumstances, your job is to listen, show empathy, and let the parents know you take the matter seriously. Explain your anti-bullying policy, and tell them you want to work with them to make school a safe place for their child (Suckling & Temple, 2002).

The parents of a child who's being harassed may press hard for severe punishment, believing it is just and necessary. Usually, however, they take this stance because they know of no other way to stop the bullying (Young, 1998). Using the Support Group Approach with difficult cases of bullying in England, Sue Young (1998) found that parents were actually much more interested in effective results than in punishment.

If you haven't seen the bullying yourself, say it's your policy to talk with parents whenever bullying is suspected. Let them know that children rarely fabricate stories about being bullied and their cooperation will make any intervention more effective.

Although you'll meet separately with the parents of the children involved, with both families it's important to keep three strategies firmly in mind:

- Show you care about the child and are trying to help him.

- Avoid blame and arguments—nothing will sabotage your efforts more quickly. Listen to the parents' concerns and try to see things from their perspective, but don't get hooked, even if they attack you.

- Remember you're presenting a problem to be solved, and the best way to solve it is with their collaboration. Parents who play an active role will feel less angry, anxious, and helpless. Be sure they realize they can support their child, help you identify the child's strengths, and figure out strategies to reinforce your efforts at home.

In other ways, your conversations with these two sets of parents may be quite different. The parents of the child who's bullying may see bullying as a normal part of growing up and deny there's a problem. Be understanding but firm. The issue is not whether bullying is acceptable; the purpose of the meeting is to find common ground and develop a strategy to stop it. Describe the school's policy (and yours!) of creating a safe and caring environment for all children (Pepler & Craig, 2000). Tell them briefly what their child has done, emphasizing it's the behavior that's unacceptable, not the child. Remember to talk about his strengths as well. Explain your expectations and the actions you've taken so far, and try to establish a shared concern for the child who was targeted. Project a sense of optimism—all parents ultimately want their child to succeed.

The parents of the child who's been harassed may feel guilty or embarrassed that their child doesn't stand up for himself. If they were bullied as youngsters, their feelings will be magnified. And they will probably continue to be angry their child has been hurt (Pepler & Craig, 2000). Listen to their concerns empathetically, explain your anti-bullying policy, and tell them what you're doing to educate all the children about bullying and prevent their child from becoming a target in the future. Be sure to inform the child about any plan you develop. Let both sets of parents know you will stay in touch and they are welcome to contact you at any time.

It's important to remember that even though bullying has probably gone on for centuries, researchers have only recently started to examine it closely. Definitive answers are still a long way off, but the field is evolving quickly, and it would be a good idea to consult the latest research literature whenever you're dealing with a bullying problem. The younger the child, the easier it is for him to learn appropriate ways to behave, and the better the outcome, both for him and for society. The most effective tool for this job is a positive, sensitive relationship.

WHAT DO YOU THINK?

1. How has your past experience influenced your attitudes about children who bully, children who are victimized, and bystanders?

2. How does what you learned in the prevention chapters (Chapters 7 and 8) relate to what you now know about bullying?

3. Which behavior do you think is the hardest to change—behavior of children who bully, behavior of children who are victimized, or behavior of bystanders? Why?

4. Based on what you have read in this chapter, what do you feel is the best way to deal with bullying? How would you respond to the child who bullies, the child who is targeted, and the bystanders?

5. Why is it important to involve parents when a bullying incident occurs?

SUGGESTED READING AND RESOURCES

Education Development Center. (2008). Eyes on bullying. www.eyesonbullying.org

Garrity, C., Jens, K., Porter, W., Sager, N., & Short-Camilli, C. (2000). *Bully proofing your school: A comprehensive approach for elementary schools* (2nd ed.). Longmont, CO: Sopris West.

Olweus, D. (1993). *Bullying at school: What we know and what we can do.* Malden, MA: Blackwell.

Operation Respect. (n.d.). *Don't laugh at me* [Video]. http://operationrespect.org/curricula/index.php

Page, M. (Producer), & Perlman, J. (Writer/Director/Animator). (2000). *Bully dance* [Video]. National Film Board of Canada. (Available from National Film Board of Canada, 1123 Broadway, Suite 307, New York, NY 10010; 1-800-542-2164;

Fax 1-866-299-9928. www.onf-nfb.gc.ca/eng/collection/film/?id=33918)

Pepler, D. J., & Craig, W. (2000). *Making a difference in bullying.* Toronto: LaMarsh Centre for Research on Violence and Conflict Resolution, York University, Report No. 60. www.yorku.ca/lamarsh/pdf/Making_a_Difference_in_Bullying.pdf

Rigby, K. (2002). *New perspectives on bullying.* London, UK: Jessica Kingsley.

U.S. Department of Education, Office of Safe and Drug Free Schools. (2010). *Exploring the nature and prevention of bullying.* Online workshop. www2.ed.gov/admins/lead/safety/training/bullying/index.html

Reflective Checklists for Chapters 7 and 8

Reflective Checklist: Social Context

Description	Always	Sometimes	Never	What I am doing	What I will do
I consistently role model caring, helpful, inclusive behavior					
I create opportunities for children to get to know one another					
I treat the children with respect and affection					
I tell the children what to do, not what not to do					
My classroom has 3–5 rules that are stated in the positive, developed with the children, and applied consistently					
I provide materials and offer activities that promote cooperation and encourage children to work/play in pairs and groups					
I hold frequent class meetings					
I help children understand their own feelings and those of others					
I teach children problem solving and encourage them to use their skills to resolve conflicts					

Adapted from the DECA Program, Devereux Foundation (1999). Used with permission of DECI, The Devereux Early Childhood Initiative.

Reflective Checklist: Physical Space

Description	Always	Sometimes	Never	What I am doing	What I will do
The classroom reflects children's families, cultures, and home languages					
Children's work is posted at their eye level					
Activity centers reflect children's current skills and interests					
Activity centers and shelves are well organized, inviting, easily accessible to the children, and strategically located					
Boundaries between areas are clear with well defined pathways from one area to another					
There is a simple system to limit the number of children who can use an area at one time					
There is a large area for group events					
Toys and materials match children's interests, abilities, cultures, temperaments, and developmental levels					
There is a sufficient variety and number of toys so each child can find something to do					
There are tactile experiences such as play dough, sand, or water play available at all times					
Each child has a place to store belongings					
There is a comfortable space that is private, but still visible to teachers					
A soothing and relaxing atmosphere with appropriate noise and activity levels is maintained throughout the day					
Children take responsibility for looking after the classroom					
Primary Grades 1–3					
Desks are arranged to encourage cooperation and collaboration and so that every student can see the board					
Students who are easily distracted are seated away from windows, doors, and pencil sharpener					

Adapted from the DECA Program, Devereux Foundation (1999). Used with permission of DECI, The Devereux Early Childhood Initiative.

275

Reflective Checklist: Routines and Transitions

Description	Always	Sometimes	Never	What I am doing	What I will do
There is a predictable schedule that includes varied and balanced quiet and active time, indoor and outdoor time, small- and large-group activities, and teacher- and child-directed activities					
There is a picture schedule posted on the wall					
I teach procedures for starting the day, transitions, going to the bathroom and/or leaving the room, cleanup, going to lunch, and ending the day					
I remind the children of the procedures and they practice them regularly					
I divide the group into smaller groups when possible					
I allow slower students more time					
I sustain student interest by using suspense, eliciting active participation, and giving frequent feedback					
I continuously scan the room					
I keep the momentum going					
I use different strategies to respond to children's individual needs					

Adapted from the DECA Program, Devereux Foundation (1999). Used with permission of DECI, The Devereux Early Childhood Initiative.

Reflective Checklist: Teaching Strategies

Description	Always	Sometimes	Never	What I am doing	What I will do
I assess the children's abilities, interests, readiness, learning styles, and culture in order to plan my lessons					
My lessons start by activating prior knowledge					
My lessons focus on the essential in a unit—what all children must learn—and provide different ways for children to understand it and be evaluated					
I use flexible grouping and multiple teaching strategies					
I create opportunities for children to make meaningful choices					
I provide varying levels of structure throughout the day, especially at free play					
I schedule between 40 and 60 uninterrupted minutes of play every day					
I provide ideas for themes that extend the content of play and choose props and toys that can be used in multiple ways					
I have high expectations for my students					
Primary Grades 1–3					
I give children a say in what they'll learn					
I adjust my teaching to maintain interest					
I build many opportunities for movement and active participation into the day's activities					

Adapted from the DECA Program, Devereux Foundation (1999). Used with permission of DECI, The Devereux Early Childhood Initiative.

The Functional Assessment Observation Form

Understanding the functional assessment observation form

Robert O'Neill and his colleagues (1997) have developed a chart for recording observations for a functional assessment. The functional assessment observation form is organized around what the authors call "problem behavior events." An event could be one challenging behavior that lasts for mere seconds (Jazmine kicks Liane) or an incident that includes several challenging behaviors (kicking, screaming, shouting) and continues for some time. The event starts when the first problem behavior begins and ends when three minutes have passed without any problem behaviors.

The functional assessment observation form indicates:

- The number of events of problem behavior
- The problem behaviors that occur together
- The times when the problem behaviors are most and least likely to occur
- The antecedent events
- Your perception of the function of the behavior
- The actual consequences

You'll find two copies of this form following this explanation. There is one form filled out for an observation of Jazmine's behavior in Chapter 10, and there is a blank one for you to use later. The form's eight sections are as follows:

A. At the top, write the child's name and the dates of the observation. You can use this form to record observations over one day or several.

B. In the column on the extreme left, indicate the time of day or the times of specific activities ("9:00–9:20 Circle"). The intervals can be different sizes if, for example, you suspect there will much more challenging behavior at circle than at naptime.

Explanation and chart adapted from O'Neill/Horner/Albin/Sprague/Storey/Newton. *Functional Assessment and Program Development for Problem Behavior*, 2/E. © 1997 Wadsworth, a part of Cengage Learning, Inc. Reproduced by permission. www.cengage.com/permissions

C. List the behaviors you want to observe (those you identified in your team's discussions and interviews) in the section labeled "Behaviors." Note each behavior separately so that you can figure out which ones occur together.

D. Just under the date, there is a space to put the antecedents that immediately precede the challenging behaviors. Again, your interviews will tell you what these are likely to be. The most common—demand/request, difficult task, transition, interruption, and lack of attention—are already listed. If you suspect other antecedents are involved, write them into the empty slots. Some likely possibilities are a particular activity, task, or setting event (such as noise) or a peer or an adult whose presence seems related to the behavior.

E. The next group of columns is for your perception of the behavior's function. What purpose does it serve for the child? Does she get something, avoid something, or change the level of stimulation? Why do you think she behaved this way? Again, the functions most often found in the literature are already listed, and there is space for you to add functions you identified in interviews and discussions.

F. The next section is for consequences. What follows the behavior? When you're setting up the chart, fill in the diagonal blanks with the consequences that actually seem to occur most often. Do you ignore the behavior, redirect the child, or put her in time-out? Does she get the tricycle? Do the other children laugh? Observing the consequences will help you see exactly what the child is getting from her behavior and provide more evidence of its function. For example, if you're using time-out when the child wants to avoid an activity, the consequence is actually reinforcing the problem behavior.

G. The last column on the right is for comments or initials. Be sure to initial the form so you'll know that you were observing during this time period even if there were no behaviors to record.

H. Finally, the bottom rows, "Events" and "Date," enable you to keep track of the number of events and the days on which you observed them. We explain how in the next section.

Using the functional assessment observation form

The first time a problem behavior occurs, write *1* in the appropriate box in the "Behaviors" column at the right time of day. As you continue to observe that behavior, continue across the form writing *1* in the appropriate boxes for the antecedents, functions, and consequences. Finally cross off the number *1* in the "Events" row at the bottom. When the second behavior occurs, write *2* in the appropriate boxes across the form, then cross off *2* in the "Events" row, and so on.

At the end of the day, draw a line after the last number you crossed off in the "Events" row and write the date beneath it. This will show you how many incidents occurred that day and allow you to compare the frequency of events over time.

You can also use this form to observe and record appropriate behaviors. Doing this will help you discover what the child enjoys and is good at—important information for developing her behavior support plan.

You should always assist a child who needs your help, even when you're observing.

Functional Assessment Observation Form

(A) Name: Jazmine

Starting Date: 11/10 - Wed   **Ending Date:** 11/12/2010

(B) Time	(C) Behaviors — Kicking	Hitting	Swearing	Spitting	(D) Antecedents — Demand/Request	Difficult Task	Transition	Interruption	No Attention	Child too close	(E) Obtain — Attention	Desired Item/Activity More/Less Stimulation	(F) Escape/Avoid — Demand/Request	Activity	Person	Consequences — Time-out	Reprimand	Stays with teacher	Ignore	(G) Comments/Initials
8 – 8:45 Free play	3	1,2 / 11 / 18							2,3 / 11, 18	1	2,3 / 11, 18				1		1,2 / 11	3 / 18		D-10/10 / D-10/11 / D-10/12
8:45 – 9 Clean-up	4 / 12	5 / 13				4,5 / 12, 13					5 / 12		4 / 13			5	4,12	13		M-10/10 / M-10/11 / G-10/12
9:30 – 10:15 Structured activity																				M-10/10 / D-10/11 / G-10/12
11:15 – 12 Outside / Clean-up	6 / 14 / 19 / 15 / 7			19	19	7 / 15		6 / 14	6 / 14 / 15	6	6 / 14 / 15	19	7			6 / 14 / 15	19 / 7			M-10/10 / M-10/11 / G-10/12
12 – 12:30 Lunch																				
2:45 – 3 Circle	20	8 / 20			20			8	8		8			20		20	8			M-10/10 / M-10/11 / M-10/12
3:15 – 4 Freeplay	21	10 / 16,17	9					9,10 / 16,17 / 21	9,10 / 16,17 / 21		9,10 / 16,17 / 21					17 / 21	16 / 10	9		L-10/10 / L-10/11 / G-10/12
4 – 4:15 Clean-up																				G-10/10 / G-10/11 / G-10/12
(H) Totals	7	14	1		2	6		12	1	1	15	1	4	1	1	5	8	7	1	

Events: 1 2 3 4 5 6 7 8 9 10 11 12 13 14 15 16 17 18 19 20 21 22 23 24 25

Date: November 10 | November 11 | November 12

Adapted from O'Neill/Horner/Albin/Sprague/Storey/Newton. *Functional Assessment and Program Development for Problem Behavior*, 2/E. © 1997 Wadsworth, a part of Cengage Learning, Inc. Reproduced by permission. www.cengage.com/permissions

280

Functional Assessment Observation Form

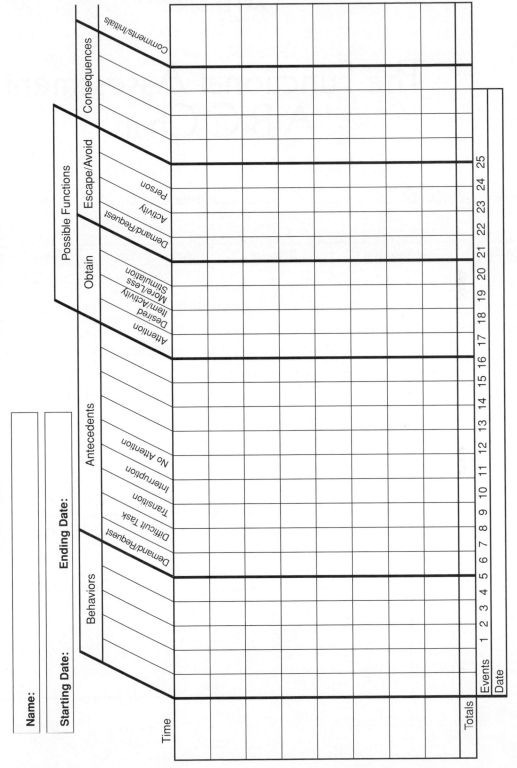

Name:

Starting Date: _____ **Ending Date:** _____

Adapted from O'Neill/Horner/Albin/Sprague/Storey/Newton. *Functional Assessment and Program Development for Problem Behavior*, 2/E. © 1997 Wadsworth, a part of Cengage Learning, Inc. Reproduced by permission. www.cengage.com/permissions

The Functional Assessment
A-B-C Chart

Child's Name: _____ Date: _____ M T W Th F

Time/Activity	Antecedent	Behavior	Consequence	Perceived Function

Setting Events:

References

Adams, R. S., & Biddle, B. J. (1970). *Realities of teaching: Exploration with videotape*. New York: Holt, Rinehart & Winston.

Adeed, P., & Smith, G. P. (1997). Arab Americans: Concepts and materials. In J. A. Banks (Ed.), *Teaching strategies for ethnic studies* (6th ed., pp. 489–510). Boston: Allyn & Bacon.

Ainsworth, M. D. S., Blehar, M., Waters, E., & Wall, S. (1978). *Patterns of attachment: A psychological study of the strange situation*. Hillsdale, NJ: Erlbaum.

Ajrouch, K. (1999). Family and ethnic identity in an Arab-American community. In M. W. Suleiman (Ed.), *Arabs in America: Building a new future* (pp. 129–139). Philadelphia: Temple University Press.

Alsaker, F. D., & Nägele, C. (2008). Bullying in kindergarten and prevention. In D. Pepler & W. Craig (Eds.), *Understanding and addressing bullying: An international perspective. PREVNet series* (Vol. 1, pp. 230–248). Bloomington, IN: AuthorHouse.

Alsaker, F. D., & Valkanover, S. (2001). Early diagnosis and prevention of victimization in kindergarten. In J. Juvonen & S. Graham (Eds.), *Peer harassment in school: The plight of the vulnerable and victimized* (pp. 175–195). New York: Guilford.

American Academy of Pediatrics, American Association of Ophthalmology, American Association for Pediatric Ophthalmology and Strabismus, & American Association of Certified Orthoptists. (2009). Joint statement—Learning disabilities, dyslexia, and vision. *Pediatrics, 124*, 837–844.

American Academy of Pediatrics Council on Communications and Media. (2009). Policy statement—Media violence. *Pediatrics, 124*, 1495–1503.

American Association of University Women. (2004). *Harassment-free hallways: How to stop sexual harassment in school*. Washington, DC: American Association of University Women Educational Foundation.

American Psychiatric Association. (2000). *Diagnostic and statistical manual of mental disorders* (4th ed., Text revision). Washington, DC: Author.

Anderson, V. (2002). Executive function in children: Introduction. *Child Neuropsychology, 8*, 69–70.

Andrews, L., & Trawick-Smith, J. (1996). An ecological model for early childhood violence prevention. In R. L. Hampton, P. Jenkins, & T. P. Gullotta (Eds.), *Preventing violence in America* (pp. 233–261). Thousand Oaks, CA: Sage.

Archer, J., & Côté, S. (2005). Sex differences in aggressive behavior: A developmental and evolutionary perspective. In R. E. Tremblay, W. W. Hartup, & J. Archer (Eds.), *Developmental origins of aggression* (pp. 425–443). New York: Guilford.

Aronson, J., & Steele, C. M. (2005). Stereotypes and the fragility of human competence, motivation, and self-concept. In C. Dweck & E. Elliot (Eds.), *Handbook of competence and motivation* (pp. 436–456). New York: Guilford.

Arseneault, L., Moffitt, T. E., Caspi, A., Taylor, A., Rijadijk, F. V., Jaffee, S. R., et al. (2003). Strong genetic effects on cross-situational antisocial behaviour among 5-year-old children according to mothers, teachers,

283

examiner-observers, and twins' self reports. *Journal of Child Psychology and Psychiatry, 44*, 832–848.

ASCD Advisory Panel on Improving Student Achievement. (1995). Barriers to good instruction. In R. W. Cole (Ed.), *Educating everybody's children: Diverse teaching strategies for diverse learners*. Alexandria, VA: Association for Supervision and Curriculum Development.

Ashman, S. B., Dawson, G., & Panagiotides, H. (2008). Trajectories of maternal depression over 7 years: Relations with child psychophysiology and behavior and role of contextual risks. *Development and Psychopathology, 20*, 55–77.

Ashman, S. B., Dawson, G., Panagiotides, H., Yamada, E., & Wilkinson, C. W. (2002). Stress hormone levels of children of depressed mothers. *Development and Psychopathology, 14*, 333–349.

Association for Supervision and Curriculum Development. (2004, September 28). The effect of state testing on instruction in high-poverty elementary schools. *ASCD Research Brief, 4*(20). Retrieved October 29, 2009, from www.ascd.org/publications/researchbrief/archived_issues.aspx

August, D., & Shanahan, T. (2006). *Developing literacy in second-language learners: Report of the National Literacy Panel on Language Minority Children and Youth*. Mahwah, NJ: Erlbaum.

Ayers, W. (2001). *To teach: The journey of a teacher* (2nd ed.). New York: Teachers College Press.

Ayoub, C. C., & Fischer, K. W. (2006). Developmental pathways and interactions among domains of development. In K. McCartney & D. Phillips (Eds.), *Handbook of early childhood development* (pp. 106–125). Malden, MA: Blackwell.

Ayres, A. J. (1979). *Sensory integration and the child*. Los Angeles: Western Psychological Services.

Bada, H. S., Das, A., Bauer, C. R., Shankaran, S., Lester, B., LaGasse, L., et al. (2007). Impact of prenatal cocaine exposure on child behavior problems through school age. *Pediatrics, 119*, 348–359.

Bagwell, C. L. (2004). Friendships, peer networking, and antisocial behavior.

In A. H. N. Cillessen & L. Mayeux (Eds.), *Children's peer relations: From development to intervention* (pp. 37–57). Washington, DC: American Psychological Association.

Bai, M. (1999, May 3). Anatomy of a massacre. *Newsweek, 133*, 24–31.

Baillargeon, R. H., Zoccolillo, M., Keenan, K., Côté, S., Pérusse, D., Wu, H.-X., et al. (2007). Gender differences in physical aggression: A prospective population-based survey of children before and after 2 years of age. *Developmental Psychology, 43*, 13–26.

Baker, J. (2002). Trilingualism. In L. Delpit & J. K. Dowdy (Eds.), *The skin that we speak: Thoughts on language and culture in the classroom* (pp. 49–61). New York: New Press.

Bakermans-Kranenburg, M. J., & van IJzendoorn, M. H. (2006). Gene-environment interaction of the dopamine D4 receptor (DRD4) and observed maternal insensitivity predicting externalizing behavior in preschoolers. *Developmental Psychobiology, 48*, 406–409.

Balaban, N. (1995). Seeing the child, knowing the person. In W. Ayers (Ed.), *To become a teacher: Making a difference in children's lives* (pp. 49–57). New York: Teachers College Press.

Ballenger, C. (1992). Because you like us: The language of control. *Harvard Educational Review, 62*, 199–208.

Bandura, A. (1977). *Social learning theory*. Englewood Cliffs, NJ: Prentice-Hall.

Barker, E. D., Boivin, M., Brendgen, M., Fontaine, N., Arsenault, L., Vitaro, F., et al. (2008). Predictive validity and early predictors of peer-victimization trajectories in preschool. *Archives of General Psychiatry, 65*, 1185–1192.

Barnett, W. S., Jung, K., Yarosz, D. J., Thomas, J., Hornbeck, A., Stechuk, R., et al. (2008). Educational effects of the Tools of the Mind curriculum: A randomized trial. *Early Childhood Research Quarterly, 23*, 299–313.

Barrera, I., & Corso, R. M. (with Macpherson, D.). (2003). *Skilled dialogue: Strategies for responding to cultural diversity in early childhood*. Baltimore: Brookes.

Barros, R. M., Silver, E. J., & Stein, R. E. K. (2009). School recess and group classroom behavior. *Pediatrics, 123*, 431–436.

Barsade, S. (2002). The ripple effect: Emotional contagion and its influence on group behavior. *Administrative Science Quarterly, 47*, 644–675.

Barton, E. J. (1986). Modification of children's prosocial behavior. In P. S. Strain, M. J. Guralnick, & H. M. Walker (Eds.), *Children's social behavior: Development, assessment, and modification* (pp. 331–372). Orlando: Academic Press.

Bauer, A. M., & Matuszek, K. (2001). Designing and evaluating accommodations and adaptations. In A. M. Bauer & G. M. Brown (Eds.), *Adolescents and inclusion: Transforming secondary schools* (pp. 139–166). Baltimore: Brookes.

Bauer, K. L., & Sheerer, M. A. (with Dettore, E., Jr.). (1997). Creative strategies in Ernie's early childhood classroom. *Young Children, 52*, 47–52.

Beam, J. M. (2004, January 20). The blackboard jungle: Tamer than you think. *The New York Times*, p. A19.

Bedell, J. R., & Lennox, S. S. (1997). *Handbook for communication and problem-solving skills training: A cognitive-behavioral approach.* New York: Wiley.

Beer, J. S. (2007). The importance of emotional-social cognitive interactions for social functioning: Insight from the orbitofrontal cortex. In E. Harmon-Jones & P. Winkielman (Eds.), *Social neuroscience: Integrating biological and psychological explanations of social behavior* (pp. 15–39). New York: Guilford.

Beland, K. R. (1996). A schoolwide approach to violence prevention. In R. L. Hampton, P. Jenkins, & T. P. Gullotta (Eds.), *Preventing violence in America* (pp. 209–231). Thousand Oaks, CA: Sage.

Bellinger, D. C. (2008). Neurological and behavioral consequences of childhood lead exposure. *PLoS Medicine, 5*(5), e115. Retrieved October 31, 2009, from www.plosmedicine.org/article/info:doi/10.1371/journal.pmed.0050115

Belsky, J. (2009). Child care composition, child care history, and social development: Are child care effects disappearing or spreading? *Social Development, 18*, 230–238.

Belsky, J., Vandell, D. L., Burchinal, M., Clarke-Stewart, K. A., McCartney, K.,

Owen, M. T., et al. (2007). Are there long-term effects of early child care? *Child Development, 78*, 681–701.

Bendersky, M., Bennett, D., & Lewis, M. (2006). Aggression at age 5 as a function of prenatal exposure to cocaine, gender, and environmental risk. *Journal of Pediatric Psychology, 31*, 71–84.

Benner, G. J., Nelson, J. R., & Epstein, M. H. (2002). Language skills of children with EBD: A literature review. *Journal of Emotional and Behavioral Disorders, 10*, 43–59.

Bennett, S., & Kalish, N. (2006). *The case against homework: How homework is hurting our children and what we can do about it.* New York: Crown.

Berkowitz, L. (1993). *Aggression: Its causes, consequences, and control.* New York: McGraw-Hill.

Berlin, L. J., Isa, J. M., Fine, M. A., Malone, P. S., Brooks-Gunn, J., Brady-Smith, C., et al. (2009). Correlates and consequences of spanking and verbal punishment for low-income white, African American, and Mexican American toddlers. *Child Development, 80*, 1403–1420.

Bhutta, A. T., Cleves, M. A., Casey, P. H., Cradock, M. M., & Anand, K. J. S. (2002). Cognitive and behavioral outcomes of school-aged children who were born preterm: A meta-analysis. *Journal of the American Medical Association, 288*, 728–737.

Bierman, K. L. (1986). Process of change during social skills training with preadolescents and its relation to treatment outcomes. *Child Development, 57*, 230–240.

Bierman, K. L., & Erath, S. A. (2006). Promoting social competence in early childhood: Classroom curricula and social skills coaching programs. In K. McCartney & D. Phillips (Eds.), *Handbook of early childhood development* (pp. 595–615). Malden, MA: Blackwell.

Biglan, A., Brennan, P. A., Foster, S. L., & Holder, H. D. (with Miller, T. R., Cunningham, P., Derzon, J. H., Embry, D. D., Fishbein, D. H., Flay, B. R., et al.). (2004). *Helping adolescents at risk: Prevention of multiple problem behaviors.* New York: Guilford.

Bijou, S. W., Peterson, R. F., & Ault, M. H. (1968). A method to integrate descriptive and experimental field studies at the level of data and empirical concepts. *Journal of Applied Behavior Analysis, 1,* 175–191.

Birch, S. H., & Ladd, G. W. (1998). Children's interpersonal behaviors and the teacher-child relationship. *Developmental Psychology, 34,* 934–946.

Blue-Banning, M., Summers, J. A., Frankland, H. C., Nelson, L. L., & Beegle, G. (2004). Dimensions of family and professional partnerships: Constructive guidelines for collaboration. *Exceptional Children, 70,* 167–184.

Blum, R. W. (2005). A case for school connectedness. *Educational Leadership, 62(7),* 16–20.

Bodrova, E., & Leong, D. J. (2003, May). Chopsticks and counting chips: Do play and foundational skills need to compete for the teacher's attention in an early childhood classroom? *Beyond the Journal.* Retrieved March 22, 2010, from www.naeyc.org/files/yc/file/200305/Chopsticks_Bodrova.pdf

Bodrova, E., & Leong, D. J. (2007). *Tools of the mind: The Vygotskian approach to early childhood education* (2nd ed.). Upper Saddle River, NJ: Pearson.

Boivin, M., Hymel, S., & Hodges, E. V. E. (2001). Toward a process view of peer rejection and harassment. In J. Juvonen & S. Graham (Eds.), *Peer harassment in school: The plight of the vulnerable and victimized* (pp. 265–289). New York: Guilford.

Boivin, M., Vitaro, F., & Poulin, F. (2005). Peer relationships and the development of aggressive behavior in early childhood. In R. E. Tremblay, W. W. Hartup, & J. Archer (Eds.), *Developmental origins of aggression* (pp. 376–397). New York: Guilford.

Bolger, K. E., & Patterson, C. J. (2003). Sequelae of maltreatment: Vulnerability and resilience. In S. S. Luthar (Ed.), *Resilience and vulnerability: Adaptation in the context of childhood adversity* (pp. 156–181). New York: Cambridge University Press.

Bollmer, J. M., Milich, R., Harris, M. J., & Maras, M. A. (2005). A friend in need: The role of friendship as a protective factor in peer victimization and bullying. *Journal of Interpersonal Violence, 20,* 701–712.

Bondy, E., & Ross, D. D. (2008). The teacher as warm demander. *Educational Leadership, 66(1),* 54–58.

Bortfeld, H., & Whitehurst, G. J. (2001). In D. B. Bailey, Jr., J. T. Bruer, F. J. Symons, & J. W. Lichtman (Eds.), *Critical thinking about critical periods* (pp. 173–192). Baltimore: Brookes.

Boulton, M. (1994). How to prevent and respond to bullying behaviour in the junior/middle school playground. In S. Sharp & P. K. Smith (Eds.), *Tackling bullying in your school: A practical handbook for teachers* (pp. 103–132). New York: Routledge.

Bovey, T., & Strain, P. (n.d.). *What works briefs 5: Using classroom activities and routines as opportunities to support peer interaction.* Center on the Social and Emotional Foundations for Early Learning. Retrieved March 18, 2010, from www.vanderbilt.edu/csefel/briefs/wwb5.pdf

Bowlby, J. (1969/1982). *Attachment and loss: Vol. 1. Attachment.* New York: Basic Books.

Bowman, B. T. (1989). Self-reflection as an element of professionalism. *Teachers College Record, 90,* 444–451.

Bowman, B. T., Donovan, M. S., & Burns, M. S. (Eds.). (2001). *Eager to learn: Educating our preschoolers.* National Research Council Committee on Early Childhood Pedagogy. Commission on Behavioral and Social Sciences and Education. Washington, DC: National Academy Press.

Boykin, A. W. (1986). The triple quandary and the schooling of Afro-American children. In U. Neisser (Ed.), *The school achievement of minority children.* Hillsdale, NJ: Erlbaum.

Brady, J. P., Posner, M., Lang, C., & Rosati, M. J. (1994). *Risk and reality: The implications of prenatal exposure to alcohol and other drugs.* Washington, DC: U.S. Department of Health and Human Services and U.S. Department of Education. Retrieved October 14, 2009, from http://aspe.hhs.gov/hsp/cyp/drugkids.htm

Bransford, J. D., Brown, A. L., & Cocking, R. R. (Eds.). (2000). *How people learn: Brain, mind, experience, and school* (expanded ed.). Commission on Behavioral and Social Sciences and Education, National Research Council. Washington, DC: National Academy Press.

Brendgen, M., Vitaro, F., Boivin, M., Dionne, G., & Pérusse, D. (2006). Examining genetic and environmental effects on reactive versus proactive aggression. *Developmental Psychology, 42*, 1299–1312.

Brendgen, M., Wanner, B., & Vitaro, F. (2006). Verbal abuse by the teacher and child adjustment from kindergarten through grade 6. *Pediatrics, 117*, 1585–1598.

Broidy, L. M., Tremblay, R. E., Brame, B., Fergusson, D., Horwood, J. L., Laird, R., et al. (2003). Developmental trajectories of childhood disruptive behaviors and adolescent delinquency: A six-site, cross-national study. *Developmental Psychology, 39*, 222–245.

Bronfenbrenner, U. (1979). *The ecology of human development: Experiments by nature and design.* Cambridge, MA: Harvard University Press.

Bronson, P., & Merryman, A. (2009). *NurtureShock: New thinking about children.* New York: Twelve.

Brooks, R. B. (1994). Children at risk: Fostering resilience and hope. *American Journal of Orthopsychiatry, 64*, 545–553.

Brooks, R. B. (1999). Creating a positive school climate: Strategies for fostering self-esteem, motivation, and resilience. In J. Cohen (Ed.), *Educating minds and hearts: Social emotional learning and the passage into adolescence* (pp. 24–39). New York: Teachers College Press.

Brophy, J. (1996). *Teaching problem students.* New York: Guilford.

Brophy, J. (1999). Perspectives of classroom management: Yesterday, today, and tomorrow. In H. J. Freiberg (Ed.), *Beyond behaviorism: Changing the classroom management paradigm* (pp. 43–56). Boston: Allyn & Bacon.

Brophy, J. (2000). *Teaching.* Geneva: International Bureau of Education. (ERIC Document No. ED440066).

Brophy, J., & McCaslin, M. (1992). Teachers' reports of how they perceive and cope with problem students. *Elementary School Journal, 93*, 3–68.

Bruce, N. K. (2007). *DECA program protective factor kit.* Lewisville, NC: Kaplan Early Learning.

Bruer, J. T. (1999). *The myth of the first three years: A new understanding of early brain development and lifelong learning.* New York: Free Press.

Bruer, J. T. (2001). A critical and sensitive period primer. In D. B. Bailey, Jr., J. T. Bruer, F. J. Symons, & J. W. Lichtman (Eds.), *Critical thinking about critical periods* (pp. 3–26). Baltimore: Brookes.

Bruer, J. T., & Greenough, W. T. (2001). The subtle science of how experience affects the brain. In D. B. Bailey, Jr., J. T. Bruer, F. J. Symons, & J. W. Lichtman (Eds.), *Critical thinking about critical periods* (pp. 209–232). Baltimore: Brookes.

Burden, P. R. (2003). *Classroom management: Creating a successful learning environment* (2nd ed.). Hoboken, NJ: Wiley.

Bushman, B., & Anderson, C. (2001). Media violence and the American public: Scientific facts versus media misinformation. *American Psychologist, 56*, 477–489.

Butchard, N., & Spencler, R. (2000). *Working effectively with violent and aggressive states.* Winnipeg, MB: WEVAS Inc.

Buyse, E., Verschueren, K., Verachtert, P., & Van Damme, J. (2009). Predicting school adjustment in early elementary school: Impact of teacher-child relationship quality and relational classroom climate. *Elementary School Journal, 110*, 119–141.

Cadoret, R. J., Yates, W. R., Troughton, E., Woodworth, G., & Stewart, M. A. (1995). Genetic-environmental interaction in the genesis of aggressivity and conduct disorders. *Archives of General Psychiatry, 52*, 916–924.

Campbell, S. B. (2002). *Behavior problems in preschool children: Clinical and developmental issues* (2nd ed.). New York: Guilford.

Campbell, S. B. (2006). Maladjustment in preschool children: A developmental psychopathology perspective. In K. McCartney & D. Phillips (Eds.), *Handbook of early childhood development* (pp. 358–377). Malden, MA: Blackwell.

Card, N. A., & Hodges, E. V. E. (2008). Peer victimization among schoolchildren: Correlations, causes, consequences, and considerations in assessment. *School Psychology Review, 23*, 451–461.

Card, N. A., Stucky, B. D., Sawalani, G. M., & Little, T. D. (2008). Direct and indirect aggression during childhood and adolescence: A meta-analytic review of gender differences, intercorrelations, and relations to maladjustments. *Child Development, 79,* 1185–1229.

Carkhuff, R. (1987). *The art of helping.* Amherst, MA: Human Resource Development Press.

Carr, A., Kikais, T., Smith, C., & Littmann, E. (n.d.). *Making friends: A guide to using the Assessment of peer relations and planning interventions.* Vancouver, BC: Making Friends.

Carr, E. G. (1994). Emerging themes in the functional analysis of problem behavior. *Journal of Applied Behavior Analysis, 27,* 393–399.

Carter, K., & Doyle, W. (2006). Classroom management in early childhood and elementary classrooms. In C. M. Evertson & C. S. Weinstein (Eds.), *Handbook of classroom management: Research, practice, and contemporary issues* (pp. 373–406). Mahwah, NJ: Erlbaum.

Carter, P. L. (2005). *Keepin' it real: School success beyond black and white.* New York: Oxford University Press.

Cartledge, G., & Milburn, J. F. (1995). *Teaching social skills to children: Innovative approaches* (3rd ed.). Needham, MA: Allyn & Bacon.

Caspi, A., Langley, K., Milne, B., Moffitt, T. E., O'Donovan, M., Owen, M. J., et al. (2008). A replicated molecular genetic basis for subtyping antisocial behavior in children with attention-deficit/hyperactivity disorder. *Archives of General Psychiatry, 65,* 203–210.

Caspi, A., McClay, J., Moffitt, T. E., Mill, J., Martin, J., Craig, I. W., et al. (2002). Role of genotype in the cycle of violence in maltreated children. *Science, 297,* 851–854.

Caspi, A., Roberts, B. W., & Shiner, R. L. (2005). Personality development: Stability and change. *Annual Review of Psychology, 56,* 17.1–17.32.

Caspi, A., & Silva, P. A. (1995). Temperamental qualities at age three predict personality traits in young adulthood: Longitudinal evidence from a birth cohort. *Child Development, 66,* 486–498.

Cauce, A. M., Stewart, A., Rodriguez, M. D., Cochran, B., & Ginzler, J. (2003). Overcoming the odds? Adolescent development in the context of urban poverty.

In S. S. Luthar (Ed.), *Resilience and vulnerability: Adaptation in the context of childhood adversity* (pp. 343–363). New York: Cambridge University Press.

Caughy, M. O., Nettles, S. M., O'Campo, P. J., & Lohrfink, K. F. (2006). Neighborhood matters: Racial socialization of African American children. *Child Development, 77,* 1220–1236.

Centers for Disease Control and Prevention. (2009). *Youth violence: National statistics.* Retrieved November 17, 2009, from www. cdc.gov/ViolencePrevention/youthviolence/ stats_at_a_glance/homicide.html

Chan, S., & Lee, E. (2004). Families with Asian roots. In E. W. Lynch & M. J. Hanson (Eds.), *Developing cross-cultural competence: A guide for working with children and their families* (3rd ed., pp. 219–298). Baltimore: Brookes.

Chandler, L. K., & Dahlquist, C. M. (1997). *Confronting the challenge: Using team-based functional assessment and effective intervention strategies to reduce and prevent challenging behavior in young children.* Presentation at SpeciaLink Institute of Children's Challenging Behaviors in Child Care, Sydney, NS.

Chandler, L. K., & Dahlquist, C. M. (2005). *Functional assessment: Strategies to prevent and remediate challenging behavior in school settings* (2nd ed.). Upper Saddle River, NJ: Prentice Hall.

Chandler, L. K., Dahlquist, C. M., Repp, A. C., & Feltz, C. (1999). The effects of team-based functional assessment on the behavior of students in classroom settings. *Exceptional Children, 66,* 101–122.

Chang, F., Crawford, G., Early, D., Bryant, D., Howes, C., Burchinal, M., et al. (2007). Spanish-speaking children's social and language development in pre-kindergarten classrooms. *Early Education and Development, 18,* 243–269.

Chao, R. K. (1994). Beyond parental control and authoritarian parenting style: Understanding Chinese parenting through the cultural notion of training. *Child Development, 65,* 1111–1119.

Chartrand, M. M., Frank, D. A., White, L. F., & Shope, T. R. (2008). Effect of parents' wartime deployment on the behavior of young children in military families. *Archives of Pediatrics and Adolescent Medicine, 162*, 1009–1014.

Chasnoff, I. J., Anson, A., Hatcher, R., Stenson, H., Laukea, K., & Randolph, L. A. (1998). Prenatal exposure to cocaine and other drugs: Outcome at four to six years. *Annals of the New York Academy of Sciences, 846*, 314–328.

Chess, S., & Thomas, A. (1989). Temperament and its functional significance. In S. I. Greenspan & G. H. Pollock (Eds.), *The course of life: Vol. 2, Early childhood* (pp. 163–228). Madison, CT: International Universities Press.

Christakis, D. A., Zimmerman, F. J., DiGiuseppe, D. L., & McCarty, C. A. (2004). Early television exposure and subsequent attentional problems in children. *Pediatrics, 113*, 708–713.

Christian, C. W., Block, R., & the Committee on Child Abuse and Neglect. (2009). Policy statement—Abusive head trauma in infants and children. *Pediatrics, 123*, 1409–1411.

Chud, G., & Fahlman, R. (1985). *Early childhood education for a multicultural society*. Vancouver: Faculty of Education, University of British Columbia.

Chud, G., & Fahlman, R. (1995). *Honouring diversity within child care and early education: An instructor's guide*. Victoria: British Columbia Ministry of Skills, Training, and Labour and the Centre for Curriculum and Professional Development.

Cicchetti, D., Ganiban, J., & Barnett, D. (1991). Contributions from the study of high risk populations to understanding the development of emotional regulation. In J. Garber & K. A. Dodge (Eds.), *The development of emotional regulation and dysregulation* (pp. 15–48). New York: Cambridge University Press.

Cicchetti, D., & Rogosch, F. A. (1997). The role of self-organization in the promotion of resilience in maltreated children. *Development and Psychopathology, 9*, 799–817.

Clonan, S. M., Lopez, G., Rymarchyk, G., & Davison, S. (2004). School-wide positive behavior support: Implementation and evaluation at two urban elementary schools. *Persistently safe schools: The National Conference of the Hamilton Fish Institute on School and Community Violence*. Retrieved April 14, 2010, from http://gwired.gwu.edu/hamfish/merlin-cgi/p/downloadFile/d/16824/n/off/other/1/name/08Clonanpdf/

Coie, J. D. (1996). Prevention of violence and antisocial behavior. In R. DeV. Peters & R. J. McMahon (Eds.), *Preventing childhood disorders, substance abuse, and delinquency* (pp. 1–18). Thousand Oaks, CA: Sage.

Coie, J. D., & Dodge, K. A. (1998). Aggression and antisocial behavior. In N. Eisenberg (Ed.), *Handbook of child psychology: Vol. 3, Social, emotional, and personality development* (5th ed., pp. 779–862). New York: Wiley.

Coie, J. D., & Koeppl, G. K. (1990). Adapting intervention to the problems of aggressive and disruptive children. In S. R. Asher & J. D. Coie (Eds.), *Peer rejection in childhood* (pp. 309–337). New York: Cambridge University Press.

Coie, J. D., Underwood, M., & Lochman, J. E. (1991). Programmatic intervention with aggressive children in the school setting. In D. J. Pepler & K. H. Rubin (Eds.), *The development and treatment of childhood aggression* (pp. 389–410). Hillsdale, NJ: Erlbaum.

Coles, G. (2008–2009). Hunger, academic success, and the hard bigotry of indifference. *Rethinking Schools, 23*(2). Retrieved October 19, 2009, from http://rethinkingschools.org/archive/23_02/hung232.shtml

Coloroso, B. (1995). *Kids are worth it! Giving your child the gift of inner discipline*. Toronto, ON: Somerville House.

Coloroso, B. (2002). *The bully, the bullied, and the bystander*. Toronto, ON: HarperCollins.

Colvert, E., Rutter, M., Beckett, C., Castle, J., Groothues, C., Hawkins, A., et al. (2008). Emotional difficulties in early adolescence following severe early deprivation: Findings from the English and Romanian adoptees study. *Development and Psychopathology, 20*, 547–567.

Committee for Children. (2002). *Second step: A violence-prevention curriculum* (3rd ed.). Seattle: Author.

Conduct Problems Prevention Research Group. (2004). The FAST Track experiment: Translating the developmental model into a prevention design. In J. B. Kupersmidt & K. A. Dodge (Eds.), *Children's peer relations: From development to intervention* (pp. 181–208). Washington, DC: American Psychological Association.

Connell, D. (2003, September). The invisible disability. *Instructor*. Retrieved September 15, 2009, from www2.scholastic.com/browse/search?query=%22invisible+disability%22

Cook, A., Blaustein, M., Spinazzola, J., & van der Kolk, B. (Eds.). (2003). *Complex trauma in children and adolescents*. National Child Traumatic Stress Network Complex Trauma Task Force. Retrieved July 15, 2009, from www.nctsnet.org/nctsn_assets/pdfs/edu_materials/ComplexTrauma_All.pdf

Cook, R. E., Klein, M. D., & Tessier, A. (with Daley, S. E.). (2004). *Adapting early childhood curricula for children in inclusive settings* (6th ed.). Upper Saddle River, NJ: Merrill Prentice Hall.

Cooper, H. (2001). Homework for all—in moderation. *Educational Leadership, 58*(7), 34–38.

Cords, M., & Killen, M. (1998). Conflict resolution in human and nonhuman primates. In J. Langer & M. Killen (Eds.), *Piaget, evolution, and development* (pp. 193–218). Mahwah, NJ: Erlbaum.

Cornelius, M. D., & Day, N. L. (2009). Developmental consequences of prenatal tobacco exposure. *Current Opinion in Neurology, 22,* 121–125.

Corsaro, W. (1988). Peer culture in the preschool. *Theory into Practice, 27*(1), 19–24.

Costello, E. J., Compton, S. N., Keeler, G., & Angold, A. (2003). Relationships between poverty and psychopathology: A natural experiment. *Journal of the American Medical Association, 290,* 2023–2029.

Côté, S. M., Boivin, M., Nagin, D. S., Japel, C., Xu, Q., Zoccolillo, M., et al. (2007). The role of maternal education and nonmaternal care services in the prevention of children's physical aggression problems. *Archives of General Psychiatry, 64,* 1305–1312.

Côté, S. M., Borge, A. I., Geoffroy, M.-C., Rutter, M., & Tremblay, R. E. (2008). Nonmaternal care in infancy and emotional/behavioral difficulties at 4 years old: Moderation by family risk characteristics. *Developmental Psychology, 44,* 155–168.

Côté, S. M., Vaillancourt, T., Barker, E. D., Nagin, D. S., & Tremblay, R. E. (2007). The joint development of physical and indirect aggression: Predictors of continuity and change during childhood. *Development and Psychopathology, 19,* 37–55.

Côté, S. M., Vaillancourt, T., LeBlanc, J. C., Nagin, D. S., & Tremblay, R. E. (2006). The development of physical aggression from toddlerhood to pre-adolescence: A nationwide longitudinal study of Canadian children. *Journal of Abnormal Child Psychology, 34,* 71–85.

Council for Exceptional Children. (n.d.a). *New IDEA delivers for students with disabilities*. Retrieved April 27, 2010, from www.cec.sped.org/AM/Template.cfm?Section=Home&CONTENTID=6234&TEMPLATE=/CM/ContentDisplay.cfm

Council for Exceptional Children. (n.d.b). *A primer on the IDEA 2004 regulations*. Retrieved May 2, 2010, from www.cec.sped.org/AM/Template.cfm?Section=Home&TEMPLATE=/CM/ContentDisplay.cfm&CONTENTID=7839

Cozolino, L. (2006). *The neuroscience of human relationships: Attachment and the developing social brain*. New York: Norton.

Craig, W. M., & Pepler, D. J. (1997). Observations of bullying and victimization in the school yard. *Canadian Journal of School Psychology, 13,* 41–60.

Crick, N. R., Casas, J. F., & Ku, H.-C. (1999). Relational and physical forms of peer victimization in preschool. *Developmental Psychology, 35,* 376–385.

Crick, N. R., & Grotpeter, J. K. (1995). Relational aggression, gender, and social-psychological adjustment. *Child Development, 66,* 710–722.

Crick, N. R., Grotpeter, J. K., & Bigbee, M. S. (2002). Relationally and physically aggressive children's intent attributions and feelings of distress for relational and instrumental peer provocations. *Child Development, 73,* 1134–1142.

Crick, N. R., Nelson, D. A., Morales, J. R., Cullerton, C., Casas, J. F., & Hickman, S. E. (2001). Relational victimization in childhood and adolescence: I hurt you through the grapevine. In J. Juvonen & S. Graham (Eds.), *Peer harassment in school: The plight of the vulnerable and victimized* (pp. 196–214). New York: Guilford.

Criss, M. M., Pettit, G. S., Bates, J. E., Dodge, K. A., & Lapp, A. L. (2002). Family adversity, positive peer relations, and children's externalizing behavior: A longitudinal perspective on risk and resilience. *Child Development, 73,* 1220–1237.

Crockenberg, S. (1981). Infant irritability, mother responsiveness, and social support influences on the security of infant-mother attachment. *Child Development, 7,* 169–176.

Cullinan, D., Evans, C., Epstein, M. H., & Ryser, G. (2003). Characteristics of emotional disturbance of elementary school students. *Behavioral Disorders, 28,* 94–110.

Cummins, J. (1999-2003). Bilingual children's mother tongue: Why is it important for education? Retrieved February 6, 2010, from www.iteachilearn.com/cummins/mother.htm

Curran, M. E. (2003). Linguistic diversity and classroom management. *Theory into Practice, 42,* 334–340.

Curtis, D. (2009, March-April). A thinking lens for reflective teaching. *Exchange, 41.* Retrieved December 20, 2009, from https://secure.ccie.com/library/5018601.pdf

Curtis, D., & Carter, M. (2003). *Designs for living and learning: Transforming early childhood environments.* St. Paul, MN: Redleaf.

Curtis, W. J., & Cicchetti, D. (2003). Moving research on resilience into the 21st century: Theoretical and methodological considerations in examining the biological contributors to resilience. *Development and Psychopathology, 15,* 773–810.

Curwin, R. L., Mendler, A. N., & Mendler, B. D. (2008). *Discipline with dignity: New challenges, new solutions* (3rd ed.). Alexandria, VA: Association for Supervision and Curriculum Development.

Cushman, K., & the students of What Kids Can Do. (2003). *Fires in the bathroom: Advice for teachers from high school students.* New York: New Press.

Darling-Hammond, L. (2004). From "separate but equal" to "No Child Left Behind": The collision of new standards and old inequalities. In D. Meier & G. Wood (Eds.), *Many children left behind: How the No Child Left Behind Act is damaging our children and our schools* (pp. 3–32). Boston: Beacon Press.

Darling-Hammond, L., & Hill-Lynch, O. (2006). If they'd only do their work! *Educational Leadership, 63*(5), 8–13.

Davidson, R. J., Putnam, K. M., & Larson, C. L. (2000). Dysfunction in the neural circuitry of emotion regulation—A possible prelude to violence. *Science, 289,* 591–594.

Dawson, G., Ashman, S. B., Panagiotides, H., Hessl, D., Self, J., Yamada, E., et al. (2003). Preschool outcomes of children of depressed mothers: Role of maternal behavior, contextual risk, and children's brain activity. *Child Development, 74,* 1158–1175.

Dearing, E., Berry, D., & Zaslow, M. (2006). Poverty during early childhood. In K. McCartney & D. Phillips (Eds.), *Handbook of early childhood development* (pp. 399–423). Malden, MA: Blackwell.

Deater-Deckard, K., Bates, J. E., Dodge, K. A., & Pettit, G. S. (1996). Physical discipline among African American and European American mothers: Links to children's externalizing behaviors. *Developmental Psychology, 32,* 1065–1072.

Deater-Deckard, K., & Cahill, K. (2006). Nature and nurture in early childhood. In K. McCartney & D. Phillips (Eds.), *Handbook of early childhood development* (pp. 3–21). Malden, MA: Blackwell.

De Bellis, M. D. (2005). The psychobiology of neglect. *Child Maltreatment, 10,* 150–172.

De Bellis, M. D., Baum, A. S., Birmaher, B., Keshavan, M. S., Eccard, C. H., et al. (1999). Developmental traumatology part I: Biological stress systems. *Biological Psychiatry, 45,* 1259–1270.

De Bellis, M. D., Keshavan, M. S., Clark, D. B., Casey, B. J., Giedd, J. N., et al. (1999). Developmental traumatology part II: Brain development. *Biological Psychiatry, 45,* 1271–1284.

Decety, J., Michalsky, K. J., Akitsuki, Y., & Lahey, B. B. (2008). Atypical empathic responses in adolescents with aggressive conduct disorder: A functional MRI investigation. *Biological Psychology, 80*(2), 203–211.

Deci, E., Koestner, R., & Ryan, R. (1999). A meta-analytic review of experiments examining the effects of extrinsic rewards on intrinsic motivation. *Psychological Bulletin, 125*, 627–668.

Deci, E., Koestner, R., & Ryan, R. (2001). Extrinsic rewards and intrinsic motivation in education: Reconsidered once again. *Review of Educational Research, 71*, 1–27.

Deci, E. L., & Ryan, R. M. (1985). *Intrinsic motivation and self-determination in human behavior.* New York: Plenum.

Delgado, J. M. R. (1979). Neurophysiological mechanisms of aggressive behavior. In S. Feshbach & A. Fraczek (Eds.), *Aggression and behavior change: Biological and social processes* (pp. 54–65). New York: Praeger.

Delgado-Gaitan, C. (1994). Socializing young children in Mexican-American families: An intergenerational perspective. In P. M. Greenfield & R. R. Cocking (Eds.), *Cross-cultural roots of minority child development* (pp. 55–86). Hillsdale, NJ: Erlbaum.

Delpit, L. (2002). No kinda sense. In L. Delpit & J. K. Dowdy (Eds.), *The skin that we speak: Thoughts on language and culture in the classroom* (pp. 31–48). New York: New Press.

Delpit, L. (2006). *Other people's children: Cultural conflict in the classroom* (updated ed.). New York: New Press.

Delpit, L. D. (1992). Education in a multicultural society: Our future's greatest challenge. *Journal of Negro Education, 61*, 237–239.

Dennis, T., Bendersky, M., Ramsay, D., & Lewis, M. (2006). Reactivity and regulation in children prenatally exposed to cocaine. *Developmental Psychology, 42*, 688–697.

Denton, P. (2008). The power of our words. *Educational Leadership, 66*(1), 28–31.

Derman-Sparks, L., & Edwards, J. O. (2010). *Anti-bias education for young children and ourselves.* Washington, DC: National Association for the Education of Young Children.

Derman-Sparks, L., & Ramsey, P. G. (with Edwards, J. O.). (2006). *What if all the kids are white? Anti-bias multicultural education with young children and families.* New York: Teachers College Press.

DeRosier, M. E. (2004). Building relationships and combating bullying: Effectiveness of a school-based social skills group intervention. *Journal of Clinical Child and Adolescent Psychology, 33*, 196–201.

Dettling, A. C., Gunnar, M. R., & Donzella, B. (1999). Cortisol levels of young children in full-day childcare centers: Relations with age and temperament. *Psychoneuroendocrinology, 24*, 519–536.

DeVries, M. W. (1989). Temperament and infant mortality among the Masai of East Africa. *American Journal of Psychiatry, 141*, 1189–1194.

Dewey, J. (1933). *How we think.* Boston: Heath.

Diamond, A., Barnett, W. S., Thomas, J., & Munro, S. (2007). Preschool program improves cognitive control. *Science, 318*, 1387–1388.

Diamond, K. E., & Stacey, S. (2002). The other children at preschool: Experiences of typically developing children in inclusive programs. In S. Sandall & M. Ostrosky (Eds.), *Natural environments and inclusion* (pp. 59–68). Denver and Longmont, CO: Division for Early Childhood of the Council for Exceptional Children.

DiPietro, J. (2002). Prenatal/perinatal stress and its impact on psychosocial child development. In R. E. Tremblay, R. G. Barr, & R. DeV. Peters (Eds.), *Encyclopedia on early childhood development* [online]. Montreal, QC: Centre of Excellence for Early Childhood Development. Retrieved October 31, 2009, from www.child-encyclopedia.com/documents/DiPietroANGxp.pdf

DiPietro, J. A. (2000). Baby and the brain: Advances in child development. *Annual Review of Public Health, 21*, 455–271.

Doble, J., & Yarrow, A. L. (with Ott, A., & Rochkind, J.). (2007). *Walking a mile: A first step toward mutual understanding.* Public Agenda. Retrieved February 6, 2010, from www.publicagenda.org/reports/walking-mile-first-step-toward-mutual-understanding

Dodge, K. A. (2003). Do social information-processing patterns mediate behavior? In

B. B. Lahey, T. E. Moffitt, & A. Caspi (Eds.), *Causes of conduct disorder and juvenile delinquency* (pp. 254–274). New York: Guilford.

Dodge, K. A. (2006). Translational science in action: Hostile attributional style and the development of aggressive behavior problems. *Development and Psychopathology, 18,* 791–814.

Dodge, K. A., Bates, J. E., & Pettit, G. S. (1990). Mechanisms in the cycle of violence. *Science, 250,* 1678–1683.

Dodge, K. A., Coie, J. D., & Lynam, D. (2006). Aggressive and antisocial behavior in youth. In W. Damon (Series Ed.) & N. Eisenberg (Vol. Ed.), *Handbook of child psychology: Vol. 3. Social, emotional, and personality development* (6th ed., pp. 719–788). New York: Wiley.

Dodge, K. A., Coie, J. D., Pettit, G., & Price, J. (1990). Peer status and aggression in boys' groups: Developmental and contextual analyses. *Child Development, 61,* 1289–1309.

Dodge, K. A., Lansford, J. E., Burks, V. S., Bates, J. E., Pettit, G. S., Fontaine, R., et al. (2003). Peer rejection and social information-processing factors in the development of aggressive behavior problems in children. *Child Development, 74,* 374–393.

Doll, B., Song, S., & Siemers, E. (2004). Classroom ecologies that support or discourage bullying. In D. L. Espelage & S. M. Swearer (Eds.), *Bullying in American schools: A socio-ecological perspective on prevention and intervention* (pp. 161–183). Mahwah, NJ: Erlbaum.

Donnellan, A. D., & Leary, M. R. (1995). *Movement differences and diversity in autism/mental retardation.* Madison, WI: DRI Press.

Donnerstein, E., Slaby, R. G., & Eron, L. D. (1994). The mass media and youth aggression. In L. D. Eron, J. H. Gentry, & P. Schlegel (Eds.), *Reason to hope: A psychosocial perspective on violence & youth* (pp. 219–250). Washington, DC: American Psychological Association.

D'Onofrio, B. M., Van Hulle, C. A., Waldman, I. D., Rodgers, J. L., Harden, K. P., Rathouz, P. J., et al. (2008). Smoking during pregnancy and offspring externalizing problems: An exploration of genetic and environmental confounds. *Development and Psychopathology, 20,* 139–164.

Donovan, M. S., & Cross, C. T. (Eds.). (2002). *Minority students in special and gifted education.* Washington, DC: National Academies Press.

Dreikurs, R. (with Soltz, V.). (1964). *Children: The challenge.* New York: Hawthorn.

Driscoll, K. C., & Pianta, R. C. (2010). Banking time in Head Start: Early efficacy of an intervention designed to promote teacher-child relationships. *Early Education and Development, 21,* 38–64.

Duncan, C., Brooks-Gunn, J., Yeung, W., & Smith, J. (1998). How much does childhood poverty affect the life chances of children? *American Sociological Review, 63,* 406–423.

Dunlap, G., & Kern, L. (1993). Assessment and intervention for children within the instructional curriculum. In J. Reichle & D. P. Wacker (Eds.), *Communicative alternatives to challenging behavior: Integrating assessment and intervention strategies* (pp. 177–204). Baltimore: Brookes.

Dunlap, G., Strain, P. S., Fox, L., Carta, J. J., Conroy, M., Smith, B. J., et al. (2006). Prevention and intervention with young children's challenging behavior: Perspectives regarding current knowledge. *Behavioral Disorders, 32,* 29–45.

Dunn, J., & Brown, J. (1991). Relationships, talk about feelings, and the development of affect regulation in early childhood. In J. Garber & K. A. Dodge (Eds.), *The development of emotional regulation and dysregulation* (pp. 89–108). New York: Cambridge University Press.

Dunst, C. J. (2002). Family-centered practices: Birth through high school. *Journal of Special Education, 36,* 139–147.

DuPaul, G. J., & Stoner, G. (2003). *ADHD in the schools: Assessment and intervention strategies* (2nd ed.). New York: Guilford.

Durand, V. M. (1990). *Severe behavior problems: A functional communication training approach.* New York: Guilford.

Durston, S. (2008). Converging methods in studying attention-deficit/hyperactivity disorder: What can we learn from neuroimaging and genetics? *Development and Psychopathology, 20,* 1133–1143.

Dweck, C. S. (2007). The perils and promises of praise. *Educational Leadership, 65*(2), 34–39.

Eaton, D. K., Kann, L., Kinchen, S., Shanklin, S., Ross, J., Hawkins, J., et al. (2008). *Youth risk behavior surveillance—United States, 2007. Morbidity and Mortality Weekly Report Surveillance Summaries*, 57 (SS04). Retrieved November 17, 2009, from www.cdc.gov/mmwr/preview/mmwrhtml/ss5704a1.htm

Egan, S. K., & Perry, P. G. (1998). Does low self-regard invite victimization? *Developmental Psychology, 34*, 299–309.

Eggers-Pieróla, C. (2005). *Connections and commitments: Reflecting Latino values in early childhood programs*. Portsmouth, NH: Heinemann.

Eisenberg, N. (2005). Temperamental effortful control (self-regulation). In R. E. Tremblay, R. G. Barr, & R. DeV. Peters (Eds.), *Encyclopedia on early childhood development* [online]. Montreal, QC: Centre of Excellence for Early Childhood Development. Retrieved September 6, 2009, from www.child-encyclopedia.com/documents/EisenbergANGxp.pdf

Eisenberg, N., Cumberland, A., Spinrad, T. L., Fabes, R. A., Shepard, S. A., Reiser, M., et al. (2001). The relations of regulation and emotionality to children's externalizing and internalizing problem behavior. *Child Development, 72*, 1112–1134.

Eisenberg, N., & Fabes, R. A. (1998). Prosocial development. In N. Eisenberg (Ed.), *Handbook of child psychology: Vol. 3, Social, emotional, and personality development* (5th ed., pp. 701–778). New York: Wiley.

Eisenberg, N., Sadovsky, A., Spinrad, T. L., Fabes, R. A., Losoya, S. H., Valiente, C., et al. (2005). The relations of problem behavior status to children's negative emotionality, effortful control, and impulsivity: Concurrent relations and prediction of change. *Developmental Psychology, 41*, 193–211.

Eisenberg, N., Spinrad, T., Fabes, R., Reiser, M., Cumberland, A., Shepard, S., et al. (2004). The relations of effortful control and impulsivity to children's resiliency and adjustment. *Child Development, 75*, 25–46.

Eisenberg, N., Valiente, C., Spinrad, T. L., Cumberland, A., Liew, J., Reiser, M., et al. (2009). Longitudinal relations of children's effortful control, impulsivity, and negative emotionality to their externalizing, internalizing, and co-occurring behavior problems. *Developmental Psychology, 45*, 988–1008.

Elias, M., & Butler, L. B. (1999). Social decision making and problem solving: Essential skills for interpersonal and academic success. In J. Cohen (Ed.), *Educating minds and hearts: Social emotional learning and the passage into adolescence* (pp. 74–94). New York: Teachers College Press.

Elias, M. J., & Schwab, Y. (2006). From compliance to responsibility: Social and emotional learning and classroom management. In C. M. Evertson & C. S. Weinstein (Eds.), *Handbook of classroom management: Research, practice, and contemporary issues* (pp. 309–341). Mahwah, NJ: Erlbaum.

Elicker, J., & Fortner-Wood, C. (1995). Adult-child relationships in early childhood programs. *Young Children, 51*(1), 69–78.

Ellis, B. (2009, Spring). Educating children who differ in susceptibility to rearing. *Florida Humanist Journal, 3*, 13–16.

Emmer, E. T., Evertson, C. M., & Anderson, L. M. (1980). Effective classroom management at the beginning of the school year. *Elementary School Journal, 80*, 219–231.

English, D. J., Upadhyaya, M. P., Litrownik, A. J., Marshall, J. M., Runyan, D. K., Graham, J. C., et al. (2005). Maltreatment's wake: The relationship of maltreatment dimensions to child outcomes. *Child Abuse and Neglect, 29*, 597–619.

Epstein, M., Atkins, M., Cullinan, D., Kutash, K., & Weaver, R. (2008). *Reducing behavior problems in the elementary school classroom: A practice guide*. Washington, DC: National Center for Education Evaluation and Regional Assistance, Institute of Education Services, U.S. Department of Education.

ERIC Clearinghouse on Disabilities and Gifted Education. (1998). *Teaching children with attention deficit/hyperactivity disorder*. Reston, VA: Author. (ERIC Digest E569).

Eron, L. D., Gentry, J. H., & Schlegel, P. (Eds.). (1994). Introduction: Experience of violence: Ethnic groups. In L. D. Eron, J. H. Gentry, & P. Schlegel (Eds.), *Reason to* hope: *A psychosocial perspective on violence & youth* (pp. 101–103). Washington, DC: American Psychological Association.

Espinosa, L. M. (2010). *Getting it right for young children from diverse backgrounds: Applying research to improve practice.* Upper Saddle River, NJ: Pearson.

Estell, D. B., Cairns, R. B., Farmer, T. W., & Cairns, B. D. (2002). Aggression in inner-city early elementary classrooms: Individual and peer-group configurations. *Merrill-Palmer Quarterly, 48,* 52–76.

Evans, G. W., & English, K. (2002). The environment of poverty: Multiple stressor exposure, psychophysiological stress, and socioemotional adjustment. *Child Development, 73,* 1238–1248.

Evertson, C. M., Emmer, E. T., & Worsham, M. E. (2003). *Classroom management for elementary teachers* (6th ed.). Boston: Allyn & Bacon.

Fabes, R. A., & Eisenberg, N. (1992). Young children's coping with interpersonal anger. *Child Development, 63,* 116–128.

Fabes, R. A., Gaertner, B. M., & Popp, T. K. (2006). Getting along with others: Social competence in early childhood. In K. McCartney & D. Phillips (Eds.), *Handbook of early childhood development* (pp. 297–316). Malden, MA: Blackwell.

Fabes, R. A., Hanish, L. D., & Martin, C. L. (2003). Children at play: The role of peers in understanding the effects of child care. *Child Development, 74,* 1039–1043.

Falvey, M. A., & Givner, C. C. (2005). What is an inclusive school? In R. A. Villa & J. S. Thousand (Eds.), *Creating an inclusive school* (2nd ed., pp. 1–11). Alexandria, VA: Association for Supervision and Curriculum Development.

Fantuzzo, J., McWayne, C., Perry, M. A., & Childs, S. (2004). Multiple dimensions of family involvement and their relations to behavioral and learning competencies for urban, low-income children. *School Psychology Review, 33,* 467–480.

Farah, M. J., Shera, D. M., Savage, J. H., Betancourt, L., Giannetta, J. M., Brodsky, N. L., et al. (2006). Childhood poverty: Specific associations with neurocognitive development. *Brain Research, 1110,* 166–174.

Farmer, T. W. (2000). Misconceptions of peer rejection and problem behavior: Understanding aggression in students with mild disabilities. *Remedial and Special Education, 21,* 194–208.

Farrington, D. P., & Ttofi, M. M. (2009). How to reduce school bullying. *Victims and Offenders, 4,* 321–326.

Fass, S., & Cauthen, N. K. (2008). *Who are America's poor children?* National Center for Children in Poverty. Retrieved October 14, 2009, from http://nccp.org/publications/pub_843.html

Fearon, R. P., Bakermans-Kranenburg, M. J., van IJzendoorn, M. H., Lapsley, A.-M., & Roisman, G. I. (2010). The significance of insecure attachment and disorganization in the development of children's externalizing behavior: A meta-analytic study. *Child Development, 81,* 435–456.

Federal Interagency Forum on Child and Family Statistics. (2009). Food security. In *America's children: Key national indicators of well-being, 2009.* Retrieved October 29, 2009, from http://childstats.gov/americaschildren/eco3.asp

Fergus, S., & Zimmerman, M. A. (2005). Adolescent resilience: A framework for understanding healthy development in the face of risk. *Annual Review of Public Health, 26,* 399–419.

Ferguson, C. (with Ramos, M., Rudo, Z., & Wood, L.). (2008). *The school-family connection: Looking at the larger picture: A review of the current literature.* Austin, TX: National Center for Family and Community Connections with Schools. Retrieved December 20, 2009, from www.sedl.org/connections/resources/sfclitrev.pdf

Fergusson, D. (2002). Tobacco consumption during pregnancy and its impact on child development. In R. E. Tremblay, R. G. Barr, & R. DeV. Peters (Eds.), *Encyclopedia on early childhood development* [online]. Montreal, QC: Centre of Excellence for Early Childhood Development. Retrieved October 29, 2009, from www.child-encyclopedia.com/pages/PDF/tobacco.pdf

Fields, M., & Boesser, C. (1998). *Constructive guidance and discipline: Preschool and primary education* (2nd ed.). Upper Saddle River, NJ: Prentice Hall.

Finkelhor, D., Ormrod, R., Turner, H., & Hamby, S. L. (2005). The victimization of children and youth: A comprehensive national survey. *Child Maltreatment, 10*, 5–25.

Finkelhor, D., Turner, H., Ormrod, R., & Hamby, S. L. (2009). Violence, abuse, and crime exposure in a national sample of children and youth. *Pediatrics, 124*, 1411–1423.

Fisher, E., & Kennedy, C. H. (2001). Access to the middle school core curriculum. In C. H. Kennedy & D. Fisher, *Inclusive middle schools* (pp. 43–59). Baltimore: Brookes.

Fisher, P. A., Gunnar, M. R., Dozier, M., Bruce, J., & Pears, K. C. (2006). Effects of therapeutic interventions for foster children on behavioral problems, caregiver attachment, and stress regulatory neural systems. *Annals of the New York Academy of Sciences, 1094*, 215–225.

Fox, L., Carta, J., Strain, P., Dunlap, G., & Hemmeter, M. L. (2009). *Response to Intervention and the pyramid model.* Tampa, FL: University of South Florida, Technical Assistance on Social Emotional Intervention for Young Children. Retrieved April 13, 2010, from www.challengingbehavior.org/do/resources/documents/rti_pyramid_web.pdf

Fox, L., Dunlap, G., & Cushing, L. (2002). Early intervention, positive behavior support, and transition to school. *Journal of Emotional and Behavioral Disorders, 10*, 149–157.

Fox, L., Dunlap, G., Hemmeter, M. L., Joseph, G. E., & Strain, P. S. (2003). The teaching pyramid: A model for supporting social competence and preventing challenging behavior in young children. *Young Children, 58*(4), 48–52.

Fox, L., Vaughn, B. J., Wyatte, M. L., & Dunlap, G. (2002). "We can't expect other people to understand": Family perspectives on problem behavior. *Exceptional Children, 68*, 437–450.

Freiberg, H. J. (1999). Sustaining the paradigm. In H. J. Freiberg (Ed.), *Beyond behaviorism: Changing the classroom management paradigm* (pp. 164–173). Boston: Allyn & Bacon.

Freire, M., & Bernhard, J. K. (1997). Caring for and teaching children who speak other languages. In K. M. Kilbride (Ed.), *Include*

me too! Human diversity in early childhood* (pp. 160–176). Toronto, ON: Harcourt Brace & Company Canada.

French, N. K. (1999). Paraeducators and teachers: Shifting roles. *Teaching Exceptional Children, 32*(2), 69–73.

Frick, P. J. (2004). Integrating research on temperament and childhood psychopathology: Its pitfalls and promises. *Journal of Clinical Child and Adolescent Psychology, 33*, 2–7.

Frick, P. J., Cornell, A. H., Bodin, S. D., Dane, H. E., Barry, C. T., & Loney, B. R. (2003). Callous-unemotional traits and developmental pathways to severe conduct problems. *Developmental Psychology, 39*, 246–260.

Frick, P. J., & Morris, A. S. (2004). Temperament and developmental pathways to conduct problems. *Journal of Clinical Child and Adolescent Psychology, 33*, 54–68.

Fried, P. A. (2002a). Adolescents prenatally exposed to marijuana: Examination of facets of complex behaviors and comparisons with the influence of in utero cigarettes. *Journal of Clinical Pharmacology, 42*, 97S–102S.

Fried, P. A. (2002b). Tobacco consumption during pregnancy and its impact on child development. In R. E. Tremblay, R. G. Barr, & R. DeV. Peters (Eds.), *Encyclopedia on early childhood development* [online]. Montreal, QC: Centre of Excellence for Early Childhood Development. Retrieved October 29, 2009, from www.child-encyclopedia.com/pages/PDF/tobacco.pdf

Friend, M. (2005). *Special education: Contemporary perspectives for school professionals.* Boston: Allyn & Bacon.

Friend, M., & Bursuck, W. D. (2002). *Including children with special needs: A practical guide for classroom teachers* (3rd ed.). Boston: Allyn & Bacon.

Frith, U., & Frith, C. D. (2003). Development and neurophysiology of mentalizing. *Philosophical Transactions of the Royal Society of London. Series B: Biological Sciences, 358*, 459–473.

Froschl, M., Sprung, B., & Mullin-Rindler, N. (with Stein, N., & Gropper, N.). (1998). *Quit it! A teacher's guide on teasing and* bullying for use with students in grades K-3. Washington, DC: NEA Professional Library.

Fry, D. P. (1988). Intercommunity differences in aggression among Zapotec children. *Child Development, 59*, 1008–1019.

Fry, P. S. (1983). Process measures of problem and non-problem children's classroom behaviour: The influence of teacher behaviour variables. *British Journal of Educational Psychology, 53*, 79–88.

Furman, E. (1986). Stress in the nursery school. In E. Furman (Ed.), *What nursery school teachers ask us about: Psychoanalytic consultations in preschools.* Madison, CT: International Universities Press.

Gable, R. A., Quinn, M. M., Rutherford, R. B., Jr., Howell, K. W., & Hoffman, C. C. (1998). *Addressing student problem behavior: Part II—Conducting a functional behavioral assessment* (3rd ed.). Washington, DC: Center for Effective Collaboration and Practice. Retrieved April 14, 2010, from http://cecp.air.org/fba/default.asp

Gagnon, C. (1991). Commentary: School-based interventions for aggressive children: Possibilities, limitations, and future directions. In D. J. Pepler & K. H. Rubin (Eds.), *The development and treatment of childhood aggression* (pp. 449–455). Hillsdale, NJ: Erlbaum.

Galinsky, E. (1988). Parents and teacher-caregivers: Sources of tension, sources of support. *Young Children, 43*, 4–12.

Ganesh, A., & Surbeck, D. (2005, December). *An investigation of the impact of standardized testing in second grade.* Presentation at National Association for the Education of Young Children, Washington, DC.

Garandeau, C. F., & Cillessen, A. H. N. (2006). From indirect aggression to invisible aggression: A conceptual view on bullying and peer group manipulation. *Aggression and Violent Behavior, 11*, 612–625.

Garbarino, J. (1999). *Lost boys: Why our sons turn violent and how we can save them.* New York: Free Press.

Garbarino, J., & deLara, E. (2002). *And words can hurt forever: How to protect adolescents from bullying, harassment, and emotional violence.* New York: Free Press.

Garcia, E. E. (2005). *Teaching and learning in two languages: Bilingualism and schooling in the United States.* New York: Teachers College Press.

García Coll, C., & Magnuson, K. (2000). Cultural differences as sources of developmental vulnerabilities and resources. In J. P. Shonkoff & S. J. Meisels (Eds.), *Handbook of early childhood intervention* (2nd ed., pp. 94–114). New York: Cambridge University Press.

Gardner, H. (1983). *Multiple intelligences: The theory in practice.* New York: Basic Books.

Garrison-Wade, D. R., & Lewis, C. W. (2006). Tips for school principals and teachers: Helping Black students achieve. In J. Landsman & C. W. Lewis (Eds.), *White teachers / diverse classrooms: A guide to building inclusive schools, promoting high expectations, and eliminating racism* (pp. 150–161). Sterling, VA: Stylus.

Gartrell, D., & King, M. (2003, November). *Guidance with boys in early childhood classrooms: An interactive exploration of boys' behavior techniques to alleviate conflict.* Presentation at National Association for the Education of Young Children, Chicago.

Gatti, U., & Tremblay, R. E. (2005). Social capital and physical violence. In R. E. Tremblay, W. W. Hartup, & J. Archer (Eds.), *Developmental origins of aggression* (pp. 398–424). New York: Guilford.

Gay, G. (2000). *Culturally responsive teaching: Theory, research, and practice.* New York: Teachers College Press.

Genesee, F. (2008). Early dual language learning. *Zero to Three, 29*(1), 17–23.

Genesee, F., Paradis, J., & Crago, M. B. (2004). *Dual language development and disorders: A handbook on bilingualism and second language learning.* Baltimore: Brookes.

Genishi, C., & Dyson, A. H. (2009). *Children, language, and literacy: Diverse learners in diverse times.* New York: Teachers College Press.

Gershoff, E. T. (2002). Corporal punishment by parents and associated child behaviors and experiences: A meta-analytic and theoretical review. *Psychological Bulletin, 128*, 539–579.

Giangreco, M. F. (2003). Working with para-professionals. *Educational Leadership, 61*(2), 50–53.

Giangreco, M. F., Edelman, S. W., Luiselli, T. E., & MacFarland, S. Z. C. (1997). Helping or hovering? Effects of instructional assistant proximity on students with disabilities. *Exceptional Children, 64*, 7–18.

Gibb, J. R. (1961). Defensive communication. *Journal of Communication, 11*, 141–148.

Giedd, J. N. (2004). Structural magnetic resonance imaging of the adolescent brain. *Annals of the New York Academy of Sciences, 1021*, 77–85.

Gilliam, W. S. (2005, May). *Prekindergarteners left behind: Expulsion rates in state prekindergarten programs*. New York: FCD Policy Brief 3. Retrieved August 31, 2009, from http://fcd-us.org/usr_doc/Expulsion PolicyBrief.pdf

Ginott, H. G. (1956). *Between parent and child*. New York: Avon.

Ginsberg, M. B. (2007). Lessons at the kitchen table. *Educational Leadership, 64*(6), 56–61.

Ginsburg, K. R. (2007). The importance of play in promoting healthy child development and maintaining strong parent-child bonds. *Pediatrics, 119*, 182–191.

Goldenberg, C. (2008). Teaching English language learners. *American Educator, 32*(2), 8–23, 42–44.

Goldenberg, C., Rueda, R. S., & August, D. (2006). Synthesis: Sociocultural contexts and literacy development. In D. August & T. Shanahan (Eds.), *Developing literacy in English-language learners: Report of the National Literacy Panel on Language Minority Children and Youth* (pp. 249–267). Mahwah, NJ: Erlbaum.

Goldschmidt, L., Day, N. L., & Richardson, G. A. (2000). Effects of prenatal marijuana exposure on child behavior problems at age 10. *Neurotoxicology and Teratology, 22*, 325–336.

Goleman, D. (1997). *Emotional intelligence*. New York: Bantam.

Goleman, D. (2006a). *Social intelligence: The new science of human relationships*. New York: Bantam.

Goleman, D. (2006b). The socially intelligent leader. *Educational Leadership, 64*(10), 76–81.

Gonzalez-Mena, J. (2003, November). Discovering my whiteness. Presentation at the National Association for the Education of Young Children, Chicago.

Gonzalez-Mena, J. (2008). *Diversity in early care and education: Honoring differences* (5th ed.). New York: McGraw-Hill.

Gonzalez-Mena, J. (2010). *50 strategies for communicating and working with diverse families* (2nd ed.). Upper Saddle River, NJ: Pearson.

Gonzalez-Mena, J., & Bernhard, J. K. (1998). Out-of-home care of infants and toddlers: A call for cultural linguistic continuity. *Interaction, 12*, 14–15.

Good, T. L., & Brophy, J. E. (2008). *Looking in classrooms* (10th ed.). Boston: Allyn & Bacon.

Gopnik, A., Meltzoff, A. N., & Kuhl, P. K. (2001). *The scientist in the crib: What early learning tells us about the mind*. New York: Perennial.

Gordon, T. (2000). *Parent effectiveness training: The proven program for raising responsible children*. New York: Three Rivers Press.

Gordon, T. (with Burch, N.). (2003). *Teacher effectiveness training*. New York: Three Rivers Press.

Gottfredson, D. (n.d.). School-based crime prevention. In L. W. Sherman, D. Gottfredson, D. MacKenzie, J. Eck, P. Reuter, & S. Bushway, *Preventing crime: What works, what doesn't, what's promising*. Washington, DC: U.S. National Institute of Justice. Retrieved October 29, 2009, from www.ncjrs.gov/works/

Gottfredson, G. D., Gottfredson, D. C., Czeh, E. R., Cantor, D., Crosse, S. B., & Hantman, I. (2004, November). *Toward safe and orderly schools—The national study of delinquency prevention in schools*. Washington, DC: National Institute of Justice. Retrieved October 29, 2009, from www.ncjrs.gov/pdffiles1/nij/205005.pdf

Graham, S., & Juvonen, J. (2001). An attributional approach to peer victimization. In J. Juvonen & S. Graham (Eds.), *Peer harassment in school: The plight of the vulnerable and victimized* (pp. 49–72). New York: Guilford.

Granot, D., & Mayseless, O. (2001). Attachment security and adjustment to school in middle childhood. *International Journal of Behavioral Development, 25,* 530–541.

Greenberg, M. T. (1999). Attachment and psychopathology in childhood. In J. Cassidy & P. R. Shaver (Eds.), *Handbook of attachment theory and research* (pp. 469–496). New York: Guilford.

Greenberg, M. T. (2006). Promoting resilience in children and youth: Preventive interventions and their interface with neuroscience. In B. M. Lester, A. S. Masten, & B. McEwen (Eds.), *Resilience in children* (pp. 139–150). Boston: New York Academy of Sciences.

Greenberg, M. T., DeKlyen, M., Speltz, M. L., & Endriga, M. C. (1997). The role of attachment processes in externalizing psychopathology in young children. In L. Atkinson & K. Zucker (Eds.), *Attachment and psychopathy* (pp. 196–222). New York: Guilford.

Greenberg, M. T., Speltz, M. L., & DeKlyen, M. (1993). The role of attachment in the early development of disruptive behavior problems. *Development and Psychopathology, 5,* 191–213.

Greene, R. W. (1998). *The explosive child: A new approach for understanding and parenting easily frustrated, "chronically inflexible" children.* New York: HarperCollins.

Greene, R. W. (2008). *Lost at school: Why our kids with behavioral challenges are falling through the cracks and how we can help them.* New York: Scribner.

Greene, R. W. (2010). *The explosive child: A new approach for understanding and parenting easily frustrated, chronically inflexible children.* New York: Harper.

Greenfield, P. M., & Suzuki, L. K. (1998). Culture and human development: Implications for parenting, education, pediatrics, and mental health. In I. E. Sigel & K. A. Renninger (Eds.), *Handbook of child psychology: Vol. 4, Child psychology in practice* (5th ed., pp. 1059–1109). New York: Wiley.

Greenman, J. (2005). *Caring spaces, learning places: Children's environments that work.* Redmond, WA: Exchange Press.

Greenough, W. T., Black, J. E., & Wallace, C. S. (1987). Experience and brain development. *Child Development, 58,* 539–559.

Greenspan, S. I. (1996). *The challenging child: Understanding, raising, and enjoying the five "difficult" types of children.* Reading, MA: Addison-Wesley.

Grigal, M. (1998). The time-space continuum: Using natural supports in inclusive classrooms. *Teaching Exceptional Children, 30*(6), 44–51.

Groves, B. M. (2002). *Children who see too much: Lessons from the Child Witness to Violence Project.* Boston: Beacon Press.

Groves, B. M., & Zuckerman, B. (1997). Intervention with parents and caregivers of children who are exposed to violence. In J. D. Osofsky (Ed.), *Children in a violent society* (pp. 183–201). New York: Guilford.

Gruber, J. E., & Fineran, S. (2008). Comparing the impact of bullying and sexual harassment victimization on the mental and physical health of adolescents. *Sex Roles, 59,* 1–13.

Guerra, N. G. (1997a). Intervening to prevent childhood aggression in the inner city. In J. McCord (Ed.), *Violence and childhood in the inner city* (pp. 256–312). New York: Cambridge University Press.

Guerra, N. G. (1997b, May). *Violence in schools: Interventions to reduce school-based violence.* Presentation at the Centre for Studies of Children at Risk, Hamilton, ON.

Guetzloe, E. C., & Johns, B. H. (2004). Instructional strategies for students with emotional and behavioral disorders in inclusive settings. In B. H. Johns & E. C. Guetzloe (Eds.), *Inclusive education for children and youths with emotional and behavioral disorders: Enduring challenges and emerging practices* (pp. 11–17). Arlington, VA: Council for Children with Behavioral Disorders.

Gunnar, M. R. (1998). Quality of early care and buffering of neuroendocrine stress reactions: Potential effects on the developing human brain. *Preventive Medicine, 27,* 208–211.

Gunnar, M. R. (2000, July). *Brain-behavior interface: Studies of early experience and the physiology of stress.* Presentation at the World Association for Infant Mental Health, Montreal, QC.

Gunnar, M. R. (2006). Social regulation of stress in early childhood development.

In K. McCartney & D. Phillips (Eds.), *Handbook of early childhood development* (pp. 106–125). Malden, MA: Blackwell.

Gunnar, M. R., & Cheatham, C. L. (2003). Brain and behavior interface: Stress and the developing brain. *Infant Mental Health Journal, 24*, 195–211.

Gunnar, M. R., & Donzella, B. (2002). Social regulation of the cortisol levels in early human development. *Psychoneuroendocrinology, 27*, 199–220.

Guzman, B. (2001, May). *The Hispanic population: Census 2000 brief.* Washington, DC: U.S. Census Bureau. Retrieved February 7, 2010, from www.census.gov/prod/2001pubs/c2kbr01-3.pdf

Haager, D., & Klingner, J. K. (2005). *Differentiating instruction in inclusive classrooms: The special educator's guide.* Boston: Allyn & Bacon.

Haager, D., & Vaughn, S. (1995). Parent, teacher, peer, and self reports of social competence of students with learning disabilities. *Journal of Learning Disabilities, 28*, 205–215, 231.

Hackman, D. A., & Farah, M. J. (2009). Socioeconomic status and the developing brain. *Trends in Cognitive Sciences, 13*, 65–73.

Hagan, J. F., Jr., & the Committee on Psychosocial Aspects of Child and Family Health, & the Task Force on Terrorism of the American Academy of Pediatrics. (2005). Psychosocial implications of disaster or terrorism on children: A guide for the pediatrician. *Pediatrics, 116*, 787–795.

Hale, J. E. (1986). *Black children: Their roots, culture, and learning styles.* Baltimore: Johns Hopkins Press.

Hale, J. E. (2001). *Learning while black: Creating educational excellence for African American children.* Baltimore: Johns Hopkins Press.

Halgunseth, L. C., Ipsa, J. M., & Rudy, D. (2006). Parental control in Latino families: An integrated review of the literature. *Child Development, 77*, 1282–1297.

Hall, E. T. (1977). *Beyond culture.* Garden City, NY: Anchor Press/Doubleday.

Hall, L. J. (2009). *Autism spectrum disorders: From theory to practice.* Upper Saddle River, NJ: Merrill.

Halle, T., Forry, N., Hair, E., Perper, K., Wandner, L., Wessel, J., et al. (2009). *Disparities in early learning and development: Lessons from the Early Childhood Longitudinal Study—Birth Cohort.* Washington, DC: Child Trends. Retrieved October 19, 2009, from http://childtrends.org/Files/Child_Trends-2009_07_10_FR_DisparitiesEL.pdf

Hamby, S., Finkelhor, D., Turner, H., & Ormrod, R. (2010). Exposure to intimate partner violence and other forms of family violence: Nationally representative rates among U.S. youth. *Office of Juvenile Justice and Delinquency Prevention.*

Hamilton, C. E. (2000). Continuity and discontinuity of attachment from infancy through adolescence. *Child Development, 71*, 690–694.

Hamre, B. K., & Pianta, R. C. (2001). Early teacher-child relationships and the trajectory of children's school outcomes through eighth grade. *Child Development, 72*, 625–638.

Hamre, B. K., & Pianta, R. C. (2005). Can instructional and emotional support in the first-grade classroom make a difference for children at risk of school failure? *Child Development, 76*, 949–967.

Hamre, B. K., Pianta, R. C., Downer, J. T., & Mashburn, A. J. (2008). Teachers' perceptions of conflicts with young students: Looking beyond problem behaviors. *Social Development, 17*, 115–136.

Handwerk, M. L., & Marshall, R. M. (1998). Behavioral and emotional problems of students with learning disabilities, serious emotional disturbance, or both conditions. *Journal of Learning Disabilities, 31*, 327–338.

Hanish, L. D., Martin, C. L., Fabes, R. A., Leonard, S., & Herzog, M. (2005). Exposure to externalizing peers in early childhood: Homophily and peer contagion processes. *Journal of Abnormal Child Psychology, 33*, 267–281.

Hargie, O., Saunders, C., & Dickson, D. (1994). *Social skills in interpersonal communication* (3rd ed.). New York: Routledge.

Harms, T., Clifford, R. M., & Cryer, D. (2005). *Early childhood environment rating scale* (Revised ed.). New York: Teachers College Press.

Harris, J. R. (1999). *The nurture assumption: Why children turn out the way they do.* New York: Touchstone.

Harwood, M., & Kleinfeld, J. S. (2002). Up front, in hope: The value of early intervention for children with fetal alcohol syndrome. *Young Children, 57*(4), 86–90.

Hawkins, D. L., Pepler, D. J., & Craig, W. M. (2001). Naturalistic observations of peer interventions in bullying. *Social Development, 10,* 512–527.

Hawkins, J. D., Guo, J., Hill, K. G., Battin-Pearson, S., & Abbott, R. D. (2001). Long-term effects of the Seattle Social Development Project on school bonding trajectories. *Applied Developmental Sciences, 5,* 225–236.

Hawkins, J. D., Smith, B. H., & Catalano, R. F. (2004). Social development and social and emotional learning. In J. E. Zins, R. P. Weissberg, W. C. Wang, & H. J. Walberg (Eds.), *Building academic success on social and emotional learning: What does the research say?* (pp. 135–150). New York: Teachers College Press.

Hawkins, J. D., Smith, B. H., Hill, K. G., Kosterman, R., & Catalano, R. F. (2007). Promoting social development and preventing health and behavior problems during the elementary grades: Results from the Seattle Social Development Project. *Victims and Offenders, 2,* 161–181.

Hay, D. F. (2005). The beginnings of aggression in infancy. In R. E. Tremblay, W. W. Hartup, & J. Archer (Eds.), *Developmental origins of aggression* (pp. 107–132). New York: Guilford.

Hay, T. (1994-1995, Winter). The case against punishment. *IMPrint, 11,* 10–11.

Hayes, N. (2000). *Section 504: It is not "unfunded" special education.* New Horizons for Learning. Retrieved May 2, 2010, from www.newhorizons.org/spneeds/inclusion/law/hayes3.htm

Hazler, R. J., & Carney, J. V. (2006). Critical characteristics of effective bullying prevention programs. In S. R. Jimerson & M. J. Furlong (Eds.), *The handbook of school violence and school safety: From research to practice* (pp. 275–291). Mahwah, NJ: Erlbaum.

Heath, S. B. (1983). *Ways with words: Language, life, and work in communities and classrooms.* New York: Cambridge University Press.

Heath, S. B. (2002). A lot of talk about nothing. In B. M. Power & R. S. Hubbard (Eds.), *Language development: A reader for teachers* (2nd ed., pp. 74–79). Upper Saddle River, NJ: Merrill Prentice Hall.

Hernandez, D. J., Denton, N. A., & Macartney, S. E. (2008). Children in immigrant families: Looking to America's future. *Social Policy Report, 22,* 3–22.

Hertz, M. F., & David-Ferdon, C. (2008). *Electronic media and youth violence: A CDC issue brief for educators and caregivers.* Atlanta: Centers for Disease Control. Retrieved May 21, 2010, from www.cdc.gov/ncipc/dvp/YVP/electronic_agression_brief_for_parents.pdf

Hewes, D. W. (2001). *W. N. Hailmann: Defender of Froebel.* Grand Rapids, MI: Froebel Foundation.

Hickman-Davis, P. (2002, Spring). "Cuando no hablan Inglés": Helping young children learn English as a second language. *Dimensions of Early Childhood,* 3–10.

Hilliard, A. G., III. (2002). Language, culture, and the assessment of African American children. In L. Delpit & J. K. Dowdy (Eds.), *The skin that we speak: Thoughts on language and culture in the classroom* (pp. 87–105). New York: New Press.

Hirsh-Pasek, K., & Golinkoff, R. M. (2008). Why play=learning. In R. E. Tremblay, R. G. Barr, R. DeV. Peters, & M. Boivin (Eds.), *Encyclopedia on early childhood development* [online]. Montreal, QC: Centre of Excellence for Early Childhood Development. Retrieved March 17, 2010, from www.child-encyclopedia.com/pages/PDF/Hirsh-Pasek-GolinkoffANGxp.pdf

Ho, D. Y. F. (1994). Cognitive socialization in Confucian heritage cultures. In P. M. Greenfield & R. R. Cocking (Eds.), *Cross-cultural roots of minority child development* (pp. 285–314). Hillsdale, NJ: Erlbaum.

Hodges, E. V. E., Boivin, M., Vitaro, F., & Bukowski, W. M. (1999). The power of friendship: Protection against an escalating cycle of peer victimization. *Developmental Psychology, 35,* 94–101.

Hodges, H. (2001). Overcoming a pedagogy of poverty. In R. W. Cole (Ed.), *More strategies for educating everybody's children* (pp. 1–9). Alexandria, VA: Association for Supervision and Curriculum Development.

Holahan, A. (2000). A comparison of developmental gains for preschool children with disabilities in inclusive and self-contained classrooms. *Topics in Early Childhood Special Education, 19*(4), 224–235.

Holden, C. (2000). The violence of the lambs. *Science, 289,* 580–581.

Holmeboe, K., & Johnson, M. H. (2005). Educating executive attention. *Proceedings of the National Academy of Sciences, 102,* 14479–14480.

Honig, A. S. (2002). *Secure relationships: Nurturing infant/toddler attachment in early care settings.* Washington, DC: National Association for the Education of Young Children.

Hoover-Dempsey, K. V., Walker, J. M. T., Sandler, H. M., Whetsel, D., Green, C. L., Wilkins, A. S., et al. (2005). Why do parents become involved? Research findings and implications. *Elementary School Journal, 106,* 105–130.

Horn, E., Lieber, J., Sandall, S. R., Schwartz, I. S., & Wolery, R. A. (2002). Classroom models of individualized instruction. In S. I. Odom (Ed.) (with P. J. Beckman, M. J. Hanson, E. Horn, J. Lieber, S. R. Sandall, I. L. Schwartz, et al.), *Widening the circle: Including children with disabilities in preschool programs* (pp. 25–45). New York: Teachers College Press.

Howard, G. R. (2007). As diversity grows, so must we. *Educational Leadership, 64*(6), 16–22.

Howes, C. (1999). Attachment relationships in the context of multiple caregivers. In J. Cassidy & P. R. Shaver (Eds.), *Handbook of attachment theory and research* (pp. 671–687). New York: Guilford.

Howes, C. (2010). *Culture and child development in early childhood programs: Practices for quality education and care.* New York: Teachers College Press.

Howes, C., & Hamilton, C. E. (1993). The changing experience of child care: Changes in teachers and in teacher-child relationships and children's social competence with peers. *Early Childhood Research Quarterly, 8,* 15–32.

Howes, C., & Hamilton, C. E. (2002). Children's relationships with caregivers: Mothers and child care teachers. *Child Development, 63,* 859–866.

Howes, C., Hamilton, C. E., & Phillipsen, L. C. (1998). Stability and continuity of child-caregiver and child-peer relationships. *Child Development, 69,* 418–426.

Howes, C., Matheson, C. C., & Hamilton, C. E. (1994). Maternal, teacher, and child care history correlates of children's relationships with peers. *Child Development, 65,* 264–273.

Howes, C., & Ritchie, S. (1999). Attachment organizations in children with difficult life circumstances. *Development and Psychopathology, 11,* 251–268.

Howes, C., & Ritchie, S. (2002). *A matter of trust: Connecting teachers and learners in the early childhood classroom.* New York: Teachers College Press.

Howes, C., & Shivers, E. M. (2006). New child-caregiver attachment relationships: Entering child care when the caregiver is and is not an ethnic match. *Social Development, 15,* 343–360.

Hu, W. (2009, March 14). Forget goofing around: Recess has a new boss. *The New York Times.* Retrieved March 18, 2010, from www.nytimes.com

Hughes, J., & Kwok, O. (2007). Influences of student-teacher and parent-teacher relationships on lower achieving readers' engagement and achievement in the primary grades. *Journal of Educational Psychology, 99,* 39–51.

Hughes, J. N., Cavell, T. A., & Willson, V. (2001). Further support for the developmental significance of the quality of the teacher-student relationship. *Journal of School Psychology, 39,* 289–301.

Huijbregts, S. C. J., Séguin, J. R., Zoccolillo, M., Boivin, M., & Tremblay, R. E. (2008). Maternal prenatal smoking, parental antisocial behavior, and early childhood physical aggression. *Development and Psychopathology, 20,* 437–453.

Human Rights Watch & American Civil Liberties Union. (2008). *A violent education: Corporal punishment of children in US public schools.* Retrieved October 10,

2009, from http://aclu.org/pdfs/humanrights/aviolenteducation_report.pdf

Humber, N., & Moss, E. (2005). The relationship of school and early school-age attachment to mother-child interaction. *American Journal of Orthopsychiatry, 75,* 128–141.

Hyman, I., & Snook, P. A. (1999). *Dangerous schools: What we can do about the physical and emotional abuse of our children.* San Francisco: Jossey-Bass.

Hymel, S., Wagner, E., & Butler, L. J. (1990). Reputational bias: View from the peer group. In S. R. Asher & J. D. Coie (Eds.), *Peer rejection in childhood* (pp. 156–186). New York: Cambridge University Press.

Ianotti, R. J. (1985). Naturalistic and structured assessments of prosocial behavior in preschool children: The influence of empathy and perspective taking. *Developmental Psychology, 21,* 46–55.

Individuals with Disabilities Education Act Amendments of 1997, P.L. 105–17.

Iwata, B. A., Dorsey, M. F., Slifer, K. J., Bauman, K. E., & Richman, G. S. (1982). Toward a functional analysis of self-injury. *Analysis and Intervention in Developmental Disabilities, 2,* 3–20.

Iwata, B. A., Vollmer, T. R., & Zarcone, J. R. (1990). The experimental (functional) analysis of behavior disorders: Methodology, applications, and limitations. In A. C. Repp & N. N. Singh (Eds.), *Perspectives on the use of nonaversive and aversive interventions for persons with developmental disabilities* (pp. 301–330). Sycamore, IL: Sycamore.

Jacobson, S. W., & Frye, K. F. (1991). Effect of maternal social support on attachment: Experimental evidence. *Child Development, 62,* 572–582.

Janssen, I., Craig, W. M., Boyce, W. F., & Pickett, W. (2004). Associations between overweight and obesity with bullying behaviors in school-aged children. *Pediatrics, 113,* 1187–1194.

Jensen, E. (2005). *Teaching with the brain in mind.* Alexandria, VA: Association for Supervision and Curriculum Development.

Joe, J. R., & Malach, R. S. (2004). Families with American Indian roots. In E. W. Lynch & M. J. Hanson (Eds.), *Developing cross-cultural competence: A guide for working with children and their families* (3rd ed., pp. 109–139). Baltimore: Brookes.

Johnson, D. W., & Johnson, R. T. (2004). The three Cs of promoting social and emotional learning. In J. E. Zins, R. P. Weissberg, W. C. Wang, & H. J. Walberg (Eds.), *Building academic success on social and emotional learning: What does the research say?* (pp. 40–58). New York: Teachers College Press.

Johnson, J., & Duffett, A. (with Farkas, S., & Wilson, L.). (2002). *When it's your own child: A report on special education from the families who use it.* New York: Public Agenda. Retrieved May 2, 2010, from www.publicagenda.org/reports/when-its-your-own-child

Jones, L. R. (2008, September 3). Teaching secrets: Bridging the gender gap. *Teacher.* Retrieved March 16, 2010, from www.edweek.org/tm/articles/2008/09/03/01tln_jones.h20.html

Jones, R. L., Homa, D. M., Meyer, P. A., Brody, D. J., Caldwell, K. L., Pirkle, J. L., et al. (2009). Trends in blood lead levels and blood lead testing among US children aged 1 to 5 years, 1998-2004. *Pediatrics, 123,* e376–e385.

Joshi, P. T., O'Donnell, D. A., Cullins, L. M., & Lewin, S. M. (2006). Children exposed to war and terrorism. In M. M. Feerick & G. B. Silverman (Eds.), *Children exposed to violence* (pp. 53–84). Baltimore: Brookes.

Joussemet, M., Vitaro, F., Barker, E. D., Côté, S., Nagin, D., Zoccolillo, M., et al. (2008). Controlling parenting and physical aggression during elementary school. *Child Development, 79,* 411–425.

Juvonen, J., & Graham, S. (2001). Preface. In J. Juvonen & S. Graham (Eds.), *Peer harassment in school: The plight of the vulnerable and victimized* (pp. xiii–xvi). New York: Guilford.

Juvenon, J., Graham, S., & Schuster, M. A. (2003). Bullying among young adolescents: The strong, the weak, and the troubled. *Pediatrics, 112,* 1231–1237.

Juvonen, J., & Gross, E. F. (2008). Extending the school grounds? Bullying experiences in cyberspace. *Journal of School Health, 78,* 496–505.

Kagan, J. (1998). Biology and the child. In N. Eisenberg (Ed.), *Handbook of child psychology: Vol. 3, Social, emotional, and personality development* (5th ed., pp. 177–235). New York: Wiley.

Kagan, J., & Snidman, N. (2004). *The long shadow of temperament.* Cambridge, MA: Belknap.

Kagan, J., Snidman, N., Kahn, V., & Towsley, S. (2007). The preservation of two infant temperaments into adolescence. *Monographs of the Society for Research in Child Development, 72,* 1–95.

Kağıtçıbaşı, C. (1996). *Family and human development across cultures: A view from the other side.* Mahwah, NJ: Erlbaum.

Kandel, E. R., Jessell, T. M., & Sanes, J. R. (2000). Sensory experience and the fine-tuning of synaptic connections. In E. R. Kandel, J. H. Schwartz, & T. M. Jessell (Eds.), *Principles of neural science* (4th ed., pp. 1115–1130). New York: McGraw-Hill.

Kaplan, H. B. (1999). Toward an understanding of resilience: A critical review of definitions and models. In M. D. Glantz & J. L. Johnson (Eds.), *Resilience and development: Positive life adaptations* (pp. 17–83). New York: Kluwer Academic/Plenum.

Kaplan, J. S. (2000). *Beyond functional assessment: A social-cognitive approach to the evaluation of behavior problems in children and youth.* Austin: Pro-Ed.

Karagammis, A., Stainback, W., & Stainback, S. (1996). Rationale for inclusive schooling. In S. Stainback & W. Stainback (Eds.), *Inclusion: A guide for educators* (pp. 3–16). Baltimore: Brookes.

Karen, R. (1998). *Becoming attached: First relationships and how they shape our capacity to love.* New York: Oxford University Press.

Karsh, K. G., Repp, A. C., Dahlquist, C. M., & Munk, D. (1995). In vivo functional assessment and multi-element interventions for problem behavior of students with disabilities in classroom settings. *Journal of Behavioral Education, 5,* 189–210.

Karten, T. J. (2005). *Inclusion strategies that work: Research-based methods for the classroom.* Thousand Oaks, CA: Corwin.

Katz, L. F., Kramer, L., & Gottman, J. M. (1992). Conflict and emotions in marital, sibling, and peer relationships. In C. U. Shantz & W. W. Hartup (Eds.), *Conflict in child and adolescent development* (pp. 122–149). New York: Cambridge University Press.

Katz, L. G., & McClellan, D. E. (1997). *Fostering children's social competence: The teacher's role.* Washington, DC: National Association for the Education of Young Children.

Kaufman, J. M. (2005). Explaining the race/ethnicity violence relationship: Neighborhood context and social psychological processes. *Justice Quarterly, 22,* 224–251.

Kay, P., Fitzgerald, M., & McConaughy, S. H. (2002). Building effective parent-teacher relationships. In B. Algonzzine & P. Kay (Eds.), *Preventing problem behaviors: A handbook of successful intervention strategies* (pp. 104–125). Thousand Oaks, CA: Corwin and Council for Exceptional Children.

Kellam, S. G., Ling, X., Merisca, R., Brown, C. H., & Ialongo, N. (1998). The effect of the level of aggression in the first grade classroom on the cause and malleability of aggressive behavior into middle school. *Development and Psychopathology, 10,* 165–185.

Keller, P. S., Cummings, E. M., Davies, P. T., & Mitchell, P. M. (2008). Longitudinal relations between parental drinking problems, family functioning, and child adjustment. *Development and Psychopathology, 20,* 195–212.

Keyser, J. (2006). *From parents to partners: Building a family-centered early childhood program.* St. Paul, MN, and Washington, DC: Redleaf and National Association for the Education of Young Children.

Kim, U., & Choi, S.-H. (1994). Individualism, collectivism, and child development: A Korean perspective. In P. M. Greenfield & R. R. Cocking (Eds.), *Cross-cultural roots of minority child development* (pp. 227–258). Hillsdale, NJ: Erlbaum.

Kitzmann, K. M., Gaylord, N. K., Holt, A. R., & Kenny, E. D. (2003). Child witnesses to domestic violence: A meta-analytic review. *Journal of Consulting and Clinical Psychology, 71,* 339–352.

Klass, C. S., Guskin, K. A., & Thomas, M. (1995). The early childhood program: Promoting children's development through and within relationships. *Zero to Three, 16(2),* 9–17.

Klass, P., & Costello, E. (2003). *Quirky kids: Understanding and helping your child who doesn't fit in—when to worry and when not to worry.* New York: Ballantine.

Klein, T. P., DeVoe, E. R., Miranda-Julian, C., & Linas, K. (2009). Young children's response to September 11th: The New York City experience. *Infant Mental Health Journal, 30,* 1–22.

Kleinfeld, J. (1975). Effective teachers of Eskimo and Indian students. *School Review, 83(2),* 301–344.

Kluth, P. (2003). *"You're going to love this kid!" Teaching students with autism in the inclusive classroom.* Baltimore: Brookes.

Knudsen, E. I. (2004). Sensitive periods in the development of the brain and behavior. *Journal of Cognitive Neuroscience, 16,* 1412–1425.

Kobak, R. (1999). The emotional dynamics of attachment relationships: Implications for theory, research, and clinical intervention. In J. Cassidy & P. R. Shaver (Eds.), *Handbook of attachment theory and research* (pp. 21–43). New York: Guilford.

Kochenderfer, B. J., & Ladd, G. W. (1996). Peer victimization: Manifestations and relations to school adjustment in kindergarten. *Journal of School Psychology, 34,* 267–283.

Kochenderfer-Ladd, B., & Skinner, K. (2002). Children's coping strategies: Moderators of the effects of peer victimization? *Developmental Psychology, 38,* 267–278.

Kochman, T. (1985). Black American speech events and a language program for the classroom. In C. B. Casden, V. P. John, & D. Hymes (Eds.), *Functions of language in the classroom* (pp. 211–261). Prospect Heights, IL: Waveland.

Koegel, R. L., & Koegel, L. K. (1995). *Teaching children with autism: Strategies for initiating positive interactions and improving learning opportunities.* Baltimore: Brookes.

Kohn, A. (1996). *Beyond discipline: From compliance to community.* Upper Saddle River, NJ: Merrill Prentice-Hall.

Kohn, A. (2001). *Five reasons to stop saying "Good job!"* Retrieved April 4, 2010, from www.alfiekohn.org/parenting/gj.htm

Kohn, A. (2006a). *The homework myth: Why kids get too much of a bad thing.* Cambridge, MA: De Capo Press.

Kohn, A. (2006b). *Unconditional parenting: Moving from rewards and punishments to love and reason.* New York: Atria.

Kokko, K., Tremblay, R. E., Lacourse, E., Nagin, D. S., & Vitaro, F. (2006). Trajectories of prosocial behavior and physical aggression in middle childhood: Links to adolescent school dropout and physical violence. *Journal of Research on Adolescence, 16,* 403–428.

Koplow, L. (2002). *Creating schools that heal: Real-life solutions.* New York: Teachers College Press.

Kostelnik, M. J., Onaga, E., Rohde, B., & Whiren, A. (2002). *Children with special needs: Lessons for early childhood professionals.* New York: Teachers College Press.

Kottler, J. A. (2002). *Students who drive you crazy: Succeeding with resistant, unmotivated, and otherwise difficult young people.* Thousand Oaks, CA: Corwin.

Kounin, J. S. (1970). *Discipline and group management in classrooms.* New York: Holt, Rinehart & Winston.

Kralovec, E., & Buell, J. (2001). End homework now. *Educational Leadership, 58(7),* 39–42.

Kranowitz, C. S. (2006). *The out-of-sync child: Recognizing and coping with sensory processing disorder* (rev. ed.). New York: Perigee.

Kreidler, W. J., & Whittall, S. T. (with Doty, N., Johns, R., Logan, C., Roerden, L. P., Raner, C. & Wintle, C.). (1999). *Early childhood adventures in peacemaking.* Cambridge, MA: Educators for Social Responsibility.

Kritchevsky, S., & Prescott, E. (with Walling, L.). (1977). *Planning environments for young children: Physical space.* Washington, DC: National Association for the Education of Young Children.

Kuhl, P. K., Williams, K. A., Lacerda, F., & Stevens, K. N. (1992). Linguistic experience alters phonetic perception in infants by 6 months of age. *Science, 255,* 606–608.

Kupersmidt, J. B., Griesler, P. C., DeRosier, M. E., Patterson, C. J., & Davis, P. W. (1995). Childhood aggression and peer relations in the context of family and neighborhood factors. *Child Development, 66,* 360–375.

Kutcher, S., Aman, M., Brooks, S. J., Buitelaar, J., van Daalen, E., Fegert, J., et al. (2004). International consensus statement on attention-deficit/hyperactivity disorder (ADHD) and disruptive behavior disorders (DBDs): Clinical implications and treatment practice suggestions. *European Neuropsychopharmacology, 14,* 11–28.

Kyle, D. W., McIntyre, E., Miller, K. B., & Moore, G. H. (2002). *Reaching out: A K-8 resource for connecting families and schools.* Thousand Oaks, CA: Corwin.

Ladd, B. K., & Ladd, G. W. (2001). Variations in peer victimization: Relations to children's maladjustment. In J. Juvonen & S. Graham (Eds.), *Peer harassment in school: The plight of the vulnerable and victimized* (pp. 25–48). New York: Guilford.

Ladd, G., & Troop-Gordon, W. (2003). The role of chronic peer difficulties in the development of children's psychological adjustment problems. *Child Development, 74,* 1344–1367.

Ladd, G. W., & Burgess, K. B. (1999). Charting the relationship trajectories of aggressive, withdrawn, and aggressive/withdrawn children during early grade school. *Child Development, 70,* 910–929.

Ladd, G. W., & Burgess, K. B. (2001). Do relational risks and protective factors moderate the linkages between childhood aggression and early psychological and school adjustment? *Child Development, 72,* 1579–1601.

Ladson-Billings, G. (1994). *The dreamkeepers: Successful teachers of African American children.* San Francisco: Jossey-Bass.

Lagae, L. (2008). Learning disabilities: Definitions, epidemiology, diagnosis, and intervention strategies. *Pediatric Clinics of North America, 55,* 1259–1268.

Lahey, B. B., & Waldman, I. D. (2003). A developmental propensity model of the origins of conduct problems during childhood and adolescence. In B. B. Lahey, T. E. Moffitt, & A. Caspi (Eds.), *Causes of conduct disorder and juvenile delinquency* (pp. 76–117). New York: Guilford.

Lake, J. F., & Billingsley, B. S. (2000). An analysis of factors that contribute to parent-school conflict in special education. *Remedial and Special Education, 21,* 240–251.

Lamb-Parker, F., LeBuffe, P. A., Powell, G., & Halpern, E. (2008). A strength-based, systemic mental health approach to support children's social and emotional development. *Infants and Young Children, 21,* 45–55.

Landsman, J. (2006a). Educating Black males: Interview with Professor Joseph White, Ph.D. In J. Landsman & C. W. Lewis (Eds.), *White teachers/diverse classrooms: A guide to building inclusive schools, promoting high expectations, and eliminating racism* (pp. 52–60). Sterling, VA: Stylus.

Landsman, J. (2006b). When truth and joy are at stake: Challenging the status quo in the high school English class. In J. Landsman & C. W. Lewis (Eds.), *White teachers / diverse classrooms: A guide to building inclusive schools, promoting high expectations, and eliminating racism* (pp. 221–233). Sterling, VA: Stylus.

LaPlante, D. P., Barr, R. G., Brunet, A., du Fort, G. G., Meaney, M., Saucier, J.-F., et al. (2004). Stress during pregnancy affects general intellectual and language functioning in human toddlers. *Pediatric Research, 56,* 1–11.

Lareau, A. (2000). *Home advantage: Social class and parental intervention in elementary school* (2nd ed.). Lanham, MD: Rowman and Littlefield.

Lareau, A., & Shumar, W. (1996). The problem of individualism in family-school policies [Extra issue]. *Sociology of Education, 69,* 24–39.

Lawrence-Lightfoot, S. (2003). *The essential conversation: What parents and teachers can learn from each other.* New York: Ballantine.

Leachman, G., & Victor, D. (2003). Student-led class meetings. *Educational Leadership, 60(6),* 64–68.

Leary, M. R., & Hill, D. A. (1996). Moving on: Autism and movement disturbance. *Mental Retardation, 34(1),* 39–55.

Lebra, T. S. (1994). Mother and child in Japanese socialization: A Japan-U.S. comparison. In P. M. Greenfield & R. R. Cocking (Eds.), *Cross-cultural roots of minority child development* (pp. 259–274). Hillsdale, NJ: Erlbaum.

LeBuffe, P. A., & Naglieri, J. A. (1999). *Devereux Early Childhood Assessment user's guide.* Lewisville, NC: Kaplan.

LeDoux, J. (2002). *Synaptic self: How our brains become who we are.* New York: Viking.

Leffert, J. S., Siperstein, G. N., & Millikan, E. (2000). Understanding social adaptation in children with mental retardation: A social-cognitive perspective. *Exceptional Children, 66*, 530–545.

Lehmann, K. J. (2004). *Surviving inclusion.* Lanham, MD: Scarecrow.

Leman, K. (1992). *The birth order book: Why you are the way you are.* New York: Bantam-Dell.

Lengua, L. J., Honorado, E., & Bush, N. R. (2007). Contextual risk and parenting as predictors of effortful control and social competence in preschool children. *Journal of Applied Developmental Psychology, 28*, 40–55.

Lenroot, R. K., & Giedd, J. N. (2006). Brain development in children and adolescents: Insights from anatomical magnetic imaging. *Neuroscience and Biobehavioral Reviews, 30*, 718–729.

Levin, D. E. (1998). *Remote control childhood? Combating the hazards of media culture.* Washington, DC: National Association for the Education of Young Children.

Levin, D. E., & Carlsson-Paige, N. (2006). *The war play dilemma.* New York: Teachers College Press.

Lewis, M. D., Granic, I., & Lamm, C. (2006). Behavioral differences in aggressive children linked with neural mechanisms of emotional regulation. *Annals of the New York Academy of Sciences, 1094*, 164–177.

Lieberman, M. D., & Eisenberger, N. I. (2006). A pain by any other name (rejection, exclusion, ostracism) still hurts the same: The role of dorsal anterior cingulate cortex in social and physical pain. In J. T. Cacioppo, P. S. Visser, & C. L. Pickett (Eds.), *Social neuroscience: People thinking about thinking people* (pp. 167–187). Cambridge, MA: MIT Press.

Li-Grining, C. P. (2007). Effortful control among low-income preschoolers in three cities: Stability, change, and individual difference. *Developmental Psychology, 43*, 208–221.

Linares, L. O., Heeren, T., Bronfman, E., Zuckerman, B., Augustyn, M., & Tronick, E. (2001). A mediational model for the impact of exposure to community violence on early child behavior problems. *Child Development, 72*, 639–652.

Litner, B. (2000). Teaching children with ADHD. In J. Andrews & J. Lupart, *The inclusive classroom: Educating exceptional children.* Scarborough, ON: Nelson Canada.

Liu, D., Diorio, J., Tannenbaum, B., Caldji, C., Francis, D., Freedman, A., et al. (1997). Maternal care, hippocampal glucocorticoid receptors, and hypothalamic-pituitary-adrenal responses to stress. *Science, 277*, 1659–1662.

Liu, J., Raine, A., Venables, P. H., & Mednick, S. A. (2004). Malnutrition at age 3 years and externalizing behavior problems at ages 8, 11, and 17 years. *American Journal of Psychiatry, 161*, 2005–2013.

Livingston, A. (2006, June). *The condition of education 2006 in brief* (NCES 2006-072). Washington, DC: U.S. Department of Education, National Center for Education Statistics. Retrieved June 20, 2010, from http://nces.ed.gov/pubs2006/2006072.pdf

Loeb, S., Bridges, M., Bassok, D., Fuller, B., & Rumberger, R. (2007). How much is too much? The influence of preschool centers on children's social and cognitive development. *Economics of Education Review, 26*, 52–66.

Loeb, S., Fuller, B., Kagan, S. L., & Carrol, B. (2004). Child care in poor communities: Early learning effects of type, quality, and stability. *Child Development, 75*, 47–65.

Loeber, R. (1985). Patterns and development of antisocial and delinquent child behavior. *Annals of Child Development, 2*, 77–116.

Loman, M. M., Gunnar, M. R., & the Early Experience, Stress, and Neurobehavioral Development Center. (2009). Early experience and the development of stress reactivity and regulation in children. *Neuroscience and Biobehavioral Reviews, 34*(6), 867–876.

Lopez, G. R. (2001). The value of hard work: Lessons on parent involvement from an (im)migrant household. *Harvard Educational Review, 71*, 416–437.

Losen, S., & Diament, B. (1978). *Parent conferences in the schools: Procedures for developing effective partnership.* Boston: Allyn & Bacon.

Lotan, R. A. (2003). Group-worthy tasks. *Educational Leadership, 60*(6), 72–75.

Lotan, R. A. (2006). Managing groupwork in the heterogeneous classroom. In C. M.

Evertson & C. S. Weinstein (Eds.), *Handbook of classroom management: Research, practice, and contemporary issues* (pp. 525–539). Mahwah, NJ: Erlbaum.

Love, J. M., Harrison, L., Sagi-Schwartz, A., van IJzendoorn, M. H., Ross, C., Ungerer, J. A., et al. (2003). Child care quality matters: How conclusions may vary with context. *Child Development, 74*, 1021–1033.

Lubeck, S. (1994). The politics of developmentally appropriate practice: Exploring issues of culture, class, and curriculum. In B. L. Mallory & R. S. New (Eds.), *Diversity and developmentally appropriate practice: Challenges for early childhood education* (pp. 17–43). New York: Teachers College Press.

Luke, S. D., & Schwartz, A. (2007). Assessment and accommodations. *Evidence for Education, 11*(1), 1–11.

Luthar, S. S. (1999). *Poverty and children's adjustment.* Thousand Oaks, CA: Sage.

Luthar, S. S. (2006). Resilience in development: A synthesis of research across five decades. In D. Cicchetti & D. J. Cohen (Eds.), *Developmental psychopathology: Vol. 3. Risk, disorder, and adaptation* (2nd ed., pp. 739–795). Hoboken, NJ: Wiley.

Luthar, S. S., Cicchetti, D., & Becker, B. (2000). The construction of resilience: A critical evaluation and guidelines for future work. *Child Development, 71*, 543–562.

Luthar, S. S., & Zelazo, L. B. (2003). Research on resilience: An integrative review. In S. S. Luthar (Ed.), *Resilience and vulnerability: Adaptation in the context of childhood adversity* (pp. 510–549). New York: Cambridge University Press.

Lynch, E. W. (2004a). Conceptual framework: From culture shock to cultural learning. In E. W. Lynch & M. J. Hanson (Eds.), *Developing cross-cultural competence: A guide for working with children and their families* (3rd ed., pp. 19–39). Baltimore: Brookes.

Lynch, E. W. (2004b). Developing cross-cultural competence. In E. W. Lynch & M. J. Hanson (Eds.), *Developing cross-cultural competence: A guide for working with children and their families* (3rd ed., pp. 41–75). Baltimore: Brookes.

Lynch, E. W., & Hanson, M. J. (2004). Steps in the right direction: Implications for interventionists. In E. W. Lynch & M. J. Hanson (Eds.), *Developing cross-cultural competence: A guide for working with children and their families* (3rd ed., pp. 449–466). Baltimore: Brookes.

Lynch, M. (2006). Children exposed to community violence. In M. M. Feerick & G. B. Silverman (Eds.), *Children exposed to violence* (pp. 29–52). Baltimore: Brookes.

Lyons-Ruth, K. (1996). Attachment relationships among children with aggressive behavior problems: The role of disorganized early attachment patterns. *Journal of Consulting and Clinical Psychology, 64*, 64–73.

Lyons-Ruth, K. (2003). Dissociation and the parent-infant dialogue: A longitudinal perspective from attachment research. *Journal of the American Psychoanalytic Association, 51*, 883–911.

Lyons-Ruth, K., & Jacobvitz, D. (1999). Attachment disorganization: Unresolved loss, relational violence, and lapses in behavioral and attentional strategies. In J. Cassidy & P. R. Shaver (Eds.), *Handbook of attachment theory and research* (pp. 520–554). New York: Guilford.

Maccoby, E. E. (2004). Aggression in the context of gender development. In M. Putallaz & K. L. Bierman (Eds.), *Aggression, antisocial behavior, and violence among girls: A developmental perspective* (pp. 3–22). New York: Guilford.

Maclean, K. (2003). The impact of institutionalization on child development. *Development and Psychopathology, 15*, 853–884.

Macmillan, R., McMorris, B. J., & Kruttschnitt, C. (2004). Linked lives: Stability and change in maternal circumstances and trajectories of antisocial behavior in children. *Child Development, 75*, 205–220.

Macrina, M., Hoover, D., & Becker, C. (2009). The challenge of working with dual language learners. *Young Children, 64*(2), 27–34.

Mandlawitz, M. (2005). *What every teacher should know about IDEA 2004.* Boston: Allyn & Bacon.

Margalit, M. (2003). Resilience model among individuals with learning disabilities: Proximal and distal influences. *Learning Disabilities Research and Practice, 18*, 82–86.

Martin, E. J., & Hagan-Burke, S. (2002). Establishing a home-school connection: Strengthening the partnership between families and schools. *Preventing School Failure, 46*(2), 62–65.

Martin, J. N., & Fox, N. A. (2006). Temperament. In K. McCartney & D. Phillips (Eds.), *Handbook of early childhood development* (pp. 126–146). Malden, MA: Blackwell.

Marzano, R. J. (with Marzano, J. S., & Pickering, D. J.). (2003). *Classroom management that works: Research-based strategies for every teacher*. Alexandria, VA: Association for Supervision and Curriculum Development.

Masten, A. S. (2001). Ordinary magic: Resilience processes in development. *American Psychologist, 56*, 227–234.

Masten, A. S. (2004). Regulatory processes, risk, and resilience in adolescent development. *Annals of the New York Academy of Sciences, 1021*, 310–319.

Masten, A. S. (2007). Resilience in developing systems: Progress and promise as the fourth wave rises. *Development and Psychopathology, 19*, 921–930.

Masten, A. S., & Coatsworth, J. D. (1998). The development of competence in favorable and unfavorable environments: Lessons from research on successful children. *American Psychologist, 53*, 205–220.

Masten, A. S., Hubbard, J. J., Gest, S. D., Telegen, A., Garmezy, N., & Ramirez, M. (1999). Competence in the context of adversity: Pathways to resilience and maladaptation from childhood to late adolescence. *Development and Psychopathology, 11*, 143–169.

Masten, A. S., & Obradovic, J. (2006). Competence and resilience in development. In B. M. Lester, A. S. Masten, & B. McEwen (Eds.), *Resilience in children* (pp. 13–27). Boston: New York Academy of Sciences.

Mathews, J. (2005, September 20). Teachers stir science, history into core classes. *Washington Post*, p. A16.

Mattson, S. N., Fryer, S. L., McGee, C. L., & Riley, E. P. (2008). Fetal alcohol syndrome. In C. A. Nelson & M. Luciana (Eds.), *Handbook of developmental cognitive neuroscience* (2nd ed., pp. 643–652). Cambridge, MA: MIT Press.

Maughan, A., & Cicchetti, D. (2002). Impact of child maltreatment and interadult violence on children's emotional regulation and socioemotional adjustment. *Child Development, 73*, 1525–1542.

McCabe, L. A., & Frede, E. C. (2007, December). *Challenging behaviors and the role of preschool education*. National Institute for Early Education Research Preschool Policy Brief, 16. Retrieved November 24, 2009, from http://nieer.org/resources/policybriefs/16.pdf

McDonald, R., Jouriles, E. N., Ramisetty-Mikler, S., Caetano, R., & Green, C. E. (2006). Estimating the number of American children living in partner-violent families. *Journal of Family Psychology, 20*, 137–142.

McEwen, B. S. (2005). Glucocorticoids, depression, and mood disorders: Structural remodeling in the brain. *Metabolism Clinical and Experimental, 54*, 20–23.

McIntosh, K., Chard, D. J., Boland, J. B., & Horner, R. H. (2006). Demonstration of combined efforts in school-wide academic and behavioral systems and incidence of reading and behavior challenges in early elementary grades. *Journal of Positive Behavior Interventions, 8*, 146–154.

McLloyd, V. C. (1998). Socioeconomic disadvantage and child development. *American Psychologist, 53*, 185–204.

Meaney, M. J. (2001). Maternal care, gene expression, and the transmission of individual differences in stress reactivity across generations. *Annual Review of Neuroscience, 24*, 1161–1192.

Meehan, B. T., Hughes, J. N., & Cavell, T. A. (2003). Teacher-student relationships as compensatory resources for aggressive children. *Child Development, 74*, 1145–1157.

Merrell, K. W., Gueldner, B. A., Ross, S. W., & Isasva, D. M. (2008). How effective are school bullying intervention programs? A meta-analysis of intervention research. *School Psychology Quarterly, 23*, 26–42.

Meyer, L. H., & Evans, I. M. (1993). Meaningful outcomes in behavioral intervention: Evaluating positive approaches to the remediation of challenging behavior. In J. Reichle &

D. P. Wacker (Eds.), *Communicative alternatives to challenging behavior: Integrating assessment and intervention strategies* (pp. 407–428). Baltimore: Brookes.

Michelson, L., & Mannarino, A. (1986). Social skills training with children: Research and clinical applications. In P. S. Strain, M. J. Guralnick, & H. M. Walker (Eds.), *Children's social behavior: Development, assessment, and modification* (pp. 373–406). Orlando: Academic Press.

Miller, E., & Almon, J. (2009). *Crisis in the kindergarten: Why children need to play in school.* Alliance for Childhood. Retrieved March 17, 2010, from www.allianceforchildhood.org/sites/allianceforchildhood.org/files/file/kindergarten_report.pdf

Miller, J. A., Tansy, M., & Hughes, T. L. (1998). Functional behavioral assessment: The link between problem behavior and effective intervention in schools. *Current Issues in Education* [on-line], *1*(5).

Miller, M. (2002). Resilience elements in students with learning disabilities. *Journal of Clinical Psychology, 58,* 291–298.

Miner, B. (1998). Embracing Ebonics and teaching Standard English: An interview with Oakland teacher Carrie Secret. In T. Perry & L. Delpit (Eds.), *The real Ebonics debate: Power, language, and the education of African-American children* (pp. 79–88). Boston: Beacon Press.

Mishna, F., Scarcello, I., Pepler, D., & Wiener, J. (2005). Teachers' understanding of bullying. *Canadian Journal of Education, 28,* 718–738.

Mize, J., & Ladd, G. W. (1990). Toward the development of successful social skills training for preschool children. In S. R. Asher & J. D. Coie (Eds.), *Peer rejection in childhood* (pp. 338–361). New York: Cambridge University Press.

Moffitt, T. E. (1997). Neuropsychology, antisocial behavior, and neighborhood context. In J. McCord (Ed.), *Violence and childhood in the inner city* (pp. 116–170). New York: Cambridge University Press.

Moffitt, T. E. (2005). The new look of behavioral genetics in developmental psychology: Gene-environment interplay in antisocial behaviors. *Psychological Bulletin, 131,* 533–554.

Moffitt, T. E., & Caspi, A. (2001). Childhood predictors differentiate life-course persistent and adolescence-limited antisocial pathways among males and females. *Development and Psychopathology, 13,* 355–375.

Moffitt, T. E., Caspi, A., & Rutter, M. (2006). Measured gene-environment interactions in psychopathology. *Perspectives on Psychological Science, 1,* 5–27.

Monk, C. S. (2008). The development of emotion-related neural circuitry in health and psychopathology. *Development and Psychopathology, 20,* 1231–1250.

Moran, S., Kornhaber, M., & Gardner, H. (2006). Orchestrating multiple intelligences. *Educational Leadership, 64*(1), 22–27.

Morrissey, T. W. (2009). Multiple child care arrangements and young children's behavioral outcomes. *Child Development, 90,* 59–76.

Moss, E., St-Laurent, D., Dubois-Comtois, K., & Cyr, C. (2005). Quality of attachment at school age: Relations between child attachment behavior, psychosocial functioning, and school performance. In K. A. Kerns & R. A. Richardson (Eds.), *Attachment in middle childhood* (pp. 189–211). New York: Guilford.

Munro, M. (2010, June 10). Study ties autism to duplicated, missing genes. *The Gazette (Montreal),* p. A3.

Nagin, D. S., & Tremblay, R. E. (2001). Parental and early childhood predictors of persistent physical aggression in boys from kindergarten to high school. *Archives of General Psychiatry, 58,* 389–394.

Nansel, T. R., Overpeck, M., Pilla, R. S., Ruan, J., Simons-Morton, B., & Scheidt, P. (2001). Bullying behaviors among US youth: Prevalence and association with psychosocial adjustment. *Journal of the American Medical Association, 285,* 2094–2100.

National Alliance of Black School Educators. (2002). *Addressing over-representation of African American students in special education: The prereferral intervention process.* Arlington, VA: Council for Exceptional Education.

National Association for the Education of Young Children. (1990, 1994). *Media violence in children's lives*. Washington, DC: Author. Retrieved March 18, 2010, from www.naeyc.org/files/naeyc/file/positions/PSMEVI98.PDF

National Association for the Education of Young Children. (1996). Time out for "time-out." Washington, DC: Author.

National Association for the Education of Young Children. (2007). *NAEYC early childhood program standards and accreditation criteria: The mark of quality in early childhood education*. Washington, DC: Author.

National Association for the Education of Young Children. (2009). Position statement: Developmentally appropriate practice in early childhood programs: Serving children from birth through age 8. In C. Copple & S. Bredekamp (Eds.), *Position statement: Developmentally appropriate practice in early childhood programs: Serving children from birth through age 8* (3rd ed.). Washington, DC: Author.

National Comprehensive Center for Teacher Quality & Public Agenda. (2008). Lessons learned: New teachers talk about their jobs, challenges, and long-range plans. *Teaching in changing times, 3*. Retrieved May 2, 2010, from www.publicagenda.org/reports/lessons-learned-issue-no-3-new-teachers-talk-about-their-jobs-challenges-and-long-range-plans

National Dissemination Center for Children with Disabilities (NICHCY). (n.d.a). *Accommodations in assessment*. Retrieved May 2, 2010, from www.nichcy.org/EducateChildren/IEP/Pages/AccommodationsinAssessment.aspx

National Dissemination Center for Children with Disabilities (NICHCY). (n.d.b). *Contents of the IEP*. Retrieved May 2, 2010, from www.nichcy.org/EducateChildren/IEP/Pages/IEPcontents.aspx

National Institute of Child Health and Human Development. (2006a, July 12). *Researchers gain insight into why brain areas fail to work together in autism*. Retrieved September 15, 2009, from www.nichd.nih.gov/news/releases/autism_brain_structure.cfm

National Institute of Child Health and Human Development. (2006b, August 16). *Study provides evidence that autism affects functioning of entire brain*. Retrieved September 15, 2009, from www.nichd.nih.gov/news/releases/autism_affects_brain.cfm

National Institute of Child Health and Human Development. (2006c, October 17). *Gene linked to autism in families with more than one affected child*. Retrieved September 15, 2009, from www.nichd.nih.gov/news/releases/gene_linked_to_autism.cfm

National Institute of Child Health and Human Development Early Child Care Research Network. (2003). Does amount of time spent in child care predict socioemotional adjustment during the transition to kindergarten? *Child Development, 74*, 976–1005.

National Institute of Child Health and Human Development Early Child Care Research Network. (2004). Trajectories of physical aggression from toddlerhood to middle childhood. *Monographs of the Society for Research in Child Development, 69*, vii–129.

National Institute of Child Health and Human Development Early Child Care Research Network. (2006). Child care effect sizes for the NICHD study of early child care and youth development. *American Psychologist, 61*, 99–106.

National Institute of Neurological Disorders and Stroke. (2009). *Autism fact sheet*. Retrieved September 15, 2009, from www.ninds.nih.gov/disorders/autism/detail_autism.htm

National Professional Development Center. (2009). Research synthesis points in early childhood inclusion. Chapel Hill: University of North Carolina, FPG Child Development Institute. Retrieved May 2, 2010, from http://community.fpg.unc.edu/resources/articles/NDPCI-ResearchSynthesis-9-2007.pdf

National Scientific Council on the Developing Child. (2004). *Children's emotional development is built into the architecture of their brains: Working paper #2*. Retrieved February 24, 2010, from http://developingchild.harvard.edu/library/reports_and_working_papers/working_papers/wp2/

National Scientific Council on the Developing Child. (2008). *Mental health problems in early childhood can impair learning and behavior for life: Working paper #6.* Retrieved October 15, 2009, from http://developingchild.harvard.edu/library/reports_and_working_papers/wp6/

Nelson, C. A. (2000). The neurobiological bases of early intervention. In J. P. Shonkoff & S. J. Meisels (Eds.), *Handbook of early childhood intervention* (2nd ed., pp. 204–227). New York: Cambridge University Press.

Nelson, C. A., & Bloom, F. E. (1997). Child development and neuroscience. *Child Development, 68,* 970–987.

Nelson, D. A., Robinson, C. C., & Hart, C. H. (2005). Relational and physical aggression of preschool-age children: Peer status linkages across informants. *Early Education & Development, 16,* 115–139.

Nemeth, K. (2009). Meeting the home language mandate: Practical strategies for all classrooms. *Young Children, 64*(2), 36–42.

New, R. S. (1994). Culture, child development, and developmentally appropriate practice: Teachers as collaborative researchers. In B. L. Mallory & R. S. New (Eds.), *Diversity and developmentally appropriate practice: Challenges for early childhood education* (pp. 65–83). New York: Teachers College Press.

Nicholas, J. S., Carpenter, L. A., King, L. B., Jenner, W., & Charles, J. M. (2009). Autism spectrum disorders in preschool-aged children: Prevalence and comparison to a school-aged population. *Annals of Epidemiology, 19,* 808–814.

Nicolet, J. (2006). Conversation—A necessary step in understanding diversity: A new teacher plans for competency. In J. Landsman & C. W. Lewis (Eds.), *White teachers / diverse classrooms: A guide to building inclusive schools, promoting high expectations, and eliminating racism* (pp. 203–218). Sterling, VA: Stylus.

Nieto, S. (2004). *Affirming diversity: The sociopolitical context of multicultural education* (4th ed.). Boston: Allyn & Bacon.

Novaco, R. W. (1975). *Anger control: The development and evaluation of an experimental treatment.* Lexington, MA: Heath.

O'Connell, P., Pepler, D., & Craig, W. (1999). Peer involvement in bullying: Insights and challenges for intervention. *Journal of Adolescence, 22,* 437–452.

O'Connor, T. G., Heron, J., Golding, J., Beveridge, M., & Glover, V. (2002). Maternal antenatal anxiety and children's behavioural/emotional problems at 4 years. *British Journal of Psychiatry, 180,* 502–508.

Odgers, C. L., Moffitt, T. E., Broadbent, J. M., Dickson, N., Hancox, R. J., Harrington, H., et al. (2008). Female and male antisocial trajectories: From childhood origins to adult outcomes. *Development and Psychopathology, 20,* 673–716.

Odom, S. L. (2000). Preschool inclusion: What we know and where we go from here. *Topics in Early Childhood Special Education, 20*(1), 20–27.

Odom, S. L., Zercher, C., Marquart, J., Li, S., Sandall, S. R., & Wolfberg, P. (2002). Social relationships of children with disabilities and their peers in inclusive preschool classrooms. In S. L. Odom (Ed.) (with P. J. Beckman, M. J. Hanson, E. Horn, J. Lieber, S. R. Sandall, I. L. Schwartz, et al.), *Widening the circle: Including children with disabilities in preschool programs* (pp. 61–80). New York: Teachers College Press.

Ogbu, J. U. (1994). From cultural differences to differences in cultural frame of reference. In P. M. Greenfield & R. R. Cocking (Eds.), *Cross-cultural roots of minority child development* (pp. 365–395). Hillsdale, NJ: Erlbaum.

Olds, D. (1997). Tobacco exposure and impaired development: A review of the evidence. *Mental Retardation and Developmental Disabilities Research Review, 3,* 257–269.

Olds, D., Henderson, C. R., Jr., Cole, R., Eckenrode, J., Kitzman, H., Luckey, D., et al. (1998). Long-term effects of nurse home visitation on children's criminal and antisocial behavior: 15-year follow-up of a randomized controlled trial. *Journal of the American Medical Association, 280,* 1238–1244.

Oliver, R. O., Hoover, J. H., & Hazler, R. J. (1994). The perceived roles of bullying in small-town Midwestern schools. *Journal of Counseling and Development, 72,* 416–420.

Olson, S. L., Sameroff, A. J., Kerr, D. C. R., Lopez, N. L., & Wellman, H. M. (2005). Developmental foundations of externalizing problems in young children: The role of effortful control. *Development and Psychopathology, 17,* 25–45.

Olweus, D. (1991). Bully/victim problems among schoolchildren: Basic facts and effects of a school-based intervention program. In D. J. Pepler & K. H. Rubin (Eds.), *The development and treatment of childhood aggression* (pp. 411–448). Hillsdale, NJ: Erlbaum.

Olweus, D. (1993). *Bullying at school: What we know and what we can do.* Malden, MA: Blackwell.

Olweus, D. (2001). Peer harassment: A critical analysis and some important issues. In J. Juvonen & S. Graham (Eds.), *Peer harassment in school: The plight of the vulnerable and victimized* (pp. 3–20). New York: Guilford.

O'Moore, M., & Minton, S. J. (2004). *Dealing with bullying in schools: A training manual for teachers, parents, and other professionals.* London, UK: Paul Chapman.

O'Neill, R. E., Horner, R. H., Albin, R. W., Sprague, J. R., Storey, K., & Newton, J. S. (1997). *Functional assessment and program development for problem behavior: A practical handbook* (2nd ed.). Pacific Grove, CA: Brooks/Cole.

Oprah Winfrey. (n.d.). In *Black history.* Gale. Retrieved August 6, 2009, from www.gale. cengage.com/free_resources/bhm/bio/winfrey_o.htm

Ormrod, J. E. (2008). *Human learning* (5th ed.). Upper Saddle River, NJ: Pearson.

Orpinas, P., & Horne, A. M. (2006). *Bullying prevention: Creating a positive school climate and developing social competence.* Washington, DC: American Psychological Association.

Osofsky, J. D., & Thompson, M. D. (2000). Adaptive and maladaptive parenting: Perspectives on risk and protective factors. In J. P. Shonkoff & S. J. Meisels (Eds.), *Handbook of early childhood intervention* (2nd ed., pp. 54–75). New York: Cambridge University Press.

Ostrov, J. M., Woods, K. E., Jansen, E. A., Casas, J. F., & Crick, N. R. (2004). An observational study of delivered and received aggression, gender, and social-psychological adjustment in preschool: "This white crayon doesn't work . . . " *Early Childhood Research Quarterly, 19,* 355–371.

Oswald, D. P., Coutinho, M. J., & Best, A. M. (2002). Community and school predictors of overrepresentation of minority children in special education. In D. Losen & G. Orfield (Eds.), *Racial inequity in special education* (pp. 1–13). Cambridge, MA: Harvard Education Publishing.

Owen, M. T., Ware, A. M., & Barfoot, B. (2002). Caregiver-mother partnership behavior and the quality of caregiver-child and mother-child interactions. *Early Childhood Research Quarterly, 15,* 413–428.

Paley, V. G. (1992). *You can't say you can't play.* Cambridge, MA: Harvard University Press.

Parke, R. D., & Slaby, R. G. (1983). The development of aggression. In P. Mussen & E. M. Hetherington (Eds.), *Handbook of child psychology: Vol. 4, Socialization, personality, and social development* (pp. 547–641). New York: Wiley.

Pashler, H., McDaniel, M., Rohrer, D., & Bjork, R. (2009). Learning styles: Concepts and evidence. *Psychological Science in the Public Interest, 9*(3), 105-119.

Pastor, P. N., & Reuben, C. A. (2008). *Diagnosed attention deficit hyperactivity disorder and learning disability: United States, 2004–2006.* National Center for Health Statistics, Vital and Health Statistics, 10(237). Retrieved September 15, 2009, from www.cdc.gov/nchs/data/series/sr_10/sr10_237.pdf

Patterson, G. R. (1982). *Coercive family process.* Eugene, OR: Castalia.

Patterson, G. R. (1995). Coercion—A basis for early age of onset for arrest. In J. McCord (Ed.), *Coercion and punishment in long-term perspective* (pp. 81–105). New York: Cambridge University Press.

Pearce, M. J., Jones, S. M., Schwab-Stone, M. E., & Ruchkin, V. (2003). The protective effects of religiousness and parent involvement on the development of conduct problems among youth exposed to violence. *Child Development, 74,* 1682–1696.

Peer-Assisted Learning Strategies. (2005). Promising Practices Network, Programs that Work. Retrieved March 18, 2010, from www.promisingpractices.net/program.asp?programid=143

Peisner-Feinberg, E. S., Burchinal, M. R., Clifford, R. M., Culkin, M. L., Howes, C., Kagan, S. L., et al. (2001). The relation of preschool child care quality to children's cognitive and social developmental trajectories through second grade. *Child Development, 72*, 1534–1553.

Pepler, D., Jiang, D., Craig, W., & Connolly, J. (2008). Developmental trajectories of bullying and associated factors. *Child Development, 79*, 325–338.

Pepler, D., Smith, P. K., & Rigby, K. (2004). Looking back and looking forward: Implications for making interventions work effectively. In P. K. Smith, D. Pepler, & K. Rigby (Eds.), *Bullying in schools: How successful can interventions be?* (pp. 307–324). Cambridge, UK: Cambridge University Press.

Pepler, D. J., & Craig, W. (2000). *Making a difference in bullying.* Toronto, ON: LaMarsh Centre for Research on Violence and Conflict Resolution, York University, Report No. 60. Retrieved May 21, 2010, from www.yorku.ca/lamarsh/pdf/Making_a_Difference_in_Bullying.pdf

Pepler, D. J., & Craig, W. (2007). *Binoculars on bullying: A new solution to protect and connect children.* Retrieved May 22, 2010, from www.knowledge.offordcentre.com/index.php?option=com_content&view=article&id=285:binoculars-on-bullying-a-new-solution-to-protect-and-connect-children-vfc&catid=73

Pepler, D. J., & Craig, W. (n.d.). *Making a difference in bullying: Understanding and strategies for practitioners.* Retrieved May 21, 2010, from www.yorku.ca/lamarsh/pdf/pedia.pdf

Perkins-Gough, D. (2004). The eroding curriculum. *Educational Leadership, 62*(1), 84–85.

Perry, D. G., Hodges, E. V. E., & Egan, S. K. (2001). Determinants of chronic victimization by peers: A review and new model of family influence. In J. Juvonen & S. Graham (Eds.), *Peer harassment in school: The plight of the vulnerable and victimized* (pp. 73–104). New York: Guilford.

Perry, D. G., Kusel, S. L., & Perry, L. C. (1988). Victims of peer aggression. *Developmental Psychology, 24*, 807–814.

Perry, D. G., Perry, L. C., & Kennedy, E. (1992). Conflict and the development of antisocial behavior. In C. U. Shantz & W. W. Hartup (Eds.), *Conflict in child and adolescent development* (pp. 301–329). New York: Cambridge University Press.

Peters, M. F. (1988). Parenting in Black families with young children: A historical perspective. In H. Pipes McAdoo (Ed.), *Black families* (2nd ed., pp. 228–241). Newbury Park, CA: Sage.

Phineas Gage's story. (2006). Retrieved July 21, 2009, from www.deakin.edu.au/hmnbs/psychology/gagepage/Pgstory.php

Pianta, R. C. (1999). *Enhancing relationships between children and teachers.* Washington, DC: American Psychological Association.

Pianta, R. C. (2006). Classroom management and relationships between children and teachers: Implications for research and practice. In C. M. Evertson & C. S. Weinstein (Eds.), *Handbook of classroom management: Research, practice, and contemporary issues* (pp. 685–709). Mahwah, NJ: Erlbaum.

Pianta, R. C., Steinberg, M. S., & Rollins, K. B. (1995). The first two years of school: Teacher-child relationships and deflections in children's classroom adjustment. *Development and Psychopathology, 17*, 295–312.

Pianta, R. C., & Stuhlman, M. W. (2004). Teacher-child relationships and children's success in the first years of school. *School Psychology Review, 33*, 444–458.

Pihl, R. O., & Benkelfat, C. (2005). Neuromodulators in the development and expression of inhibition and aggression. In R. E. Tremblay, W. W. Hartup, & J. Archer (Eds.), *Developmental origins of aggression* (pp. 261–280). New York: Guilford.

Pikas, A. (1989). The Common Concern Method for the treatment of mobbing. In E. Roland & E. Munthe (Eds.), *Bullying: An international perspective.* London, UK: Fulton.

Pluess, M., & Belsky, J. (2009). Differential susceptibility to rearing experience: The case of childcare. *Journal of Child Psychology and Psychiatry, 50*, 396–404.

Pollak, S., & Tolley-Schell, S. (2003). Selective attention to facial emotion in physically abused children. *Journal of Abnormal Psychology, 112*, 323–338.

Posada, G., Gao, Y., Wu, F., Posada, R., Tascon, M., Schoelmerich, A., et al. (1995). The secure-base phenomenon across cultures: Children's behavior, mothers' preferences, and experts' concepts. In E. Waters, B. E. Vaughn, G. Posada, & K. Kendo-Ikemura (Eds.), Caregiving, culture, and cognitive perspectives on secure-base behavior and working models: New growing points for attachment theory and research. *Monographs of the Society for Research in Child Development, 60*(2-3, Serial No. 244), 27–48.

Posner, M. I., & Rothbart, M. K. (2000). Developing mechanisms of self-regulation. *Development and Psychopathology, 12*, 317–334.

Powell, D. R. (1989). *Families and early childhood programs.* Washington, DC: National Association for the Education of Young Children.

Powell, D. R. (1998). Reweaving parents into the fabric of early childhood programs. *Young Children, 53*(5), 60–66.

Power, B. M. (2002). Crawling on the bones of what we know: An interview with Shirley Brice Heath. In B. M. Power & R. S. Hubbard (Eds.), *Language development: A reader for teachers* (2nd ed., pp. 81–88). Upper Saddle River, NJ: Merrill Prentice Hall.

Pranksy, K. (2009). There's more to see. *Educational Leadership, 66*(7), 74–78.

Pretti-Frontczak, M., & Bricker, D. (2004). *An activity-based approach to early intervention* (3rd ed.). Baltimore: Brookes.

Price, J. M., & Dodge, K. A. (1989). Peers' contributions to children's social maladjustment. In T. J. Berndt & G. W. Ladd (Eds.), *Peer relationships in child development* (pp. 341–370). New York: Wiley.

Public Agenda. (2004, May). *Teaching interrupted: Do discipline policies in today's public schools foster the common good?* New York: Author. Retrieved May 10, 2010, from www.publicagenda.org/files/pdf/teaching_interrupted.pdf

Putallaz, M., & Sheppard, B. H. (1992). Conflict management and social competence. In C. U. Shantz & W. W. Hartup (Eds.), *Conflict in child and adolescent development* (pp. 330–355). New York: Cambridge University Press.

Putallaz, M., & Wasserman, A. (1990). Children's entry behavior. In S. R. Asher & J. D. Coie (Eds.), *Peer rejection in childhood* (pp. 60–89). New York: Cambridge University Press.

Putnam, S. P., & Stifter, C. A. (2008). Reactivity and regulation: The impact of Mary Rothbart on the study of temperament. *Infant and Child Development, 17*, 311–320.

Quay, L. C., Weaver, J. H., & Neel, J. H. (1986). The effects of play materials on positive and negative social behaviors in preschool boys and girls. *Child Study Journal, 16*(1), 67–76.

Quinn, M. M., Gable, R. A., Rutherford, R. B., Nelson, C. M., & Howell, K. W. (1998). *Addressing student problem behavior: Part I— An IEP team's introduction to functional behavior assessment and behavior intervention plans.* Washington, DC: Center for Effective Collaboration and Practice. Retrieved April 14, 2010, from http://cecp.air.org/fba/default.asp

Quinn, M. M., Osher, D., Warger, C. L., Hanley, T. V., Bader, B. D., & Hoffman, C. C. (2000). *Teaching and working with children who have emotional and behavioral challenges.* Longmont, CO: Sopris West.

Raikes, H. H., & Edwards, C. P. (2009). *Extending the dance in infant and toddler caregiving: Enhancing attachment relationships.* Baltimore: Brookes.

Raine, A. (1993). *The psychopathology of crime: Criminal behavior as a clinical disorder.* San Diego: Academic Press.

Raver, C. C. (2002). Emotions matter: Making the case for the role of young children's emotional development for early school readiness. *Social Policy Report, 16*, 3–18.

Raver, C. C., Garner, P. W., & Smith-Donald, R. (2007). The roles of emotional regulation and emotional knowledge for children's academic readiness: Are the links causal? In R. C. Pianta, M. J. Cox, & K. L. Snow (Eds.), *School readiness and the transition to kindergarten in the era of accountability* (pp. 121–147). Baltimore: Brookes.

Ray, A., Bowman, B., & Robbins, J. (2006). *Preparing early childhood teachers to successfully educate all children*. Foundation for Child Development. Retrieved February 5, 2010, from www.fcd-us.org/resources/resources_show.htm?doc_id=463599

Readdick, C. A., & Chapman, P. L. (2000). Young children's perceptions of time out. *Journal of Research in Childhood Education, 15*, 81–87.

Rebora, A. (2008, September 10). Making a difference. *Teacher, 02*(01), 26, 28–31.

Regalado, M., Sareen, H., Inkelas, M., Wissow, M., & Halfon, N. (2004). Parents' discipline of young children: Results from the National Survey of Early Childhood Health. *Pediatrics, 113*, 1952–1958.

Reiss, A. J., Jr., & Roth, J. A. (Eds.). (1993). *Understanding and preventing violence*. Washington, DC: National Academy Press.

Renken, B., Egeland, B., Marvinney, D., Mangelsdorf, S., & Sroufe, L. A. (1989). Early childhood antecedents of aggression and passive-withdrawal in early elementary school. *Journal of Personality, 57*, 257–281.

Repp, A. C., Karsh, K. G., Munk, D., & Dahlquist, C. M. (1995). Hypothesis-based interventions: A theory of clinical decision-making. In W. T. O'Donohue & L. Krasner (Eds.), *Theories of behavior therapy: Exploring behavior change* (pp. 585–608). Washington, DC: American Psychological Association.

Rhee, S. H., & Waldman, E. D. (2002). Genetic and environmental influences on antisocial behavior: A meta-analysis of twin and adoption studies. *Psychological Bulletin, 128*, 490–529.

Rice, C. (2009). Prevalence of autism spectrum disorders—Autism and Developmental Disabilities Monitoring Network, United States, 2006. *Morbidity and Mortality Weekly Report, 58*(SS10), 1–20.

Richards, M. H., Larson, R., Miller, B. V., Luo, Z., Sims, B., Parrella, D. P., et al. (2004). Risk and protective contexts and exposure to violence in urban African American young adolescents. *Journal of Child and Adolescent Psychology, 33*, 138–148.

Rideout, V., & Hamel, E. (2006). *The media family: Electronic media in the lives of infants, toddlers, preschoolers and their parents*. Kaiser Family Foundation. Retrieved October 21, 2009, from www.kff.org/entmedia/upload/7500.pdf

Rigby, K. (1998). *Bullying in schools and what to do about it*. Markham, ON: Pembroke Publishers.

Rigby, K. (2001a). Health consequences of bullying and its prevention in schools. In J. Juvonen & S. Graham (Eds.), *Peer harassment in school: The plight of the vulnerable and victimized* (pp. 310–331). New York: Guilford.

Rigby, K. (2001b). What is bullying? Defining bullying: A new look at an old concept. Retrieved May 21, 2010, from www.education.unisa.edu.au/bullying/define.html

Rigby, K. (2002). *New perspectives on bullying*. London, UK: Jessica Kingsley.

Rigby, K., & Johnson, B. (2006). Expressed readiness of Australian schoolchildren to act as bystanders in support of children who are being bullied. *Educational Psychology, 26*, 425–440.

Rigby, K., Smith, P. K., & Pepler, D. (2004). Working to prevent school bullying: Key issues. In P. K. Smith, D. Pepler, & K. Rigby (Eds.), *Bullying in schools: How successful can interventions be?* (pp. 1–12). Cambridge, UK: Cambridge University Press.

Rimm-Kaufman, S. E., Curby, T. W., Grimm, K. J., Nathanson, L., & Brock, L. L. (2009). The contribution of children's self-regulation and classroom quality to children's adaptive behaviors in the kindergarten classroom. *Developmental Psychology, 45*, 958–972.

Rimm-Kaufman, S. E., Early, D. M., Cox, M. J., Saluja, G., Pianta, R. C., Bradley, R. H., et al. (2002). Early behavioral attributes and teachers' sensitivity as predictors of competent behavior in the kindergarten classroom. *Applied Developmental Psychology, 23*, 451–470.

Ritchie, S. (2009, November). *The FirstSchool framework for pre-K to third grade: Ensuring success for vulnerable children*. Presentation at the National Association for the Education of Young Children, Washington, DC.

Roberts, W. B., Jr. (2006). *Bullying from both sides: Strategic interventions for working with bullies and victims*. Thousand Oaks, CA: Corwin.

Robin, A. L., Schneider, M., & Dolnick, M. (1976). The turtle technique: An extended case study of self-control in the classroom. *Psychology in the Schools, 13,* 449–453.

Robinson, G., & Maines, B. (2000). *Crying for help: The No Blame Approach to bullying.* Bristol, UK: Lucky Duck.

Rodd, J. (1996). *Understanding young children's behavior: A guide for early childhood professionals.* New York: Teachers College Press.

Rodriguez, R. (1982). *Hunger of memory: The education of Richard Rodriguez.* New York: Dial Press.

Rogers, C., & Freiberg, J. (1994). *Freedom to learn* (3rd ed.). New York: Merrill.

Roland, E., & Galloway, D. (2002). Classroom influences on bullying. *Educational Research, 44,* 299–312.

Ross, S. W., & Horner, R. H. (2009). Bully prevention in positive behavior support. *Journal of Applied Behavior Analysis, 42,* 747–759.

Rothbart, M. K. (2004). Commentary: Differentiated measures of temperament and multiple pathways to childhood disorders. *Journal of Clinical Child and Adolescent Psychology, 33,* 82–87.

Rothbart, M. K., & Bates, J. E. (2006). Temperament. In W. Damon (Series Ed.) & N. Eisenberg (Vol. Ed.), *Handbook of child psychology: Vol. 3. Social, emotional, and personality development* (6th ed., pp. 105–176). New York: Wiley.

Rothbart, M. K., & Jones, L. B. (1998). Temperament, self-regulation, and education. *School Psychology Review, 27,* 479–491.

Rothbart, M. K., Posner, M. I., & Kieras, J. (2006). Temperament, attention, and the development of self-regulation. In K. McCartney & D. Phillips (Eds.), *Handbook of early childhood development* (pp. 338–357). Malden, MA: Blackwell.

Rotheram-Borus, M. J. (1988). Assertiveness training with children. In R. H. Price, E. L. Cowen, R. P. Lorion, & J. Ramos-McKay (Eds.), *Fourteen ounces of prevention: A casebook for practitioners.* Washington, DC: American Psychological Association.

Rothstein-Fisch, C., & Trumbull, E. (2008). *Managing diverse classrooms: How to build on students' cultural strengths.* Alexandria, VA: Association for Supervision and Curriculum Development.

Rothstein-Fisch, C., Trumbull, E., & Garcia, S. G. (2009). Making the implicit explicit: Supporting teachers to bridge cultures. *Early Childhood Research Quarterly, 24,* 474–486.

Rowe, M. (1986). Wait time: Slowing down may be a way of speeding up! *Journal of Teacher Education, 37,* 43–50.

Rubin, K. H., Bukowski, W., & Parker, J. G. (1998). Peer interactions, relationships, and groups. In N. Eisenberg (Ed.), *Handbook of child psychology: Vol. 3, Social, emotional, and personality development* (5th ed., pp. 619–699). New York: Wiley.

Rueda, M. R., Rothbart, M. K., McCandliss, B. D., Saccomanno, L., & Posner, M. I. (2005). Training, maturation, and genetic influences on the development of executive attention. *Proceedings of the National Academy of Sciences, 102,* 14931–14936.

Rueda, R. S., August, D., & Goldenberg, C. (2006). The sociocultural context in which children acquire literacy. In D. August & T. Shanahan (Eds.), *Developing literacy in English-language learners: Report of the National Literacy Panel on Language Minority Children and Youth* (pp. 319–339). Mahwah, NJ: Erlbaum.

Rutter, M. (1987). Psychosocial resilience and protective mechanisms. *American Journal of Orthopsychiatry, 57,* 316–331.

Rutter, M. (2000). Resilience reconsidered: Conceptual considerations. In J. P. Shonkoff & S. J. Meisels (Eds.), *Handbook of early childhood intervention* (2nd ed., pp. 651–682). New York: Cambridge University Press.

Rutter, M. (2006a). *Genes and behavior: Nature-nurture interplay explained.* Malden, MA: Blackwell.

Rutter, M. (2006b). Implications of resilience concepts for scientific understanding. In B. M. Lester, A. S. Masten, & B. McEwen (Eds.), *Resilience in children* (pp. 1–12). Boston: New York Academy of Sciences.

Rutter, M. (2006c). The promotion of resilience in the face of adversity. In A. Clarke-Stewart & J. Dunn (Eds.), *Families count: Effects on child and adolescent development* (pp. 26–52). New York: Cambridge University Press.

Rutter, M., Giller, H., & Hagell, A. (1998). *Antisocial behavior by young people.* New York: Cambridge University Press.

Rutter, M., Moffitt, T. E., & Caspi, A. (2006). Gene-environment interplay and psychopathology: Multiple varieties but real effects. *Journal of Child Psychology and Psychiatry, 47*, 226–261.

Rutter, M., O'Connor, T. G., & the English and Romanian Adoptees Study Team. (2004). Are there biological programming effects for psychological development? Findings from a study of Romanian adoptees. *Developmental Psychology, 40*, 81–94.

Saft, E. W., & Pianta, R. C. (2001). Teachers' perceptions of their relationships with students: Effects of child age, gender, and ethnicity of teachers and children. *School Psychology Quarterly, 16*, 125–141.

Salend, S. J. (1999). Facilitating friendships among diverse students. *Intervention in School and Clinic, 35*(1), 9–15.

Salmivalli, C. (1999). Participant role approach to school bullying: Implications for interventions. *Journal of Adolescence, 22*, 453–459.

Salmivalli, C. (2001). Group view on victimization: Empirical findings and their implications. In J. Juvonen & S. Graham (Eds.), *Peer harassment in school: The plight of the vulnerable and victimized* (pp. 398–419). New York: Guilford.

Salmivalli, C. (2010). Bullying and the peer group: A review. *Aggression and Violent Behavior, 15*, 112–120.

Salmivalli, C., Kaukiainen, A., & Lagerspetz, K. (1998). Aggression in the social relations of school-aged girls and boys. In P. T. Slee & K. Rigby (Eds.), *Children's peer relations* (pp. 60–75). New York: Routledge.

Salmivalli, C., Kaukiainen, A., & Voeten, M. (2005). Anti-bullying intervention: Implementation and outcome. *British Journal of Educational Psychology, 75*, 465–487.

Sameroff, A. (2005). Early resilience and its developmental consequences. In R. E. Tremblay, R. G. Barr, & R. DeV. Peters (Eds.), *Encyclopedia on early childhood development* [online]. Montreal, QC: Centre of Excellence for Early Childhood Development. Retrieved August 6, 2009, from www.child-encyclo-pedia.com/pages/PDF/ResilienceANG.pdf

Sameroff, A. J., & Fiese, B. H. (2000). Transactional regulation: The developmental ecology of early intervention. In J. P. Shonkoff & S. J. Meisels (Eds.), *Handbook of early childhood intervention* (2nd ed., pp. 135–159). New York: Cambridge University Press.

Sampson, R. J. (1997). The embeddedness of child and adolescent development: A community-level perspective on urban violence. In J. McCord (Ed.), *Violence and childhood in the inner city* (pp. 31–77). New York: Cambridge University Press.

Sandall, S. R., & Schwartz, I. S. (with Joseph, G. E., Chou, H.-Y., Horn, E. M., Lieber, J., Odom, S. L., & Wolery, R.). (2002). *Building blocks for preschoolers with special needs.* Baltimore: Brookes.

Sandomierski, T., Kincaid, D., & Algozzine, B. (n.d.). Response to Intervention and positive behavior support: Brothers from different mothers or sisters from different misters? Retrieved April 13, 2010, from http://flpbs.fmhi.usf.edu/FLPBS%20and%20RtI%20article.pdf

Saunders, W. M., & O'Brien, G. (2006). Oral language. In F. Genesee, K. Lindholm-Leary, W. M. Saunders, & D. Christian (Eds.), *Educating English language learners: A synthesis of research evidence* (pp. 14–63). New York: Cambridge University Press.

Schaps, E., Battistich, V., & Solomon, D. (2004). Community in school as key to student growth: Findings from the Child Development Project. In J. E. Zins, R. P. Weissberg, W. C. Wang, & H. J. Walberg (Eds.), *Building academic success on social and emotional learning: What does the research say?* (pp. 189–205). New York: Teachers College Press.

Scherer, M. (2006). Celebrate strengths, nurture affinities: A conversation with Mel Levine. *Educational Leadership, 64*(1), 8–15.

Schwartz, C. E., Wright, C. I., Shin, L. M., Kagan, J., & Rauch, S. L. (2003). Inhibited and uninhibited infants "grown up": Adult amygdalar response to novelty. *Science, 300*, 1952–1953.

Schwartz, D., Dodge, K. A., & Coie, J. D. (1993). The emergence of chronic peer victimization in boys' play groups. *Child Development, 64*, 1755–1772.

Schwartz, D., Dodge, K. A., Pettit, G. S., & Bates, J. E. (1997). The early socialization of aggressive victims of bullying. *Child Development, 68*, 665–675.

Schwartz, D., & Proctor, L. J. (2000). Community violence exposure and children's social adjustment in the school peer group: The mediating roles of emotional regulation and social cognition. *Journal of Consulting and Clinical Psychology, 68*, 670–683.

Schwartz, D., Proctor, L. J., & Chen, D. H. (2001). The aggressive victim of bullying: Emotional and behavioral dysregulation as a pathway to victimization by peers. In J. Juvonen & S. Graham (Eds.), *Peer harassment in school: The plight of the vulnerable and victimized* (pp. 147–174). New York: Guilford.

Schwartz, J. M., Stoessel, P. W., Baxter, L. R., Martin, K. M., & Phelps, M. E. (1996). Systematic changes in cerebral glucose metabolic rate after successful behavior modification treatment of obsessive-compulsive disorder. *Archives of General Psychiatry, 53*, 109–113.

Segall, M. H., Dasen, P. R., Berry, J. W., & Poortinga, Y. H. (1990). *Human behavior in global perspective: An introduction to cross-cultural psychology.* New York: Pergamon.

Seikaly, M. (1999). Attachment and identity: The Palestinian community of Detroit. In M. W. Suleiman (Ed.), *Arabs in America: Building a new future* (pp. 25–38). Philadelphia: Temple University Press.

Serbin, L., Cooperman, J. M., Peters, P. L., Lehoux, P. M., Stack, D. M., & Schwartzman, A. E. (1998). Intergenerational transfer of psychosocial risk in women with childhood histories of aggression, withdrawal, or aggression and withdrawal. *Developmental Psychology, 34*, 1246–1262.

Shackman, J. E., Wismer-Fries, A. B., & Pollak, S. D. (2008). Environmental influences on brain-behavioral development. In C. A. Nelson & M. Luciana (Eds.), *Handbook of developmental cognitive neuroscience* (2nd ed., pp. 869–881). Cambridge, MA: MIT Press.

Shankaran, S., Lester, B. M., Das, A., Bauer, C. R., Bada, H. S., Lagasse, L., et al. (2007). Impact of maternal substance use during pregnancy on childhood outcome. *Seminars in Fetal and Neonatal Medicine, 12*, 143–150.

Shantz, C. U., & Hartup, W. W. (1992). Conflict and development: An introduction. In C. U. Shantz & W. W. Hartup (Eds.), *Conflict in child and adolescent development* (pp. 1–11). New York: Cambridge University Press.

Sharifzadeh, V.-S. (2004). Families with Middle Eastern roots. In E. W. Lynch & M. J. Hanson (Eds.), *Developing cross-cultural competence: A guide for working with children and their families* (3rd ed., pp. 373–414). Baltimore: Brookes.

Sharp, S., & Cowie, H. (1994). Empowering pupils to take positive action against bullying. In P. K. Smith & S. Sharp (Eds.), *School bullying: Insights and perspectives* (pp. 57–83). New York: Routledge.

Sharp, S., Cowie, H., & Smith, P. K. (1994). How to respond to bullying behaviour. In S. Sharp & P. K. Smith (Eds.), *Tackling bullying in your school: A practical handbook for teachers* (pp. 79–101). New York: Routledge.

Sharp, S., & Smith, P. K. (1994). Understanding bullying. In S. Sharp & P. K. Smith (Eds.), *Tackling bullying in your school: A practical handbook for teachers* (pp. 1–6). New York: Routledge.

Sharp, S., & Thompson, D. (1994). The role of whole-school policies in tackling bullying behaviour in schools. In P. K. Smith & S. Sharp (Eds.), *School bullying: Insights and perspectives* (pp. 57–83). New York: Routledge.

Shatz, C. J. (1992). The developing brain. *Scientific American, 267*, 60–67.

Shaw, P., Eckstrand, K., Sharp, W., Blumenthal, J., Lerch, J. P., Greenstein, D., et al. (2007). Attention-deficit/hyperactivity disorder is characterized by a delay in cortical maturation. *Proceedings of the National Academy of Sciences, 104*, 19649–19654.

Sheridan, S. M. (2000). Considerations of multiculturalism and diversity in behavioral consultation with parents and teachers. *School Psychology Review, 29*, 344–353.

Shonkoff, J. P., & Phillips, D. A. (Eds.). (2000). *From neurons to neighborhoods: The science of early childhood development.* National Research Council and Institute of Medicine, Committee on Integrating the Science of Early Childhood Development, Board on Children, Youth, and Families, Commission on Behavioral and Social Sciences and Education. Washington, DC: National Academy Press.

Siegel, A. E., & Kohn, L. G. (1959). Permissiveness, permission, and aggression: The effects of adult presence or absence on aggression in children's play. *Child Development, 36,* 131–141.

Silver, R. B., Measelle, J. R., Armstrong, J. M., & Essex, M. J. (2005). Trajectories of classroom externalizing behavior: Contributions of child characteristics, family characteristics, and the teacher-child relationship during the school transition. *Journal of School Psychology, 43,* 39–60.

Simpson, G. A., Cohen, R. A., Pastor, P. N., & Reuben, C. A. (2006). *U.S. children 4–17 years of age who received treatment for emotional or behavioral difficulties: Preliminary data from the 2005 National Heath Interview Survey.* National Center for Health Statistics. Retrieved September 16, 2009, from www.cdc.gov/nchs/products/pubs/pubd/hestats/children2005/children2005.htm

Slaby, R. G. (1997). Psychological mediators of violence in urban youth. In J. McCord (Ed.), *Violence and childhood in the inner city* (pp. 171–206). New York: Cambridge University Press.

Slaby, R. G., Roedell, W. C., Arezzo, D., & Hendrix, K. (1995). *Early violence prevention: Tools for teachers of young children.* Washington, DC: National Association for the Education of Young Children.

Slavin, R. E. (1995). *Cooperative learning: Theory, research, and practice* (2nd ed.). Boston: Allyn & Bacon.

Slee, P. (1993). Bullying: A preliminary investigation of its nature and the effects of social cognition. *Early Child Development and Care, 87,* 47–57.

Smith, I., & Ellsworth, C. (Eds.). (2004). *Supporting children with autism in child care settings.* Halifax, NS: Department of Child and Youth Study, Mount St. Vincent University. Retrieved September 15, 2009, from http://msvu.ca/child_youth/coeei/files/scaccs_workbook.pdf

Smith, J. D., Schneider, B. H., Smith, P. K., & Ananiadou, K. (2004). The effectiveness of whole-school antibullying programs: A synthesis of evaluation research. *School Psychology Review, 33,* 547–560.

Smith, L. M., LaGasse, L. L., Derauf, C., Grant, P., Shah, R., Arria, A., et al. (2008). Prenatal methamphetamine use and neonatal neurobehavioral outcome. *Neurotoxicology and Teratology, 30,* 20–26.

Smith, P. K., Cowie, H., & Sharp, S. (1994). Working directly with pupils involved in bullying situations. In P. K. Smith & S. Sharp (Eds.), *School bullying: Insights and perspectives* (pp. 193–212). New York: Routledge.

Smith, P. K., Morita, Y., Junger-Tas, J., Olweus, D., Catalano, R., & Slee, P. (Eds.). (1999). *The nature of school bullying: A cross-national perspective.* New York: Routledge.

Smith, P. K., & Shu, S. (2000). What good schools can do about bullying: Findings from a survey in English schools after a decade of research and action. *Childhood, 7*(2), 193–212.

Smith, P. K., Shu, S., & Madsen, K. (2001). Characteristics of victims of school bullying: Developmental changes in coping strategies and skills. In J. Juvonen & S. Graham (Eds.), *Peer harassment in school: The plight of the vulnerable and victimized* (pp. 332–351). New York: Guilford.

Smith, R. (2004). *Conscious classroom management: Unlocking the secrets of great teaching.* San Rafael, CA: Conscious Teaching Publications.

Smitherman, G. (1998). Black English/Ebonics: What it be like? In T. Perry & L. Delpit (Eds.), *The real Ebonics debate: Power, language, and the education of African-American children* (pp. 29–37). Boston: Beacon Press.

Snyder, J., Brooker, M., Patrick, M. R., Snyder, A., Schrepferman, L., & Stoolmiller, M. (2003). Observed peer victimization during early elementary school: Continuity, growth, and relation to risk for child antisocial and depressive behavior. *Child Development, 74,* 1881–1898.

Snyder, J., Horsch, E., & Childs, J. (1997). Peer relationships of young children: Affiliative choices and the shaping of aggressive behavior. *Journal of Clinical Child Psychology, 26,* 145–156.

Snyder, J., Prichard, P., Schrepferman, L., Patrick, M. R., & Stoolmiller, M. (2004). Child impulsiveness-inattention, early peer experiences, and the development of early onset conduct problems. *Journal of Abnormal Child Psychology, 32,* 579–594.

Snyder, J., Schrepferman, L., McEachern, A., Barner, S., Johnson, K., & Provines, J.

(2008). Peer deviancy training and peer coercion: Dual processes associated with early-onset conduct problems. *Child Development, 79*, 252–268.

Snyder, J., Schrepferman, L., Oeser, J., Patterson, G., Stoolmiller, M., Johnson, K., et al. (2005). Deviancy training and association with deviant peers in young children: Occurrence and contribution to early-onset conduct problems. *Development and Psychopathology, 17*, 397–413.

Sobel, J. (1983). *Everybody wins: Noncompetitive games for young children.* New York: Walker.

Solomon, D., Watson, M. S., Delucci, K. L., Schaps, E., & Battistich, V. (1988). Enhancing children's prosocial behavior in the classroom. *American Educational Research Journal, 25*, 527–555.

Soodak, L. C., & McCarthy, M. R. (2006). Classroom management in inclusive settings. In C. M. Evertson & C. S. Weinstein (Eds.), *Handbook of classroom management: Research, practice, and contemporary issues* (pp. 461–489). Mahwah, NJ: Erlbaum.

Spencer, M. B., Fegley, S. G., & Harpalani, V. (2003). Theoretical and empirical examination of identity as coping: Linking coping resources to the self processes of African American youth. *Applied Developmental Science, 7*, 181–188.

Spivack, G., & Shure, M. B. (1974). *Social adjustment of young children. A cognitive approach to solving real-life problems.* San Francisco: Jossey-Bass.

Sroufe, L. A. (1983). Infant-caregiver attachment and patterns of adaptation in preschool: The roots of maladaptation and competence. In M. Perlmutter (Ed.), *Minnesota symposium on child psychology* (Vol. 16, pp. 41–83). Hillsdale, NJ: Erlbaum.

Stainback, S., & Stainback, W. (1996). *Inclusion: A guide for educators.* Baltimore: Brookes.

Stanwood, G. D., & Levitt, P. (2008). The effects of monoamines on the developing nervous system. In C. A. Nelson & M. Luciana (Eds.), *Handbook of developmental cognitive neuroscience* (2nd ed., pp. 83–94). Cambridge, MA: MIT Press.

Statistics Canada. (2009). *Homicide offences, number and rate, by province and territory.* Retrieved November 17, 2009, from www40.statcan.gc.ca/l01/cst01/legal12a eng.htm

Stewart, R. M., Benner, G. J., Martella, R. C., & Marchand-Martella, N. E. (2007). Three-tier models of reading and behavior. *Journal of Positive Behavior Interventions, 9,* 239–253.

Strain, P. S., & Danko, C. D. (1995). Caregivers' encouragement of positive interaction between preschoolers with autism and their siblings. *Journal of Emotional and Behavioral Disorders, 3*(1), 2–12.

Strasburger, V. C., Wilson, B. J., & Jordan, A. B. (2009). *Children, adolescents, and the media* (2nd ed.). Thousand Oaks, CA: Sage.

Strayhorn, J. M., & Strain, P. S. (1986). Social and language skills for preventive mental health: What, how, who, and when. In P. S. Strain, M. J. Guralnick, & H. M. Walker (Eds.), *Children's social behavior: Development, assessment, and modification* (pp. 287–330). Orlando: Academic Press.

Strizek, G. A., Pittsonberger, J. L., Riordan, K. E., Lyter, D. M., & Orlofsky, G. F. (2006, April). *Characteristics of schools, districts, teachers, principals, and school libraries in the United States 2003-04. Schools and staffing survey* (NCES 2006-313 revised). Washington, DC: U.S. Department of Education, National Center for Education Statistics. Retrieved February 7, 2010, from http://nces.ed.gov/pubsearch/pubsinfo.asp? pubid=2006313

Suckling, A., & Temple, C. (2002). *Bullying: A whole-school approach.* London, UK: Jessica Kingsley.

Sugai, G. (n.d.). *School-wide positive behavior support and Response to Intervention.* Retrieved April 13, 2010, from www.rtinetwork.org/ Learn/Behavior/ar/SchoolwideBehavior

Sugai, G., & Horner, R. H. (2002). Introduction to the special series on positive behavior support in schools. *Journal of Emotional and Behavioral Disorders, 10*, 130–135.

Sugai, G., Horner, R. H., Dunlap, G., Hieneman, M., Lewis, T. J., Nelson, C. M., et al. (2000). Applying positive behavior support and functional behavioral assessment in schools. *Journal of Positive Behavior Interventions, 2,* 131–143.

Sugai, G., Horner, R., & Gresham, F. M. (2002). Behaviorally effective school environments. In M. Shinn, H. Walker, &

G. Stoner (Eds.), *Interventions for academic and behavior problems II: Preventive and remedial approaches* (pp. 315–350). Bethesda, MD: National Association of School Psychologists.

Suina, J. H., & Smolkin, L. B. (1994). From natal culture to school culture to dominant society culture: Supporting transitions for Pueblo Indians. In P. M. Greenfield & R. R. Cocking (Eds.), *Cross-cultural roots of minority child development* (pp. 115–131). Hillsdale, NJ: Erlbaum.

Sullivan, K., Cleary, M., & Sullivan, G. (2004). *Bullying in secondary schools: What it looks like and how to manage it*. Thousand Oaks, CA: Corwin.

Surgeon General's Scientific Advisory Committee on Television and Social Behavior. (1972). *Television and growing up: The impact of televised violence*. Washington, DC: U.S. Government Printing Office.

Sutherland, K. S., Wheby, J. H., & Gunter, P. L. (2000). The effectiveness of cooperative learning with students with emotional and behavioral disorders: A literature review. *Behavioral Disorders, 25*, 225–238.

Sutton, J., & Smith, P. K. (1999). Bullying as a group process: An adaptation of the participant role approach. *Aggressive Behavior, 25*, 97–111.

Sutton, J., Smith, P. K., & Sweetenham, J. (1999). Bullying and "theory of mind": A critique of the "social skills deficit" view of anti-social behaviour. *Social Development, 8*, 117–127.

Sutton, R. E., & Wheatley, K. F. (2003). Teachers' emotions and teaching: A review of the literature and directions for future research. *Educational Psychology Review, 15*, 327–358.

Swearer, S. M., & Doll, B. (2001). Bullying in schools: An ecological framework. In R. A. Geffner, T. Loring, & C. Young (Eds.), *Bullying behavior: Current issues, research, and interventions* (pp. 7–47). New York: Haworth.

Swearer, S. M., Song, S. Y., Cary, P. T., Eagle, J. W., & Mickelson, W. T. (2001). Psychosocial correlates in bullying and victimization: The relationship between depression, anxiety, and bully/victim status. In R. A. Geffner, T. Loring, & C. Young (Eds.), *Bullying behavior: Current issues, research, and interventions* (pp. 95–121). New York: Haworth.

Szalacha, L. A., Erkut, S., García Coll, C., Fields, J. P., Alarcón, O., & Ceder, I. (2003). Perceived discrimination and resilience. In S. S. Luthar (Ed.), *Resilience and vulnerability: Adaptation in the context of childhood adversity* (pp. 414–435). New York: Cambridge University Press.

Tabors, P. O. (2008). *One child, two languages: A guide for preschool educators of children learning English as a second language* (2nd ed.). Baltimore: Brookes.

Talge, N. M., Neal, C., Glover, V., & the Early Stress, Translational Research and Prevention Science Network: Fetal and Neonatal Experience on Child and Adolescent Mental Health (2007). Antenatal maternal stress and long-term effects on child neurodevelopment: How and why? *Journal of Child Psychology and Psychiatry, 48*, 245–261.

Tarullo, A. R., Obradovic, J., & Gunnar, M. R. (2009). Self-control and the developing brain. *Zero to Three, 29*, 31–37.

Tarullo, A. R., Quevedo, K., & Gunnar, M. R. (2008). The LHPA system and neurobehavioral development. In C. A. Nelson & M. Luciana (Eds.), *Handbook of developmental cognitive neuroscience* (2nd ed., pp. 63–82). Cambridge, MA: MIT Press.

Tatum, B. D. (1997). *"Why are all the Black kids sitting together in the cafeteria?" and other conversations about race*. New York: Basic Books.

Tharp, R. G. (1994). Intergroup differences among Native Americans in socialization and child cognition: An ethnogenetic analysis. In P. M. Greenfield & R. R. Cocking (Eds.), *Cross-cultural roots of minority child development* (pp. 87–106). Hillsdale, NJ: Erlbaum.

Thomas, A., Chess, S., & Birch, H. G. (1968). *Temperament and behavior disorders in children*. New York: New York University Press.

Thomas, W. P., & Collier, V. P. (2003). The multiple benefits of dual language. *Educational Leadership, 61*(2), 61–64.

Thompson, M., & Grace, C. O. (with Cohen, L. J.). (2001). *Best friends, worst enemies: Understanding the social lives of children*. New York: Ballantine.

Thompson, R. A., & Lagattuta, K. H. (2006). Feeling and understanding: Early emotional development. In K. McCartney &

D. Phillips (Eds.), *Handbook of early childhood development* (pp. 317–337). Malden, MA: Blackwell.

Thompson, T. (2007). *Making sense of autism.* Baltimore: Brookes.

Thornton, T. N., Craft, C. A., Dahlberg, L. L., Lynch, B. S., & Baer, K. (2000). *Best practices of youth violence prevention: A sourcebook for community action.* Atlanta: Centers for Disease Control and Prevention, National Center for Injury Prevention and Control. Retrieved February 25, 2010, from www.cdc.gov/violenceprevention/pub/YV_bestpractices.html

Tobin, J. J., Wu, D. Y. H., & Davidson, D. (1989). *Preschool in three cultures: Japan, China, and the United States.* New Haven: Yale University Press.

Tomlinson, C. A. (1999). *The differentiated classroom: Responding to the needs of all learners.* Alexandria, VA: Association for Supervision and Curriculum Development.

Tomlinson, C. A. (2001). *How to differentiate instruction in mixed-ability classrooms* (2nd ed.). Alexandria, VA: Association for Supervision and Curriculum Development.

Tomlinson, C. A. (2005). Traveling the road to differentiation in staff development. *Journal of Staff Development, 26*(4). Retrieved March 18, 2010, from www.nsdc.org/news/getDocument.cfm?articleID=480

Tracey, C. (2005). Listening to teachers: Classroom realities and No Child Left Behind. In G. L. Sunderman, J. S. Kim, & G. Orfield (Eds.), *No Child Left Behind meets school realities: Lessons from the field* (pp. 81–103). Thousand Oaks, CA: Corwin.

Tremblay, R. E., Gervais, J., & Petitclerc, A. (2008). *Early learning prevents youth violence.* Montreal, QC: Centre of Excellence for Early Childhood Development. Retrieved November 24, 2009, from www.excellence-jeunesenfants.ca/documents/Tremblay_AggressionReport_ANG.pdf

Tremblay, R. E., Nagin, D. S., Séguin, J. R., Zoccolillo, M., Zelazo, P. D., Boivin, M., et al. (2004). Physical aggression during early childhood: Trajectories and predictors. *Pediatrics, 114,* e43–e50.

Tremmel, R. (1993). Zen and the art of reflective practice in teacher education. *Harvard Educational Review, 63,* 434–458.

Trumbull, E., Rothstein-Fisch, C., & Greenfield, P. M. (2000). *Bridging cultures in our schools: New approaches that work.* Retrieved March 18, 2010, from www.wested.org/online_pubs/lcd-99-01.pdf

Trumbull, E., Rothstein-Fisch, C., Greenfield, P. M., & Quiroz, B. (with Altchech, M., Daley, C., Eyler, K., Hernandez, E., Mercado, G., Pérez, A. I., et al.). (2001). *Bridging cultures between home and school: A guide for teachers with a special focus on immigrant Latino families.* Mahwah, NJ: Erlbaum.

Turnbull, A., Turnbull, R., Erwin, E. J., & Soodak, L. C. (2006). *Families, professionals, and exceptionality: Positive outcomes through partnerships and trust* (5th ed.). Upper Saddle River, NJ: Merrill Prentice Hall.

Twemlow, S. W., Fonagy, P., & Sacco, F. C. (2004). The role of the bystander in the social architecture of bullying and violence in schools and communities. *Annals of the New York Academy of Science, 1036,* 215–232.

Tyre, P. (2008). *The trouble with boys: A surprising report card on our sons, their problems at school, and what parents and educators must do.* New York: Crown.

Underwood, M. K. (2003). *Social aggression among girls.* New York: Guilford.

Ungar, M. (2004). *Nurturing hidden resilience in troubled youth.* Toronto, ON: University of Toronto Press.

United Nations Office of the High Commission on Human Rights. (1989). *Convention on the rights of the child.* Retrieved May 10, 2010, from www2.ohchr.org/english/law/crc.htm

United Nations Office on Drugs and Crime. (2010). *Homicide statistics, criminal justice and public health sources—Trends (2003–2008).* Retrieved May 24, 2010, from www.unodc.org/unodc/en/data-and-analysis/homicide.html

U.S. Census Bureau. (2003, June 18). *Hispanic population reaches all-time high of 38.8 million, new Census Bureau estimates show.* Retrieved February 7, 2010, from www.census.gov/Press-Release/www/releases/archives/population/011193.html

U.S. Census Bureau. (2006). *Children who speak a language other than English at home by region: 2006. American community survey: B16003.* Retrieved February 7, 2010, from www.census.gov/compendia/statab/2009/tables/09s0227.pdf

U.S. Census Bureau. (2010). *Current population survey, 1955–2008. School enrollment of the population 3 years old and over, by level and control of school, race, and Hispanic origin: October 2008.* Retrieved February 5, 2010, from www.census.gov/population/www/socdemo/school/cps2008.html

U.S. Department of Education, Office for Civil Rights. (2005a). *Frequently asked questions about racial harassment.* Retrieved May 21, 2010, from http://ed.gov/about/offices/list/ocr/qa-raceharass.html

U.S. Department of Education, Office for Civil Rights. (2005b). *Sexual harassment: It's not academic.* Retrieved May 21, 2010, from http://ed.gov/about/offices/list/ocr/docs/ocrshpam.html

U.S. Department of Education, Office for Civil Rights. (2009). *Protecting students with disabilities: Frequently asked questions about Section 504 and the education of children with disabilities.* Retrieved May 4, 2010, from www2.ed.gov/about/offices/list/ocr/504faq.html

U.S. Department of Education, Office of Safe and Drug Free Schools. (2010). *Exploring the nature and prevention of bullying.* Retrieved May 22, 2010, from www2.ed.gov/admins/lead/safety/training/bullying/index.html

U.S. Department of Education, Office of Special Education and Rehabilitative Services. (2000, July). *A guide to the Individualized Education Program.* Retrieved May 2, 2010, from http://ed.gov/parents/needs/speced/iepguide/index.html

U.S. Department of Education, Office of Special Education and Rehabilitative Services. (n.d.). *IDEA reauthorized statute: Disproportionality and overidentification.* Retrieved May 1, 2010, from www2.ed.gov/policy/speced/guid/idea/tb-overident.pdf

U.S. Department of Education, Office of Special Education Programs. (2004). *Teaching children with ADHD: Instructional strategies and practices.* Retrieved March 18, 2010, from www.ed.gov/teachers/needs/speced/adhd/adhd-resource-pt2.pdf

U.S. Department of Education, Office of Special Education Programs. (2006). *Discipline.* Retrieved May 2, 2010, from http://idea.ed.gov/explore/view/p/%2Croot%2Cdynamic%2CTopicalBrief%2C6%2C

U.S. Department of Education, Office of Special Education Programs, Data Analysis System. (2008a). *Table 1.1. Children and students served under IDEA, Part B, by age group and state: Fall 2007.* Retrieved May 1, 2010, from https://www.ideadata.org/TABLES31ST/AR_1-1.htm

U.S. Department of Education, Office of Special Education Programs, Data Analysis System. (2008b). *Table 1-3. Students ages 6 through 21 served under IDEA, Part B, by disability category and state: Fall 2007.* Retrieved May 1, 2010, from https://www.ideadata.org/TABLES31ST/AR_1-3.htm

U.S. Department of Education, Office of Special Education Programs, Data Analysis System. (2008c). *Table 1-19. Students ages 6 through 21 served under IDEA, Part B, by race/ethnicity and state: Fall 2007.* Retrieved May 1, 2010, from https://www.ideadata.org/TABLES31ST/AR_1-19.htm

U.S. Department of Education, Office of Special Education Programs, Data Analysis System. (2008d). *Table 1-19c. Students ages 6 through 21 with mental retardation served under IDEA, Part B, by race/ethnicity and state: Fall 2007.* Retrieved May 1, 2010, from https://www.ideadata.org/TABLES31ST/AR_1-19.htm

U.S. Department of Education, Office of Special Education Programs, Data Analysis System. (2008e). *Table 8.1. Infants and children receiving early intervention services under IDEA, Part C, by age and state: Fall 2007.* Retrieved May 1, 2010, from https://www.ideadata.org/TABLES31ST/AR_8-1.htm

U.S. Department of Education, Office of Special Education Programs, Data Analysis System. (2008f). *Table C-8. Estimated resident population ages 6 through 21, by race/ethnicity and state: 2007.* Retrieved May 1, 2010, from https://www.ideadata.org/tables31st%5Car_C-8.htm

U.S. Department of Health and Human Services. (2003). *Children's mental health facts: Children and adolescents with mental, emotional, and behavioral disorders.* Washington, DC: SAMHSA's Mental

Health Information Center. Retrieved October 29, 2009, from http://mentalhealth.samhsa.gov/publications/allpubs/CA-0006/default.asp

U.S. Department of Health and Human Services, Administration on Children, Youth and Families. (2009). *Child maltreatment 2007*. Washington, DC: U.S. Printing Office. Retrieved October 28, 2009, from www.acf.hhs.gov/programs/cb/pubs/cm07/cm07.pdf

U.S. Department of Health and Human Services, Office of the Surgeon General. (2005, February 21). *U.S. Surgeon General releases advisory on alcohol use in pregnancy*. Retrieved June 20, 2010, from www.surgeongeneral.gov/pressreleases/sg02222005.html

U.S. Department of Justice, Federal Bureau of Investigation. (2009). *Crime in the United States, 2008: Murder*. Retrieved November 17, 2009, from www.fbi.gov/ucr/cius2008/offenses/violent_crime/murder_homicide.html

Vacca, D. M. (2001). Confronting the puzzle of nonverbal learning disabilities. *Educational Leadership, 59*(3), 26–31.

Vaillancourt, T. (2005). Indirect aggression among humans: Social construct or evolutionary adaptation? In R. E. Tremblay, W. W. Hartup, & J. Archer (Eds.), *Developmental origins of aggression* (pp. 158–177). New York: Guilford.

Vaillancourt, T., Brittain, H., Bennett, L., Arnocky, S., McDougall, P., Hymel, S., et al. (2010). Places to avoid: Population-based study of student reports of unsafe and high bullying areas at school. *Canadian Journal of School Psychology, 25*, 40–54.

Vance, E., & Weaver, P. J. (2002). *Class meetings: Young children solving problems together*. Washington, DC: National Association for the Education of Young Children.

Vandell, D. L., Nenide, L., & Van Winkle, S. J. (2006). Peer relationships in early childhood. In K. McCartney & D. Phillips (Eds.), *Handbook of early childhood development* (pp. 455–470). Malden, MA: Blackwell.

Van den Bergh, B. R. H., & Marcoen, A. (2004). High antenatal maternal anxiety is related to ADHD symptoms, externalizing problems, and anxiety in 8- and 9-year-olds. *Child Development, 75*, 1085–1097.

van den Boom, D. C. (1994). The influence of temperament and mothering on attachment and exploration: An experimental manipulation of sensitive responsiveness among lower-class mothers with irritable infants. *Child Development, 65*, 1457–1477.

van den Boom, D. C. (1995). Do first-year intervention effects endure? Follow-up during toddlerhood of a sample of Dutch irritable infants. *Child Development, 66*, 1798–1816.

van der Wal, M. F., de Wit, C. A. M., & Hirasing, R. A. (2003). Psychosocial health among young victims and offenders of direct and indirect bullying. *Pediatrics, 111*, 1312–1317.

van IJzendoorn, M. H. (1995). Adult attachment representations, parental responsiveness, and infant attachment: A meta-analysis on the predictive validity of the Adult Attachment Interview. *Psychological Bulletin, 117*, 387–403.

van IJzendoorn, M. H., & DeWolff, M. S. (1997). In search of the absent father: Meta-analysis of infant-father attachment. *Child Development, 68*, 604–609.

van IJzendoorn, M. H., & Sagi, A. (1999). Cross-cultural patterns of attachment: Universal and contextual dimensions. In J. Cassidy & P. R. Shaver (Eds.), *Handbook of attachment theory and research* (pp. 713–734). New York: Guilford.

van IJzendoorn, M. H., Schuengel, C., & Bakermans-Kranenburg, M. J. (1999). Disorganized attachment in early childhood: Meta-analysis of precursors, concomitants, and sequelae. *Development and Psychopathology, 11*, 225–249.

Vartuli, S. (2005). Beliefs: The heart of teaching. *Young Children, 60*(5), 76–86.

Viadero, D. (2009). Research hones focus on English language learners. *Education Week, 28*(17), 22–25.

Viding, E., Williamson, D. E., Forbes, E. E., & Harir, A. R. (2008). The integration of neuroimaging and molecular genetics in the story of developmental cognitive neuroscience. In C. A. Nelson & M. Luciana (Eds.), *Handbook of developmental cognitive neuroscience* (2nd ed., pp. 351–366). Cambridge, MA: MIT Press.

Villegas, A. M., & Lucas, T. (2007). The culturally responsive teacher. *Educational Leadership, 64*(6), 28–33.

Vitaro, F., Barker, E. D., Boivin, M., Brendgen, M., & Tremblay, R. E. (2006). Do early difficult temperament and harsh parenting differentially predict reactive and proactive aggression? *Journal of Abnormal Child Psychology, 34*, 685–695.

Vitaro, F., & Brendgen, M. (2005). Proactive and reactive aggression: A developmental perspective. In R. E. Tremblay, W. W. Hartup, & J. Archer (Eds.), *Developmental origins of aggression* (pp. 178–201). New York: Guilford.

Vitaro, F., & Tremblay, R. E. (1994). Impact of a prevention program on aggressive children's friendships and social adjustment. *Journal of Abnormal Child Psychology, 22*, 457–475.

Vossekuil, B., Fein, R. A., Reddy, M., Borum, R., & Modzeleski, W. (2002). *Final report and findings of the Safe School Initiative: Implications for the prevention of school attacks in the United States.* Washington, DC: U.S. Department of Education, Office of Elementary and Secondary Education, Safe and Drug-Free Schools Program, and U.S. Secret Service. Retrieved May 21, 2010, from www.ed.gov/admins/lead/safety/preventingattacksreport.pdf

Votruba-Drzal, E., Coley, R. L., & Chase-Lansdale, P. L. (2004). Child care and low-income children's development: Direct and moderated effects. *Child Development, 75*, 296–312.

Vreeman, R. C., & Carroll, A. E. (2007). A systematic review of school-based interventions to prevent bullying. *Archives of Pediatric and Adolescent Medicine, 161*, 78–88.

Walker, H. M., & Buckley, N. K. (1973). Teacher attention to appropriate and inappropriate classroom behavior. *Focus on Exceptional Children, 5*, 5–11.

Walker, H. M., Ramsey, E., & Gresham, R. M. (2004). *Antisocial behavior in school: Evidence-based practices* (2nd ed.). Belmont, CA: Wadsworth.

Wallis, C., Thomas, C. B., Crittle, S., & Forster, P. (2003, December 15). Does kindergarten need cops? *Time.* Retrieved October 29, 2009, from www.time.com/time/magazine/article/0,9171,1006435,00.html

Walsh, M. (2009). English language learners and the law: Statutes, precedents. *Education Week, 28*(17), 8–9.

Walther-Thomas, C., Korinek, L., McLaughlin, V. L., & Williams, B. T. (2000). *Collaboration for inclusive education.* Boston: Allyn & Bacon.

Warner, T. D., Behnke, M., Eyler, F. D., Padgett, K., Leonard, C., Hou, W., et al. (2006). Diffusion tensor imaging of frontal white matter and executive functioning in cocaine-exposed children. *Pediatrics, 118*, 2014–2024.

Warren, J. S., Bohanon-Edmonson, H. M., Turnbull, A. P., Sailor, W., Wickham, D., Griggs, P., et al. (2003). School-wide positive behavior support: Addressing behavior problems that impede student learning. *Educational Psychology Review, 18*, 187–198.

Waters, E., Merrick, S., Treboux, D., Crowell, J., & Albersheim, L. (2000). Attachment security in infancy and early adulthood: A twenty-year longitudinal study. *Child Development, 71*, 684–689.

Waters, E., Weinfeld, N. S., & Hamilton, C. E. (2000). The stability of attachment security from infancy to adolescence and early adulthood: General discussion. *Child Development, 71*, 703–706.

Watson, M. (with Ecken, L.). (2003). *Learning to trust: Transforming difficult elementary classrooms through developmental discipline.* San Francisco: Jossey-Bass.

Watson, M., & Battistich, V. (2006). Building and sustaining classroom communities. In C. M. Evertson & C. S. Weinstein (Eds.), *Handbook of classroom management: Research, practice, and contemporary issues* (pp. 253–279). Mahwah, NJ: Erlbaum.

Watson, M., Solomon, D., Battistich, V., Schaps, E., & Solomon, J. (n.d.). Developmental discipline. Retrieved April 4, 2010, from http://tigger.uic.edu/~lnucci/MoralEd/practices/practice2watson.html

Way, N., & Hughes, D. (2007, March 25). The middle ages. *The New York Times.* Retrieved October 24, 2010, from www.nytimes.com

Weber, R., Ritterfeld, U., & Mathiak, K. (2006). Does playing violent video games induce aggression? Empirical evidence of a functional magnetic resonance imaging study. *Media Psychology, 8*, 39–60.

Webster-Stratton, C., & Herbert, M. (1994). *Troubled families—problem children: Working with parents: A collaborative process.* Chichester, UK: Wiley.

Weinfeld, N. S., Sroufe, L. A., & Egeland, B. (2000). Attachment from infancy to early adulthood in a high-risk sample: Continuity, discontinuity, and their correlates. *Child Development, 71,* 695–702.

Weinfeld, N. S., Sroufe, L.A., Egeland, B., & Carlson, E. A. (1999). The nature of individual differences in infant-caregiver attachment. In J. Cassidy & P. R. Shaver (Eds.), *Handbook of attachment theory and research* (pp. 68–88). New York: Guilford.

Weinstein, C. S. (2003). This issue. *Theory into Practice, 42,* 266–268.

Weiss, H. B., Kreider, H., Lopez, M. E., & Chatman, C. C. (Eds.). (2005). *Preparing educators to involve families: From theory to practice.* Thousand Oaks, CA: Sage.

Weist, M. D., & Ollendick, T. H. (1991). Toward empirically valid target selection: The case of assertiveness in children. *Behavior Modification, 15,* 213–227.

Werner, E. E. (1984). Resilient children. *Young Children, 40,* 68–72.

Werner, E. E. (2000). Protective factors and individual resilience. In J. P. Shonkoff & S. J. Meisels (Eds.), *Handbook of early childhood intervention* (2nd ed., pp. 115–132). New York: Cambridge University Press.

Werner, E. E., & Johnson, J. L. (1999). Can we apply resilience? In M. D. Glantz & J. L. Johnson (Eds.), *Resilience and development: Positive life adaptations* (pp. 259–268). New York: Kluwer Academic/Plenum.

Werner, E. E., & Smith, R. S. (1982). *Vulnerable but invincible: A longitudinal study of resilient children and youth.* New York: McGraw-Hill.

White, K. J., & Kistner, J. (1992). The influence of teacher feedback on young children's peer preferences and perceptions. *Developmental Psychology, 28,* 933–975.

Whitfield, A. L., Anda, R. F., Dube, S. R., & Felitti, V. J. (2003). Violent childhood experiences and the risk of intimate partner violence in adults. *Journal of Interpersonal Violence, 18,* 166–185.

Whitney, I., Smith, P. K., & Thompson, D. (1994). Bullying and children with special educational needs. In P. K. Smith & S. Sharp (Eds.), *School bullying: Insights and perspectives* (pp. 213–240). New York: Routledge.

Wilczenski, F. L., Steegmann, R., Braun, M., Feeley, F., Griffin, J., Horowitz, T., et al. (1994). Promoting "fair play": Interventions for children as victims and victimizers. Workshop at the National Association of School Psychologists, Seattle. (ERIC document No. ED380744).

Williams, D. L. (2008). What neuroscience has taught us about autism: Implications for early intervention. *Zero to Three, 28*(4), 11–17.

Williams, L. R. (1994). Developmentally appropriate practice and cultural values: A case in point. In B. L. Mallory & R. S. New (Eds.), *Diversity and developmentally appropriate practice: Challenges for early childhood education* (pp. 155–165). New York: Teachers College Press.

Willicutt, E. G., & Pennington, B. F. (2000). Co-morbidity of reading disability and attention-deficit/hyperactivity disorder: Differences by gender and subtype. *Journal of Learning Disabilities, 33,* 179–191.

Willis, C. (2009). Young children with autism spectrum disorder: Strategies that work. *Young Children, 64*(1), 81–89.

Willis, W. (2004). Families with African American roots. In E. W. Lynch & M. J. Hanson (Eds.), *Developing cross-cultural competence: A guide for working with children and their families* (3rd ed., pp. 141–177). Baltimore: Brookes.

Wilson, B. J. (2008). Media and children's aggression, fear, and altruism. *Future of Children, 18,* 87–118.

Wilson, D. B., Gottfredson, D. C., & Najaka, S. S. (2001). School-based prevention of problem behaviors: A meta-analysis. *Journal of Quantitative Criminology, 17,* 247–272.

Wolfgang, C. H. (2001). *Solving discipline and classroom management problems: Methods and models for today's teachers* (5th ed.). New York: Wiley.

Wong, H. K., & Wong, R. T. (2001). *The first days of school: How to be an effective teacher.* Mountain View, CA: Harry K. Wong Publications.

Wong Fillmore, L. (1991). When learning a second language means losing the first. *Early Childhood Research Quarterly, 6,* 323–346.

Wood, G. (2004). A view from the field: No Child Left Behind's effects on classrooms and schools. In D. Meier & G. Wood (Eds.), *Many children left behind: How the No Child Left Behind Act is damaging our children and our schools* (pp. 33–50). Boston: Beacon Press.

Wright, J. P., Deitrich, K. N., Ris, M. D., Hornung, R. W., Wessel, S. D., Lanphear, B. P., et al. (2008). Association of prenatal and childhood blood lead concentrations with criminal arrests in early adulthood. *PLoS Medicine, 5*(5), e101. Retrieved October 31, 2009, from www. plosmedicine.org/article/info:doi/10.1371/journal.pmed.0050101

Wyman, P. A. (2003). Emerging perspectives on context specificity of children's adaptation and resilience: Evidence from a decade of research with urban children in adversity. In S. S. Luthar (Ed.), *Resilience and vulnerability: Adaptation in the context of childhood adversity* (pp. 293–317). New York: Cambridge University Press.

Xue, Y., Leventhal, T., Brooks-Gunn, J., & Earls, F. J. (2005). Neighborhood residence and mental health problems of 5- to 11-year-olds. *Archives of General Psychiatry, 62,* 554–563.

Yale University Office of Public Affairs. (2008). *Bullying-suicide link explored in new study by researchers at Yale.* Retrieved May 21, 2010, from http://opa.yale.edu/news/article. aspx?id=5913#

Yates, T. M., Egeland, B., & Sroufe, L. A. (2003). Rethinking resilience: A developmental process perspective. In S. S. Luthar (Ed.), *Resilience and vulnerability: Adaptation in the context of childhood adversity* (pp. 243–266). New York: Cambridge University Press.

Yehle, A. K., & Wambold, C. (1998, July/August). An ADHD success story: Strategies for teachers and students. *Teaching Exceptional Children, 30*(6), 8–13.

Yoshikawa, H. (1994). Prevention as cumulative protection: Effects of early family support and education on chronic delinquency and its risks. *Psychological Bulletin, 115,* 28–54.

Young, J. (1998). The Support Group Approach to bullying in schools. *Educational Psychology in Practice, 14,* 32–39.

Zelazo, P. D. (2005, May 13). *The development of executive function in infancy and early childhood.* Retrieved July 14, 2009, from www.aboutkidshealth.ca/News/Executive-Function-Part-Two-The-development-of-executive-function-in-infancy-and-early-childhood.aspx?articleID=8036&categoryID= news-poh3

Zelazo, P. D., Carlson, S. M., & Kesck, A. (2008). The development of executive functions in childhood. In C. A. Nelson & M. Luciana (Eds.), *Handbook of developmental cognitive neuroscience* (2nd ed., pp. 553–574). Cambridge, MA: MIT Press.

Ziegler, S., & Pepler, D. (1993). Bullying at school: Pervasive and persistent. *Orbit, 24,* 29–31.

Zimmerman, F. J., Glew, G. M., Christakis, D. A., & Katon, W. (2005). Early cognitive stimulation, emotional support, and TV watching as predictors of subsequent bullying among grade-school children. *Archives of Pediatric and Adolescent Medicine, 159,* 384–388.

Zionts, L. T. (2005). Examining relations between students and teachers: A potential extension of attachment theory? In K. A. Kerns & R. A. Richardson (Eds.), *Attachment in middle childhood* (pp. 231–254). New York: Guilford.

Zoccolillo, M., Romano, E., Joubert, D., Mazzarello, T., Côté, S., Boivin, M., et al. (2005). The intergenerational transmission of aggression and antisocial behavior. In R. E. Tremblay, W. W. Hartup, & J. Archer (Eds.), *Developmental origins of aggression* (pp. 353–375). New York: Guilford.

Zull, J. E. (2002). *The art of changing the brain: Enriching the practice of teaching by exploring the biology of learning.* Sterling, VA: Stylus.

Zuniga, M. E. (2004). Families with Latino roots. In E. W. Lynch & M. J. Hanson (Eds.), *Developing cross-cultural competence: A guide for working with children and their families* (3rd ed., pp. 179–217). Baltimore: Brookes.

Photo Credits

Index